DATE DUE

OCT 7 1987		
OCT 2 1 1987		
FEB 1 5 1989		
FEB 2 5 1991		
JUN 8		
FEB 2 8 1994		

DEMCO NO. 38-298

Politics in Three Worlds:
An Introduction to Political Science

POLITICS IN THREE WORLDS: AN INTRODUCTION TO POLITICAL SCIENCE

Paul J. Best
Kul B. Rai
David F. Walsh

Southern Connecticut
State University

John Wiley & Sons
New York · Chichester · Brisbane · Toronto · Singapore

Cover photo by Michael Malyszko
Cover design by Karin Gerdes Kincheloe

Library of Congress Cataloging in Publication Data:

Best, Paul J. (Paul Joseph), 1939-
  Politics in three worlds.

  Includes indexes.
  1. Political science. 2. Comparative government.
3. Comparative economics. I. Rai, Kul B. II. Walsh,
David F., 1944-   . III. Title.

JA71.B48 1986   320   85-12397
ISBN 0-471-87809-X

Printed in the United States of America

10 9 8 7 6 5 4 3 2 1

Preface

The student of introductory political science is confronted with two general
tasks: understanding the great diversity of contemporary political systems
and political behavior, and developing a conceptual and methodological
framework sufficient to permit more advanced study. Modern social science
scholarship demands that these tasks be accomplished within a nonsexist
framework in which value biases are understood and controlled. In addition,
introductory learning material is most useful when its data and studies are
carefully integrated.

Politics in Three Worlds: An Introduction to Political Science addresses
itself to the needs of the modern student. It presents a tightly constructed,
comparative model of three political worlds, the West (the United States,
Canada, Japan, and the states of Western Europe), the Communist states
(the Soviet bloc countries, Albania, China, Cuba, North Korea, Yugoslavia,
and the states of Indochina), and the Third World (the less-developed
countries of Africa, Asia, Latin America, and the Middle East). The three
political worlds are explained as the result of the interaction of two factors,
namely, the level of political development and the element of human choice.
The level of political development is the general political setting of the state
consisting of the natural and financial resources available to the state, the
size and capacity of existing political institutions, and the political orientation of the general population toward the state. The study identifies three
levels of political development: preindustrial, industrial, and postindustrial.

The element of human choice includes both the general political culture and the elite ideology. Both specify particular values and attitudes about politics. Although the level of political development establishes the general characteristics of the political process, the selection of individual issues for national attention and the implementation of specific policies reflect the value preferences of political actors. The Western political process results from the application of liberal and social liberal (social democratic) ideologies to a postindustrial social setting. The political process in the Communist states reflects the application of Marxist–Leninist ideology to both preindustrial and industrial social settings. The politics of the Third World is explained as the interaction of diverse national ideologies combining both modern and traditional political values with a preindustrial level of political development.

The work includes several important features. The general model integrates more than 100 concepts and studies from the literature of political science and employs tables, graphs, and other devices to present the material. Individual chapters are devoted to the level of development, elite political ideologies, the origin of the state, government structures, interest groups, political parties, the role of women, and international relations. In addition, three chapters consider the political economies of the three worlds and incorporate some of the most recent theoretical material from the field of comparative politics.

Paul J. Best
Kul B. Rai
David F. Walsh

Acknowledgments

This textbook originated in the years 1978–1980 when two of the authors took part in a project encouraging a global approach to teaching in public higher education in Connecticut. That project was funded by an Undergraduate International Studies and Foreign Language Program grant from the Center for International Education, United States Department of Education. We wish to acknowledge our debt to the Department of Education for turning our thinking to a global framework for the study of politics.

Additionally, we wish to thank Richard F. Staar, Senior Fellow at the Hoover Institution on War, Revolution and Peace at Stanford University and James Dull, Professor of Political Science at the University of New Haven, for reading our manuscript and offering many useful suggestions. Our colleagues at Southern Connecticut State University, Professors John O. Iatrides and Harriet B. Applewhite, also assisted us by pointing out our errors and omissions. We appreciate their efforts. We wish to give special thanks to Debra Fratello of John Wiley & Sons, Inc. for her support & cooperation in the production of this book. We would have never finished this project without the able assistance of Jean Alberino, the Political Science secretary at our University, and Mrs. Kathleen Walsh.

Of course, the authors accept sole responsibility for the content of the book.

David F. Walsh wishes to dedicate this book to his mother and father.

Contents

CHAPTER 1

Politics and Political Science

Political science is the study of the process of making public decisions and of the individuals and the institutions that participate in this process. The process of making public decisions is called politics. The central questions in the study of politics concern power, authority, and conflict.

Although the study of political questions as a separate branch of knowledge called political science is about 100 years old, the concern with such questions is as old as human society. Ancient Greeks were the first to study political questions systematically. Philosophy, history, and law have had considerable influence on the study of politics. Sociology, psychology, economics, and some other disciplines have also influenced the study of politics and the development of political science as a separate discipline.

Several approaches are used to study political science. They can be grouped under three major categories: traditional, behavioral, and postbehavioral. These three categories are often considered separate schools of study in political science.

Human knowledge can be usefully divided into three groups: exact sciences, social sciences, and humanities. Political science is one of the eight social sciences, the other seven being anthropology, communication, economics, geography, history, psychology, and sociology. Political science is divided into several fields and subfields.

In theory at least, in the First World and, to a considerable extent in the Third World, objectivity is the ideal in political science. Of course, all governments, to some extent, interfere with freedom of expression for social scientists. Pressure to see the world and politics in a particular way is also exerted by sources outside the government. In the Second World the possibility of or even the need for objectivity is emphatically denied. Yet objective studies, though from a Marxist point of view, are not altogether absent in the Second World.

ERA rally in July of 1978, Washington, D.C.

On March 22, 1972, the U.S. Congress proposed a historic amendment to the Constitution—the Equal Rights Amendment (ERA). The amendment stated that "equality of rights under the law shall not be denied or abridged by the United States or by any state on account of sex." As stipulated in the U.S. Constitution, although an amendment is proposed by the Congress, it still needs ratification by the legislatures of three-fourths of the states before it becomes a part of the Constitution. Congress set March 22, 1979, as the deadline for ratification by state legislatures and later extended this date to June 30, 1982. During these ten years (1972–1982), the ERA was debated not only in state legislatures, but also in the media and in other public forums as well as in private homes. Women's groups campaigned for the ratification of the ERA and so did many men. When the deadline of June 30, 1982, approached, the ERA had been ratified by 35 state legislatures, 3 short of the required three-fourths majority. The ERA was not ratified; however, many women and men vowed to continue the fight for its adoption at some later date.

In August 1980, the government of Poland made an unprecedented decision for a Communist country. Workers were granted the right to form independent trade unions and to strike. This decision was made after Poland

Warsaw, Poland—Demonstrators run for cover as riot police fire tear gas during demonstrations which marked the second anniversary of the founding of Solidarity.

had experienced economic unrest for several months. Inflation was high and essential goods were in short supply; overall, the Polish economy's perform-ance was very poor. Restless workers resorted to work stoppages, which spread to several parts of the country. Strikes by workers became common. The government's decision regarding the workers' right to form independent trade unions and to strike was aimed at placating them. The Polish workers, led by Lech Walesa, demanded further reforms including free elections. The government was not ready for these reforms and responded by outlawing Solidarity, the largest workers' union in Poland, and jailing Walesa, its leader. On December 13, 1981, martial law was imposed in Poland. Two years later martial law was lifted, although more in appearance than in reality.

In 1979 Iran experienced a revolution and a drastic change in govern-ment. Shah Mohammed Reza Pahlavi, the king of Iran, was ousted and the country became an Islamic republic under the leadership of the Ayatollah Khomeini. Several of the decisions made by Khomeini concerned the rights and role of women in Iran. The Shah was an authoritarian ruler, but one of the positive aspects of his rule had been the improvement in the status of women in Iran. During his reign, great numbers of women went to school and college and many of them joined professions. Khomeini put a virtual stop to this trend. Women were completely segregated from men in public places and their role in the society became far less visible. Decisions on the role of women in the society were made without public debate in Iran. The

Iranian traditionalist demonstrates support for the Ayatollah Khomeini, Teheran, Iran.

only consideration kept in view was adherence to the tenets of Islam (according to Khomeini's interpretation of them) as written in the Koran (the holy book of the Moslems).

The events in the United States, Poland, and Iran just described reveal the process of making public decisions as it occurs in different countries. It is this process that we call *politics*. Decisions that concern only one's self, family, or close friends are of a private nature. All other decisions made by individuals are public. Sometimes a person acting as a private citizen may make decisions of a public nature, for example, when a rich man buys a large amount of silver or some other commodity, thus forcing up the price of that commodity. Most public decisions are, however, made by individuals acting on behalf of some organization.

Political science is the study of the process of making public decisions and of the individuals and the institutions that participate in this process. A number of organizations, such as churches and labor unions, make public decisions. However, in the study of political science the process by which governmental decisions are made is emphasized. Sometimes people make decisions for the government through a referendum (in which the people directly vote on an issue, rather than acting through their representatives). Most governmental decisions are, however, made by the institutions and the agencies of the government. The people do provide inputs into this process.

Such inputs are much more substantial in the democratic countries than in the nondemocratic countries. Governments seek such inputs because it makes them appear responsive to the public concerns. More important, this process helps a government acquire *legitimacy*. In other words, the people consider such a government appropriate for meeting their needs and will support it. People may also have selfish motives in providing inputs into the governmental decision-making process. Governmental decisions distribute values, that is, the benefits and opportunities that people seek. These values are distributed authoritatively in the sense that the distribution has the force of law. As the resources to provide such values are limited in every country, different groups of people, and in some cases individuals, attempt to obtain as large a share of the pie as possible. This competition is one of the major reasons of conflict among different groups and individuals in every society.

CENTRAL QUESTIONS IN POLITICS

The central questions in the study of politics concern power, authority, and conflict. Many political scientists include political behavior in this list. *Power* has been defined in several ways. A generally accepted definition of power in political science can be expressed in the following manner: A has power over B if A can get B to do something that B would not otherwise do. Implied in this definition is the notion that A has the ability to influence B's behavior, by coercion if necessary. The other important aspects of this definition are that it expresses a relationship between individuals and groups and it refers to the exercise of power regarding some specific issue.

Legitimate (conforming to established rules and procedures) *power*, or the legitimate exercise of power, is termed *authority*. A hijacker may have power over the plane crew and the passengers, but he has no authority. A police officer who stops a speeding car on the highway exercises legitimate power: the officer has the authority to make a driver stop and to issue a speeding ticket. Even legitimate power can be and is challenged. However, power when combined with authority is less likely to be challenged than is power without authority.

Decisions on authoritative distribution of values in a society are made by those who hold positions of authority in the political system. As mentioned earlier, conflict in a society arises because individuals and groups seek a favorable distribution of such values. Either holding a position of authority or having access to and influence on those in authority assures an individual or a group disproportionately greater benefits and opportunities. As individuals and groups compete for positions of authority or attempt to influence those in authority, conflict is the inevitable result. The exercise of power by those in authority in making people accept an authoritative distribution of values also leads to *conflict*, because those who receive less than what they perceive to be their share want a change in such distribution.

Political behavior indicates a perspective or an approach as well as subject matter for study. The behavioral approach is considered later in this chapter. The subject matter of political behavior concerns observable human behavior in politics, in other words, the observable behavior of individuals and groups in politics. Several political scientists who study political behavior place greater emphasis on individual behavior than on group behavior on the ground that group behavior is nothing more than the behavior of the individuals who constitute the group.

POLITICAL SCIENCE: PAST AND PRESENT

Concern with political questions is as old as human society, but the study of these questions as a separate branch of knowledge called political science is only about 100 years old. The first graduate department of political science in the United States was established at Columbia University in 1880. Almost 35 years later less than 40 American colleges and universities had separate departments of political science.[1] The establishment of political science departments in colleges and universities, and along with it the recognition of political science as a separate branch of knowledge, has taken place gradually in the twentieth century.

In ancient, medieval, and early modern times scholars had a holistic attitude toward knowledge. All knowledge was considered under the heading of philosophy. The distinction between natural sciences and social sciences did not emerge, even in a rudimentary form, until the seventeenth century. The title of philosophy was retained, however: "natural philosophy" for the natural sciences and "moral philosophy" for what later became social sciences. Of the social sciences (considered later in this chapter), political science was virtually the last to be recognized as a separate discipline, that is, a body of well-organized knowledge with distinct concepts, questions, and a history.

Ancient Greeks were the first to study political questions systematically. Writing in the fifth century B.C., the Greek historian Herodotus classified all governments into three types—monarchy, aristocracy, and democracy. These governments were distinguished by the number of persons exercising ultimate power. *Monarchy* was considered a government by one person, an *aristocracy* by a few, and a *democracy* by many or all. About a century later Aristotle revised this classification with the inclusion of another criterion—in whose interest the rulers exercise their power. Monarchy, aristocracy, and polity (government by many) were considered governments in which power was exercised in the interest of all; *tyranny* (government by one), *oligarchy* (government by a few), and *democracy* (government by many) represented governments in which the rulers served only their own interests.

Another political question that preoccupied the Greeks concerned the ideal state or utopia. Plato, the mentor of Aristotle, is best known for depicting such an ideal state in the *Republic*. A central question considered in Plato's *Republic* is justice. Justice to Plato meant that every individual performed tasks for which he was best suited by innate qualities and training. This, Plato believed, would bring harmony within an individual as well as within the state. Good citizens and an ideal state would result from such harmony and justice.

Political questions such as classification of governments and justice in the society were considered by the Greeks as a part of the study of philosophy. As indicated earlier, the tradition of studying politics (and other subjects) as a part of philosophy continued for centuries. The writings of political philosophers became the source of knowledge on politics. These philosophers differed, as could be expected, with regard to their focus on politics. Although some, notably Niccolo Machiavelli (1469–1527), emphasized pragmatic aspects of politics, most of the political philosophers wrote as social ethicists or as social critics and sometimes assumed both of these roles. Some of the great social ethicists or social critics whose writings still form an important part of the study of politics are St. Augustine (354–430), Thomas Aquinas (1225–1274), John Locke (1632–1704), Jean Jacques Rousseau (1712–1778), Immanuel Kant (1724–1804), Thomas Jefferson (1743–1826), Karl Marx (1818–1883), and James Bryce (1832–1922).

Besides philosophy, history and law have had considerable influence on the study of politics and the development of the discipline of political science. When political science emerged in the nineteenth century as a separate discipline, it was an offshoot of history. Even after recognition of political science as a distinct branch of knowledge, political science courses commonly were taught within the departments of history or within the joint departments of history and political science. (In some U.S. colleges and universities, joint departments of these two disciplines still exist.) Political science courses were not much different from history courses. When political institutions such as cabinets or political parties were considered, the emphasis was on their history; courses in international relations or foreign policy stressed the history of international relations and foreign policy. Even today the influence of history on political science is quite evident. In fact, some political scientists are indistinguishable from historians in their teaching and research. Alan Isaak calls such political scientists "historians of the present."[2] These political scientists "give detailed descriptions of contemporary political events, done in the narrative style of the historians."[3]

Political science is generally distinguished from other social sciences by its emphasis on government and laws. It seems logical, therefore, that the study of law influenced the development of political science. Isaak mentions two important factors responsible for the "inclination toward legalism in U.S. political science."[4] One is the training in law the nineteenth-century U.S. political science professors received, often at European, usually German, universities. The other factor, clearly more important, is the nature of the U.S. political system with its "doctrine or folkway of the rule of law." In theory at least, the rule of law has supremacy over the rule of individuals in the U.S. political system, so it is no surprise that such subjects as the legal system, judicial interpretations of the executive and the legislative decisions, and individual rights guaranteed by the Constitution are given much attention in U.S. political science.

The influence of philosophy, history, and law made the study of politics interdisciplinary. A deliberate effort to incorporate sociology and psychology into this study began in the early twentieth century. Arthur Bentley argued in his 1908 book, now considered a classic, that the best way to understand the political process was through the study of groups, large and small.[5] In studying groups Bentley's concern was not so much with formal rules, prescribed by laws, as with the response of individual members of groups to these rules and members' interactions within groups. About the same time Graham Wallas, an English thinker, advocated a psychological perspective of politics with an emphasis on the irrational in human behavior.[6]

The use of sociology and psychology for the study of politics acquired a greater acceptance among political scientists with the publication of another great work, *New Aspects of Politics*.[7] Charles Merriam originated the tradition in political science of studying observable human political behavior with the help of sociology and psychology. It was this tradition that encouraged the emergence of behavioralism in political science after World War II. Polling techniques and other research methods developed in the 1930s; they supplemented interdisciplinary endeavors in political science.

Since the end of World War II, political science has become even more interdisciplinary, making use not only of sociology and psychology, but also of economics and some other disciplines. Methods used in mathematics and statistics have been borrowed and computers are commonly used to analyze political data. Some political scientists are even interested in the biological aspects of politics. Such diverse perspectives and new methods have led to the development of several subfields within political science. These perspectives and methods have also contributed to some disagreements between political scientists of different orientations.

APPROACHES TO POLITICAL SCIENCE

Several approaches are used to study political science. They can be grouped under three major categories: traditional, behavioral, and postbehavioral. These three categories can be considered separate schools within the discipline of political science. However, although each of these schools has some distinct features, each complements the other two in certain respects.

Traditional Political Science

Traditionalism in political science, the oldest of the three schools, provided the predominant perspective for the study of politics up to and just after World War II. Questions of value judgment are given prominence in this school. To say that democracy is a good form of government and every country should strive for it is to express a value judgment or a value preference. Such a statement cannot be verified empirically, that is, by observable data in the world, for though we may agree on what democracy is, it is virtually impossible to find commonly accepted criteria for determining what a good form of government is. Everyone has a different view of good forms of government. For example, one person may consider guarantees of freedom of expression the most important ingredient of a good form of government, but another may attach greatest importance to the availability of basic necessities of life.

Of the major fields of political science discussed in this chapter, value judgments are made most frequently in political philosophy. Political philosophy may be called value or normative theory (as distinguished from empirical or scientific theory, which is discussed with behavioral political science) because the discussion of values and norms has been the primary preoccupation of political philosophers. The first essential characteristic of such theory or political philosophy is morality.[8] Although political philosophy does not ignore the empirical world altogether, its central message is almost invariably moral. Machiavelli and the Indian philosopher Kautilya are two major exceptions in the history of political philosophy in this respect, for they divorced politics almost completely from morality.

Most political scientists make some use of history. Traditional political scientists, however, make hardly any distinction between history and political science. Traditional international relations (another field within political science), for example, has often meant the chronological study of international events during a certain period. With the use of this approach the study of contemporary events is no less historical than the study of past events. Such a study of the Vietnam War, for instance, would be primarily a chronological description of the events that took place during the course of this war, with very little effort at explaining the process of policy making.[9]

In considering political institutions of a country, traditional political scientists emphasize the history and structures of these institutions, and their formal processes as prescribed by a nation's constitution and laws. The structures and formal processes of the political institutions are described without much attention to the roles of the individual actors within these institutions. In some traditional studies, the political institutions are discussed with emphasis on the court decisions concerning them.[10]

Behavioral Political Science

Behavioralism in political science can be traced to the 1920s. This approach, however, is usually considered a post–World War II phenomenon. Behavioralism has presented a serious challenge to traditionalism. The key terms in this approach are political behavior and political process. By emphasizing the study of political behavior and political process, behavioralists go beyond the traditional focus on the structures and formal processes of political institutions. It is important to know the structure of a political institution; however, for behavioralists it is even more important to understand how individual political actors *behave* within an institution and by which processes, formal as well as informal, they make policy. The diverse interests and personalities of individual political actors within an institution and their interpersonal relations and conflicts for power are issues of interest to behavioralists. Policy content is not ignored in behavioral political science, but the decision-making process for arriving at the policy is given at least as much attention.

Behavioral political scientists claim to use the scientific method in their studies. They verify hypotheses about politics with empirical data and then attempt to explain and even predict political phenomena. Statistics and computers are often used in behavioral political science.

There is little room, if any, for value judgments in behavioral political science. Several behavioralists argue that the use of the scientific method excludes value judgments from the study of politics. A great deal of controversy exists among political scientists over the use of the scientific method and of value judgments.

In its approach to the study of political science behavioralism is interdisciplinary. Social sciences, especially economics, psychology, and sociology, are applied in such studies. The behavioral argument is that human life is not completely political even in politics, so other social sciences must be employed to ensure that the study of politics is as complete and comprehensive as possible.

A very important, perhaps the ultimate, goal of behavioralists is to develop a political theory that would incorporate verifiable generalizations about the observable political world. This goal is to be achieved by heavy reliance on the scientific method. Such political theory is very different from traditional political theory (philosophy), which is normative in its orientation. Political theory in behavioralism is not normative; rather, it is "positive" (i.e., as opposed to normative theory, it does not incorporate value judgments) and certainly empirical (in that it deals with the observable world). As David Easton, one of the first to use behavioralism in political science, states, the verifiable generalizations in this theory express "discoverable uniformities in political behavior."[11] Uniformities can be discovered in several aspects of political behavior, for example, political party behavior or voting behavior.

Postbehavioralism in Political Science

Postbehavioralism began in the late 1960s as a reaction to behavioralism. Some political scientists consider the postbehavioral approach revolutionary. Easton expressed such an opinion in 1969.[12] Yet Easton did not perceive postbehavioralism as antagonistic to behavioralism; instead he considered the two complementary.[13]

The emphasis in postbehaviorism is on issues and objectives, not on methods. Postbehavioralists believe that behavioral political scientists have been much too preoccupied with the scientific method and have consequently failed to identify and resolve the major problems facing society. The argument is that behavioral overemphasis on refining methods does just that: it refines methods at the cost of the study of issues in politics. When the Vietnam War and racial riots were major crises in America, U.S. political scientists committed to behavioralism had little to say about these problems except to suggest which approaches and techniques could be used for their analysis.

Postbehavioralists do not wish to make the study of politics less scientific or even less interdisciplinary; rather, they advocate a far greater emphasis on the substance of politics. The postbehavioral approach goes a step further—it not only advocates scientific and interdisciplinary study of politics, it suggests that action be taken by political scientists and other social scientists to resolve major problems. In emphasizing solutions to problems and action for such solutions, postbehavioralists maintain that value judgments must be made. The postbehavioral argument is fairly straightforward: when we propose solutions to problems and attempt to have them accepted in the political sphere, we make value judgments. Value judgments are also made when we evaluate action taken by others, for the criteria used to evaluate such action are clearly based upon our values.

Although the strict adherents of each of the three schools can be quite dogmatic, tolerance of different approaches is on the increase in the discipline of political science. Some political scientists use the approaches of two or all three of these schools in teaching and research. The decision as to which of the approaches should be used and when more than one should be used depends not only on one's orientation toward politics but also on the nature of the topic being investigated and the type of data available. For example, in studying U.S. foreign aid, one acknowledges that it is part of a larger and very significant issue of the relationship between rich and poor nations. The issue of foreign aid plays an important role in the formulation of U.S. foreign policy. Suppose we want to find why some countries receive large amounts of aid while others receive small amounts of aid or no aid at all from the United States. The question is deceptively simple; its answer is not. A number of factors are considered by officials in determining the varying amounts of aid to be given to different countries. We can attempt to find these factors through historical research by studying available government documents or we may employ statistical techniques. For the latter, we need data amenable to such analysis. Such data must be quantitative in nature, that is, it must be data that we can express in numbers. The historical approach is traditional; use of statistical techniques makes the study behavioral. However, there is no reason the historical approach and the statistical techniques cannot be combined. It seems clear that if we do not adhere strictly to only one of the three schools discussed in this chapter and if the nature of the topic and the available data justify the combination of different approaches, our understanding of politics would certainly improve.

EXACT SCIENCES, SOCIAL SCIENCES, AND THE HUMANITIES

From the definition of politics and political science given here one can appreciate the scope of this book. Still, one might ask in what sense is political science a science?

Human knowledge may be usefully divided into the exact sciences, the social sciences (of which political science is one), and the humanities. The term "science" derives from the Latin verb *scio*—"to know" and the noun *scientia*—"knowledge." In general, science means any systematic approach to the acquisition of knowledge, the classification of knowledge concerning some subject or group of subjects, or simply an organized body of knowledge. Using these definitions, we can see how political science is a science, but we must differentiate it from the popular connotation of "science" as a physical or exact science, dealing with physical and biological (material) phenomena and numbers. The exact sciences (e.g., mathematics, physics, chemistry, biology, and earth science) have the feature of replicability; that is, results can be duplicated exactly if the same conditions, materials, or numbers are available. For example, mathematical equations using a number system as we know it would be the same anywhere in the universe, and steel can be made anywhere if the requisite conditions are present whether in Pittsburgh or Tasmania. Without this replicability modern civilization could not exist. If one could not be sure of the results of an applied physical science process—meaning different results would occur each time something was tried—manufacturing would be impossible.

Political science does not really resemble the studies and activities known as the humanities either. The humanities encompass literature (rhetoric, prose, poetry), language, sculpture, painting, music, and dance, and the study of the meaning of life as found in philosophy and theology. The modern humanities have their source in classical Greek and Roman culture and the Renaissance. The humanities do not attempt to use scientific methodology, relying on human judgment rather than objectivity. Both the humanities and social sciences deal with the same subject, human beings; the difference between them is methodological. The exact and social sciences share a common pattern of research and are known as empirical sciences, those based on experiment or observation and experience, using rigorous methodology, logical reasoning, and an objective approach. In the exact and social sciences the researcher is led to the results by following the trail of evidence rather than forcing data into some preconceived notion. Emotional involvement with a subject is considered unscientific. The two major differences between the exact and social sciences are subject matter—material and numbers for the former and human beings for the latter—and results of research. Political science has not been able to formulate rules of political behavior accurate enough to predict future events, and it does not seem likely that such rules will ever be discovered in view of the large number of variables involved in human activity.

As mentioned earlier, political science does not stand alone but is part of a group of sciences that have the same object of study—that is, human beings—and hence are called "social" sciences. It is commonly accepted that there are eight social science disciplines. Besides political science, these include the following:

Anthropology. The study of human beings in general, the physical facts concerning human development (archaeology), and the history, geographic distribution, ethnology and culture of people. It resembles sociology but emphasizes primitive and preliterate society.

Communications. The study of speech, the origin and structure of language (linguistics, phonetics, and semantics), and how we transfer information by verbal and nonverbal signals, including print and nonprint media. Social scientists, linguists, and biological scientists cooperating in this field use the term *semiotics* (Greek *semeion,* "mark," "sign," and *otic,* an adjectival ending meaning "pertaining to," "about"). Semiotics is understood by them to be "the study of all sign processes from their psycho-biological foundations to their expression in animal and human communication. It pays special attention to all human sign systems, verbal and non-verbal, and the messages and texts they generate."[14]

Economics. How people make a living—the production, distribution, and consumption of wealth. Its major concern is modern complex civilization. Economics attempts to determine how to most efficiently utilize scarce resources to derive the greatest production of goods and services desired by society.

Geography. The interrelationship of humans and their environment. It emphasizes spatial characteristics of natural and human phenomena-seeking patterns and explanations for these patterns.

History. The sequential order of human events, especially the unique sequence based on written records.

Psychology. The study of the mind and mental and emotional processes and their influence on behavior.

Sociology. Human institutions and their functions, and human interactions with an emphasis on group interaction in contemporary society.

It is convenient to divide human knowledge into the exact sciences, the social sciences, and the humanities, but it is not an altogether satisfactory solution to the problem. The three great groupings of knowledge are overlapping and interdependent. For instance, one's theological convictions greatly affect one's view of the exact sciences. It would be impossible for a believer in the specific creation of each individual species by a Creator to deal with evolution and become a paleontologist (one who studies prehistoric life by examining fossils). A geographer cannot ignore the earth sciences, an anthropologist needs to use the latest exact science instruments, the political scientist may use mathematics and the computer. Social science writers cannot ignore the requisites of literature, as found in the humanities, in publishing their research, especially when seeking to reach a wide audience. Moreover, the social science disciplines include economic history, economic geography, political economy, political sociology, and political psychology. Such interdependence of knowledge defeats efforts to separate it into discrete units. Why, then, bother dividing it at all? The simple reason is that human knowledge is so broad that no one person could possibly claim to be able to encompass it all. This is also true within the disciplines. Political science very rarely produces a generalist in the subject;

rather, each scholar specializes in a field of political science or even in a subfield.

FIELDS OF POLITICAL SCIENCE

There are six major fields within the discipline of political science: political theory and political philosophy; methodology; national, state (provincial), and local government; comparative politics; international relations; and political dynamics. Most traditional political scientists use the terms *political theory* and *political philosophy* interchangeably. Behavioral political scientists make a distinction between the two. According to their viewpoint, political theory explains and predicts diverse political phenomena, whereas political philosophy concentrates on questions of value judgment. In the study of political philosophy, its history and the ideas of great political thinkers such as Plato, Aristotle, Hobbes, Locke, John Stuart Mill, and Karl Marx are examined.

Methodology is a system of approaches and techniques used in a discipline. Some form of methodology is used in every field (and subfield) of political science. Concern with the methods for studying politics is as old as Aristotle's comparisons of the Greek city-state constitutions. However, the emphasis on political methodology has increased so much within the last 30 years or so that it is now considered a separate field. Most political scientists who specialize in methodology want to make the study of this discipline similar to that of the exact sciences. Some of those interested in political methodology study epistemology (the origin, nature, and limits of knowledge) and philosophy of science (the assumptions and general principles of science). Many experts in political methodology are concerned with computer techniques, statistical analysis, and polling techniques.

In *national, state (provincial), and local government,* the political system of one country is considered. In U.S. government, the major field of political science in the United States, national, state, and local governments are studied. Similarly, the field of Canadian government includes governments at the three levels. Several specialists in U.S. or Canadian government also study political behavior of participants in politics. Thus, the roles of congressmen (in the United States) or members of Parliament (in Canada) are of interest to these political scientists.

In *comparative politics,* comparison of contemporary governments and politics of different countries is emphasized. In the United States and Canada this field is further divided into subfields comprising geographical areas such as Western Europe, the Soviet Union and Eastern Europe, Africa, Latin America, the Middle East, South Asia, and Oceania. Outside of North America the study of U.S. or Canadian government is part of comparative politics.

The study of *international relations* focuses on interactions among nations. Foreign policies of nations, considered separately or on a comparative basis, are an integral part of this field. The field of international relations also includes international organizations and international law. Some examples of worldwide international organizations are the United Nations, World Bank, and UNESCO. Organizations such as the European Economic Community, the Organization of African Unity, and the Organization of Petroleum Exporting Countries have limited membership, but are included in the study of international organizations. International law deals with legal issues in the relations of nations; an example is the immunities and privileges of diplomats.

Political dynamics is the study of public opinion, interest groups (sometimes called "lobbies," pressure groups, or special interests), voting behavior—why people vote as they do, what influences voters, why people do not vote—and political parties—organized groups that attempt to win political control. Of course, these topics overlap with national, state (provincial), and local government and comparative politics, but as specialization within the discipline of political science has increased, political dynamics has become a separate field.

Two other fields—public policy and public administration—have become very prominent in political science. (Some political scientists consider public policy and public administration one field instead of two separate fields.) Although these fields concentrate on certain aspects of government, the study of which is not altogether new, attention given them in teaching and research in recent years is such that they can be considered separate. These fields provide training for working within the government. Public policy encompasses such areas as health, education, science, and defense. Public policy students are trained to do research to aid policy making in these areas and to analyze and evaluate such policies. The study of public administration is chiefly concerned with the implementation of public policy, although in actual practice experts in public administration do participate in the policy-making process as well.

The foregoing list of political science fields is not all-inclusive.[15] A comprehensive list of fields and subfields of political science prepared by the American Political Science Association follows:[16]

Administrative Law
Administration
Constitutional Law
Executive
Foreign Policy
Government Regulation of Business

International Law
International Organization and Administration
International Politics
Legislature
Methodology
Metropolitan and Urban Government and Politics
National Security Policy
Personnel Administration
Political and Constitutional History
Political Parties and Elections
Political Psychology
Political Socialization
Political Theory and Philosophy (Empirical)
Political Theory and Philosophy (Historical)
Political Theory and Philosophy (Normative)
Public Opinion
Revolution and Political Violence
State and Local Government and Politics
Voting Behavior
American National Government
Interest Groups
Political Development
Policy Studies
Communications
Federalism
Mathematics and Politics
Science and Government

POLITICAL SCIENTISTS IN THREE WORLDS

The Western (First) World's, and to a considerable extent the less-developed Third World's, official view of what a political scientist should be both as a person and as a researcher can be summed up in the terms *integrity* and *objectivity*. In theory, the researcher should follow where the evidence leads rather than forcing the evidence onto a preestablished path. A conclusion is reached by the rigorous and objective study of the phenomenon in question without emotional or *a priori* (preconceived) judgments. One may well question whether objectivity is possible when one examines the actions of another, and whether social and political pressures or one's philosophical and theological predelictions might not influence the conclusion. Yet, at least in theory, objectivity is considered the ideal.[17]

That is not to say that political scientists, governments, or politicans perceive the study of politics in the same light. All governments, to some extent, attempt to influence the mass of the population concerning the rectitude of the government's policies. In some countries any statements that might be construed as critical of or in opposition to government policies can bring about punishment of some sort. In the First World there have been a number of aberrations in regard to freedom of expression for social scientists and others. The United States has suffered through several critical periods since World War II, during which freedom of inquiry and expression was under severe attack. The most notorious assault occurred in the early 1950s when Senator Joseph McCarthy claimed to have discovered a plot within U.S. society to sell out the country to the Communists, a plot led by "red" intellectuals. The effects of this period are felt up to this very day. *The Chronicle of Higher Education* of September 2, 1982 (pp. 2–3), carried a story entitled "Temple Reinstates Professor Fired in McCarthy Era."

> Barrows Dunham, who lost his job at Temple University in 1953 after he refused to testify before the House Un-American Activities Committee, has been named an emeritus professor by Temples Board of Trustees [28 years later]. Mr. Dunham, now 75, taught at Temple 16 years and became chairman of the philosophy department before he was called to testify. He was held in contempt of Congress after refusing to answer a question about the date and place of his birth and was later found by the University to be in violation of a Pennsylvania loyalty statute.
>
> He has since taught at Beaver College, the University of Pennsylvania, and Montgomery Community College. Temple will pay Mr. Dunham a small stipend, a university spokesman said.

A film, *The Front,* by the popular actor/director Woody Allen, portrays a fictionalized account of the persecution of writers during the McCarthy period. It is true that the U.S. Senate finally condemned Senator McCarthy and he died in disgrace; nevertheless, the pressures of his activities were felt throughout society and the pain and suffering has not yet ended.

A second period of pressure to conform to policy took place during the Vietnam War era. For example, the Federal Bureau of Investigation launched *Cointelpro* (Counter-intelligence Program) which was meant to suppress criticism of the war, especially in college circles. False accusations, anonymous denunciations, behind-the-scenes pressure, and defamatory and libelous letters were used to attempt to silence and/or remove from teaching staffs "politically unreliable" professors.

The decline of support for the war even in government circles led to a reduction of and eventual end to *Cointelpro* activities. Subsequent "Freedom of Information" inquiries have brought much of this sordid business to light but certainly not all of it, as some vital records have been destroyed.

Today pressure to see the world, politics, and particularly religion in a particular way is being brought to bear in North America by the political right, conservatives and religious fundamentalists. The most active of this new wave are adherents of fundamental Christianity, which is mainly represented by the so-called Moral Majority organization. These people see today's world as a battleground between good and evil. The good clearly is that which conforms to their notions of God, country, and government. Those who do not view the world in the same way are seen as ideological enemies and if these unbelievers are in the teaching profession they are labeled pejoratively "secular humanists" who, in the "battle for the mind," do Satan's work. Thus certain teachers are seen as "purveyors of pornography, promiscuity, and perversion." So far these latest attacks have been fended off, but this has not prevented the religious right from attempting and actually getting their followers elected to public office. Laws have even been passed that, although so far overthrown in the courts, would force the teaching of "Creation Science"—a doctrine that says all material existence came into being some 6000 to 10,000 years ago by the acts of a Creator in a six-day period of 24-hour days—in public schools as an alternative to evolution. Freedom of expression and inquiry in North America and the First World has been saved, in part at least, by the existence of independent courts, professional organizations (such as U.S. and Canadian political science associations, American Association of University Professors, Canadian Association of University Teachers, and American Federation of Teachers), associations such as the American Civil Liberties Union, and individuals who fight to prevent the collapse of freedom. So far they have been successful.

The Third World unfortunately does not yet have a strong infrastructure that can resist social and governmental pressure to see society and politics as some would have them seen. Although lip service, in many cases, is given to freedom of research and inquiry, a political scientist must think long and hard about whether he or she might wish to say or write something that does not conform to conventional wisdom. Banning (house arrest, and the prohibition of being in company of more than two people who are not one's family) in the Republic of South Africa is quite effective in silencing opposition by the white population; for coloreds, blacks, and Asians, being killed "while trying to escape," having a "heart attack," and "committing suicide" when in the hands of the police are sufficient.[18] In Zambia arrest and indefinite detention quiets dissidents; in Argentina's military regime (which ended in 1983) "disappearance" under mysterious circumstances was the norm. A firing squad settles matters in Iran. Loss of work or a year or two of solitary confinement takes care of any problems caused by intellectuals in many states. India is among the few Third World countries that permit freedom of research and inquiry, but even there such freedom was suppressed during the Emergency (1975–1977).

In the Second (Communist) World the possibility or even need for objectivity is emphatically denied. The idea of a nonideological approach to social science problems is considered a pretense, something to be scoffed at, a bourgeois (First World) prejudice foisted on the suppressed proletarians (industrial workers) to fool them into supporting the status quo. Western political scientists are, in the last analysis, paid agents of the ruling capitalist class no matter whether they are college professors or government officials.

The Communists claim that only they have a true social science—in fact a true exact science—which tells them where the human race has been, where it is, and where it needs to and shall go. The writings of Karl Marx, Friedrich Engels, Vladimir Ilyich Ulyanov (Lenin), and on occasion certain specified successors such as Stalin, Mao, Castro, Tito, and Ceausescu are transformed into dogmatic "laws" of human behavior every bit as exact as the laws of physics and chemistry. Because these laws were contained in the "classics" of Marx, Engels, and Lenin, for a long time Communist regimes denied the need for and hindered the development of separate social sciences, political science in particular. All the politics, economics, history, sociology and anthropology necessary to understand the modern world was to be found in the classics and commentaries on them. Very slowly, over the three decades since Stalin's death, each of the Communist states has allowed some sort of political science disciplinary development, from the nearly nonexistent as in China, to the rudimentary as in the USSR, and to the highly developed discipline in Poland. Officially, political science in a Communist state is treated as little more than another tool for political indoctrination. Mikhail Suslov, considered the official ideologist of the Communist party of the Soviet Union, writing in 1972 in the journal *Kommunist,* in an article entitled "The Social Sciences: An Effective Weapon of the Party in the Building of Communism," stated:

> Social science teachers at higher education establishments. . . [are] expected to be concerned with man's inner world, to help him develop a correct,

Marxist–Leninist outlook, to make him into a convinced builder of communism.[19]

Does this mean all political science in the Second World is fake? The answer is an emphatic no. A Marxist approach to the study of politics can be as legitimate as any other and is frequently used by Western political scientists, as long as it is heuristic (used as a guide or reference for discovery).[20] It is the rigid dogmatic approach that is nonscientific, not the Marxist method itself, as when the explanation of the phenomenon studied is only given within the lines of a preconceived political mold required for propaganda purposes. In reading Second World political studies one is not likely to find anything of value in the area of *macropolitics* (an overall view of a political system) because any new ideas might call the whole system into question—which cannot be allowed. So far, doubts about the correctness of contemporary ruling Communist party policies have led not to change but to repression (East Germany—1953, Hungary—1956, Czechoslovakia—1968, Poland—1981). One, however, may find some useful studies produced by Communist political scientists on the *micropolitical* level (small unit studies, studies of specific political phenomena)—especially after the first few pages in which required references must be made to Marx, Engels, Lenin, and the current leader—because such work would not "undermine the foundations of the socialist state," a specific crime in many Communist countries.

One, then, finds both extremes in the Second World, turgid propaganda passed off as scientific work and objective studies, although from a Marxist point of view.

The principal arena for the meeting of political scientists of the First, Second, and Third World is provided by the International Political Science Association (IPSA), a body consisting of 40 national political science associations plus individual members. IPSA has international conferences every few years which so far have been held in East and West Europe and North and South America. Besides the international conferences, meetings of the 22 recognized research committees and 21 study groups deal with problems ranging from "Conceptual and Terminological Analysis" to "Political Education."[21] To both the world conventions and the research meetings come political scientists from all areas of the world, making this a truly international forum for the exchange of ideas.

NOTES

1. See Robert C. Bone, *Action and Organization: An Introduction to Contemporary Political Science* (New York: Harper & Row, 1972), p. 24.

2. Alan C. Isaak, *Scope and Methods of Political Science* (Homewood, Ill.: Dorsey Press, 1981), p. 35.
3. Ibid.
4. Ibid., p. 37.
5. Arthur Bentley, *The Process of Government* (Chicago: University of Chicago Press, 1908).
6. Graham Wallas, *Human Nature in Politics* (Lincoln: University of Nebraska Press, 1962; originally published in England in 1908).
7. Charles E. Merriam, *New Aspects of Politics* (Chicago: University of Chicago Press, 1924).
8. See George Kateb, *Political Theory: Its Nature and Uses* (New York: St. Martin's Press, 1968), p. 2.
9. See for example Frederick L. Schuman, *International Politics,* 7th ed. (New York: McGraw-Hill, 1969), pp. 424–442.
10. An example of such a study is Edward S. Corwin, *The President: Office and Powers* (New York: New York University Press, 1957). See also Department of State, Office of Legal Advisor, "The Legality of United States Participation in the Defense of Vietnam," *Yale Law Journal* 75 (June 1966): 1085–1108.
11. David Easton, "The Current Meaning of Behavioralism," in James C. Charlesworth, ed., *Contemporary Political Analysis* (New York: Free Press, 1967), p. 16.
12. See David Easton, "The New Revolution in Political Science," *American Political Science Review* 3 (December 1969): 1060. About nine years later John C. Wahlke, another prominent American political scientist, suggested that political behavior research was still in a prebehavioral stage. (This indicates the extent of disagreement within political science.) See John C. Wahlke, "Pre-Behavioralism in Political Science," *American Political Science Review* 73 (March 1979): 9–31.
13. Easton, "The New Revolution," p. 1060.
14. From a flyer announcing a new journal of the Semiotic Society of America, *American Journal of Semiotics* (Fall 1981). See also "Scholars Sign on with Semiotics," Sunday *New York Times,* "Week in Review," October 18, 1981, p. 11.
15. Considerable disagreement exists within the discipline of political science regarding what should be studied and by which methods it should be studied. See Michael Mandelbaum, "A Discipline Shaped Not by Accord but by Disagreement," Sunday *New York Times* "Week in Review," March 27, 1977, p. 18.
16. This list of subfields is from the "classification of members by fields of interest" found on pages 650–712 of the 1968 *Biographical Directory* of the American Political Science Association. A somewhat different breakdown of the discipline appears in the 1973 *Directory*; yet another list is in the 1980 *Directory*.
17. For an interesting study of a psychologist gone awry in regard to honesty and objectivity, see L. S. Heanshaw, *Cyril Burt: Psychologist* (Ithaca, N.Y.: Cornell University Press, 1979).
18. South Africa is a First World country for the white population but a Third World country for its some 80% nonwhite inhabitants.

19. This is translated in M. Suslov, *The CPSU: The Party of Creative Marxism* (Moscow: Novosti Press Agency Publishing House, 1972), pp. 51–52.
20. See Irving M. Zeitlin, *Marxism: A Re-Examination* (Princeton, N.J.: Van Nostrand, 1967), esp. pp. 152–155.
21. *IPSA Participation* [Newsletter], "Supplement 1985," pp. 2–15.

2

The Contemporary Political World: The Rationale for a Three World Approach

The contemporary political world is characterized by great diversity. Modern states display a wide variety of political structures, issues, and political styles which the student of politics must attempt to understand. Modern political systems can best be understood as products of the interaction of two factors, the level of development and the political culture. The level of development is determined by the social setting of the state. The social setting determines the dominant elite and the political issues on which political discussion will focus. Preindustrial, industrial, and postindustrial social settings exist in the contemporary world.

The political culture is the particular set of beliefs, attitudes, and orientations that are dominant in a society. At every level of development specific choices are available regarding the manner in which national problems are defined, demands are made on government, and standards of political morality are developed. By influencing such choices, the political culture affects the pattern of politics. The political beliefs of elite groups are the most important element of the national political culture because these groups dominate political decision making and are in direct control of the government. The political beliefs of the elite constitute the operative ideology of the system.

A comparative study of the contemporary political world which employs the concepts of the level of development and the political culture reveals the existence of three political worlds. The pattern of politics in the Western or First World is the product of the interaction of industrial and postindustrial social settings with liberal political beliefs. The pattern of politics in the Communist or

Second World reveals the interaction of Marxist–Leninist political beliefs with either a social setting of advanced industrialization (the Communist states of Europe) or a setting of preindustrialism (the Communist states outside Europe). Finally, the political systems of the Third World are the products of preindustrial social settings and belief systems combining traditional values with either liberal or Marxist–Leninist political values.

CONTEMPORARY POLITICAL DIVERSITY

When students undertake to study the modern political world, they are confronted with a great diversity of institutional forms, issues, and political styles. Even a superficial comparison of such states as the United States, the Soviet Union, and Iran reveals the degree of diversity present in modern political life. Although the diversity took much of the twentieth century to develop, it has only been fully recognized in the study of politics in the past few decades. Earlier generations of students were convinced that all of the areas of the world would eventually come to resemble the states of the West, especially the democratic states of the United States and Great Britain, and that it was not important to study other varieties of political systems because they would soon disappear. In 1914, 84% of the world's land area was under

President Ronald Reagan chairs a cabinet meeting.

the political control of Europeans or North Americans. Britain, France, Belgium, the Netherlands, Spain, and Portugal had imposed colonial rule over areas of Africa and Asia which exceeded many times the geographic size of Europe. Despite some significant differences from area to area, local values and institutions were suppressed, and Western political values and Western political institutions were imposed on the populations of the controlled areas. In addition, by 1914 the development of a fledgling democratic movement in Russia and the existence of social welfare legislation in Germany beneficial to common workers led many Europeans to believe that even the monarchies of Europe had begun the evolution toward democracy. The political world temporarily achieved the appearance of homogeneity, but the facade of homogeneity was short-lived.

The Russian Revolution of 1917 brought to power the Bolshevik faction of the Russian Social Democratic Labor party which was committed to a new system of political values called Marxism. More precisely, the Bolsheviks advocated Marxism–Leninism, Marxism as interpreted by their leader Vladimir Ilych Ulyanov (Lenin). Although developed in Western Europe, Marxist theory differed greatly from the political thought that prevailed in the rest of Europe and North America. The new value system was ultimately extended to all of Eastern Europe as well as to China and other parts of Asia, although in a modified form, and came to constitute the major alternative to the older political values of the West. The commitment to Marxist–Leninist ideology has led to the creation of a political style in the Second World different from that of the Western states.

After World War II, the diversity of the political world was further increased as decolonization led to the creation of more than 100 newly independent states in Africa, Asia, the Middle East, and Latin America. This is more than the total number of states in existence in 1914. Native values were reasserted throughout the Third World, and political institutions were developed that reflected both the traditional cultures of those areas and the interaction of those traditional cultures with the political values of the First or Second World. Although the new states shared the common characteristic of being less developed than the states of either the West or the Second World, they differed greatly from one another. In many areas of the Third World, unique regional, racial, and ethnic rivalries that predated the colonial period reemerged to influence the political process. By the 1970s it was also clear that the new states differed greatly in terms of economic potential. Some states rich in oil or other strategic natural resources made significant economic progress. Included in this group are Venezuela, Kuwait, and several other members of the Organization of Petroleum Exporting Countries (OPEC). The term *Fourth World* has been applied by some analysts to states such as Bangladesh and Somalia which lack such strategic resources and have been less successful in their attempts at economic development. Recently, the term *Fifth World* has also been used to identify the "microstates" or the states smallest in territory and population, such as Barbados, Grenada, and Malta.

Why Ronald Reagan, Why the Ayatollah Khomeini?

The diversity of contemporary politics is apparent from even a cursory comparison of the elites, political issues, and political institutions in different countries. In 1979 the traditional religious leader Ayatollah Khomeini swept to power in Iran by advocating a doctrine of militant Islam which called for a return to the fundamental teachings of the Islamic religion and the punishment of forces, both domestic and foreign, that sought to modernize Iranian society. As part of his conservative revolution, women returned to wearing veils, alcoholic beverages and Western music were banned, and social crimes such as prostitution and homosexuality were made punishable by death. Although some resistance developed from ethnic minorities and leftish students, Khomeini and his program received the overwhelming support of the majority of the Iranian population.

The emergence of traditional leaders displaying a heroic leadership style has not been restricted to Iran. The possession of charisma (personal attributes or qualities recognized by others as extraordinary) and identification with historic events are often prerequisites to political leadership in the Third World. Important leaders such as Muammar Qaddafi of Libya and Mohammed Zia ul-Haq of Pakistan regularly wear uniforms to demonstrate

Colonel Muammar Qaddafi, Libya's leader.

their ties to the military. It is also common for members of the elite to seek political support by appealing to tradition. Arab oil ministers attend meetings of the international oil cartels donned in traditional dress. In addition, political parties and interest groups often develop from traditional social groups such as tribes and ethnic communities or from national liberation movements and retain the names of the original structures. Political life in the Third World has been shaped by the colonial experience, especially the reaction to it, and by the pressure to attain more of the economic achievements of the states of the West and the Soviet bloc. Political elites in the Third World are interested in issues that are relevant to political life in states at lower levels of development. Foremost among these issues are demands for global decolonization, including an end to the interference of outside states in their domestic affairs, and programs to speed the economic development of the state.[1]

Different elites, political issues, and institutions dominate in the more developed political systems of the West and the Soviet bloc. Elite members in these systems affect a bureaucratic style and behave as political managers or problem solvers. Decisions are made in the context of large bureaucracies (e.g., the U.S. Department of Defense) and, although political in nature, decisions are often justified on the basis of formal studies and scientific reports. High-ranking members of the government bureaucracy usually possess considerable scientific and technological expertise. Members of the Western political elite are often recruited from business and academic circles and may, as in the case of former U.S. National Security Advisor Henry Kissinger, serve in a political role only temporarily. Members of the elite of the industrialized Communist states have backgrounds comparable to their Western counterparts. Many Communist party leaders in the Soviet Union and Eastern Europe have professional backgrounds in either state industry or state agriculture. Although a compelling political actor in Iran, a figure such as the Ayatollah Khomeini would be an irrelevant anachronism in both the West and the Second World.

Political issues in the developed world also differ from those of the Third World. Contemporary politics in the West reflects a concern for the maintenance of economic affluence, environmental quality, individual privacy, control over bureaucracy, equality for women, and a need for more meaningful participation by the majority in political decision making.[2] Some of these issues, such as protection of the environment, are also common in the Second World. However, the commitment to Marxist–Leninist ideology produces a wide range of unique issues concerned with the maintenance of a socialist-totalitarian system in the Communist states. Such issues include the establishment of official artistic, cultural, and educational standards to which all persons must conform and programs to strengthen the control of the Communist party over the rest of society. Political decision making in the Communist states also takes place within a bureaucratic context. The agencies of the Soviet state and the Communist party together constitute the largest political bureaucracy in the world. This bureaucracy is required to implement Marxist–Leninist ideology, which establishes rules and guidelines for every area of life.

TWO KEY VARIABLES: POLITICAL DEVELOPMENT AND HUMAN CHOICE

Understanding contemporary political diversity is the first task of the modern student of politics. The differences in the political process which distinguish the Western states, the Communist World, and the Third World are the result of the interaction of two sets of factors, the level of political development and the element of human choice.

Level of Political Development

The level of political development is the general political setting of the state, which consists of three elements: (1) the natural and financial resources available to the political system, (2) the size and capability of existing political institutions, and (3) the political orientation of the general population. The political orientation determines the willingness of the general population to accept political authority and to support the political system. Support for the political system tends to increase as citizens encounter authority in schools and the work place and are educated about the national political system. States at higher levels of development are distinguished from those at lower levels by the possession of greater resources, larger and more efficient political institutions, and populations more willing to accept authority and to support the state.

The level of political development is important in determining the range of political issues that are discussed because different political problems develop at different levels of development. The agenda of political issues in most Third World states includes the need to develop a national identity and create loyalty to the state. The manipulation of traditional symbols by elites and the rhetorical attacks on the industrialized states common in the Third World are part of the effort to create a national identity. Because most of the states of the West have overcome the problem of creating a national identity, symbolic issues of this type are not prominent in the politics of these systems. The dominant political issues in the West are the maintenance of economic prosperity, and to a lesser extent, quality-of-life concerns. These issues are largely irrelevant in the Third World where political systems are attempting to cope with more basic problems. In addition, the level of political development places absolute limits on the functions that the political system can perform. Given the limited resources in the states of the Third World, it is impossible for any of them to develop a military capability equal to that of the United States or the Soviet Union even if this became the primary goal of the elite.

Human Choice

The level of political development is not an absolute determinant of the pattern of politics. At every stage of development, alternate issues are available for discussion and alternative public policies (authoritative decisions made by governments or ruling political parties) are possible for dealing with societal problems. Within the limits set by the level of political development, the range and quality of political issues and the selection of specific policies are the results of human choice. Differences in the policies of Italy and the Soviet Union, both advanced industrial states, and of India and Tanzania, both less-developed countries (LDCs), demonstrate the effects of human choice. In political life the element of human choice is reflected in the political culture. Political culture is the amalgam of political values, attitudes, and orientations present in a political system. It is the mental dimension of politics, the feelings and beliefs that exist within the general population of a state. Political cultures differ from one nation to the next. All members of a society hold political values and attitudes whether or not they are capable of expressing them in a coherent and systematic fashion. However, because political decisions in the contemporary world are made by small groups of elites who have disproportionate power and influence, the most important element of any political culture is the belief system of the elite. The belief system that guides the political behavior of the elite is called the *operative ideology*.[3] It is through political culture and the operative ideology that the element of human choice enters the political process. The pattern of politics that characterizes any political system over a substantial period of time is the result of the interaction of the factors of political development with the elements of political culture, especially the operative ideology of the elite.

By employing a comparative framework based on an understanding of the stages of political development and the role of political culture, the diversity of modern political life becomes both manageable and intelligible. The use of this framework reveals the existence of three political worlds, the West or First World, the Communist or Second World, and the Third World. (see Table 2.1) The political style of the Third World develops from the preindustrial nature of the society and economy. Social and economic problems associated with underdevelopment dominate political life. In most cases, the population consists largely of parochials (rural persons primarily interested in family affairs and a traditional life-style) who have only recently been brought under the authority of the state and whose support for the state is uncertain. The presence of a majority of parochials requires that the elites adopt a traditional and heroic style of leadership. The Third World encompasses the LDCs of Africa, Asia, Latin America, and the Middle East (see Table 2.2).

The Communist World consists of two distinct economic and social settings, a developed setting in the states of Europe and a less-developed, agrarian setting in the Communist states outside Europe. The political style of the European Communist states (with the exception of Albania; see Table 2.3) develops from the advanced industrial nature of their societies. Elites are selected on the basis of political loyalty and the possession of scientific and technical knowledge relevant to modern industry and agriculture. They operate within the context of large-scale bureaucracies and adopt a bureaucratic and managerial style. Issues related to the development and expansion of the industrial complex dominate the political agenda. In the area of human choice, all significant elite groups embrace Marxist–Leninist political and social values. In the Communist states outside Europe elites have also chosen to adopt Marxist–Leninist values, but they operate within the context of a preindustrial and agrarian social setting. Confronted with the existence of a rural majority and the problems connected with underdevelopment, they frequently adopt a heroic and charismatic style of leadership. The issue of how to develop a modern industrial complex preoccupies the political system.

The political style of the states of the Western World develops from their industrial and postindustrial social settings (see Table 2.4). As in the Communist states of Europe, elites are recruited on the basis of the possession of scientific and technical knowledge, and issues associated with maintaining acceptable rates of economic growth dominate the political agenda. However, the pattern of politics in the West differs from that of the Communist World because Western elites are committed to different political values, the values of liberalism, social liberalism, and social welfare theory (see Chapter 4). It is the element of human choice that accounts for the different patterns of politics in the First and Second Worlds.

POLITICS AND LEVEL OF DEVELOPMENT: A USEFUL MODEL

Many models exist to help us to understand the relationship between the social and economic environment of the state and the political process. A

Table 2.1 The Three Political Worlds

	The West (First World)	The Communist (Second) World	The Third World
States	United States, Canada, Great Britain, France, German Federal Republic, Denmark, Norway, Sweden, Switzerland, Luxembourg, Netherlands, Belgium, Japan, Australia, New Zealand, Italy, Portugal, Ireland, Spain, Israel, etc.	*Europe:* USSR, Czechoslovakia, Hungary, German Democratic Republic, Poland, Romania, Bulgaria, Yugoslavia, and Albania *Outside Europe:* China, North Korea, Cuba, Vietnam, Laos, Kampuchea, Mongolia, and Afghanistan	Less-developed countries (LDCs) of Africa, Asia, the Middle East, and Latin America
Social setting	Postindustrial and advanced industrial settings	Advanced industrial and industrial setting in Europe; preindustrial setting outside of Europe and Albania	Preindustrial, modernizing settings: limited industrial roles; agricultural roles predominate
Majority coalition (dominant elite)	Technocrats: scientific and technological elites	Industrial and agricultural specialists within the Communist party and state bureaucracy	Civilian and military bureaucrats; large landowners; heroic–charismatic style
Agenda of politics	Preservation of affluence; quality-of-life issues	*Europe:* Industrial growth, improved mass welfare, Communist party control of society *Outside Europe:* Rapid modernization, rhetoric of world revolution, Communist party control of society	Increased rate of development: nation-building; anti-colonialism

Political structures	High bureaucratic specialization and proliferation	High bureaucratic specialization and proliferation	Low bureaucratic specialization and proliferation
General population: Outlook on authority	Majority employed in large-scale enterprises; majority accepts authority	*Europe*: Majority accepts authority *Outside Europe*: Parochial majority	Parochial majority; parochial view of authority prevails
Political ideology	Liberalism, social liberalism, and social welfare theory	Marxism–Leninism	Combinations of traditional values, Western social liberalism, and Marxism–Leninism

Table 2.2 Comparative Resources: The Third World

State	GNP million U.S. $	GNP per capita Rank	GNP per capita U.S. $
Algeria	39,363	56	2,091
Angola	6,299	82	902
Argentina	123,138	37	4,361
Bahrain	2,932	24	8,474
Bangladesh	11,392	138	129
Barbados	822	48	3,301
Benin	1,114	117	322
Bolivia	5,839	76	1,071
Botswana	797	84	886
Brazil	245,110	57	2,002
Brunei	2,620	6	14,162
Burma	5,894	134	171
Burundi	881	131	210
Cameroon	6,373	90	743
Central African Republic	771	115	333
Chad	498	139	113
Chile	27,548	51	2,506
Colombia	32,600	70	1,251
Congo	1,574	80	1,014
Costa Rica	4,623	58	1,923
Cyprus	2,199	44	3,496
Dominican Republic	6,784	72	1,175
Ecuador	10,891	66	1,358
Egypt	25,273	99	600
El Salvador	3,420	92	725
Equatorial Guinea	152	98	608
Ethiopia	4,094	136	137
Gabon	3,389	38	4,279
Gambia	227	112	384
Ghana	4,359	114	359
Guatemala	556	75	1,096
Guinea	1,581	118	315
Guyana	7,805	95	680
Haiti	1,436	124	266
Honduras	2,414	96	633
India	159,766	128	230
Indonesia	69,467	105	460
Iran	83,709	55	2,160
Iraq	36,647	48	2,791
Ivory Coast	9,950	71	1,235

Table 2.2 Comparative Resources: The Third World

State	GNP million U.S. $	GNP per capita Rank	GNP per capita U.S. $
Jamaica	2,398	77	1,069
Jordan	3,596	73	1,154
Kenya	6,769	109	412
Korea, South	54,915	65	1,388
Kuwait	33,524	3	24,434
Laos	300	140	87
Lebanon	na		na
Lesotho	676	102	505
Liberia	977	101	515
Libya	30,540	20	10,119
Madagascar	3,172	113	366
Malawi	1,491	126	248
Malaysia	22,728	62	1,623
Mali	1,354	133	196
Mauritania	622	108	414
Mauritius	968	81	1,011
Mexico	181,611	50	2,590
Morocco	18,283	85	872
Mozambique	4,774	110	394
Nepal	2,029	137	135
Nicaragua	2,090	87	837
Niger	1,795	116	325
Nigeria	79,806	79	1,035
Oman	4,780	31	5,365
Pakistan	25,043	121	292
Panama	3,193	61	1,666
Paraguay	4,367	67	1,346
Peru	18,607	78	1,056
Philippines	35,881	91	728
Quatar	6,644	1	28,034
Rwanda	1,156	128	226
Saudi Arabia	117,595	11	12,484
Senegal	2,717	103	471
Sierra Leone	1,049	119	306
Singapore	10,674	35	4,422
Somalia	1,519	122	283
Sri Lanka	4,138	123	279
Sudan	7,844	107	418
Swaziland	455	89	786
Syria	13,027	63	1,481

Table 2.2 Comparative Resources: The Third World

State	GNP million U.S. $	GNP per capita	
		Rank	U.S. $
Taiwan	40,137	54	2,255
Tanzania	4,919	125	264
Thailand	32,928	94	691
Togo	1,001	111	388
Trinidad and Tobago	6,106	32	5,268
Tunisia	8,440	69	1,301
Turkey	61,078	68	1,327
Uganda	6,000	104	468
United Arab Emirates	27,555	2	27,975
Upper Volta (Burkina)	1,358	130	221
Uruguay	9,811	46	3,398
Venezuela	60,743	43	3,726
Yemen, Arab. Rep.	3,084	100	578
Yemen, Peoples Dem. Rep.	810	106	423
Zaire	5,756	132	201
Zambia	3,514	97	609
Zimbabwe	5,424	93	718

Source: Statistics from Ruth Leger Sivard, *World Militry and Social Expenditures 1983* (Washington, D.C.: World Priorities, 1983). Cited with permission of the author.

model is a mental construct by which political events can be understood. Models help us to organize our thoughts and to understand complex relationships between political variables. Everett Ladd has developed a model that employs the concept of the sociopolitical period to explain this relationship (see Figure 2.1).[4] Each sociopolitical period consists of four interdependent elements: (1) the social setting, (2) the majority coalition, (3) the agenda of politics, and (4) the political party system. In this discussion Ladd's work will be combined with the findings of other studies.

The Social Setting

At any point in time, a dominant set of economic and social relationships defines the general nature of the society. The social setting may be preindustrial (agricultural), industrial, or postindustrial. A preindustrial social setting is one in which most economic activity occurs within the context of small-scale agricultural or family enterprises. The great majority of the population lives in the rural countryside and is preoccupied with the

Table 2.3   Comparative Resources: The Communist World

State	GNP million U.S. $	GNP per capita Rank	GNP per capita U.S. $
Bulgaria	37,390	39	4,219
Czechoslovakia	89,260	28	5,821
Germany, East	120,940	21	7,226
Hungary	44,990	40	4,200
Poland	139,780	41	3,929
Romania	85,500	42	3,851
USSR	1,212,030	34	4,564
Other Communist States			
Afghanistan	3,661	127	240
Albania	2,400	83	898
China	300,000	120	298
Kampuchea	—	—	—
Korea, North	20,500	74	1,151
Laos	300	140	87
Mongolia	1,420	86	854
Vietnam	8,600	135	161
Yugoslavia	59,132	49	2,651
Cuba	18,000	60	1,864

Source: Statistics from Ruth Leger Sivard, *World Military and Social Expenditures 1983* (Washington, D.C.: World Priorities, 1983). Cited with permission of the author.

affairs of the local community. A minority of the population, usually between 5 and 30% lives in cities and is engaged in industrial or service employment.[5] The urban group is better educated, receives more government services, and is exposed to foreign influences that do not reach the countryside. The rural and urban groups are culturally isolated from one another and significant tension exists between them. In many preindustrial states the urban group constitutes an important force for change toward social, economic, and political arrangements similar to those in the more developed states.

In an industrial social setting a substantial portion of the population, usually between 30 and 70%, is employed in industry or service enterprises and lives in urban areas.[6] The development of the industrial complex is well under way and communication and transportation networks extend into most rural areas. Large government and private bureaucracies also exist with which the majority of the population must interact on a daily basis. A rural subculture may persist and some parochial groups may abstain from economic and political activities, but a modern and urban outlook dominates

Leaders of the Soviet Union on the rostrum of the Lenin Mausoleum, outside the Kremlin in Moscow.

the society. Many scholars believe it is useful to distinguish between the early stages of industrialization in which society is preoccupied with building more and larger industries and the advanced stages of industrialization in which concern develops for the regulation of industry and the extension of social welfare benefits to the general population.

The postindustrial setting is defined as one of the relative mass affluence in which both the tasks of industrialization and increased regulation have been completed. The term *mass affluence* does not mean that the majority possesses great wealth. Rather, it defines a condition in which basic questions of economic survival no longer concern the majority of the population and poverty is confined to a distinct minority. (see Chapter 3). A large majority of the labor force, over 70%, works within a bureaucratic setting and the number of government and private bureaucracies exceeds that of the earlier industrial period.[7] In addition, white-collar employees in the service industries (health, banking, tourism, education, and secretarial services) outnumber blue-collar production workers. Only the most affluent political systems of the West, which provide their citizens with the full protections of a developed welfare state, have attained this level.

The Majority Coalition

In every society political life is dominated by small elite groups that possess great influence and power. The dominant elite group or groups, which Ladd

Table 2.4 Comparative Resources: The Western World

State	GNP million U.S. $	GNP per capita Rank	GNP per capita U.S. $
Australia	145,328	21	9,943
Austria	79,364	17	10,508
Belgium	118,404	13	12,023
Canada	244,683	19	10,159
Denmark	64,059	10	12,504
Finland	49,390	18	10,333
France	654,120	12	12,156
Germany, West	824,886	8	13,399
Greece	42,273	36	4,384
Iceland	2,738	14	12,009
Ireland	17,322	33	5,074
Israel	21,237	29	5,635
Italy	393,925	27	7,012
Japan	1,048,168	23	8,975
Luxembourg	5,204	5	14,297
Malta	1,240	45	3,406
Netherlands	161,227	15	11,399
New Zealand	23,954	25	7,727
Norway	54,578	9	13,357
Portugal	23,657	52	2,393
South Africa[a]	68,552	53	2,387
Spain	208,040	30	5,550
Sweden	116,027	7	13,962
Switzerland	103,362	4	16,188
United Kingdom	516,004	22	9,213
United States	2,583,700	16	11,347

[a] Because of the official policy of apartheid, separation of the races, only white South Africans experience a political existence based on a high level of development and a Western political culture. Blacks and whites opposed to apartheid are denied the right to interact freely.
Source: Statistics from Ruth Leger Sivard, *World Military and Social Expenditures 1983* (Washington, D.C.: World Priorities, 1983). Cited with permission of the author.

calls the majority coalition, develop from the social setting. These groups possess the skills and expertise most necessary to the society at the stage of development defined by the social setting. In the case of a preindustrial, agrarian society, the majority coalition consists of groups whose status is based on landownership. At this stage of development, close ties exist between large landowners and the military.

In an industrial setting, business entrepreneurs and labor leaders dominate. These groups possess the skills necessary to organize the two

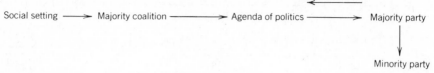

Figure 2.1. The Sociopolitical Period (Everett Ladd).

elements most essential to the completion of the process of industrialization—capital and manpower. The political power of the labor elite usually increases in the latter stages of the industrial process when low wages and worker insecurity lead to a demand for industrial regulation.

In the postindustrial social setting, the majority coalition consists of elites possessing the scientific and technological expertise necessary to manage the complex problems of society such as pollution, citizen alienation, and depletion of natural resources. Control of such problems is a prerequisite to the maintenance of mass affluence.

Regardless of the level of development, the majority coalition never constitutes the majority in a numerical sense. In Ladd's theory, the majority coalition refers to the group that possesses a majority of power and influence in the society. As an elite group, it constitutes only a small percentage of the total population. Karl Deutsch estimates that elite groups that identify important problems in society and raise them to the level of major political issues are limited to those individuals who are in the top 5% of the population in education, income, and occupational status.[8] According to Deutsch, the elite groups that make decisions about those issues and implement specific policies may constitute a group as small as 50 persons per million in the general population.

The Agenda of Politics

It is the majority coalition that determines the agenda of politics, the major political issues discussed at a given time. Political issues emerge to dominate the political scene because they are relevant to the values and interests of the majority coalition. In a preindustrial society the dominant political issues center on the particular form that the new political system should take. Of special concern is the issue of the proper role of the majority of the population in the political process. The agenda of politics in an industrial setting changes as different political elites assume a powerful position in the society. In the early stages of industrialization, the agenda of politics is dominated by business or governmental elites concerned with industrial development. The major issues revolve around the identification and achievement of the conditions necessary for the rapid completion of the process of industrialization.[9] In the latter stages of industrialization, the agenda of politics is increasingly influenced by labor groups. These groups generate issues involving reform of the industrial system and the redistribution of the wealth of society to provide unemployment insurance, pensions, and other benefits to workers.

In the postindustrial setting, the agenda of politics is composed of the issues created by the scientific and technological elite. The general theme of those issues is the preservation of the prevailing mass affluence and the protection of the quality of life. Most quality-of-life issues actually are preservation issues in disguise—the preservation of the environment from pollution, the preservation of privacy in the face of the growing power of government, and the preservation and extension of the concept of equality to women in economic life. The emergence of a preservationist agenda accentuates the problem of citizen apathy and alienation. Complex scientific and sociological issues are difficult for the majority to understand and are generally not issues around which mass political movements form. Since the 1960s, many states of the West have experienced increasing political apathy among their citizens. This apathy has become a major concern of social scientists and political leaders.

The political agenda of the Communist states of Europe reflects the transitional nature of the social setting between advanced industrialization and postindustrialization in the Soviet Union. Certain quality-of-life issues exist, but they are less prominent than in the West. The Soviet political agenda is still dominated by issues concerned with the expansion of the industrial complex. The Marxist-Leninist commitment to collective political action also discourages the development of quality-of-life issues oriented toward the individual. The preoccupation with industrial expansion is almost total in the Communist states.

The Political Party System

The majority coalition combined with the agenda of politics determines the nature of partisan political competition. Political discussion centers on the issues of the political agenda. The political party or coalition of parties that most closely represents the issues of the political agenda, and works to translate the interests of the majority coalition into government policy, becomes the dominant political party or coalition in the system. This status is achieved as a result of the support of the majority coalition. Minority parties, those not supported by the majority coalition, must constantly react to the items of the political agenda as defined by the majority party. When minority parties attempt a direct challenge of the prevailing agenda of politics they are opposed by the full resources of the majority coalition.

Change in the Sociopolitical period

According to Ladd's model, once the majority coalition, agenda of politics, and dominant party are established, they will not change as long as the social setting remains the same. A change in the social setting, such as from agriculture to beginning industrialization, signals the onset of a new sociopolitical period. In this period, a new majority coalition will initiate a changed agenda of politics. The political party that was dominant in the first period may maintain its position if it succeeds in attracting the support of the new majority coalition, or a new dominant party may emerge. As Ladd notes, incremental changes in the social setting occur constantly. The sociopolitical periods he identifies are analytical abstractions intended only to help us to understand the dynamics of major social and political change.[10]

POLITICAL STRUCTURES AND POLITICAL DEVELOPMENT

The preindustrial, industrial, and postindustrial social settings are also characterized by the existence of political structures (organizations) with different characteristics and capabilities. Governmental structures and political parties in both the postindustrial states of the West and the industrial states of the Communist World are complex, large-scale, specialized bureaucracies. Control of bureaucracy is a persistent political issue in the West. The behavior and role expectations of Western civil servants and Communist state bureaucrats are shaped by different ideological commitments, but the organizational settings of which they are part are similar. In both systems governmental structures possess the capability to regulate most areas of human activity. Because of the strong belief in individualism in the West, however, governments do not always utilize this capability.

In the preindustrial states of the Third World, governmental structures tend to be less specialized and smaller in scale. The concentration of power in the hands of small groups of military officers and bureaucrats is common. The creation of effective governmental structures constitutes a major political issue. Many groups, regions, and areas of human activity remain resistant to regulation by government. Political parties are also less developed than in the industrialized world and frequently are so weak that they play only a symbolic role in the political process.

Political Structures and Four Problems of Development

Structural proliferation (an increase in the number of political organizations) and structural differentiation (increased specialization in political organizations) are among the most important elements of political development.

Structural proliferation and specialization occur when the political system confronts new and complex problems that demonstrate the inadequacy of existing structures. Political structures in the industrialized states of the West and the Communist World are more specialized than in the Third World because the former systems have confronted certain problems and conditions that prompted the development of more sophisticated structures. Historically, four basic problems have challenged political systems and led to the development of new structures. They are state building, nation building, participation, and distribution.[11] State building involves the establishment of political authority over the entire territory of the state. Nation building constitutes the task of developing loyalty and commitment to the political system among the populace. The problems of participation and distribution occur at later stages of development. The problem of participation results from the demands of groups in society for a larger role in political decision making. The issue of distribution concerns the demands of groups in society for a redistribution of economic resources and benefits.

Political structures in the West and in the industrialized Communist states are more specialized than in the Third World because the former systems have faced the four problems of development over a long period of time. In the states of Western Europe, army and police bureaucracies evolved over several centuries in response to the problems of state building and nation building. The nineteenth century witnessed the proliferation and development of political parties, interest groups, and popularly elected legislatures in response to demands for increased political participation. In the twentieth century, the social setting of advanced industrialization produced a political agenda that included the demand for the redistribution of economic benefits. This led to the development of education, health, and social agencies associated with the modern welfare state.

The political infrastructures of the Communist states of Europe are also extensive and highly specialized. Governmental and Communist party bureaucracies successfully penetrate every area of the society. In assessing the Soviet Union, one study has noted that the Soviet political system has a regulative capability greater than that of any other human experiment in political rule.[12] The rise of the Polish labor union Solidarity is indicative of the increased concern for industrial reform emerging in the most industrially advanced Communist states, Czechoslovakia, Poland, East Germany, Hungary, and the Soviet Union. The desire to develop an agenda of industrial reform has met with the opposition of the Communist parties of these states, however, which continue to favor an agenda of increased industrialization and to seek to reaffirm their control over the society.

In the states of Third World, the problems of political development have only recently been confronted. In most of the states of Africa and Asia,

political activity has centered on the development of governmental structures capable of accomplishing state-building and nation-building tasks.
These structures frequently consist of small-scale bureaucracies with only
moderate specialization. The agenda of politics in a preindustrial setting
does not emphasize issues concerned with participation or distribution.
Consequently, political parties and legislative bodies remain largely symbolic. Political structures in the Communist states outside Europe are similar
to those of the Third World because they also develop from preindustrial
social settings that have not experienced the political issues associated with
advanced industrialization. Regulative and police agencies in the Communist
states tend to be larger and more specialized than those in most Third World
states, however, because of the importance Communist party elites assign to
the mobilization and control of the general population.

SOCIAL SETTING AND POLITICAL BEHAVIOR

Before completing our discussion of social setting, one final point must be
made. The social setting also has an important effect on the political
behavior of the general population. At each stage of development individuals
encounter economic and social institutions that prepare them to react to
political structures and political authority in different ways. In this context,
some studies of political development have identified changes in the composition of the work force to be among the most important aspects of
political development.[13] Such studies have found that citizens readily accept
political authority only after constant exposure to the authority of managers,
supervisors, and executives at their place of work. The exposure to
authority is most constant where the majority of the work force is employed
in large-scale organizations such as factories and corporate bureaucracies.
As the number of such large-scale enterprises increases at higher levels of
development, the percentage of the population that accepts authority as a
fact of daily life also increases. Citizens who accept authority are the source
of such supports for the political system as taxes, national service, and
demonstrations of loyalty. The existence of such groups is essential for the
performance of any major political task. In the social settings of the West
and the industrialized Communist states, groups that accept political authority constitute the vast majority of the population.

Groups that do not accept the modern concept of authority are often
referred to as *parochials*. Parochials view the exercise of authority as an
assertion of status. They accept authority as legitimate only if they recognize
the superior status of the person involved. Consequently, parochials accept
the direction of family members, clerics, and local notables whom they know
personally and judge to have superior status, but view the authority of the

state as an illegitimate intrusion into their lives.[14] The existence of the parochial view of authority is a barrier to the achievement of political tasks requiring modern organization and direction by officials of the political system. The parochial view of authority is common to groups employed in agriculture and small-scale family enterprises. In the preindustrial social settings of the Third World and some of the Communist states outside Europe, parochials frequently constitute a majority of the population. In such states parochial groups are a major barrier to rapid development and are often subjected to force. The treatment of the population of Kampuchea (Cambodia) by the Communist Khmer Rouge regime of Pol Pot is an extreme example of the use of force in which an estimated 2 million people were killed.

HUMAN CHOICE: POLITICAL CULTURE AND IDEOLOGY

Every political system, regardless of the level of development, operates within an environment of ideas that we call political culture. The contemporary political culture of any state is the product of the human choices of the past in which certain values and beliefs were selected as superior over others. Successive generations acquire or learn the elements of the national political culture through the process of political socialization. For the individual this process begins as soon as one is old enough to understand the spoken language or to observe the reactions of adults to political authority figures or national symbols such as the flag. Political values are transmitted by parents, schools, military organizations, employers, unions, political parties, and government elites and agencies. Although the inclusion of new beliefs produces incremental change, a political culture tends to persist over long periods of time and its major elements are resistant to change.[15]

Unlike a political structure, political culture cannot be observed and studied directly. It must be inferred or abstracted from human behavior.[16] We can see only its effects and these effects are only meaningful if they are compared to the effects of political culture in other systems. In this context, some social scientists believe that a great deal can be learned by observing and comparing the behavior of the police and the general populace toward one another in different states. It is argued that this behavior reveals the attitudes and expectations of the general population toward political authority as well as the perceptions of those in power toward the rest of society. As with other aspects of political culture, such a comparative study yields a wide variety of patterns ranging from unarmed British bobbies who are widely respected to the South African Security Force which is seen as a hated symbol of political oppression by the majority of the population.

Political culture affects behavior because actions and events are not neutral. Studies of political culture refer to its "shaping" and "screening" effects on responses to political problems.[17] Problems are shaped or interpreted according to the preexisting mental framework of the groups that encounter them. Similarly, political culture acts as a screen in selecting from a universe of potential issues and problems those few which, according to prevailing values, are considered significant and deserving of national attention. A simple stimulus–response model is inadequate for an understanding of political behavior because it ignores the cultural intermediary.[18] Differences in the politics of states can only be understood if the importance of culture is fully realized.

The content of the political culture affects the nature and development of the political system in many ways. The supports available to the political system in the form of taxes, national service, and symbolic demonstrations are conditioned by the underlying attitudes toward the state and its symbols. In Italy where cynicism and distrust of government are common, strikes, protests, and tax evasion occur frequently. This situation contrasts sharply with Great Britain where tax and other laws are generally observed and public opinion polls reveal considerable skepticism about certain forms of protests and demonstrations.[19] Standards of political conduct and political morality also develop from the basic value structure of the political culture. Notions of what constitutes political corruption, as well as the degree of compliance with formal laws against corruption, differ with the individual political culture. In many Third World states, laws similar to those in the West exist against acts of nepotism that would grant special benefits to the relatives of government employees. These laws are often ignored or are not rigorously enforced, however, because cultural values emphasize traditional obligations and kinship ties.[20]

The political culture also determines the type of demands made on the political system. Canadian political beliefs place great emphasis on individual freedom, and citizens regularly demand that the government respect and protect their privacy. Such demands and expectations do not exist in the Soviet Union where political thinking is dominated by collectivist and totalitarian conceptions (see Chapter 7).

The political beliefs of elite groups constitute the most important element of the national political culture because these groups dominate political decision making and are in direct control of the government. In the contemporary political world, elite groups are frequently drawn from the most affluent or best-educated segments of the society.[21] Although their political views may differ from those of the majority, elite groups are usually successful in imposing many of their beliefs on the general population. The rules and values that guide the actions of the elite constitute the operative ideology of the system.

The operative ideology determines the specific response of a state to its social setting. As noted earlier, the general content of the agenda of politics is established by the social setting, but the social setting does not determine the agenda's final form. The agenda of politics is always selective and biased. At any level of development a large number of potential political issues exist from which elite groups select those around which conflict and discussion will center. In the screening process, elites select issues on the basis of their perceptions and value preferences. They also define the issues subjectively on the basis of the same mental framework.

In the public policy process, elites make decisions about how issues will be resolved and values allocated on the basis of their ideological preferences. The decisions are made within the context of political structures or institutions that also reflect elite preferences about such matters as centralization versus decentralization and the proper role of the general population in the governmental process.

The West

In the states of the West, the political process has been shaped by the system of beliefs we call liberalism. Liberal ideology is dominated by the logic of political conflict which accepts as inevitable the pursuit of self-interest by the individual members of society.[22] Political institutions exist to resolve peacefully the resulting political conflict. Liberal values include the concepts of individual rights, political equality, limited government, modified economic freedom, decentralization, and the rule of law. Due to differences in political culture, the states of the West vary in their degree of commitment to several of these principles. Cultural factors are responsible for differences in the pattern of politics within the three worlds as well as between the three worlds.

The Communist World

In the Communist World the pattern of politics has been shaped by Marxist–Leninist ideology. This ideology contains two themes; one is emphasized in the preindustrial Communist states outside Europe and the other is dominant in the industrial states of Eastern Europe and the Soviet Union. In the preindustrial states, the prevailing theme is that Communist political systems are the major actors in an evitable process of world revolution. In order to facilitate the revolutionary process, the ideology prescribes the rapid expansion and modernization of industry at almost any cost in human welfare.[23]

In the industrial states of Europe, the theme of world revolution and

First World leaders at summit meeting in London, June, 1984.

forced development has been deemphasized since the 1950s. A second theme of increased industrialization combined with a concern for the improvement of the welfare of the general population now holds sway.[24] The nature of the improvements and the speed of their implementation are to be dictated and strictly controlled by the Communist party elite. Despite similar social settings of advanced industrialization, the ideological differences between the Communist states and the West are sufficient to produce distinct political patterns.

Both forms of Marxist–Leninist thought emphasize certain common elements. These common elements include elite rule, centralization of power, conformity to official standards, collectivism in political life, and obligation to the revolutionary cause as defined by the Communist party.

The Third World

In discussing the influence of ideology on the politics of the Third World, one must speak of patterns of politics rather than of a single pattern. Third World elites have borrowed political concepts from the West and the Communist World. Frequently, elites have also retained traditional values unique to their political system. In some states, Western or Soviet values are clearly predominant, but in most cases the political ideologies in the Third World states are combinations of two or even three systems of thought.

Third World ideologies are above all blueprints for political development. Ideologies like that of India which borrow heavily from Western political thought advocate economic modernization, but only under conditions in which democratic institutions are preserved.[25] Ideologies incorporating Marxist–Leninist concepts place economic development ahead of all other considerations and generally view traditional institutions and values as impediments to development which should be removed. Ideologies retaining traditional values simultaneously emphasize economic modernization and retention of elements of the traditional life-style that are considered compatible with the goal of development. The Libyan regime of Colonel Qaddafi employs an operative ideology known as Islamic socialism which advocates rapid economic development but retains the Koran as the basis for the official constitution of the state.[26] In the Third World various political ideologies have combined with the factors of underdevelopment to produce patterns of politics different from that found in either the West or the Communist World.

NOTES

1. For a discussion of issues in preindustrial states see Gabriel A. Almond and G. Bingham Powell, Jr., *Comparative Politics Today: A World View* (Boston: Little, Brown, 1980), pp. 145–46.
2. Richard L. Siegel and Leonard B. Weinberg, *Comparing Public Policies* (Homewood, Ill.: Dorsey Press, 1977), p. 5.
3. H. Mark Roelofs, *Ideology and Myth in American Politics: A Critique of a National Political Mind* (Boston: Little, Brown, 1976), p. 4.
4. Everett Carll Ladd, Jr., *American Political Parties: Social Change and Political Response* (New York: Norton, 1970), pp. 1–7. Ladd applies his concepts only to the United States in this study. We are using his concepts as the basis for a comparative study of other political systems as well as the United States.
5. For a discussion of the levels of development see G. Lowell Field, *Comparative Political Development: The Precedent of the West* (Ithaca, N.Y.: Cornell University Press, 1967), pp. 37–78.
6. *Ibid.*, pp. 54–58.
7. *Ibid.*
8. Karl W. Deutsch, *Politics and Government: How People Decide Their Fate*, 3d ed. (Boston: Houghton Mifflin, 1980), pp. 46–48.
9. For a discussion of the development of the industrial agenda in the United States see Ladd, p. 115.
10. *Ibid.*, p. 3.
11. Gabriel A. Almond and G. Bingham Powell, Jr., *Comparative Politics: A Developmental Approach*, 1st ed. (Boston: Little, Brown, 1966), p. 35.
12. Ibid., p. 278.
13. Field, pp. 37–42.

14. Ibid., pp. 175–178.
15. Donald J. Divine, *The Political Culture of the United States* (Boston: Little, Brown, 1972), p. 31. See also David Easton, *A Framework for Political Analysis* (Englewood Cliffs, N.J.: Prentice-Hall, 1965), pp. 119–135.
16. Heinz Eulau, *The Behavioral Persuasion in Politics* (New York: Random House, 1966), p. 63.
17. See the discussion of the work of Alfred Kroeber and Clyde Kluckholn in Divine, pp. 7–8.
18. Eugenia V. Nomikos and Robert C. North, *International Crisis* (Montreal: McGill-Queen's University Press, 1976), pp. 244–252.
19. Richard Rose, "Politics in England," in Almond and Powell, p. 171.
20. James C. Scott, *Comparative Political Corruption* (Englewood Cliffs, N.J.: Prentice-Hall, 1976), pp. 9–11.
21. Robert D. Putnam, *The Comparative Study of Political Elites* (Englewood Cliffs, N.J.: Prentice-Hall, 1976), pp. 21–28.
22. Mark E. Kann, *Thinking about Politics* (New York: West, 1980), pp. 15–42.
23. A. F. Organski, *The Stages of Political Development* (New York: Knopf, 1965), p. 178.
24. Ibid.
25. Monte Palmer, *Dilemmas of Political Development*, 2d ed. (Ithaca, Ill.: Peacock, 1980), p. 12.
26. Ibid.

CHAPTER 3

Levels of Development

The countries that make up the world are clearly at different levels of political, social, and economic development. There are three general levels of development at which states may be found. These three levels—"preindustrial," "industrial," and "postindustrial"—are presented as tools to assist the student in understanding the politics in different states of the world. The social setting of politics, the political styles of the elites, the size and capability of the political institutions of the states, and the types of issues that arise in the various states of the world are related to their particular levels of development.

First World societies are complex and predominantly postindustrial in makeup. Social, economic, and political issues are quite different from those of the Second and the Third Worlds. Communist states have a special social and political situation because of the existence of Communist party domination. Second World countries are either preindustrial or industrial; the former are mainly Asian, whereas the latter are mainly European.

The preindustrial Third World presents the most complex setting because of vast differences in the various countries' social, political, and economic levels. The various elites in contention for power, the influence of religion and what kind of religion, the level of economic development, and the political ideology predominating in a given country are determinants of the patterns of politics in the Third World.

PREINDUSTRIAL, INDUSTRIAL, AND POSTINDUSTRIAL LEVELS OF DEVELOPMENT

The level of development is defined in Chapter 2 as the general political setting of the state consisting of the natural and financial resources available to the political system, the size and capability of existing political institutions, and the political orientations of the general population. Three levels of society and economy are considered in that chapter: preindustrial, industrial, and postindustrial. Most Third World countries are at the preindustrial level, Communist countries are at the preindustrial and industrial levels, and Western countries are at the industrial and postindustrial levels. Individual countries are at different stages of advancement at one of these levels and some are in transition between two levels.

The level of political development in a country often reflects its level of economic development. The relationship between these two types of development is such that if one is achieved without the other, the result can be violent conflict and even chaos. The revolution in Iran in 1979 is an example of a country that had achieved economic development to some extent without concomitant political development. India is at a higher level of political development than most other Third World countries. However, because economic development in India has been very slow, the political system has not been able to meet the demands generated by the progress in political development. The result has been frequent unrest in the country.

Economic development as indicated by the three levels—preindustrial, industrial, and postindustrial—influences several aspects of political development, four of which we consider more important: political styles of the elites, the size and capability of political institutions, the nature of political issues, and the political orientations of the general population.

Political Styles of Elites

At the preindustrial level the number of the elite members is relatively small. As countries advance to an industrial and then to a postindustrial level of development, the elites become somewhat more numerous. With economic and educational advancement, a relatively large number of individuals acquire influence and other attributes usually associated with the elites. The opportunities for becoming members of the elites expand at the same time, as the size and capability of the political institutions as well as the diversity and complexity of political issues increase. With changes in the political institutions and the issues, new decision-making centers are created that absorb a larger number of the elite members.

At the preindustrial level the elites appeal to the sentiments of the general population in the name of tradition. Even some military leaders, who are generally considered modern in their outlook, display traditional political style. Colonel Qaddafi and General Zia, the military leaders of Libya and Pakistan respectively, are examples. Several members of elites in the preindustrial countries have been educated in the West and have absorbed Western values. However, in order to stay in power, they must temper their enthusiasm for the West with appeals to the traditional values such as respect for religion and the acceptance of tribal norms. Appeals to traditional values sometimes give rise to heroic leadership. A number of countries in the Third World (for example, Argentina, Egypt, Ghana, India, Indonesia, and Kenya) have experienced heroic leadership.

Elite members in countries at the industrial and postindustrial levels also appeal to the sentiments of the general population. Thus "traditional American values" such as freedom and competitiveness are often extolled by U.S. leaders. However, elites in the West or in industrialized Communist countries cannot remain in power by merely appealing to such sentiments. Through the use of the media and other devices they cultivate and project an image of competence and efficiency. Because a large number of problems, often requiring technical expertise, have to be resolved in these countries, the elites attempt to develop a political style with an image of problem solving.

Size and Capability of Political Institutions

At the preindustrial stage the political institutions are relatively small in size and limited in capabilities. Economic development creates problems that must be resolved politically. It also provides revenue for resolving problems. Economic development, for example, increases life expectancy and the number of older citizens, thus necessitating a system of old-age pensions and medical care for the elderly. New problems and the need to resolve them increase the size and capability of political institutions. Bureaucracy, in particular, proliferates in countries at the industrial and postindustrial levels. This development is even more noticeable in the Communist countries, as the state owns the means of production and regulates the lives of the citizens far more than is the case in the West.

The size and capability of the political institutions have increased so much in some industrial and postindustrial countries that a demand for reducing them has arisen. When Ronald Reagan became president of the United States in 1981, he attempted to decrease the size of the federal bureaucracy. Such developments have taken place in other Western countries also, notably in Britain and Sweden.

Nature of Political Issues

At the preindustrial level a major issue is economic development at an accelerated pace. The issue of accelerated economic growth is important in the politics of even the poorest countries. Elites in a majority of the Third World countries also perceive the development of a national identity as a major political issue. Outside influence, especially by Western countries, is often viewed as an impediment to economic growth and the development of a national identity. In the Third World countries the reduction of such influence, if not its elimination, has become a significant political issue.

As countries become industrialized, they continue to be concerned with economic development. However, issues such as environmental quality, privacy, control over bureaucracy, equality for women, and a need for more meaningful participation in political decision making have also become significant in the West. Along with economic development, a major issue in Communist countries continues to be the maintenance of the totalitarian system. An issue that remains important in the Communist World as well as in the West and the Third Worlds is the distribution of income and other economic benefits.

Political Orientations

Political orientations are defined in Chapter 2 as the general willingness of the population to accept political authority and to support the political system. Such willingness is often lacking at the preindustrial stage. As a country develops economically and the living standards of the people improve, acceptance of the political authority and support of the political system also increase. Acceptance of political authority and support of the political system cannot be explained in economic terms only. Elites in the industrialized countries of the West appeal to the sentiments of the people by using symbols and slogans (e.g., "American dream," "American way of life") to keep their support. Such an appeal to emotions is a form of propaganda. In totalitarian countries support of the people is maintained with the help of a much greater use of propaganda (and a greater show of force) than in the West.

Lack of acceptance for political authority and of support for the political system increases the possibility of violent changes in the government. This is a major reason for the frequent government changes by military coups in many Third World countries.

THE FIRST WORLD

The Social Setting of Western Politics

In any society the political system performs two general functions. First, it resolves conflicts arising from competing demands for scarce resources, and second, it promotes community-building activities necessary to sustain the political system. The existence of mass demonstrations and political violence in many areas of the world testifies to the fact that these functions are not performed to the satisfaction of the individuals who make up the state.

To perform either conflict resolution or community-building functions, a political system must be congruent or compatible with the society it attempts to regulate. Both political institutions and political actors must be relevant to the daily life of the society at its particular level of development. Political institutions gain legitimacy and are obeyed because citizens judge them to be rational and necessary based on their daily social experiences. Political actors gain positions of political power because they raise issues that are judged by the majority of people to promise solutions to the current problems confronting the society. To be successful members of the political elite, they must adopt a political style and employ political symbols that can be understood in the context of the societies in which they live.

In a very real sense the social setting of the state is the major determinant of the political process.[1] All political activity occurs within a social and economic environment determined by the level of development of the society. The social and economic factors are like cards dealt to a group of players. The strength or weakness of the hands may be interpreted differently, and different strategies may be developed for playing the hand, but in the end the face value of the cards cannot be changed and the cards must be played. The presence or absence of such factors as large industries, bureaucratic structures, or an educated population will greatly affect the nature of the political process. These factors determine what goals are possible or impossible and which problems and issues will dominate political life. In addition, they determine whether leadership groups must adopt a heroic style of leadership in order to appeal to the general population or whether a bureaucratic style of politics will prevail in which leaders gain support by demonstrating knowledge and expertise. A discussion of the social setting is an important starting point in the study of political life in the Western world.

In comparative perspective the social setting of the West is unique because the most advanced societies such as the United States and Sweden have reached the highest level of development presently attained. Social scientists have designated these societies as postindustrial to indicate that they have evolved beyond even the level of an industrial society. More will be said about industrialism and postindustrialism later. Of course, the evolution of society will not end at the postindustrial stage and students of the future will undoubtedly recognize higher levels of development. However, the fact that Western societies have been the first to reach this level has had important political consequences. First, Western societies and the political leaders who have attempted to regulate them have been free from the pressure to emulate or "catch up" with more advanced societies. This pressure has been the overriding political preoccupation in the states of the Third World and the Communist World. Second, being at the highest level of development has meant that the Western societies and their political leaders have been in the forefront of social change and have been confronted with a series of problems without historical precendents. Between the period of the American Revolution and the end of the Civil War (1775–1865), Great Britain, Germany, and the United States were the first states to experience the industrial revolution. These same states along with Sweden and Canada were also the first to experience the achievements and problems of postindustrial society. Third, for the last two centuries Western political leaders have been able to offer to the world their development as the model to be followed by other states. Although other states have not always accepted the democratic political structures of the West, the most advanced Second and Third World states have sought to duplicate the economic development by creating industrial states like those in the West.

Contemporary Western society is considered to be the most developed because it is the most complex.[2] In the case of societal development, complexity refers to the number of roles and structures (institutions) that exist in a society.[3] In a primitive society one individual or a small-scale institution may perform many roles at the same time. In a simple agrarian system, a single chief or king may be a soldier, judge, legislator, diplomat, and policeman, and also assume responsibility for seeing that sufficient crops are harvested to feed the population. In such a society roles are relatively unspecialized and structures are few in number. In modern Western society roles have become highly specialized and institutions have proliferated in number. Using the United States as an example, it is unthinkable that any one person or group would attempt to simultaneously play the role of soldier, judge, legislator, diplomat, policeman, and supervisor of food production. Instead, each of these functions is performed by a series of specialized large-scale institutions such as the Department of Defense, the courts, the Congress, Department of State, Department of Justice, and the Department of Agriculture. The function of providing food is performed by thousands of nongovernmental business structures that are separated into growers, packers, shippers, wholesale and retail merchandisers, most of whom deal only in specialized areas of the food industry such as dairy products, meat packing, bakery goods, frozen foods, and so on.

Specialization has led to an additional element of complexity in the West, the increasing dependency of the groups in society on one another.[4] In less-developed societies, especially those in which the majority of the population is engaged in agriculture or other family enterprises, it is common for people to grow their own food and meet many other basic needs. In such a society a high degree of self-sufficiency is achieved. However, beginning with the onset of industrialization an increasing division of labor occurs. Tasks such as providing food are divided up into a series of specialized functions in order to increase efficiency and the rate of production. Both specialization and interdependence multiply in postindustrial society. As in the example above, food production is now accomplished in a complicated series of activities, for example growing, packing, shipping, and merchandising. An interruption in any of the stages of the process, such as a strike by shippers, will result in a cessation of the distribution of food and serious social distress.

In the recent history of the West, the economic and social development that produced role specialization, structural proliferation, and societal interdependence has placed great burdens on the political system. Beginning with the industrial revolution, political institutions and actors have been confronted with the problem of having to perform conflict resolution and community-building functions in an increasingly complex society. The economic and social development has fostered political development. As social and economic structures have risen in number and become more specialized, the political structures that must regulate them have evolved in a similar manner. The size and sophistication of government bureaucracies in the major states of the West stand as testimony to this point. In addition, the increasing interdependence of the groups in society and their vulnerability to disruption have created an unprecedented need for planning by political leaders. This, in turn, has led to the development of a highly specialized political elite that displays the same educational credentials and bureaucratic style as the business managers and social leaders that it must attempt to regulate. Most important, the particular characteristics of postindustrial society have created unique concerns and political issues that distinguish the politics of the West from the politics of the other two worlds. Because of their importance in shaping Western politics, certain economic and social characteristics of postindustrial society must be discussed further.

Postindustrialism: Social and Economic Dynamics

Politics in the West takes place in an economic setting ranging from advanced industrialization in Great Britain and Italy to postindustrialization in the United States, West Germany, Sweden, and Canada. In both industrial and postindustrial societies the majority of the population is employed in the large bureaucracies of factories and office buildings. These societies differ from those at a preindustrial level of development because the majority of the population is no longer employed in agriculture or small family enterprises. Postindustrial society is distinguished from industrial society by the predominance of white-collar jobs over blue-collar jobs, and the predominance of service industries over manufacturing. In postindustrial society the sale of services such as financial advice, medical expertise, entertainment, recreation, and education contributes more to the gross national product than do the profits from the production of industrial goods. Workers in service industries also constitute a larger percentage of the work force than do workers employed in industrial production and agriculture combined (50% or more in the service sector). A study on Western European politics has summarized the development of Western society:

> Industrial society differed from preindustrial society because of the declining role of agriculture in the economy and the lower percentage of persons employed in the agricultural sector, especially when compared with the growing ranks of the industrial proletariat. By the same token, postindustrial society differs from industrial society because of the increasing importance of the service sector in relation to both agriculture and industry and the growing ranks of persons employed in the service sector as compared with both agriculture and industry.[5]

The occupational pursuit of the majority of the population is a vitally important aspect of any society because the work place is the chief socialization agency for people in their adult years.[6] It is while interacting with bosses, union officials, and other workers that adults acquire the factual knowledge, emotional beliefs, and judgments about politics that determine their political behavior. (Of course, these learnings are in addition to those attitudes acquired as children from parents and school.) In general, persons employed in different occupational pursuits are likely to develop different political expectations and interests. In societies in which the majority of the population is involved in industrial production, political conflict is likely to revolve around issues of class in which lower and lower-middle-class workers demand a more egalitarian distribution of values.[7] In the United States this stage occurred in the years before World War II and culminated in the period of reform known as the New Deal, which began with the election of Franklin Roosevelt as president in 1932. During this period political conflict revolved around the demands by workers and their unions for unemployment insurance, guaranteed pensions, workers' compensation, and other benefits. In postindustrial societies in which the majority of the population is employed in white-collar jobs in the service sector, political conflict no longer centers on class interests. Instead, important interest groups develop from the various parts or institutions of the service sector. In his book on postindustrial society, Daniel Bell has identified some of the units he believes will constitute the major interest groups in future political conflicts. They include the scientific community, government bureaus, universities and research centers, social complexes (hospitals and social service centers), the military, and individual economic enterprises.[8] Each of these groups will seek to attain values for itself and will not engage in broad-based appeals to class interests.

The transition from class politics to service sector politics has not been uniformly realized in the West because not all of the states have achieved postindustrial development. In addition, in several states service sector employment has only recently reached 50% and the new interest groups have not had sufficient time to develop. The United States, Sweden, and Canada were the first states to achieve postindustrial development, reaching this level before 1960. Several other states, including Belgium, the Netherlands, Luxembourg, West Germany, Norway, Australia, and New Zealand, reached the postindustrial level by the early 1970s.[9] Statistics for Japan indicate that by 1970 and perhaps as early as 1968, more than 50% of the work force was employed in the service sector.[10] France joined the list of postindustrial states in 1976 with 51% of the work force in this service sector, 38% in industrial production, and 11% in agriculture.[11] At present, several Western states including Britain and Italy have not attained 50% employment in the service sector, although Britain is close to this figure. In Britain and Italy class issues continue to dominate the political agenda. In Italy the pattern of politics since World War II has been shaped by the conflict between the ruling Christian Democratic coalition and its opponents, the Italian Communist party (PCI) and the small Italian Socialist party (PSI).[12] Both the PCI and PSI have taken positions on unemployment, inflation, and government social programs that favor greater benefits for working-class groups. In Britain, the term of Conservative Prime Minister Margaret Thatcher has been marked by sharp conflict between her party and British trade unions representing working-class interests.[13] In Britain, as in Italy, the pattern of political conflict remains that of an industrial rather than postindustrial society.

In the states that have attained postindustrialization, class issues continue to exist side-by-side with the new issues of the postindustrial agenda. By definition, a political interest is a shared attitude to which a group of people have become committed or attached. Such an attachment takes time to form and once learned tends to persist, so individuals in Western society who reached adulthood during the period before the attainment of postindustrialization are likely to remain committed to the older concerns of the industrial agenda. A study by Ronald Inglehart has shown that persons in the states of Western Europe who experienced the trauma of World War II and the subsequent economic dislocation tend to assign greatest importance to such issues as economic welfare and maintaining order in the nation, concerns called materialistic values. In contrast, persons born in the postwar years expressed greater concern for issues reflecting postmaterialist values, such as greater opportunity for political participation, protection of free speech, and progress toward a less impersonal and more humane society.[14] Similar studies have found that the postwar generation shows greater interest in environmental protection, equal opportunity for women, and other quality-of-life issues than does the older generation, which remains most concerned with the earlier class issues. The economic difficulties experienced in the West since the early 1970s, including high unemployment and persistent inflation, have strengthened the concern for jobs, government benefits, and economic stability even among those born after World War II. Consequently, even in a state such as the United States, which was the first to attain postindustrial development, the political agenda is a mixed one of industrial and postindustrial issues. Successful political actors and parties must appeal simultaneously to two different constituencies, a blue-collar one concerned with class issues and a professional one concerned with quality-of-life issues. In the United States, the Democratic party contains members, such as House Speaker Thomas (Tip) O'Neill and Senator Theodore (Ted) Kennedy, with close ties to the labor movement, as well as individuals such as ex-Senator George McGovern and Senator William Proxmire, who have sought to identify themselves with environmental and quality-of-life issues. The existence of a dual constituency and a dual political agenda reveals an important point about modern Western society; namely, that it is presently in a period of transition. The concept of a postindustrial society is only a model or analytical tool developed by social scientists to help us understand contemporary Western society. Data currently available about Western society seem to provide evidence that the concept has explanatory value and that Western societies will conform more and more to the model of postindustrialization in the future. However, people and institutions currently in existence in the West are products of both industrial and postindustrial culture. The real political and social world will continue to reflect the duality for some time to come.

Other Characteristics of Postindustrial Society

In addition to the shift to service sector employment, Daniel Bell has identified other dimensions of postindustrial development:[15]

1. *The centrality of theoretical knowledge.* The unprecedented growth of theoretical knowledge forms the basis for a succession of dynamic innovations in technology such as the development of the modern computer.
2. *The creation of a new intellectual technology.* Through the use of new research techniques developed by mathematicians and other scien-

tists, we can chart more efficient, "rational" solutions to economic and perhaps social problems.

3. **The spread of a knowledge class.** In a society in which information and knowledge plays a central role, the fastest growing group in society is the technical and professional group or "class."

4. **A change in the character of work.** Work in the service sector involves person-to-person activities (doctor and patient, teacher and pupil) rather than contact with nature as in farming or with products and artifacts as in industrial production. For the first time in history, success at work depends on one's ability to interact with other people.

5. **A new role for women.** The growth of the service sector of the economy creates new employment opportunities for women. For the first time women have a secure base for economic independence.

6. **A new role for science in the society.** For the first time in history, science has become inextricably intertwined with technology, the military, social needs, and other state-directed goals.

7. **Meritocracy.** In a technological society, the possession of education and skills is more important than inheritance or property.

The conditions discussed by Bell explain much about the style of politics that dominates in the West. As mentioned previously, social complexity and economic development often act as a catalyst for political development, although political development is by no means inevitable. In the West the evolution to postindustrial society has led to political development with the qualification that political institutions and actors only partly reflect postindustrial norms. Again it must be kept in mind that because Western society is in a state of transition, so is the style of Western politics.

The growth of economic bureaucracies (factories and corporations), which began with the industrial revolution and continued with the expansion of the service sector, has been paralleled by the development of large and specialized government bureaucracies. If, as some social scientists believe, structural (organizational) proliferation and specialization is a central feature of political development, then it can be said that growing societal complexity stimulated political development. The need to regulate increasingly sophisticated economic activities and to deal with such problems as pollution, occupational training, consumer protection, and sex discrimination in employment has led to the development of government bureaucracies that employ millions and in some states constitute the largest single employer. In the West political decision making is undertaken by committees within large bureaucracies not unlike those of large corporations. These range in size from presidential cabinets with a dozen members to "superministries" that employ several hundred undersecretaries and thousands of lower-level employees.

The growth of government bureaucracy has been accompanied by the development of a "class" of government experts. In postindustrial society where a high premium is placed on the possession of technical skills and the ability to use theoretical knowledge, education and experience have become increasingly important in elite recruitment (meritocracy), especially at the lower and middle levels of the civil service. In a study of politics in the postindustrial states Lawrence Mayer and John Burnett have argued that the rapid development and spread of technology has made the growth of a specialized bureaucracy inevitable.[16] Citing the example of the growth of the commercial aviation industry, which requires extensive safety and traffic regulations, the authors believe that each new invention creates new problems that government must regulate. High-level political leaders in the West, especially those who must seek popular election, are still recruited on the basis of a number of factors, including loyalty, political reliability, party affiliations as well as education and expertise.[17] However, in recent elections candidates in all of the states of the West have increasingly sought electoral support on the basis of a display of knowledge and the pledge to be good managers of the affairs of the society. This new "managerial" approach to campaigning has been utilized by all of the presidential candidates in France since the resignation in 1970 of Charles de Gaulle, who may have been the last chief of state of the heroic–charismatic type in the West. In any society, political actors who seek to lead must develop programs and appeals that are relevant to the economic and social interests of the majority of the population.

Postindustrial Political Issues

The emergence of postindustrial society creates a series of political issues that have become increasingly important in the politics of the West. Although these issues exist in some form in the Second and Third Worlds, they do not receive or are not allowed to receive the attention that they do in the West. The increase in the size of government bureaucracies and the use of sophisticated technology (e.g., computers) has caused concern in some segments of Western society that the civil rights and privacy of citizens may be violated. This concern is based on the belief that as the number of areas subject to government regulation increases, it will become more difficult to assure that the activities of civil servants conform to the law. In several Western states *ombudsmen,* officials with independent investigatory powers, have been established to protect the interests of clients in their relations with bureaucrats,[18] and interest groups have formed that advocate the protection of individual privacy from both public and private bureaucracies (e.g., corporations, unions, universities). In addition to the issue of privacy, the cause of women's equality has received increasing attention in the postindustrial societies of the West. The development of this political issue is related to the expanded employment opportunity available to women in the service sector. As women achieve positions of economic importance in rising numbers and recruitment on the basis of ability becomes the norm, discrimination on sexual grounds, especially in employment, becomes more and more unacceptable. The increasing political strength of the women's rights movement also reflects the fact that as a group's economic importance in society increases, its political influence grows and greater priority is given to its political demands. Other political issues such as environmental protection, arms control, and the use of nuclear energy are also more prominent in the West than anywhere else in the world. These issues are dependent on a high level of mass education and an understanding of the impact of technology on the quality of life, two factors present in postindustrial societies.

The most important political issue to emerge in postindustrial society may ultimately prove to be the survival of crisis. Studies have shown that postindustrial societies in the West are experiencing crises of participation, identity, and distribution, which are the result of postindustrial development.[19] Crises of participation occur when new groups are politically mobilized and seek direct involvement in the political system but institutions are not available to effectively accommodate their participation. Crises of identity and distribution are related.[20] Crises of identity occur when groups in a society feel a lack of common identity with the political system. Such groups are likely to reject the political symbols of the system and may engage in acts of violence as a form of protest. Groups are likely to feel such a lack of identity if the political system has failed to distribute to them the basic values that they demand (jobs, equality, and so on). If basic demands go unmet for a prolonged period, a crisis of distribution occurs. Many social scientists used to believe that such crises occurred only at lower levels of development and that problems of identity, participation, and distribution had been overcome in the developed states of the West. We now know that such a view failed to take into account the political problems resulting from the complexity of postindustrial development. In a study of the United States, J. Rogers Hollingsworth found that crises of participation, identity, and distribution were present.[21] High levels of urbanization, literacy, and education, combined with extensive mass media, have caused an increase in the level of political participation. Unfortunately, this new demand for participation has coincided with a decline in the strength and importance of political parties and elected assemblies, the two institutions most necessary if increased participation is to be accommodated. Real political power and control of government in the United States is now passing into the hands of trained specialists within the government bureaucracy and to powerful organized interest groups. As Hollingsworth notes, at the same time more Americans are seeking meaningful political participation, "America has become a society of giant organizations in labor, industry, government, and education, and in each sector the citizen has yielded to the power of the organization."[22] Since the 1960s the United States has also experienced a crisis of distribution. The same factors of urbanization, literacy, and education that created the demand for political participation also produced a rising expectation on the part of blacks and other minorities, which led to demands for greater equality of opportunity. When the political system was slow to deliver on the demands for equality, these groups became disenchanted. They also felt that the government specialists on whom they had depended were unresponsive to their desire for participation in decisions that affect their lives. As Hollingsworth notes, "the tension between bureaucrats and frustrated clients has involved not only the poor but many groups that feel they have no control over 'establishment' officials who 'manage' their lives."[23] The nonratification of the Equal Rights Amendment led many women to experience similar feelings of frustration. Groups such as the black community, dissatisfied with the present distribution of benefits and opportunities, have lost their sense of identity with the American political system, which they feel has not adequately served their interests. As a result, they have become increasingly isolated from the other groups in American society.

Other political problems have become apparent in the postindustrial societies of the West beyond those associated with participation, identity, and distribution. A study of California politics found that higher levels of confusion and political conflict accompanied efforts by government specialists in that state to provide more public services.[24] The expanded government activity produced an intense political debate about the proper size of government and the cost of public service programs. In addition, the general population became disturbed when many programs did not live up to general expectations, and a loss of confidence in government resulted. Other studies have documented an increasing "elite-mass strain" in Japan[25] and growing difficulty in making private corporations, trade unions associations, and universities responsive to the needs of society.[26] The existence of these problems clearly indicates that in postindustrial society, complexity does not equal utopia, and that politics in the West will be preoccupied with issues related to the resolution of difficult problems.

An Environment of Affluence

No discussion of postindustrial development would be complete without reference to the fact that Western political and social activities take place in an environment of affluence. It may seem strange to speak of affluence when fluctuating industrial production, inflation, and unemployment plague many of the states of the West, but the most important distinction between these states and the rest of the world is their level of affluence. The states of the West presently contain less than 10% of the world's population but possess approximately 35% of the world's wealth. In 1976 the world had an average per capita gross national product (GNP) of $1651, whereas the United States and the states of Western Europe had a per capita GNP ranging from a high of $9014 in Sweden to $3968 in the United Kingdom. The real meaning of these statistics is that in every area of life—education, health, job training, the arts, leisure—the states of the West are able to provide their citizens with benefits far beyond those available to people in the Second and Third Worlds. In the 1960s, several social scientists argued that the states of the West had attained a condition of "mass affluence."[27] The term "mass affluence" referred to a state in which the age-old problem of the scarcity of basic resources (food, housing, basic medical services) had been overcome for the majority of the population. According to this argument, government welfare programs (e.g., unemployment insurance, workmen's compensation, and pension plans) guaranteed the basic necessities of life even to those who found themselves temporarily unemployed or physically incapacitated. Union contracts and company-sponsored programs also protected workers against the hazards of life. In an article written in 1965, Robert Lane argued that only 15% of the U.S. population was without protection against the hazards of life, and that this group was composed largely of nonwhite and non–English speaking individuals.[28] Since the 1960s terms such as mass affluence appear less often in social science literature as rising unemployment and inflation have reduced the standard of living of some groups in Western societies. However, the basic point made by the advocates of the concept of mass affluence is still valid. Politics in the West occurs in an economic environment in which the majority of the population expects the satisfaction of its basic needs and pursues additional benefits and opportunities unavailable to most of the rest of the world. It is only in such an environment that political issues such as privacy, environmental protection, and other quality-of-life concerns can be raised to the level of importance they receive in the West.

Czechoslovak textile factory.

THE SECOND WORLD

Two Political Worlds

An understanding of the social setting of Communist politics requires above all a recognition of the economic and social diversity that exists in the Second World. In an economic and social sense, there are at least two "Communist worlds": (1) the systems of Europe including the Soviet bloc countries (German Democratic Republic, Czechoslovakia, the USSR, Hungary, Poland, Romania, and Bulgaria) and Yugoslavia, and (2) the systems outside Europe consisting of the Asian states of China, Mongolia, North Korea, Viet Nam, Kampuchea, Laos, and Afghanistan, and Cuba in Latin America. (For purposes of analysis, the European Communist state of

Albania should be grouped with the Communist states of the Third World because it is at the same lower level of development.) Political life in the seven states of the Soviet bloc takes place within an economic setting ranging from middle to advanced industrialization. The majority of the population is employed in large, bureaucratic enterprises and comes in contact with authority and management on a daily basis. The percentage of the population involved in agriculture has declined steadily since World War II, and in many cases persons employed in agriculture encounter political authority on a regular basis within the state-controlled collective farm systems. Economic and social life in the European states increasingly has come to involve complex organizations, urbanization, and the introduction of new technology typical of industrial states in the Western World.[29] The challenge posed by the more-developed states of the West continues to act as a catalyst for further development in the Soviet bloc. The Soviet Union is the outstanding example of a Communist state seeking to equal or surpass Western achievements in science, medicine, space exploration, industrial production, and military procurement. By contrast, the Communist states outside of Europe have primarily agricultural social settings. Economic and social life is characterized by the same conditions that prevail in much of the Third World: large rural populations, the predominance of an agrarian life-style, low levels of education, a shortage of scientific and technical knowledge, a scarcity of capital for investment, and a low level of technology in industry and agriculture. The social setting of these Communist states is one of economic, social, and technological underdevelopment. In addition to the distinction between the Communist states inside and outside Europe, significant economic and social differences exist between the states in each group. A comparative study of the Second World has identified several factors responsible for the economic and social differences between the Communist states of Europe. These factors include (1) different initial conditions before the establishment of Communist regimes (natural resource endowment, size, the longevity of statehood, and so on), (2) the existence of nationality problems, (3) war damage, reparations, and war-related transfers, (4) ownership patterns in agriculture, (5) current defense burdens, (6) critical political events that have affected economic activities (e.g., worker riots in Poland in 1956), and (7) special economic and political links between member states, especially those involving the Soviet Union.[30] Many of the same factors are also responsible for the differences existing between the Communist states outside Europe.

European Communist States. The transition toward an industrial social setting in the European Communist states was greatly accelerated by World War II. In each state, prewar governments, Nazi occupation authorities, and

their Soviet successors sought to expand the industrial complex by mobilizing human and natural resources to meet the needs of the war. With regard
to industrialization, development in the states of Eastern Europe was
uneven before the war. In the 1930s the percentage of the work force
employed in industry was 30% in Czechoslovakia, 24% in Hungary, and 19%
in Poland, but only 8% in Romania and Bulgaria and 10% in Yugoslavia.[31] By
the beginning of World War II, Germany, of which the current German
Democratic Republic was part, and Czechoslovakia were industrialized
nations; Hungary and Poland were at the first stage of industrialization and
possessed developed industrial sectors; and Romania, Bulgaria, Yugoslavia,
and Albania were essentially very poor agricultural societies (with Albania
lagging far behind the others).[32] Soviet domination of Eastern Europe after
World War II helped to speed the movement toward industrial society. The
Soviet model of economic development was imposed on the states of the
region. These included Albania, which retained the model even after it
renounced Soviet influence, and initially, Yugoslavia, which later deviated
in several important aspects after being forced out of the bloc in 1948. The
model was designed to produce rapid growth of the industrial complex and
included the following elements: (1) the share of investment in the national
income was increased to very high levels at the expense of consumption; (2)
investment was concentrated in industry; and (3) investment in industry was
concentrated on machine building and metallurgy.[33] In the period after the
death of Josif Stalin (1953), the imposition of a common plan for industrial
development was relaxed as local problems and conditions were finally
recognized. Soviet economic involvement in Eastern Europe left behind a
mixed legacy. Soviet exploitation of the Eastern European economy included the dismantling and removal of factories, near confiscatory payment
for raw materials, and forced industrialization. On the one hand, this
exploitation retarded development, and the Soviet master plan for industrialization produced many of the same problems that are common to the
Soviet Union—duplication, economic imbalance, bureaucratic inefficiency,
and chronic shortages of consumer goods. On the other hand, Eastern
Europe achieved high or acceptable economic growth rates, an enlarged and
increasingly skilled work force, a solution to the problem of unemployment
(in most of these states unemployment is at 1% or less), and at least a
minimum standard of living for most citizens.[34] Throughout the period, the
trend toward increasing industrialization was clear. By the 1950s the
approximate percentages of the work force employed in industry was the
following: 55% in Czechoslovakia, 60% in the German Democratic Republic,
60% in Hungary, 50% in Poland, 28% in Romania, 35% in Bulgaria, and 28%
in Yugoslavia.[35] By 1980 the percentage of the work force outside agriculture
had reached the following levels: Czechoslovakia, 86%; German Democratic

Republic, 93%; Hungary, 77%; Poland, 68%; Romania, 60%; Bulgaria, 27%; Yugoslavia, 52%; and Albania, 39%. Contemporary Eastern Europe possesses all of the attributes of industrial society, including large urban centers, extensive bureaucracies, and even the deterioration of the environment common at this level of development. Demands for more consumer goods and other industrial reforms in several of the states of the Soviet bloc indicate the achievement of advanced industrialization.

The Soviet Union. In the Soviet Union the process of industrialization also began before the assumption of power by Communist forces. As W. W. Rostow has noted, the origin of modern industrialization dates to the mid-nineteenth century and perhaps two decades before.[36] By the 1880s the Tsarist state had undertaken specific programs to promote the development of industry. After a brief period of industrial stagnation, a period of industrial expansion occurred after 1908 which marked the beginning of the drive to technological maturity.[37] By 1913 the percentage of the work force employed in industry was 19%. The upheaval produced by World War I and the subsequent civil war prevented any increase in the industrial component through the year 1928.[38] Beginning in the late 1920s, Stalin and the Communist party undertook the task of rapid industrialization. The first Five-Year Plan (1928–1932) and successive plans featured a command-type economic system, centralized planning, nationalization of property, collectivization of agriculture, investment of nearly all available resources in industry, and the use of force against opponents of the program.[39] As Gary Bertsch has noted, although the human costs of Stalin's programs were high, the economic benefits were substantial, and the Communist regime in the USSR reached the stature of a world power by 1953.[40] By 1980, 76% of the labor force was employed in industry. By 1981 the GNP of the Soviet Union was $967,820 million, a figure that exceeded the GNP of every Western state except that of the United States. With over three-quarters of the Russian work force involved in industry today, the Soviet Union is clearly at the stage of advanced industrialization and is approaching the level of postindustrial development.

The Communist World outside Europe. James Townsend, an authority on China, has noted that a number of social and economic factors combined in the first half of the twentieth century to limit economic growth. These included high rents and taxes, usurious credit, small and fragmented farms, traditional farming methods, low productivity, illiteracy, and external disturbances.[41] Despite the existence of these conditions, a small but significant industrial establishment centered in the coastal cities developed after 1840, largely as a result of the foreign presence in China.[42] However, conflict between Chinese nationalists and foreigners preoccupied the country until the victory of the Chinese Communists in 1949. As a result, the Communists inherited a backward country with an industrial sector that had been almost totally destroyed during World War II and the ensuing civil war. After a brief period of careful reconstruction from 1949 to 1952, Mao Zedong and the Communist leadership undertook the first Five-Year Plan (1953–1957) based on the Stalinist model of economic development. By 1956, most private enterprises had been replaced by a cooperative form of state/private management.[43] After the success of the initial Five-Year Plan, economic growth was interrupted by the failure of the Great Leap Forward program, a radical plan to make China a major industrial power in a matter of decades, and by the loss of Soviet foreign aid after the deterioration of relations between the two states in 1960. Economic development was further retarded by the upheaval of the Great Proletarian Cultural Revolution of 1965 to 1969. Since the death of Mao, modest economic growth has been achieved, but the Chinese leadership no longer entertains expectations of ultrarapid industrial growth. At present, over 80% of the Chinese work force remains in the agricultural sector, and China's per capita production is modest even by Third World standards. China's economic and industrial development remains largely potential.

The same factors that have prevented the modernization of the Chinese economy have had a similar impact on the other Communist states outside Europe. The predominance of traditional economic roles, illiteracy, and penetration by external forces have worked to retard economic development. Conflict with foreigners has been especially important in Laos, Vietnam, and Kampuchea, as well as in Afghanistan where Communist forces are still seeking to consolidate their political power. Although the elites in these states embrace Marxist–Leninist ideology, which prescribes industrial development and modernization, they exist in a socioeconomic setting of underdevelopment.

The economic and social differences between the Communist states inside and outside Europe have had a profound effect on the pattern of politics. In the Communist states of Europe, high-level elite members are recruited on the basis of the possession of scientific knowledge about industry or agriculture from within the party and government bureaucracies. Such leaders embrace a bureaucratic style and develop political issues that center on the development and expansion of the industrial complex. In the states outside Europe, Communist leaders often take on a heroic or charismatic style, as in the cases of Fidel Castro and Mao Zedong. Such a style is typical of leadership groups in the less-developed countries (LDCs) of the Third World. These elites have modified Marxist–Leninist theories to fit the special conditions that prevail in an agrarian social setting. Like the leaders of other LDCs, Communist elites outside Europe are preoccupied with the issue of how to achieve economic and political development in the shortest possible time.

THE THIRD WORLD

Elites

Elites in the Third World can be divided into two broad categories—traditional and westernized. A third category, closer to the westernized than to the traditional, is that of the military elite. Although traditional elites have existed in the Third World since the precolonial period, westernized elites emerged during the colonial period and after the achievement of independence by the Third World countries from the Western powers. Military elites are, for the most part, a post–World War II phenomenon in Africa and Asia. In Latin America, however, military elites date back to the early nineteenth century when wars of independence were fought against Spain.

Members of the traditional elite derive their authority from three major sources—religion, tribe, and caste (in the case of India). The influence of religious elites is particularly strong in the Moslem countries of the Middle East where a resurgence of Islam has been under way since the late 1970s. In contrast to the Western concept of the separation of church and state, these two institutions have almost coalesced in some of these countries. Except in Iran, *mullahs* (Moslem teachers or interpreters of the religious law) do not wield political power directly at the highest level. However, their influence on the governmental decision-making process, especially in the judiciary, is substantial. In countries such as Saudi Arabia, Libya, and Pakistan (geographically, Pakistan falls in South Asia, not the Middle East) the Koran forms the basis of the law. Even in those Middle Eastern countries that are considered relatively modern or westernized, the elites give the appearance of strict adherence to religion in order to stay in power. An example is that of Anwar el-Sadat, late President of Egypt, who sometimes prayed in traditional religious manner on television.

Traditional elites, based on tribe, are prominent in the black African nations. Their influence, however, is much greater at the local than at the national level. In his study of political leadership in five African countries (Benin [formerly Dahomey], Central African Republic, Niger, Senegal, and Upper Volta [now called Burkina]), Victor Le Vine observes that he restricted himself to "actors on the modern scene, since in most of these countries traditional leaders are no longer important except locally."[44] The same observation could apply to the Indian elites, which are based on caste, a hierarchical structure that divides the society into four major groups. The national elites in Africa or India do not ignore their traditional ties with tribe or caste. On the contrary, whenever feasible, they exploit them to their political advantage. However, as every black African nation has a large number of tribes, the national elites must at least to some extent dissociate themselves from their particular tribes for the sake of national unity. Members of the Indian elites behave similarly at the national level.

In Africa, India, and most other Third World countries, elites at the national level are westernized or modern. Members of these elites do not necessarily forsake their ties with the traditions of religion, tribe, or caste, but their position and status in the political system are based on their Western-oriented education and occupation rather than tradition. The westernized elites in the African and Asian nations emerged during the colonial period when the colonial powers deemed it necessary to educate some of the natives for carrying out essential functions of the colonial administration in civil service, police, military, commerce, and education. Even the educated natives held only minor government positions under the colonial rule. As Monte Palmer points out, they did constitute the core of the westernized elite.[45]

As the colonies gained independence after the Second World War, some natives with Western education became members of the central or highest elite. It is important to remember, however, that individuals who held the highest political positions in their countries after independence were often those who had waged a struggle for freedom against the colonial powers. Although most former colonies in Africa and Asia emphasize learning of indigenous languages and attach a great deal of significance to their own cultures, the importance of Western education has not diminished in these countries. As a result, Western education has become almost a prerequisite for holding decision-making positions in these political systems.

The masses in Africa and Asia are still very traditional. The national elites, therefore, follow certain traditions or give the appearance of doing so in order to stay in power. For example, many political leaders in India and in some African countries dress in traditional clothes in public.

Military elites are divided by one scholar into two broad categories: "a professional military [elite] under the direct supervision of civilian political leaders, and a political military [elite] which considers itself responsible for the definition and delegation of political authority."[46] Political military elites can be further divided into two subcategories: (1) ruling military elites with direct control over the government; and (2) supportive military elites whose support is considered indispensable by the civilian leadership in power. Although some Third World countries, notably Costa Rica, India, Malaysia, Mexico, Saudi Arabia, Sri Lanka, Tanzania, and Zambia, have professional military elites under the direct supervision of civilian political leaders, most have either ruling military elites or supportive military elites.

Several Latin American nations have experienced ruling military elites for over a century and a half. African and Asian nations that were colonies of the Western nations experimented with democracy after achieving independence. In a majority of the cases, democracy did not work and ruling military elites took over. In some Middle Eastern countries (such as Egypt and Jordan) civilian governments depend on the support of the military elites.

When a military coup occurs, the ruling military elites often promise a return to democracy at the appropriate time. In most cases, the appropriate time never arrives. An interesting exception is that of Ghana, where civilian rule was restored to the country in 1979 after an interval of seven years of military rule. However, two years later, the same military officer (Jerry Rawlings), who was instrumental in ending the military rule in 1979, staged a coup, ending the civilian rule. Nigeria, which returned to democracy in 1979 after military rule of thirteen years, also came under military rule again, five years later.

Ruling military elites promise speedy economic recovery, an end to internal strife, and a "clean" government without corruption. They do bring some order to the country at the cost of human rights, but there is little evidence that the economy fares better or that corruption is less under military compared with civilian rule. Military elites, whether ruling or supportive, invariably increase defense spending, often by buying arms abroad and thus diverting funds from the more pressing needs of the country.

Some leaders in the Third World have had charismatic qualities. In discussing types of legitimate authority and the basis of the validity of their claims, Max Weber defines charismatic grounds as "resting on devotion to the specific and exceptional sanctity, heroism or exemplary character of an individual person, and of the normative patterns or order revealed or ordained by him."[47] Such devotion to a leader can be expected in Third World countries where the elites often make appeals to the sentiments of the masses. Leaders such as Kemal Ataturk (Turkey), Jomo Kenyatta (Kenya), Gamal Abdel Nasser (Egypt), Jawaharlal Nehru (India), Kwame Nkrumah (Ghana), and Juan Domingo Peron (Argentina) are said to have possessed such qualities.

There have been fewer charismatic leaders in the Third World in the 1970s and 1980s than in the previous two decades. A possible explanation is that rising expectations of the people have become rising frustrations in many cases. If members of the ruling elites in a country are unable to resolve economic and related problems, the masses cannot be expected to show the kind of devotion that "charisma" demands.

Political Institutions

In those countries of Africa and Asia that were formerly colonies of the European powers, contemporary political institutions have developed as a combination of indigenous and Western institutions. When Europeans gained control over Africa and Asia (most of the colonies in Africa and Asia were acquired in the nineteenth century), they invariably established a central government with a governor or a viceroy, who held the highest political office in a colony. Of the two powers with the largest empires, Britain and France, the former used the existing indigenous institutions for governing a colony at the local level, supplementing these institutions with a bureaucratic structure. The British also showed some respect for the cultures and the languages of the colonies. Furthermore, they made an attempt, albeit limited and belated, to train the upper strata of the indigenous populations in self-government. The British form of colonial rule came to be known as indirect rule. In contrast to the British indirect rule, the French believed in governing their colonies directly from Paris, leaving little initiative, even at the local level, in the hands of the indigenous people. After losing Indochina in the battle of Dien Bien Phu in 1954, the French realized that they could not hold on to their empire for long and adopted a policy similar to that of the British.[48]

Other European colonial powers, namely, the Netherlands, Belgium, Portugal, and Spain, had smaller empires in Africa and Asia and paid little attention to the indigenous political institutions of their colonies. In this region, the United States had only one major colony (the Philippines) which it had acquired from Spain in 1898, after the Spanish–American War. The U.S. colonial policy in the Philippines was closer to the British policy of indirect rule than to that of the French or any other European colonial power.

The Western institutions were established by the colonial powers to maintain law and order in the colonies. As the colonies have become free, the adaptation of these institutions to the additional task of social and economic development has proven to be very difficult. At the national level this task is often carried on primarily by the executive and the bureaucracy. As several former colonies have adopted military rule, the legislative and even the judicial branches of government have become less important. At the local level the bureaucratic structure, established by the colonial powers, has been retained in most of the former colonies. In some countries, this structure has been augmented with new institutions necessitated by the social and economic policies. In India, for example, the bureaucracy of the colonial era has been retained, but a whole new hierarchy of institutions has been created that deal primarily with such issues as increasing food production and controlling population. Similarly, in Tanzania the policy to reduce income inequality, to dissuade villagers from moving to urban areas, and to increase self-reliance and local initiative, all under the aegis of "African socialism (*ujamaa*)," has led to the emergence of new institutions.

In Latin America, the prevalence of military rule has prevented the emergence of effective legislative and judicial branches in many cases. The executive branch and the bureaucracy under it are the major institutions responsible for governing these countries as well as for bringing about social and economic change. Because the government can change unexpectedly through a military coup, bureaucracies that have to work under the guidance and supervision of the executives have not developed traditions of effective responsibility and competence. Government changes by military coups or attempts at such changes have been common in Africa and the Middle East. In contrast to these three regions, Asia has been relatively stable.[49] In Latin American countries that have civilian rule, often the executive is so powerful that the bureaucracy is not left with much initiative. This is particularly true of Mexico.

Political Issues

In any Third World country, a great diversity of political issues requires decisions by those in power. Of the major issues common to most of these countries, we consider the following most important: type of government, economic development, distribution of income, national identity (especially in those former colonies of Africa and Asia with a great deal of tribal, ethnic, and linguistic diversity), independence from foreign powers and corporations, corruption, and return to fundamentalism in religion in some of the Moslem countries in the Middle East and Pakistan.

The debate on the type of government concerns a choice between Western-style democracy with a free enterprise or limited state intervention system or some form of Marxist–Leninist socialism, resembling rather remotely the Soviet or the Chinese model. A few Third World nations, primarily Saudi Arabia and the sheikhdoms in the Middle East, being still traditional societies, are virtually immune to this debate. Even in those Latin American countries where military government is the general rule, the issue of the type of government is significant, though the debate takes a somewhat different form. In such countries movements demanding the human rights generally associated with Western democracies have emerged.

Notwithstanding the high hopes of economic development after the end of colonial rule, the African and Asian nations have made poor headway in their economies. In the Third World as a whole, only a few nations (such as Argentina, Brazil, South Korea, Singapore, and Taiwan) have made signif-

A traditional market in the Andes mountains, Peru.

icant economic progress based on industrialization. The oil-rich nations have increased their incomes very substantially in the last decade as a result of rising oil prices. For most of the Third World nations, economic development remains a crucial issue for which there appears to be no solution in the near future.

One of the major reasons for the slow economic progress in the Third World countries is the unchecked population growth rate, an important issue by itself in these countries. The annual growth rate of populations is the highest in Latin America (2.7%), followed by Africa (2.6%) and Asia (2.0%).[50] These growth rates are not likely to slow. According to one estimate, of the additional 2 billion people expected to be added to the global population in the next two decades, at least 90% will be in the developing parts of the world, that is, the Third World.[51] Hence, whatever economic progress is achieved by these countries will be vastly diminished in per capita terms.

The distribution of income is more uneven in the Third World than in the First or the Second World. Several Third World countries have adopted various forms of socialism—African socialism, Arab socialism, democratic socialism—in order to reduce the extremes of wealth and poverty and to make income distribution equitable. However, instead of decreasing, income inequalities in most Third World countries have increased. One expert states that in these countries "it is not uncommon for the richest fifth of the nation to command 60 percent or more of the national income, while the poorest fifth has 3 to 5 percent of it."[52]

The issue of national identity is significant in the new nations of Africa and Asia, but not in Latin America. Diversity within the African and Asian nations is such that instead of perceiving themselves as members of a nation, people in these countries think primarily in terms of their association with a relatively smaller group such as a tribe, a caste, an ethnic group, a religious group, or a linguistic group. The lack of a national identity and the great differences among such groups sometimes result in violence. Africa has had several tribal conflicts and India has experienced not only caste, but also linguistic riots. The civil war in Nigeria in the late 1960s had its roots in tribal differences; the Lebanese civil war beginning in 1975 was fought along religious lines. Leaders in the Third World have attempted to forge a feeling of national identity by use of symbols as well as policies. So far the goal of national identity has proven to be elusive for most countries of Africa and Asia.

Because the countries in Africa and Asia were dominated by Western powers during the colonial era, it is not surprising that they value their independence. The Latin American countries, although free of direct colonial domination since the early nineteenth century, have been dependent on the United States for trade and capital inflows for investment. The influence of U.S. corporations in Latin America (and other parts of the world) has given rise to what is called *neocolonialism*. The U.S. multinational corporations have immense assets; however, because of the uncertain stability of the Third World and fears of nationalization, corporations have been increasing their investments in the developed countries and decreasing them in the less-developed countries.[53] On the other hand, notwithstanding their criticism of neocolonialism, the Third World countries have felt compelled to seek Western investment, foreign aid, and trade concessions. Foreign aid and, to a lesser extent, trade concessions, also are sought from the Communist states.

No political system in the world is entirely free of corruption. If we define corruption as granting or receiving of favors in violation of laws, then the total value of such favors is greater in the First World and possibly the Second World than in the Third World. In the Third World countries, however, corruption is more pervasive and visible than in the First or the Second World. Thus, in some of the countries in Africa, Asia, and Latin America, it is virtually impossible to get anything done without a bribe. The leaders in these countries often claim that they would eliminate all corruption from the society. More often than not, they fall prey to the temptation of corruption themselves.

With a resurgence of Islam in Moslem countries, return to the fundamentals of Islam has become a major issue. Iran and Pakistan are two major examples. In Egypt President Sadat was assassinated by religious zealots who felt that he did not adhere strictly to holy writ.

Political Orientations

During the colonial era, the European powers ruled Africa and Asia by force and sought legitimacy by attempting to cultivate a subservient attitude among the native populations. For the common people, the government was a remote entity that did little for them. Laws were obeyed solely out of fear. When the colonies achieved independence, the fear of government lessened. As government was no longer in the hands of foreigners, acceptance of the political system, even commitment to it, rose. The people also expected more from *their* governments. The phenomenon of rising expectations in the Third World took place partly because of the end of colonialism and the establishment of indigenous governments. In most countries, the governments have not been able to deliver—the economic gains achieved have been marginal and very few social welfare programs have been successful. At the same time, politicization of the general populace has taken place, as the result of rising expectations and greater opportunities for political participation.

Political orientations in African and Asian countries are ambivalent indeed. The masses have little faith in the efficacy of particular governments, yet they feel a sense of some commitment to *their* political system. A somewhat similar ambivalence exists in those Latin American countries that have been free a long time and have developed a national identity. The case of Mexico is particularly interesting. Although the people do not believe that the government can produce any beneficial results for them, they feel committed to the political system.[54]

Political socialization in the Third World countries is such that not much attention is paid to the laws passed by the government. It is far more common, for example, to conceal income than to report it for income tax. Of course, in Western nations many people and corporations devise methods for cheating the government of taxes. In the West, however, such cheating is done as carefully as possible, keeping in view the letter of the law. In the Third World, income tax violations take place blatantly with generous use of bribes by the affluent. In some countries, prominently India, Pakistan, and Bangladesh, the phrase "black money" is commonly used to indicate unreported income. It is not only in income tax payments that the laws are ignored in the Third World. A general impression has developed that anything can be accomplished with money, no matter what the laws are. *Baksheesh,* an Arab word for a tip, a gratuity, and more appropriately, a bribe, plays a very prominent role in getting things done, often against the laws, in Arab as well as non-Arab countries of the Third World.

Another commonly used method in Third World countries to accomplish something is violence. Research indicates that the countries in Africa, Asia, and Latin America experience a high incidence of violence with political goals.[55] Not only military coups, often combined with executions, but also assassinations, terrorism, and riots take place more frequently in the Third World than in the First or the Second World. The Iranian revolution of early 1979 and the civil wars in Lebanon and Nigeria are examples.

Violence generally results from frustrations caused by a lack of achievement of one's expectations. Such frustrations exist in every country. In relative terms, however, frustrations are more severe in the Third World than in the First or the Second World. That is one major reason for the higher incidence of violence in the Third World.

NOTES

1. It should be noted that an alternate explanation of the political process is that it is the product of unique historical events and the particular culture that has developed. For example, some historians have argued that cultural factors and important historical events were more important in shaping the pattern of politics of modern France than developmental factors. Although both types of factors can be important, we believe that factors related to the general level of development have greater explanatory power in understanding Western politics.
2. For a good introduction to the concept of complexity and the dynamics of development from an agrarian to industrial society see William A. Faunce, *Problems of Industrial Society* (New York: McGraw-Hill, 1968).
3. For a theoretical discussion of structural differentiation and role specialization see Gabriel A. Almond and G. Bingham Powell, Jr., *System, Process and Policy: Comparative Politics,* 2d ed. (Boston: Little, Brown, 1978), pp. 20–22, 68–72.
4. Faunce, p. 31.
5. David Wood, *Power and Policy in Western European Democracies,* 2d ed. (New York: Wiley, 1978), p. 37.
6. For the theoretical meaning of the work force in political development see G. Lowell Field, *Comparative Political Development: The Precedent of the West* (Ithaca, N.Y.: Cornell University Press, 1967).
7. See Field, pp. 53–48, 117–170.
8. Daniel Bell, *The Coming of Post-industrial Society: A Venture in Social Forecasting* (New York: Basic Books, 1976), p. xvii.
9. See G. Lowell Field's discussion of Level 4, pp. 121–124.
10. Taketsugu Tsurutani, "Japan as a Postindustrial Society," in Leon N. Lindberg,

ed., *Politics and the Future of Industrial Society* (New York: McKay, 1976), p. 100.

11. Wood, p. 38.
12. For a discussion of a recent Italian election see Howard R. Penniman, ed., *Italy at the Polls, 1979: A Study of the Parliamentary Elections* (Washington, D.C.: American Enterprise Institute for Public Policy Research, n.d.)
13. For a contemporary discussion of industrial relations in Britain see Douglas E. Ashford, *Policy and Politics in Britain: The Limits of Consensus* (Philadelphia: Temple University Press, 1981), esp. pp. 136–167.
14. Ronald Inglehart, "The Nature of Value Change in Postindustrial Societies," in Lindberg, pp. 61–73.
15. Bell, pp. xvi–xviii.
16. Lawrence C. Mayer and John H. Burnett, *Politics in Industrial Societies: A Comparative Perspective* (New York: Wiley, 1977), p. 220.
17. For a discussion of the criteria employed in the selection of elites see Robert D. Putnam, *The Comparative Study of Political Elites* (Englewood Cliffs, N.J.: Prentice-Hall, 1977), pp. 57–64.
18. For a discussion of these "citizen protectors" in Sweden see M. Donald Hancock, *Sweden: The Politics of Postindustrial Change* (Hinsdale, Ill.: Dryden Press, 1972), pp. 235–240.
19. Raymond Grew, "The Crises and Their Sequences," in Raymond Grew, ed., *Crises of Political Development in Europe and the United States* (Princeton, N.J.: Princeton University Press, 1978), pp. 3–4.
20. J. Rogers Hollingsworth, "The United States," in Grew, pp. 163–197.
21. Ibid., pp. 188–194.
22. Ibid., p. 189.
23. Ibid., p. 190.
24. Todd LaPorte and C. J. Abrams, "Alternative Patterns of Post-industria: The Californian Experience," in Lindberg, pp. 19–56.
25. Tsurutani, in Lindberg pp. 100–125.
26. Charles W. Anderson, "Public Policy and the Complex Organization: The Problem of Governance and the Further Evolution of Advanced Industrial Society," in Lindberg, pp. 209–219.
27. For an interesting presentation of this view see Everett Carll Ladd, Jr., *American Political Parties: Social Change and Political Response* (New York: Norton, 1970), pp. 243–248.
28. Robert Lane, "The Politics of Consensus in the Age of Affluence," *American Political Science Review* 59 (December 1965): 874–895.
29. Lenard J. Cohen and Jane P. Shapiro, eds., *Communist Systems in Comparative Perspective* (New York: Anchor Books, 1974), pp. xxvii–xxxiv.
30. Paul Marer, "East European Economies: Achievements, Problems, Prospects," in Teresa Rakowska-Harmstone, ed., *Communism in Eastern Europe* (Bloomington: Indiana University Press, 1979), pp. 245–250. See also Richard F. Staar, *The Communist Regimes in Eastern Europe*, 4th ed. (Stanford, Calif.: Hoover Institution Press, 1982).

31. Gary Bertsch, *Power and Policy in Communist Systems,* 2d ed. (New York: Wiley, 1982), p. 36.
32. Marer, p. 246.
33. Ibid., p. 262.
34. Ibid., p. 286.
35. For a discussion of these statistics see Field, pp. 158–167.
36. W. W. Rostow, *The World Economy: History and Prospect* (Austin: University of Texas, 1978), p. 462.
37. Ibid., p. 428.
38. Ibid., p. 428.
39. Bertsch, p. 36.
40. Ibid., p. 36.
41. James R. Townsend, "Politics in China," in Gabriel A. Almond and G. Bingham Powell, Jr., eds., *Comparative Politics Today: A World View* (Boston: Little, Brown, 1980), p. 385.
42. Rostow, p. 522.
43. Bertsch, p. 37.
44. Victor T. Le Vine, *Political Leadership in Africa* (Stanford, Calif.: Hoover Institution Press, 1967), p. 89.
45. See Monte Palmer, *Dilemmas of Political Development,* 2d ed. (Itasca, Ill. Peacock, 1980), p. 82.
46. Irving L. Horowitz, "The Military Elites," in Seymour Martin Lipset and Aldo Solari, eds., *Elites in Latin America* (New York: Oxford University Press, 1967), p. 148.
47. Max Weber, *The Theory of Social and Economic Organization* (New York: Macmillan, 1947), p. 328.
48. See John G. Stoessinger, *The Might of Nations* (New York: Random House, 1982), pp. 110–11.
49. For some statistics on government changes by military coups in the Third World, see Kevin Kennedy, *The Military in the Third World* (New York: Scribners, 1974), Appendix A.
50. The source for these statistics is Population References Bureau, *1977 World Population Data Sheet* (Washington, D.C., 1977).
51. Ruth Leger Sivard, *World Military and Social Indicators, 1980* (Leesburg, Va.: World Priorities, 1980), p. 19.
52. Ibid., p. 16.
53. See David H. Blake and Robert S. Walters, *The Politics of Global Economic Relations* (Englewood Cliffs, N.J.: Prentice-Hall, 1976), p. 79.
54. See Gabriel A. Almond and Sidney Verba, *The Civic Culture* (Boston: Little, Brown, 1965), p. 203. The Mexican Revolution that began in 1910 played a major role in helping the Mexicans develop a national identity.
55. See, for example, Ivo K. Feierabend, Rosalind L. Feierabend, and Ted Robert Gurr, eds., *Anger, Violence and Politics: Theories and Research* (Englewood Cliffs, N.J.: Prentice-Hall, 1972).

4

The Element of Human Choice: Political Ideology in Three Worlds

Political actors make certain choices that help to determine the political patterns of their countries. These choices are determined by the political culture of a given society and the perceptions people have of political activity.

The political elites of the three worlds have different views of what politics is all about. The First World elites look at political activity as an arena of struggle for self-interest in which fairness also must be observed. Liberalism, capitalism, and social welfare theory have influenced the First World's views of politics, concepts of justice, perceptions of the role of government, and notions of public versus private rights.

The Second World's political elites have chosen to base their political views on those of Marx, Engels, and Lenin. These views present the world as a place of struggle between the emerging "socialist-Communist" forces and those of the receding "capitalists." The role of government has expanded greatly in the Second World, whereas the individual has become submerged for the sake of the development of society.

Third World nations have selected from First and Second World political outlooks, adapting them to particular local conditions. African socialism and Taiwanese and South Korean free enterprise are examples of the different choices made.

POLITICAL DEVELOPMENT AND HUMAN CHOICE

Although level of development is a major determinant of the pattern of politics of any state, a second determinant is also present, the element of human choice. At every level of development from preindustrial to postindustrial, choices and alternatives are available to political actors. These choices are shaped and influenced by the general level of political development. It is the level of political development that establishes the ultimate limits on the scope of choice. Such factors as a low level of industrial development and the existence of a large population of rural parochials presently deny most Third World states the option of playing a major role in world affairs. However, political actors in the Third World as in all states are confronted with choices and options that influence the general pattern of politics. Decisions about which areas of social life the political system should regulate, the nature of political morality and immorality, and the proper role of the masses in politics produce differences in the pattern of politics of all states, even those at the same level of development.

Both the United States and the Soviet Union are industrialized states at an advanced level of development. As such, political actors in both states share a preference for efficiency in government, political decision making by small groups of experts (such as those in the Politburo or the president's Cabinet), and require a background of specialized education and bureaucratic experience of those seeking to become members of the political elite. These similarities have caused some observers to argue that a convergence of political thought is taking place in the two superpowers. Beyond these common elements, however, other decisions and choices serve to differentiate the two systems. American political actors have chosen to place great emphasis on civil liberties, the rights of the individual, and the role of private enterprise in development, whereas the Soviet Union has chosen to build its industrial state through forced and voluntary collectivization and a centralized economy. It is difficult to deny that these choices have produced meaningful differences in the political styles of the two states.

Determinants of Choice

Political choices are the result of the application of political values, attitudes, and preconceptions to specific political problems. Political values and attitudes are components of a state's political culture, and political cultures differ from state to state. Political culture constitutes the second important variable of the political process. The political process of any state is the result of the interaction of the factors of development with the elements of the national political culture.

Political Culture

The political culture of any state includes a vast array of components encompassing all of the knowledge, beliefs, judgments, and feelings about politics held by both the elite and general population. Included in the political culture is the totality of factual knowledge about the political system, the emotional feelings toward the institutions, personalities and symbols of the political system, and evaluational judgments about the political system and political life. Some components of political culture are more important than others in determining the pattern of politics. Because political elites possess disproportionate power and influence and have control over the major institutions in society, their value preferences and attitudes have a greater influence on the political process than do those of the other elements of society. Similarly, the values and attitudes of groups within the general population which interact regularly with the major institutions are more important than those of parochial groups which abstain from the conventional political process. Groups that are alienated from the prevailing pattern of politics and "drop out" of political life may have strong value preferences, but, short of revolution or major civil upheaval, their values do not influence the political system.

In understanding the differences between political systems, the most important component of political culture is the *operative ideology of the elite*. The operative ideology of the elite is the set of rules governing elite political behavior. Central to the elite ideology are six elements: (1) a general view of politics, (2) a conception of justice or morality in politics, (3) a preference for the way political decisions should be made, (4) a view of the proper scope of governmental activity and involvement in the society, (5) a view of the proper relationship between public and private power, and (6) a conception of the proper role of the masses in the political process. The operative ideology may also include certain political goals on which national elites share a consensus. The operative ideology may be openly proclaimed in public, denied to the public in any coherent form, or concealed by another belief system that is proclaimed publicly but not followed. All elite groups are guided by an operative ideology that may be either observed directly or inferred from their actions and behavior.

Perceptions of Politics

In this discussion, the elements of the operative ideology are referred to as *elite perceptions of politics*. This phrase is preferred because it avoids the implication that the values and attitudes that guide elite behavior in the contemporary political world are identical to the traditional ideologies of fascism, Communism, and capitalism. Contemporary belief systems often contain many new value combinations and conceptions not contained in these ideologies. Elite thought in the United States and Great Britain may be used to illustrate this point. Contemporary elites in these states favor decision making by small groups of specialized experts, although such limited decision making was not a part of traditional democratic theory. The term "elite perceptions of politics" also permits recognition of the fact that other political attitudes that are not part of the operative ideology of the elite also shape the pattern of politics in a society. Mass attitudes play a role, although a less important role, in shaping the pattern of politics because members of this segment of society do interact with major political institutions. In a world where strikes, boycotts, acts of violence, or demonstrations of support may affect the political fortunes of the elite, mass attitudes do affect the pattern of politics. The overthrow of the Shah of Iran by popular forces embracing traditional religious values stands as testimony to this point.

The most important mass political perceptions concern three points: (1) mass attitudes toward participation, (2) mass expectations of system performance and (3) the degree of mass support for political symbols and institutions. Mass attitudes toward participation in the political system include both those attitudes toward partisan political activity in which demands are made on the system and those toward system-sponsored activities in which services are performed for the political system (paying taxes, conscription, accepting regulations). Mass expectations of system performance constitute the demands made on the political system for services, benefits, and rights. In the contemporary Communist World, for example, the pattern of politics in Poland is distinguished from that of other Soviet satellite states by a higher level of mass demands for services. Finally, supports for political institutions and symbols include attitudes toward both actual political institutions and those toward such symbols as flags, crests, and the "national political tradition." These attitudes reveal the degree of grass-roots support available to the political system.

ELITE PERCEPTIONS OF POLITICS IN THREE WORLDS: AN OVERVIEW

In the three political worlds of the West, the Communist World, and the Third World, different political conceptions and values prevail in the six fundamental areas. In the West, politics is generally viewed as a conflict process in which groups of individuals pursue their self-interests. Political morality requires only that the competition be "fair" and that the same legal and political rights be available to all parties, not that the conflict process result in an equitable distribution of values to all groups. Because of the concern for the private individual, Western political conceptions prescribe a limited-to-moderate role for government and permit private institutions such as corporations, unions, and charities to play an important part in the allocation of wealth and opportunity. Western political attitudes also reflect the concern for specialization, expertise, and efficiency typical of societies at the stage of advanced industrialization. Decision making by small groups such as judges and Cabinet members is permitted, although high-level members of the elite must be accountable to the general population at election time. Western political values require that members of the general population be treated with respect and civility, and that their civil liberties be observed.

Political perceptions in the Communist World reflect the interaction of Marxist–Leninist theory with the concerns for efficiency, specialization, and expertise common to industrial societies. Politics is viewed as a conflict process in which class antagonisms are resolved according to an inevitable historical scheme. Although theoretically conflict occurs only between the members of different classes, Communist political thought has been forced to recognize the existence of conflict even within the Communist party. Justice is defined as the egalitarian distribution of values; however, dispro-portionate status, benefits, and opportunities are permitted for members of the Communist party. Rigorous participation is required of members of the masses, but the participation is limited to demonstrations of support for the political system and acts of conformity to official standards. Finally, Communist political perceptions legitimize the regulation and manipulation of all areas of the society by the Communist party.

Political perceptions in the Third World reflect both the concern for rapid development and the tendency to adopt the political values of the more-developed states. Politics is viewed as a two-stage process in which the conflict associated with anticolonialism is followed by a community-building process during which national consensus and loyalty to the state develop. Conceptions of justice vary considerably from state to state, but the developed world is attacked as immoral and unjust either because of the inequitable distribution of values in the world or its failure to respect traditional values. Elite decision making by small cliques, coercive regula-tion of society, and suppression of private power are justified in most Third World states as measures necessary to accomplish rapid development. Third World political attitudes place great emphasis on symbolic political partici-pation by the masses. Symbolic displays are frequently used to demonstrate the commitment to national unity or to conceal the failure of national development programs. The states of the Third World display a greater diversity of thought than do the states of the West or the Communist World.

THE FIRST WORLD

The Influence of Liberalism, Capitalism, and Social Welfare Theory

Contemporary Western political perceptions are the product of the three ideologies that have shaped modern Western society, namely, liberalism, capitalism, and social welfare theory. To understand the meaning of Western political life is to understand the manner in which these three ideologies have interacted since the sixteenth century to produce political attitudes and values unique in the world. The present preoccupation in the West with the rights of the individual, an open and "fair" political process, and limited government are but a few of the examples of the influence of the three ideologies.

Liberalism, capitalism, and social welfare theory are three separate belief systems or "layers of thought." The values and ideals of each were introduced into Western society at different periods, beginning with liberalism in the late seventeenth century, followed by capitalism in the eighteenth and nineteenth centuries, and social welfare theory in the nineteenth and twentieth centuries. As each new school of thought gained acceptance, new values were added to the older ones and the nature of Western political culture changed. In some areas the three ideologies offered competing and contradictory prescriptions for political life. Major political conflicts have occurred when groups within the same political system adopted contradictory values, especially those contained in liberalism and social welfare theory. Foremost among these conflicts has been the issue of how much government assistance can be given to disadvantaged groups without forfeiting the freedom of other individuals who must pay for such assistance or must submit to additional government regulations. In this case liberalism and social welfare theory have left a contradictory and confused set of values, making it difficult to decide which should take precedence, the welfare theorist's concern for greater equality in society or the liberal's preoccupation with the economic freedom of the individual.

In addition to the conflicts that have arisen from commitment to contradictory values, the three belief system: ave had different degrees of influence in the various states of the West rld. William Bluhm has referred to the United States as a system wl "sm is established" because of the American preoccupation v dom, limited government, and the rights of the indiv of Canada).[1] Charles Andrain has argu element of social welfare theory, has the other Scandinavian states than on a Many of the differences between Western st decisions result from varying degrees of acceptance of one or more of the basic belief systems.

Despite the differences, contemporary Western states are more alike in the area of political beliefs than they are different. It is possible to speak of a Western "political mind" and of Western political perceptions that are present with some variations in all of the states of the West. In terms of their political beliefs, the states of the West display greater similarity than do either the Communist states or the states of the Third World. The terms "democracy" and "welfare state" are applicable to each of the Western political systems because of their common acceptance of certain basic values of liberalism and social welfare theory.

The Influence of Liberalism

From its inception in the seventeenth century, liberalism was the doctrine of the middle-class commercial segment of Western society, the *bourgeoisie*. This group sought to end royal interference in trade and commerce and to gain full political and legal rights. First in England and later on the continent, the bourgeoisie became an important political force. The primary concern of liberal theorists was to justify individual freedom and the right to engage in economic activity free of government interference. They succeeded in establishing a rich tradition of human rights and respect for the individual, which has persisted in Western thought to the present day. As a theory of democracy, however, liberalism sought to free only a small minority of the population, the middle class, from the control of the much smaller group, the aristocracy. It was consequently a limited theory of democracy. As the power of the bourgeoisie grew, its members gave it an increasingly narrow class interpretation.[3] The important concepts of freedom, justice, and the proper role of government were defined in ways that were compatible with the political interests of the bourgeoisie.

From the time of the classical liberal theorists (in the seventeenth and eighteenth centuries) to the present, the concepts of individual freedom and *laissez-faire* (limited) government have been at the center of liberal thought. Classical liberals argued that the individual constituted the most important element in human life, and that progress and human happiness were possible only if the rights of the individual were respected. Classical liberal theorists, such as the Englishman John Locke (1632–1704), the French-Swiss Jean Jacques Rousseau (1712–1778), and the American Thomas Jefferson (1743–1826), argued that individuals were born free with natural and inalienable rights to life, liberty, and property, which could not be denied. By forming governments individuals did not forfeit their rights, but instead established a new means to better protect them, providing that the power of

John Locke.

government was carefully limited. John Locke maintained in his work, *Of Civil Government* (1690), that governments must be established by a specific agreement or social contract and that acts of government were binding on individuals only if they consented to them. In addition, Locke argued that the functions of government should be severely limited. The French liberal, Charles Louis de Secondat, the Baron de Montesquieu (1689–1755), in his work *Spirit of the Laws* sought to protect the freedom of the individual by separating the powers of government into distinct legislative, executive, and judicial departments. In the United States, Thomas Jefferson authored the "Bill of Rights," the first ten amendments to the U.S. Constitution, which listed the rights of the individual that government could not abridge.

Collectively, liberal theorists sought to build a world where the individual could enjoy the freedoms of conscience, speech, the press, religion, and the right to form economic and political associations.[4] Because of the political and economic position of the bourgeoisie, much attention was devoted to the issue of economic associations and activities. Early liberal thought placed great emphasis on economic freedom, and in the hierarchy of freedoms, economic freedom was assigned a predominant position in the works of several prominent liberals. Freedom was defined in a negative way, as the absence of government restrictions and regulations. Individuals were considered to be free when they were left alone by government to succeed or fail on the basis of their own actions. Later social welfare theorists argued that freedom was not merely the absence of restrictions, but rather the presence of opportunities for personal development such as an education and a job. In some cases the government would provide these opportunities. However, this conception of freedom had to wait for the nineteenth and twentieth centuries when there was a greater concern for the economic condition of the majority.

Liberals embraced a conception of justice known as "justice as fairness."[5] According to this concept, justice is achieved in the political system when the same neutral rules apply equally to all participants in economic or political competition. A just society is one in which the same legal rights apply to all individuals, and no group receives special advantages or restrictions. This conception of justice was entirely preoccupied with process, and did not extend to political outcomes or to the manner in which political and economic values were actually distributed. If the fair process led to a result in which a few individuals won all the economic values at the expense of the majority, this was both acceptable and just as long as all the competitors had competed under genuinely similar conditions. The early development of the concept of justice as fairness prevented the development of other conceptions of justice until the late nineteenth and early twentieth centuries.

Liberalism had its greatest influence in Britain and in the English "transplant societies" of the United States, Canada, New Zealand, and Australia. On the European continent liberal political concepts were opposed by groups advocating older authoritarian beliefs. The French Revolution of 1789 marked the partial victory of liberalism in France and began its spread throughout Europe. In France, Germany, and Italy, however, the final victory of liberalism did not occur until after World War II. The most important liberal theorists included Voltaire, Rousseau, Diderot, and Montesquieu in France; Locke, Hume, and Adam Smith in Britain; Goethe, Lessing, and Kant in Germany; Vico and Beccaria in Italy; and Jefferson, Franklin, and Paine in America.[6]

The Influence of Capitalism

Capitalism is often referred to as "liberal economics" because it was the application of liberal principles to the field of economics, especially to the issue of the proper relationship between government and business. Beginning with the classic work of Adam Smith, *The Wealth of Nations* (1776), capitalist theorists sought to demonstrate that economic welfare and development are fostered not by government regulation or planning, but by freeing economic activity completely from restriction and control.[7] This thesis was pursued with remarkable consistency by successive generations of capitalist thinkers well into the twentieth century. As early as 1770 capitalism was widely accepted in Europe, and it became the dominant school of economic thought throughout the states of the West by the time the industrial revolution reached maturity in the mid-nineteenth century.[8]

Capitalism reinforced many of the beliefs of liberalism, but placed an even greater emphasis on the need for economic freedom. According to classical capitalist theory, human happiness and individual and national wealth could best be promoted by the free market instrument. The free market was defined as the meeting place or point of interaction of free individuals who—propelled by self-interest—buy, sell, invest, borrow, loan, seek employment, and enter into contractual relationships.[9] The free market system produced maximum human productivity because it offered the opportunity for profit. The underlying assumption of capitalism was that human beings were by nature competitive, acquisitive, and self-interested. As long as the opportunity for additional wealth and property (profit) were present, people would continue vigorous economic activity. Capitalists argued that the free market system was guided by natural laws or by an "invisible hand" to assure that entrepreneurs make profit, laborers find employment, consumers pay reasonable prices, and that new products be produced and distributed.

Given the self-regulating nature of the free market, capitalist theorists reemphasized the need for limited or laissez-faire government.[10] Government intervention would invariably produce harm and upset the natural forces that guided the free market. Any attempt to interfere with private property (e.g., by progressively taxing the rich) was especially dangerous as it removed the opportunity for profit, the sole motive for economic activity. Capitalists sought to confine governmental activity to two areas, the protection of private property and the maintenance of the security of the state. By confining the government to these tasks, the state became the protector of the capitalist system.

When the industrialization process produced great disparities between the rich and poor in the nineteenth century, capitalist theorists clung tenaciously to their opposition to government intervention on behalf of the disadvantaged. They argued that great disparities in wealth and the existence of poverty proved that the free market system was working to reward those that had been successful in economic competition. Those who temporarily found themselves in a state of poverty had no one to blame but themselves because they had failed to take advantage of the opportunities of the free market. It was not possible to help them without destroying the free market mechanism, and only through methods of self-help would their conditions be improved.

Like liberalism, capitalism emphasized two aspects of political life, competition and the pursuit of self-interest. The good citizen in a liberal-capitalist society was, as President Woodrow Wilson later described him, the "man on the make" who vigorously pursued his own economic and political self-interest.[11] Because capitalism specified no common or commu nity goals, no one was expected to participate in collective programs for the benefit of others. The capitalist state constituted a community only in the sense that its members had agreed to create a political environment in which the individual could be free to compete with others.

The Influence of Social Welfare Theory

By the mid-nineteenth century the industrialization process in the West produced social and economic conditions that many observers considered to be morally and socially unacceptable. Beginning in Germany and Britain, a system of beliefs called *democratic socialism* developed, challenging some of the fundamental conceptions of liberal economics. The important advocates of democratic socialism in Europe included Eduard Bernstein (1850–1932) in Germany, the Fabian Society (founded in 1883) and the British Labour party (founded in 1906) in Britain, Jean Juares (1859–1914) in France, and Ernst Wigforss in Sweden. Within a few decades a second set of beliefs, *social liberalism*,[12] arose in the United States and Canada; it also attacked the prevailing liberal economic theories.

As originally developed, democratic socialism and social liberalism differed in several important respects. Early democratic socialists called for public ownership (ownership by a democratically elected government) of major industries, utilities, and transportation systems. In theory they also sought to impose limits on the accumulation of private property, and social democrats in several countries developed master plans for the eradication of both the upper and lower classes and the creation of homogeneous middle-class societies. Most social liberals in the United States did not seek the public ownership of industry and did not attack the institution of private property. In addition, U.S. and Canadian social liberals rejected grandiose social planning schemes to restructure society. As they evolved, however, neither democratic socialism nor social liberalism maintained its orthodoxy or consistency. Democratic socialists moderated both their demands for public ownership and their attacks on private property. For their part, social liberals accepted increasing government intervention and planning. In the years after World War II, a limited convergence took place around a set of beliefs common to both democratic socialism and social liberalism.[13] This common set of beliefs, called social welfare theory, formed the theoretical foundation for the modern welfare state that developed with minor variations in each of the states of the West between the end of World War I and the end of World War II.

Social welfare theory offered definitions of freedom and justice that differed from those of liberalism and capitalism. It also placed greater emphasis on the value of equality and added the concept of the positive state. According to the new definitions, social welfare theorists argued that justice required not only that individuals compete under identical and fair conditions (justice as fairness), but also that the actual distribution of values be to some degree equal. Although they accepted economic competition, welfare state theorists argued that all individuals must be guaranteed the basic essentials of life, including food, housing, and medical services. Programs providing these services were developed in various forms in each of the Western nations by the end of World War II. The new conception of equality also went beyond the liberal idea of legal and political equality. Equality now was defined as the creation of an environment in which every person was free to fulfill aspirations to a legitimate career, regardless of wealth, sex, or family background, and to receive fair compensation for his or her services.[14] Social welfare theory also replaced the limited definition of freedom of liberalism. Freedom was no longer defined as the absence of government restrictions, but rather as the presence of real opportunities for human development including an education, a job, protection of one's health, and meaningful leisure activities. Such opportunities were seen as necessary to prevent the development of two evils in the political system: (1) insecurity among persons experiencing the hardships of modern economic and social life, and (2) an economically inefficient system in which only the human potential of the affluent members of society was developed while the majority of persons were ignored.[15]

Social welfare theory also included a positive conception of the state, which contrasted sharply with the negative conception of government contained in liberalism and capitalism. The democratically elected government was seen as a potentially positive force in the affairs of both society and the individual. The important programs guaranteeing the essentials of life, such as pension plans, employees' insurance, aid to dependent children, and welfare entitlement programs were to be financed at the public expense and administered directly by the government. The new economic guarantees were viewed as "economic civil liberties" guaranteeing individual freedom, not interfering with it. In addition, it was argued that government planning was necessary to prevent depressions and other economic catastrophies and to protect special groups such as minorities, women, children, and the handicapped from societal discrimination and the loss of opportunity.

From the earliest pronouncements to the present, social welfare theorists maintained that the welfare state would be developed without excessive interference with the political freedoms that liberalism had established. They accepted that the scope of welfare state activities would fluctuate according to the prevailing political sentiments of the electorate. In addition, twentieth-century theorists have argued that the welfare state is not incompatible with economic responsibility. The attempt by social welfare theorists to accommodate liberal values demonstrated the pervasive effect of liberalism even on those critical of some of the results it had produced.

Contemporary Elite Perceptions

Contemporary elite perceptions are derived from the three systems of thought that prevail in the West, liberalism, capitalism, and social welfare theory. Unfortunately, for the modern student of politics, no one belief system is clearly dominant in all of the six major areas of political perceptions (nature of politics, concept of justice, the proper scope of government, public versus private power, assumptions about decision making, and view of the masses). Western political perceptions are the combination of the three belief systems and reflect the interaction of liberal, capitalist, and social welfare goals. In general, elite perceptions are based on a foundation of liberal beliefs modified by social welfare values. In summary, Western elites view politics as a conflict process, but one in which the losers must be guaranteed some minimal level of values. The conception of justice is primarily one of justice as fairness although some concern is given to the equitable distribution of values. Western elites embrace a positive view of the state and accept limited-to-moderate government intervention in economic and social life. However, they also favor a major role for private institutions such as businesses, unions, and charities in the distribution of values. Western elites share an outlook toward political decision making known as "democratic elitism." Democratic elitism assumes that most political decisions will be made by the elite and that the masses will play only a limited role in the decision-making process.

General View of Politics. Western elites share a general view of politics mostly influenced by the liberal–capitalist tradition but also modified by social welfare theory. They view politics as a qualified conflict process in which individuals and groups compete for values such as wealth, status, and influence but in which even the losers must be provided with certain minimal values necessary to guarantee their status as citizens in a democracy. In determining their own political roles, elite members accept the "logic of political conflict."[16] They view political life as a continuous competition for values that all persons covet. Rational political behavior is seen to consist of involvement in activities that will permit the pursuit of economic and political self-interest for themselves as individuals and for the client groups they represent. Such activities, known as conflict representation activities, include influencing public opinion in ways consistent with one's own political interests, the exercise of organizational and leadership skills, and involvement in the activities of political parties and interest groups.[17] In accepting the logic of political conflict, elite members assume the fact that the other political actors with whom they interact are also rational and motivated by self-interest. This assumption leads to attempts at bargaining, compromise, and deal making, which are common features of political life in the West.

The pursuit of self-interest by elite groups is so common in the West that it is appropriate to speak of the "normalcy of politics." In every Western state, unions, businesses, farmers' organizations, environmentalists, professional groups, women's rights advocates, and minority group activists regularly and openly compete for economic benefits and opportunities. In addition, it is accepted that lobbyists meet regularly with the government officials to work for the interest of their clients and that legislators and other elected officials serve the interests of those groups that supported their election. The scope of political competition is also wide in contemporary Western politics and extends to many different issues. Recently, elite groups have attempted to politicize such issues as prostitution, pornography, abortion, homosexuality, smoking, and corporal punishment of children by parents. In so doing, these groups have sought to impose their views of morality on the rest of society. Such conflicts, as well as the more conventional ones involving economics, testify to the persistence of the liberal–capitalist concepts of individual competition, and the pursuit of self-interest.

Despite the emphasis on the logic of political conflict, Western elites have come to accept limits on competition. Since World War II, elites in every Western state have endorsed the assumption of social welfare theory that the distribution of values in society must be to some degree equitable. Although the elites of the various Western states differ on the extent of equality required, they agree that certain minimal benefits must be made available to all persons through government programs financed at public expense. These benefits include an education, access to a job, workers' compensation, unemployment insurance, retirement benefits, and basic medical services.[18] In Europe and Canada these benefits and several others are considered entitlements that must be guaranteed to every citizen as a matter of principle. In the United States such benefits are granted more on the basis of temporary need than as permanent entitlements. Elites on both sides of the Atlantic endorse progressive taxation, mandatory employer contributions, government regulations, and other limitations on free market competition in order to make available these benefits or public goods.

Concept of Justice. Western elites embrace a modified view of justice as fairness. Because of the emphasis on the logic of political conflict inherited from the liberal–capitalist tradition, great importance is assigned to the development and maintenance of fair and equal procedures in the competition for political values. The freedoms of speech, assembly, association, and the press are guaranteed in every Western political system either by a bill of rights or by specific statutes. In addition, the concept of equality before the law and the right to vote are also firmly established in the Western political tradition. In general, Western elites demonstrate a respect for the rights of the individual citizen unequaled anywhere else in the world. In a comment on the attitudes of local government elites in the United States, Robert Dahl noted that they behaved according to a "democratic creed" observing customary civility, the right to dissent, bargaining, varying degrees of good faith and trust, and the laws of electoral conduct.[19] These comments might well have been made about the national elite of any Western nation.

Although Western elites see as the foremost requirement for a just society the development of equal competitive conditions, their definition of justice is not limited entirely to this point. Western political elites also believe that a just society must provide every individual with certain basic opportunities such as an education and a job necessary for human development. Some analysts refer to this concept of justice as "justice as goodness" and argue that it is incompatible with the concept of justice as fairness.[20] In contemporary Western thought, however, both conceptions of justice are present, although greater emphasis is given to the concept of fairness. The concept of justice as fairness is especially strong in the United States, whereas the concept of justice as goodness is the most developed in Sweden.

Proper Scope of Government. Since the 1930s, Western elites have accepted the positive role of the state. Despite the increasing acceptance of government involvement in economic and social affairs, Western elites favor only a limited-to-moderate role for government when compared with elites of the Third World and the Communist states. In this area, elite beliefs have been influenced by the value systems of liberalism and capitalism, which traditionally view government activity with suspicion. Resistance to government intervention is the strongest in the United States, where liberalism has had its greatest influence. The scope of government activity is broadest in the continental European systems where liberal values have had to compete with social democratic, Communist, and conservative belief systems. Although European elites have more readily accepted the need for government regulation of economic life and even government ownership of certain industries, they advocate only a moderate role for government. In Sweden, France, and Italy, where government ownership is the most advanced, more than 85% of all industry remains under private ownership and the role of the state is predominately one of regulation rather than outright ownership.

Among Western European elite groups, only the Communists presently advocate greatly increased public (government) ownership.

Western elites have traditionally considered certain important areas of life to be outside the proper scope of government activity. These areas include religious practice, family relations, artistic and cultural expression, and academic life. Western elites are strongly influenced by the liberal ideal that individuals should be free to establish their own life-styles and value preferences.

Public versus Private Power. In Western political systems, private (nongovernmental) groups are assigned an important role in the public (governmental) policy process. Western elites accept that private interest groups must be consulted in the making of all public policies and that important public policy decisions, especially those in the economic area, must involve the participation of both public and private elite groups. In a study of economic policy in seven Western political systems (the United States, Canada, Britain, West Germany, Sweden, France, and Italy), Charles Andrain found that government, private business corporations, and labor unions jointly formulate and carry out public policies.[21] The blurring of public and private sources of power is especially obvious in Canada and the states of Western Europe, where business and labor leaders are consulted on all policy decisions involving inflation, unemployment, income distribution, nationalization, and government regulation of economic activities.[22] Although central government bureaucrats may take the lead in planning and proposing public policies, an important role is reserved for private interest groups in other areas of public policy. Private physicians work with government health officials to develop public health policies, government and industry scientists consult over pollution control standards, and private business firms receive government subsidies to train the unemployed. In Britain, labor leaders and business representatives maintain regular contacts with cabinet members and high-level civil servants, whose roles are institutionalized in special committees. In a study of the political economy of the United States, Charles Lindblom found that business leaders have a great influence on public policy.[23]

The important role assigned to private interest groups develops from several different political assumptions. In the United States it is part of the liberal tradition of limited government and the right of groups to pursue their self-interest. In Great Britain since the late 1960s attempts have been made to end labor unrest and to increase economic output through the development of economic policies mutually acceptable to trade unions, business, and government. In Sweden, where social democratic theory has had its greatest influence, the inclusion of private groups in the public policy process is seen as an extension of equality from economic areas to political matters. Despite the different theoretical foundations, Charles Lindblom has concluded that all the states of the West constitute a unique type of political system that he calls a *polyarchy* (many centers of power), in which elected officials and government bureaucrats share authority and decision-making power with well-organized private groups.[24]

Political Decision Making: Role of the Elite and the Masses. Most Western elites embrace a conception of decision making known as democratic elitism.[25] Democratic elitism assigns the major role in political decision making to the elite and only a limited role to the masses. Western elites believe that the problems confronting modern political systems are too difficult and complex to be understood by the general population except when presented in some simplified form, as in election campaign issues. As in other fields, such as medicine and science, specialization is required in the making of political decisions. Only elite members who possess political experience, education, and special expertise are competent to deal with such problems as nuclear deterrence, inflation, and the shortage of natural resources. In light of the complicated nature of modern politics, the role of the masses must be confined to choosing at election time between competing slates of elites who will make the important political decisions for them.

Western elites argue that dominance of the decision-making process by elite groups is democratic because the following conditions are present: (1) elite groups genuinely compete with one another, (2) the elites are accountable to the general population at election time, (3) elites are open to lobbying efforts and other communications from the masses, and (4) elites defend the civil liberties of all citizens and respect the right to dissent.[26] In theory every citizen is free to pursue an elective position which will enable him or her to become a decision maker and every citizen retains his or her civil liberties as required by liberal theory. The barriers that limit the participation of the general population are not legal or political, but rather are based on competence, interest, and expertise. Such obstacles are not seen as incompatible with democracy.

Examples of elite decision making abound in modern Western political systems. Once elected, Western legislators serve for the duration of their terms free from the direct control of the public. Legislative decision making, although theoretically open to the public, usually involves inputs only from the representatives of organized interest groups. In addition, executive and administrative decisions that often involve secret sessions and appointed rather than elected officials have increased greatly in recent years. Studies of political activism in the West put the percentage of the population that regularly engages in political activities at approximately 5%. Political

Marx, Engels, Lenin, and Stalin.

activity in the West is clearly sustained by a subculture of activists contained within a larger population not involved in a meaningful way in political decision making.

The theory of democratic elitism gained prominence in the West during the late nineteenth and early twentieth centuries when specialization and elite dominance by entrepreneurs and managers became the mode of operation in factories and businesses. Democratic elitism developed from capitalist thought stressing efficiency and the need for rational organization of workers to increase production. The theory of democratic elitism is most firmly established in the United States, Great Britain, and Germany, where the influence of capitalism was the greatest. In Sweden, where social democratic theory seriously challenged capitalist thought, a different conception of decision making also developed. In Sweden, members of the Social Democrat party and their allies have sought to promote the involvement of new groups in the political decision-making process at the local and national levels. Before their defeat in the 1976 election, the Social Democrats had proposed legislation that would have made worker participation mandatory in the business decisions of some industries, a conception of decision making known as *industrial democracy*. Many nonsocialist critics have attacked what they call a "socialist concentration of power" at the apex of the Swedish political system.[27]

THE SECOND WORLD

It might appear at first that a discussion of political perceptions in the Second World would be fairly simple. Communist politicians, after all, appear to share a monolithic (single, undivided) view, based on the writings of the German social scientists and philosophers Karl Marx (1818–1883) and Friedrich Engels (1820–1895), and of the Russian revolutionary Vladimir Ilyich Ulyanov (Lenin) (1870–1924). The situation, however, is analogous to that of the three great monotheistic religions: Judaism, based on the Old Testament writings, has three main branches; Christianity, with its New Testament foundation, has four major interpretations; and Islam, founded on a single book, the Koran, is divided into two camps. Communist political "classics" (the writings of Marx, Engels, and Lenin) are also interpreted in various ways. In order to understand the different types of Communism it is necessary to consider, first, the unifying features of Communist doctrine and then the disjunctive forces at work in the Communist World.

Unifying Features of Communist Political Doctrine

Besides the common experience of the seizure of power through force, the basic unity of Communist elites is promoted by acceptance of the "classics." Unique adjustments and interpretations have been made to fit local political circumstances (such as Mao's theory that revolution in the Third World would be promoted by peasants rather than factory workers); however, the general theory is unified by common acceptance of Marxist-Leninist political beliefs. Communist Party members believe they have the only correct, coherent, and comprehensive political view that explains human past and present, and identifies the direction of future development. The "forces of history" moving along a "dialectical" path will show to all that the Communist party is correct in its explanation of human existence. The shared feelings of correctness in understanding life, of being part of a worldwide movement, and of pursuing the goal of a Communist utopia are powerful psychological inducements to unity.

Before the Socialist-Communist stage is reached, history passes through four stages: primitive communalism, slavery, feudalism, and capitalism. These stages are determined by economic factors; specifically, the means of production used in a given stage of history and the socioeconomic class that controls these means. The countries of the Second World today are in the first part of the Socialist-Communist stage. Karl Marx referred to this as early Communism; Lenin, however, called it socialism. When the final step to full-scale Communism will be made is not clear in the Marxist-Leninist doctrine. Nikita Khrushchev, the Soviet leader who succeeded Stalin, wanted Soviet society to reach the Communist utopia by 1980.[28] This goal is not within the reach of the Soviet leaders in the near future. However, the idea of the imminent arrival of full-scale Communism—a stateless, classless society of freedom and abundance—is still maintained and propaganda is used by the ruling elites to convince the masses that much of what Marx perceived as Communism has already been achieved.

In explaining history, Karl Marx borrowed some ideas from the German philosopher G.W.F. Hegel (1770–1831). Hegel perceived history as a dialectical process reflected in the conflict of ideas. Marx, on the other hand, interpreted history as a conflict between humans and nature and, more important, between socioeconomic classes of people within a society. A class is defined in terms of the possession or nonpossession of the means of production at a particular stage in history. Except for the beginning (primitive communal stage) and the final stage (Socialism–Communism), two major classes exist within society—the class whose members own the means of production, and the class whose members do not own the means of production. Exploitation of the latter class (the have-not class) by the former and struggle between the two classes are inevitable. This class struggle continues until the final stage, Socialism–Communism, is reached. Throughout this process the government is controlled by the class that owns the means of production. The state thus is used not for the good of all, but for the benefit of the owning class, primarily as a means of repressing the propertyless class.

Karl Marx lived in capitalism, the stage of history that had replaced feudalism. Under capitalism, the ruling class that owns the means of production is the bourgeoisie and the propertyless class is made up of the industrial workers or the "proletariat." To Marx, a revolution by the proletariat and the end of capitalism, leading to the Socialist–Communist stage, was inevitable. The proletarian revolution would occur because of the increasing concentration of capital into fewer and fewer hands and the deteriorating conditions of the expanding worker class.

The ultimate goal of Marxism–Leninism is the attainment of Communism in the entire world. A world revolution was, therefore, predicted. Lenin considered the alternative of only some or even one country establishing Communism first and the rest of the world following at some indeterminable time.

The elites of societies that believe in the basic tenets of Marxism–Leninism have some common perceptions. They do not tolerate dissent and treat dissenters harshly. The regime inevitably becomes repressive. Use of force is essential to keep the masses (and any nonconforming elite members) in line. Maintaining unity of the nation becomes a primary goal and a combination of propaganda, symbols, and force is used to achieve this goal.[29] A facade of democracy is constantly supported.

The Nature of Politics. Politics in the Second World is quite different from the

First World's liberal democracy and the Third World's authoritarianism, for it is "totalitarian" in nature—politics is an all-embracing activity. Jacob L. Talmon in his seminal study of the origins of both liberal and totalitarian democracy has described the nature of totalitarian mass democracy in the following manner.

> The essential difference between the two schools of democratic thought as they have evolved is not, as is often alleged, in the affirmation of the value of liberty by one, and its denial by the other. It is in their different attitudes to politics. The liberal approach assumes politics to be a matter of trial and error, and regards political systems as pragmatic contrivances of human ingenuity and spontaneity. It also recognizes a variety of levels of personal and collective endeavour, which are altogether outside the sphere of politics.
>
> The totalitarian democratic school, on the other hand, is based upon the assumption of a sole and exclusive truth in politics. It may be called political Messianism in the sense that it postulates a preordained, harmonious and perfect scheme of things to which men are irresistibly driven, and at which they are bound to arrive. It recognizes ultimately only one plane of existence, the political. It widens the scope of politics to embrace the whole of human existence. It treats all human thought and action as having social significance, and therefore as falling within the orbit of political action. Its political ideas are not a set of pragmatic precepts or a body of devices applicable to a special branch of human endeavour. They are an integral part of an all-embracing and coherent philosophy. Politics is defined as the art of applying this philosophy to the organization of society, and the final purpose of politics is only achieved when this philosophy reigns supreme over all fields of life.[30]

Every human activity is considered to have social and political significance. The clubs one joins, the books one reads, the type of films one sees, whether one attends religious services, and the individuals with whom one has contacts are of interest to the state. The state apparatus attempts to control and regulate all economic, social, political, religious, and personal activities. Nothing is spared from pervasive control of the Communist party.

Concept of Justice. The main claim of the Communist states is that Communism is a just system. It is said that without economic justice and equality, the economic foundation of personal, social, and political life, the rest of the so-called freedoms are farcical. According to Communist theory, a fair distribution of a society's resources should be based on the principle "From each according to his ability, to each according to his needs."[31] Before the final victory of Communism, however, the needs of the revolution are the overriding factor in deciding what is just. Actions that advance the revolution are good, and those that impede it are bad. Individual rights must be subordinated to revolutionary necessity.

Proper Scope of the Government. A Communist party regime is made up of two parts, the party itself, where decision making and supervision of all aspects of life take place, and the government or state apparatus, which implements and enforces Communist party decisions. The government not only exercises centralized control over the economy, but directly owns and operates economic enterprises. In actual practice, however, some degree of private enterprise may continue to exist. Education, trade (domestic and international), communications, and transportation are always state monopolies. The government also seeks to control labor unions and other social organizations, as well as religious groups.

Public versus Private Power. In Communist theory private power is explicitly denied and the Communist party is granted a monopoly of power, which it exercises on behalf of the people. Before coming to power in the Soviet Union, Lenin established the principle of leadership by the "vanguard of the proletariat." According to this principle, in the interim period between the establishment of socialism in one country and the final world revolution, the actions of the working class must be guided by an elite group which possesses an advanced revolutionary consciousness (the most politically knowledgeable, experienced, and astute members of the working class). In the states of the Second World, the members of the Communist party are seen to constitute this group, and Lenin's principle is used to legitimize Communist party rule. If a socialist society is to be maintained at home and the cause of world revolution is to be advanced, it is argued that the Communist party must control and direct all activities in the society. The principle of Communist party rule over all groups and institutions is central to the maintenance of a totalitarian dictatorship, and this principle is advocated by Communist party elites throughout the Second World. Within the context of Communist party rule, involvement by private interest groups (those outside of the party and government) in political decision making is impossible. The now-defunct Polish labor union Solidarity constitutes the only example of a full-scale attempt by a major nonparty, nongovernmental interest group to enter the public policy process in the Soviet bloc. Solidarity was vehemently opposed by Communist party elites not only in Poland, but also in the Soviet Union, Czechoslovakia, and East Germany.

In actual practice, a type of interest group politics does exist in the Communist states, but it is carried out by groups *within* the Communist party. Military leaders, scientists, industrial managers, collective farm leaders, and others have sought to advance the interests of their respective groups, but their efforts have been undertaken within the Communist party.

Prevailing political perceptions in the Communist World preclude the establishment of independent interest groups like those found in the Western polyarchies which communicate directly with the public and expect to be consulted in the making of all important political decisions.

Political Decision Making: Role of the Elite and the Masses. Decision making in Communist party systems is exclusively in the hands of the members of the Communist party. Some local, rather unimportant decisions are made without the formal participation of the party, but all major decisions are made by the Communist party. The reason for this is the Communist party's view of the contemporary world. The Communist party states claim to be in the first period (the socialist period) of the final stage of history (Socialism-Communism), and during this period the Communist party lays the groundwork for the evolution to Communism, uniting within its ranks all the most advanced political thinkers. People are admitted to party membership only upon reaching the highest level of political consciousness. All others are not yet capable of taking part in decision making. In full-scale Communism every person will be politically competent to make decisions. Before that stage, however, the Communist party has the right and *duty* to rule. In theory, the masses give their assent to this because they recognize the superiority and legitimacy of the Communist party.

Disjunctive Factors within Ruling Communist Party Systems

All ruling Communist parties have come to power by violent overthrows of previous regimes or as a result of major wars. There has yet to be a democratically elected Communist government. In the USSR, China, Yugoslavia, Albania, Cuba, and Vietnam, the forces that came to power were indigenous, but their violent seizure of power disaffected large segments of the population. The Soviet army has been an important factor in the establishment of Communist regimes. In East Germany, Poland, Czechoslovakia, Hungary, Romania, Bulgaria, and North Korea, Communism was imposed more or less directly by the Russian army as a result of World War II. The Soviet army has also maintained a Communist government in Afghanistan since 1979. In Laos and Cambodia, Vietnam, with the help of the Soviet Union, placed puppet regimes in control. The Russian army also played a decisive role in Mongolia during 1922. In all of these countries, however, there remains resistance to Communist party rule, occasionally even by Communist party members themselves (German Democratic Republic—1953; Czechoslovakia—1968; Poland—1956, 1968, 1970, 1976, 1981). Most of these regimes have never gained full legitimacy. They must constantly look to their sponsors (i.e., the USSR or Vietnam) or to internal security forces to remain in power.

Another major disjunctive feature is the level of economic development that each of these states had reached at the time of the Communist seizure of power. Marx and Engels had said that only when the capitalist state had reached its final development, that is, when the country was fully industrialized, would the workers be able to take power.[32] However, none of the states of the Second World had attained that level of development at the time the Communist party assumed power. It took some adroit mental gymnastics for Lenin to "prove" that Russia was really a mature capitalist country in 1917 and, therefore, worthy of a Communist revolution.[33] He, nevertheless, believed that the Russian revolution would be the spark or catalyst for revolution in at least one advanced capitalist country, Germany, and perhaps in others.

Nationalism also creates problems for the unity of Communist doctrine. Despite the condemnation of this phenomenon as a capitalist method of dividing workers along nationality lines, nationalism still exists in Communist party states. The Union of Soviet Socialist Republics is a multinational state, and despite Communist ideology, many of its ethnic groups have maintained strong, independent identities. In addition, it is fairly clear that Chinese remain Chinese despite ideology, as do Poles, Czechs, Germans, Bulgarians, and so on. This persistence of nationalism has led to armed clashes between Communist party members of different nationalities— Russians and Hungarians, 1956; Chinese and Russians, 1960s; Chinese and Vietnamese, 1970s; and Vietnamese and Cambodians, since 1979.

Finally, personality has caused major rifts to occur among Communist elites. In spite of the denial of any substantial role for the individual-as-leader in history and the clear proposition that the masses are the movers of social change, individual personalities have been of critical importance. No one except the most dogmatic Communist ideologue would deny that Lenin as an individual was of vital importance to the Russian Revolution. His successor, Stalin (Josif Vissarionovich Djugashvili), had a major clash with Leon Trotsky (Lev Davidovich Bronstein) whom he defeated politically and eventually had murdered.

Intense conflict also developed between Stalin and Josip Broz (Tito) of Yugoslavia. Tito survived but Yugoslavia, while remaining Communist, left the Soviet bloc. After Stalin's death (1953) Nikita Khrushchev competed for influence with Mao Zedong of China, and Enver Hoxha of Albania, further splintering the Communist movement. Today Fidel Castro of Cuba, Kim Il-Sung of North Korea, and Nicolae Ceausescu of Romania exercise strong personal influence both within their own countries and throughout the Communist World.[34]

THE THIRD WORLD

Elite perceptions in the Third World have been shaped by the impact of the Western and Communist ideologies as well as by indigenous influences. During the colonial era, members of the elites in African and Asian countries were educated either in the West, where they read works on capitalism, liberalism, and other Western ideologies, or they attended universities at home that had patterned their curricula after Western education. Exposure to Communist ideologies came through university education in the West or at home and in some cases through travel to the Communist countries. The end of the colonial era did not diminish the influence of Western education on the newly independent countries. Most of these countries continue to rely on Western-style education. Education of elite members from the Third World in the West (as well as in the Soviet Union) has increased as has their travel to Western and Communist nations.

Indigenous influences have been those of tradition, especially religion and tribe, and underdevelopment. Tradition has tempered enthusiasm for capitalism and liberalism, and underdevelopment has strengthened the appeal of socialism and Communism. According to some experts, the problems of underdevelopment have made liberal democracy unworkable in the Third World. B. K. Nehru, an Indian diplomat, argues that liberal democracy as practiced in the West is not suitable for the Third World countries because of their "extreme material poverty."[35]

It is not possible to find a replica of Western-style liberal democracy in the Third World. However, one Third World country, India, comes close. Most members of the Indian elites believe in liberalism and practice it to a considerable extent. Richard Park and Bruce Bueno de Mesquita write: "Liberalism, particularly in its British garb, remains an important ingredient in the political thought of many senior politicians in India today."[36] A major deviation from liberalism occurred in India during the 21-month period of the Emergency (1975–1977). The fact that India returned to democracy attests to the strong hold of liberalism on the political thinking of the Indian elites. Members of the Indian elites firmly believe in basic civil and political rights of the individual. Equality before the law is accepted and the right of the people to elect those entitled to govern is not questioned. Following the British system of government, India has devised controls over the exercise of power by the different branches of government. The principle of civilian control over the military is also well entrenched.

Most Third World nations, however, do not practice Western-style liberal democracy because of their overwhelming economic problems (which may necessitate government controls over individual freedom anathematic to liberalism), the lack of an indigenous liberal tradition, and the ineffectual opposition to the regimes in power. In some of these countries the role of the military is being accepted in a form that is far removed from the concept of civilian control over the military. An observer of elite politics in Pakistan writes that it would be "in order to give the military a constitutional role, that is, to take over the political arena under certain conditions."[37] The writer elaborates: "It would not mean giving the military a license to rule; on the contrary their role would be clearly defined for performing two functions: first, to remove the governing elites and, secondly, to remain in power for a limited period to resolve a political crisis."[38] As we are well aware, very few military leaders who assume political power are willing to give it up voluntarily. The military rulers of Pakistan have given no indication of turning over power to civilian leaders. Western liberal thought, it seems, is being given up by the elites of Pakistan.

Indonesia has found a middle ground between India's acceptance of Western liberalism and Pakistan's virtual rejection of it. Though rights of the individual are respected in Indonesia, national integration and unity stand above any such rights.[39] Indonesia has qualified Western liberal values with the primacy of its own traditions.[40] Democracy in this country has been redefined to include monotheism, nationalism, humanism, and social justice.[41]

Capitalism is accepted by the elites in a large number of the Third World countries, especially in Latin America. However, as stated earlier, problems of underdevelopment have increased the appeal of socialism and Communism. It is socialism, not Communism, that appeals as a predominant ideology to the elites in several Third World countries. Communism has had large numbers of adherents in some Asian countries such as Burma, Indonesia, Malaysia, the Philippines, and Thailand. The force of Communism has now ebbed in these countries and the elites have not accepted Communist ideology.

India is a major non-Communist nation in the Third World with substantial numbers of elite members who are imbued with Communist ideology. It is important to note here that Communism in India is a regional rather than a national force and the national elites have among them only a small minority of believers in Communism. Furthermore, in those states in India where Communists have exercised power, some of the basic tenets of liberalism, especially the necessity of opposition to government, have not been questioned.

Socialism as an elite ideology in the Third World takes various forms, such as democratic socialism, African socialism, and Arab or Islamic socialism. All these forms of socialism have borrowed ideas from socialism as it developed as an ideology in the West; they also contain some elements of Communist ideology. (The ruling parties in four African states—Angola,

Sukarno, first President of the Republic
of Indonesia.

Ethiopia, Mozambique, and Zimbabwe—have adopted the tenents of
Marxism–Leninism as official ideology.) An important aspect of these
varieties of socialism is that they have adapted the outside ideas to the
indigenous conditions with an emphasis on tradition and culture. Democratic
socialism in India, an ideology shared by most members of the Indian
national elites, attempts to introduce socialism by way of public ownership
of the major industries and services in a democratic political structure.
Public ownership coexists with private ownership in India. For several
members of the elite, democratic socialism also entails a belief in social
welfare programs and advancing the society toward egalitarian goals through
laws and change in attitudes.

　　African socialism has been interpreted in various ways. Max Mark
summarizes the characteristics of African socialism as follows: "(1) the
absence of class struggle, with the resultant definition of the political public
not by particular classes but as the people as a whole; (2) the single-party
system; (3) elitist leadership; (4) relative flexibility in the definition of the
national sector of the economy vis-a-vis the private sector; and (5) willingness to accept foreign investments within well-defined rules."[42] Julius
Nyerere of Tanzania, who introduced the *ujamaa* concept of rural socialism
in his country with emphasis on communal or cooperative village farming,
considers the avoidance of self-interest conflicts as a central element of
African socialism.[43] Individual freedom is not considered of any great
significance in African socialism, for "the freedom on which all other

Julius K. Nyerere, President of Tanzania.

freedoms depend is freedom from the fear of starvation, and only their type of system (African socialism) can liberate the people from this fear."[44]

Arab or Islamic socialism combines socialist ideology with religion—a very unusual combination indeed. Among its adherents Nasser of Egypt and Qaddafi of Libya can be mentioned. This form of socialism stresses those aspects of the Islamic faith that are compatible with the modernization implied by socialism.[45] Thus, redistribution and sharing of wealth, albeit to a limited extent, are emphasized.

In some Third World countries liberalism or socialism has little relevance for the elites; instead, elite ideology is determined primarily by tradition. Examples of such elites are in Saudi Arabia, Kuwait, and some other oil-rich sheikhdoms. Of course, tradition plays a role in the ideologies of other Third World countries also—Indonesia and Tanzania were discussed earlier. Tradition in these countries is a major, but not the primary factor in determining elite ideology. In Saudi Arabia "a highly traditional, tribally-oriented, patriarchal Muslim elite"[46] has control over economic and social change. Islam, as interpreted by the elite, dictates the rules to be followed in virtually every aspect of life, political or otherwise. A similar situation prevails in oil-rich sheikhdoms of the Persian Gulf and in Iran under Khomeini.

Monte Palmer argues that the desire to keep "the traditional religious and tribal underpinnings of their thrones" has had a major impact on the values of the elites in Saudi Arabia and oil-rich sheikhdoms of Persian Gulf regarding modernization.[47] Economic modernization cannot be ignored entirely in these countries, because their oil revenues are very substantial.

To introduce economic modernization and social reform programs on a large scale might make the masses question the special status of the elites. Therefore, "they have tended to follow a pattern of distributing their oil revenues as broadly as necessary, but allowing foreigners to provide most technical services, thereby minimizing structural changes in society."[48]

The elite ideologies just considered are followed in various forms in the countries of the Third World, but African and Asian elites, especially in countries that formerly were colonies, share belief in another ideology, nationalism. In these countries nationalism means not only a group consciousness of belonging together, as it is commonly perceived, but also a strong desire to maintain national independence against possible encroachments of the major powers. Nationalistic feelings of the African and Asian elites are understandable in view of the domination of their countries during the colonial rule and the struggle that often had to be waged against the colonial powers for independence.

Nationalism, for the African and Asian elites, is not only political in importance, it also has economic and cultural relevance. In the economic field the elites want to decrease their countries' dependence on the major powers. Remedies for economic problems are sought more through development of exports and trade relations with outside countries than through foreign aid. Extreme economic nationalism means complete economic self-sufficiency, which is virtually impossible in modern times. In Africa and Asia (and in Latin America) economic nationalism indicates a desire to maintain control over foreign corporations, to minimize and perhaps eliminate domination by outside powers, and to develop the country's economic potential. Cultural nationalism means maintaining traditions of the country so that they are not engulfed by foreign, especially Western, influences.

Some leaders of Third World nations have thought more in regional or even continental terms than in national terms. To Nasser of Egypt, Arabism was more important than Egyptian nationalism and Nkrumah of Ghana dreamed of Pan-Africanism in which all the African nations would be brought into a confederation (a loose union of independent states in which limited powers are given to a central authority and the states retain the right to secede). The elites in Ghana and to a lesser extent in Egypt have given up such concepts and now think primarily in terms of their own nations.

In formulating any ideology, Latin American elites suffer certain disadvantages when compared with their African and Asian counterparts.[49] Neither liberalism nor socialism has had much appeal for the Latin American elites. Because independence was won in the early nineteenth century, nationalism is a nonissue. Some writers take the extreme position that Latin American elites have no ideologies. Peter Smith, in a study of political recruitment in Mexico, maintains that Mexican leaders are not guided by ideologies.[50] We do not accept such an extreme viewpoint. Ideology does not play as important a role in Latin American countries as it does in other Third World countries. Certain major values in the belief systems of the Latin American elites are, however, discernible. Most members of the Latin American elites believe in private enterprise and find socialism or Communism unacceptable. There are prominent exceptions, however, for example Nicaragua today and Chile under Salvador Allende. Another important aspect of Latin American elites' values is resentment against U.S. domination of their economies. It was not a coincidence that *dependencia* theory in international relations, which explores the economic dependence of the Latin American and other Third World nations on the Western powers, has its origins in the writings of the Latin American scholars.

Although Latin American elites resent U.S. domination over their economies, they are opposed to any major reforms in their countries that would upset their own economic advantages and special status. Of course, elites in other countries also do not want their special status upset by reforms. However, the belief in social change that is a part of socialistic ideologies of the Africans and the Asians is lacking in Latin America.

General View of Politics. Not unlike Western elites, Third World elites perceive politics as a process of conflict to pursue self-interest. Many Third World elites exceed Western elites in placing limits on competition. Because of the influence of socialism and Communism, they want a more equitable distribution of values than the Western theory of social welfare permits. On the other hand, elites in several third World countries have not even developed a view of politics in which losers are accepted in the political game as legitimate players who deserve another chance in the future. Instances in which a former ruler is killed (Liberia, 1980) or executed after a trial (Pakistan, 1979) are uncommon, but the leaders of Third World military coups treat their predecessors unkindly and attempt to minimize their prospects of coming back to power.

Family and kinship ties play an important role in shaping Third World elites' general view of politics. In several countries it is an accepted rule of the game that one cannot advance much in the political hierarchy without such connections. "Outsiders" sometimes do reach the upper echelons of politics, but these are exceptions.

Concept of Justice. In the Third World the concept of "justice as fairness," which stipulates establishment of procedures for the protection of the rights of the individual, is accepted more in theory than in practice. Constitutions of several Third World countries incorporate bills of rights similar to those in the Western constitutions; however, these rights are practiced more in their violation than in observance. When a military coup occurs, a constitution is often suspended temporarily and sometimes abrogated, thus ending even lip service to any rights. In general, the record of the Third World countries in protecting rights of the individual is poor. Some flagrant violations of these rights have occurred in Argentina, Brazil, Pakistan, the Philippines, South Korea, and Uganda. Democracies in the Third World (e.g., Costa Rica, India, and Sri Lanka) do protect rights of the individual to a considerable extent, but their records are not comparable to those of the Western nations.

The concept of "justice as goodness" is accepted by elites in those Third World countries that advocate socialism in some form. As opposed to the Western notion of providing every individual with opportunites for human development, "justice as goodness" in the Third World context means first satisfying people's basic needs for food, shelter, and health care, and then considering human development.

In some Moslem countries such as Libya, Iran, and Saudi Arabia, the Islamic concept of justice is followed. The Koran is interpreted by the *mullahs* for the dispensation of justice. In these countries rights of the individual are protected in a negative manner in the sense that crime against an individual is punishable with what may appear to many in the West "cruel and unusual punishment." A convicted thief could, for example, lose a body limb.

Proper Scope of Government. In considering the proper scope of government, Third World elites advocate a far greater role for the government than the concept of liberalism permits. The starting point of elite thinking in most Third World countries is that the government exists as much for performing economic functions as political ones. It is considered the government's responsibility to redistribute land, expropriate foreign corporations, nationalize domestic industries, and introduce innovative programs to improve the economic well-being of the masses. Third World elites want their governments not simply to regulate economic activities but to be active participants in the economic arena.

In African and Asian countries the elites perceive the development of a national identity as a major function of the government. Achievement of a national identity in Third World nations is hindered by separateness of the tribes, castes, or linguistic groups. The elites consider a national identity essential for political unity as well as for economic progress, because separateness often leads to divisiveness and unrest detrimental to the economy.

Elites in some Moslem countries in the Middle East, (e.g., Iran, Libya, and Saudi Arabia) consider the regulation of morality also a government function. In these countries, contrary to the Western concept of the separation of church and state, the two institutions have coalesced into what may be called a politico-religious state.

Public versus Private Power. Elites in the Third World assign a relatively unimportant role to nongovernmental groups in the decision-making processes of the government. In some countries groups generally considered as nongovernmental—an example is the church—are a part of the government. In others, especially those with military rule, power is so concentrated in the hands of one or a few that consultation with outside groups is insignificant. Even in countries where lobbying by private groups is permitted (India is a prominent example), interest groups often function within the umbrella of the political parties. Their role in decision-making processes of the government is not independent of the role of the parties.

In some cases private groups do exert substantial amounts of influence on governmental policy processes. Such influence is generally the result of personal and family connections rather than of established political traditions. It is not uncommon for private groups, especially those in business, to influence government leaders with money, that is, with bribes and "kickbacks."

Political Decision Making: Role of the Elites and the Masses. Although Western elites accept a limited role for the masses in decision making and are open to communications with the masses, the masses are often ignored by elites in the Third World. In military regimes no role for the masses is expected. In the politico-religious states of the Middle East the masses can petition to the government for the redress of grievances or for some favors, but have no say in the policy-making processes of the government. Even in the democracies of the Third World, the masses' role in politics is limited to the selection of leaders during elections. The peaceful expression of mass concern over a major issue seldom occurs, although the masses sometimes do express their frustrations and anger through violent means, which may influence government policy.

NOTES

1. William T. Bluhm, *Ideologies and Attitudes* (Englewood Cliffs, N.J.: Prentice-Hall, 1974), p. 67.
2. Charles F. Andrain, *Politics and Economic Policy in Western Democracies* (North Scituate, Mass.: Duxbury, 1980), pp. 224–225.
3. Max Mark, *Modern Ideologies* (New York: St. Martin's Press, 1973), p. 27.

4. Ibid., p. 26.
5. For a discussion of the concept of justice as fairness see Mark E. Kann, *Thinking about Politics: Two Political Sciences* (New York: West, 1980), pp. 46–54.
6. Salwyn Schapiro, *Liberalism: Its Meaning and History* (New York: Van Nostrand, 1958), p. 16.
7. Frederick M. Watkins, *The Age of Ideology—Political Thought 1750 to the Present* (Englewood Cliffs, N.J.: Prentice-Hall, 1964), p. 12.
8. John Vaizey, *Revolutions of Our Time: Capitalism* (New York: Praeger Publishers, 1972), p. 13.
9. Roy C. Macridis, *Contemporary Political Ideologies* (Cambridge, Mass.: Winthrop, 1980), p. 22.
10. For an introduction to the "political creed" of capitalism see Reo M. Christenson, Alan S. Engel, Dan N. Jacobs, Mostafa Rejai, and Herbert Waltzer, *Ideologies and Modern Politics* (New York: Dodd, Mead, 1971), pp. 218–222.
11. Cited by H. Mark Roelofs, *Ideology and Myth in American Politics: A Critique of a National Political Mind* (Boston: Little, Brown, 1976).
12. This term is employed by Schapiro, p. 58.
13. For a discussion of this argument see Norman Furness and Timothy Tilton, *The Case for the Welfare State: From Social Security to Social Equity* (Bloomington: Indiana University Press, 1979), pp. 22–26.
14. Ibid., p. 29.
15. Ibid., pp. 36–37.
16. For a discussion of the logic of political conflict see Kann, pp. 18–27.
17. For a discussion of conflict representation activities see Dan Nimmo and Thomas D. Ungs, *American Political Patterns: Conflict and Consensus* (Boston: Little, Brown, 1967), pp. 13–14.
18. For a general discussion of social welfare policies in the Western political systems see Richard L. Siegel and Leonard B. Weinberg, *Comparing Public Policies: United States, Soviet Union, and Europe* (Homewood, Ill.: Dorsey Press, 1977), pp. 200–233.
19. Cited in David Ricci, *Community Power and Democratic Theory: The Logic of Political Analysis* (New York: Random House, 1971), p. 139. See also Robert Dahl, *Who Governs?* (New Haven, Conn.: Yale University Press, 1961), pp. 52–59.
20. For a discussion of justice as fairness see Kann, pp. 311–329.
21. Andrain, p. 219.
22. Ibid., p. 220.
23. Cited in Andrain, p. 53. For a discussion of the privileged position of business in Western society see Charles E. Lindblom, *Politics and Markets: The World's Political-Economic Systems* (New York: Basic Books, 1977), pp. 170–189.
24. For a discussion of polyarchical systems see Lindblom, pp. 131–143.
25. For a discussion of the origin and development of the concept of democratic elitism see Peter Bachrach, *The Theory of Democratic Elitism: A Critique* (Boston: Little, Brown, 1967).

26. Henry Kariel, ed., *Frontiers of Democratic Theory* (New York: Random House, 1970), pp. 31–35.

27. M. Donald Hancock, *Sweden: The Politics of Postindustrial Change* (Hinsdale, Ill.: Dryden Press, 1972), p. 72.

28. See Robert H. McNeal, *The Bolshevik Tradition,* 2d ed. (Englewood Cliffs, N.J.: Prentice-Hall, 1975), p. 192.

29. Cf. Macridis, pp. 90–91.

30. J. L. Talmon, *The Origins of Totalitarian Democracy* (New York: Praeger, 1960), pp. 1–2.

31. For a useful discussion of this issue see Alfred G. Meyer, *Communism,* 4th ed., (New York: Random House, 1984), esp. p. 103–119.

32. Henry B. Mayo, *Introduction to Marxist Theory* (New York: Oxford University Press, 1960), pp. 142–143.

33. See Robert C. Tucker, ed., "The Revolutionary Taking of Power," *The Lenin Anthology* (New York: Norton, 1975), pp. 293–414.

34. Three books that offer an adequate analysis of communist systems are Gary K. Bertsch, *Power and Policy in Communist Systems* (New York: Wiley, 1978); Richard C. Gripp, *The Political System of Communism* (New York: Dodd, Mead, 1973); and Robert G. Wesson, *Communism and Communist Systems* (Englewood Cliffs, N.J.: Prentice-Hall, 1978).

35. B. K. Nehru, "Western Democracy and the Third World," *Third World Quarterly* 1 (April 1979): 69–70.

36. Richard L. Park and Bruce Bueno de Mesquita, *India's Political System* (Englewood Cliffs, N.J.: Prentice-Hall, 1979), p. 40.

37. Asaf Hussain, *Elite Politics in an Ideological State* (Kent, England: Dawson, 1979), p. 145.

38. Ibid.

39. See Geoffrey C. Gunn, "Ideology and the Concept of Government in the Indonesian New Order," *Asian Survey* 19 (August 1979): 757.

40. Ibid., p. 752.

41. Ibid.

42. Mark, p. 169. Also see William H. Friedland and Carl G. Rosberg, Jr., eds., *African Socialism* (Stanford, Calif.: Stanford University Press, 1964), esp. pp. 3–11.

43. Raymond F. Hopkins, *Political Roles in a New State: Tanzania's First Decade* (New Haven, Conn.: Yale University Press, 1971) p. 98. On the working of *ujamaa* and some policy recommendations concerning this concept, see Goran Hyden, *Beyond Ujamaa in Tanzania* (London: Heinemann, 1980).

44. Mark, p. 171.

45. See Monte Palmer, *Dilemmas of Political Development* (Itasca, Ill.: Peacock, 1980), p. 12.

46. This phrase is borrowed from Frank Tachau, ed., *Political Elites and Political Development in the Middle East* (New York: Wiley, 1975), p. 181.

47. Palmer, p. 12.

48. Ibid.

49. Cf. Seymour Martin Lipset, "Values, Education, and Entrepreneurship," in Seymour Martin Lipset and Aldo Solari, eds., *Elites in Latin America* (New York: Oxford University Press, 1967), p. 36.

50. Peter H. Smith, *Labyrinths of Power* (Princeton, N.J.: Princeton University Press, 1979), p. 57.

CHAPTER 5

The State in Three Worlds

The contemporary political world includes more than 160 states, and for the last three centuries states have been the major actors in the international system. Traditionally, states have been defined as institutions possessing four attributes: a fixed territory, a specific population, a government recognized as legitimate, and sovereignty. In today's international system, however, states frequently lack one or more of these characteristics. Despite this fact, the significance of the states can hardly be overestimated. States divide the world's population into competing units and create discontinuities in such areas of human activity as trade, travel, and communications.

The first modern states emerged in Western Europe in the two centuries between the mid-1600s and the mid-1800s. Their development shattered the myth of a unified Christian commonwealth. By the time of the French Revolution the concept of the nation-state was born as the state became identified with the nationality group inhabiting its territory. In every period, the development of the state was fostered by elite groups whose careers, power, and prestige depended on the maintenance of a strong state.

Marxist–Leninist thought includes a specific theory of the origin and development of the state, which has influenced perceptions of the state in the Second World. The contemporary state is seen as the product of one stage of an inevitable historical process that will ultimately lead to the "withering away" of the state and the achievement of full-scale Communist society. Despite such theories, ruling Communist parties have constructed powerful states frequently referred to as totalitarian.

A majority of the contemporary states are in the Third World. Most of these states developed as a result of the process of decolonization and, in their modern form, are of only recent origin. For this reason many Third World states lack well-defined borders, clearly defined populations, and effective governments. The experience of many Third World states suggests that state-building and nation-building processes are in an early stage of development.

A WORLD OF STATES

We live in a political world dominated by institutions called states. The United Nations has approximately 160 member states and, as we have already learned, each of the three political worlds consists of separate states. Today most important political activity occurs within or between states. Political activity contained within the borders of a single state is called domestic politics; political activity that crosses national borders (that is, transnational activity) is called international politics. Historians have referred to the period of the last three centuries as the era of "state supremacy" or "state hegemony" because the state has proven better able to win and maintain human allegiance than any other social, religious, or political institution. In the service of the state citizens have performed great acts of heroism and committed unspeakable crimes. In our era the populations of Israel, Poland, and Vietnam have demonstrated once again the willingness to endure great hardships so that the state might exist.

The division of the world into separate states is a political fact of great importance. Donald Puchala has noted that the system of states creates a pattern of political discontinuities (interruptions or breaks) in vital areas of human existence.[1] He observes that "the political map of the world is like a patchwork quilt on which each separate state is represented by an irregularly shaped, different-sized piece."[2] Each piece or state is a community with unique laws, political institutions, political symbols, currency, patterns of communication, and often distinct languages and cultures.[3] As people, goods, and ideas pass from one state to the next, their movement is regulated or even prevented. A passport (a travel document issued by one's state) and a visa (an entry permit placed in the passport allowing one to enter a foreign country and indicating conditions for entry) are required for travel to most countries. Quotas and tariffs are used to restrict trade. Governments use methods ranging from electronic devices to legal penalties, found in laws against sedition and treason, to prevent the entry of hostile ideas into the state. Most important, states create and reinforce a sense of separate identity among their citizens, which works to divide the world's population. Some sources refer to this phenomenon as the "we–they" mentality. From early childhood the citizens of every state are taught to identify with and respect their national political symbols, leaders, heroes, and traditions with the understanding, either explicit or implicit, that their institutions are superior to those of other states. This mentality contributes to intense competition. The separation of the world into states also encourages attempts to solve problems at the national rather than global level. Today poverty, disease, and even pollution are most often conceived as "national" problems, and each state attempts its own solution. States also strive for self-sufficiency in food and natural resources, a condition called *autarky,* because they fear that other states may deprive them of these essentials.

Unfortunately, it may well be that many problems confronting mankind are more amenable to solution at global or regional levels rather than at national levels. In addition, autarky may be impossible to attain in a world in which vital natural resources are becoming increasingly scarce. After World War II the belief that recovery efforts by individual states would be inadequate to rebuild Europe led six states of Western Europe to form regional organizations devoted to the solution of their common economic and social problems. In theory, by joining these organizations whose policies are approved by a modified majority rule, each state lost control of policy making over important areas of economic and social life. However, this action stands as an exception in an era in which states have jealously guarded their independence and generally have succeeded in retaining the loyalty of their citizens. The existence of states has divided the world's population and contributed to human competition. Because states have had such important political consequences, the origin and nature of the states in each of the three worlds will be examined in the following sections.

STATES, NATIONALITY GROUPS, NATION-STATES, PATRIOTISM, AND NATIONALISM

An appreciation of the dynamics of the modern state system requires an understanding of certain key concepts. In the general literature on politics the terms state, nation, and country are often used interchangeably, but they are not synonymous. The term *state* has a precise meaning both in international law and in traditional international relations theory. A state is a political institution possessing a distinct territory, population, and government, and the attribute of sovereignty. The state is formally recognized as a legal entity or subject under international law. The United States, Canada, France, and the Soviet Union are examples of states. The term *nation-state* can only be understood with reference to the concept of nationality. A *nationality group* is a collection of people sharing a common identity or feeling of unity that separates them from other groups. The identity is often based on such factors as a common language, similar ethnic and racial characteristics, a common religion, and a common historical tradition. Nationality groups are not just groups having a common biological descent, however; they are "psychological" or "belief" groups. Members of the group believe that they are a unique community separate from all others and that the members of the group constitute the "we" of political life and all others constitute the "they." When the population of a nationality group is

The storming of the Bastille prison during the French Revolution (1789).

located within the geographic boundaries of a single state, an especially strong bond of loyalty is created. Loyalty to the state is reinforced by loyalty to the nationality group (sometimes called a "unitary" state).

The term nation-state can be strictly applied to a state only if it is inhabited and dominated by a single nationality group. Many states, however, have more than one important nationality group residing within their borders and are called pluralistic states. Examples of pluralistic states are Canada which contains both an English-speaking and a French-speaking nationality group, Yugoslavia which has Croatian, Serbian, and other Slavic and non-Slavic elements, and the Soviet Union which has well over 100 such groups although Russians makeup about 50% of the population.

Patriotism and nationalism are ideologies or belief systems. Historically the ideals of nationalism and patriotism have served to promote loyalty to the state by acting as the "intellectual glue" binding the citizens to the state. *Patriotism* is the identification with and love of the "fatherland," the territory of one's birth. Patriotism teaches admiration for the institutions of one's state as well as the belief that citizens derive strength from the territorial state. Patriotism developed early in the history of Western Europe, beginning as pride in local principalities, and became an important force after the formation of the first modern states in 1648. *Nationalism* first emerged in its modern form during the French Revolution (1789). In the words of Hans Kohn, "nationalism is a state of mind in which the supreme loyalty of the individual is felt due to the nation state".[4] Nationalism promotes the identity of the individual with both the nationality group of which he or she is a part and the national political unit (nation-state) that the group inhabits.[5] Nationalism teaches both the superiority of one's nationality group and the superiority of one's nation-state. The nation-state is considered the political expression of the group. Nationalism has often taken extreme and violent forms and has fostered intense competition between nations. Nationalism has had great popular appeal and since its development has been the most compelling political force in the world. The development of the modern state and the growth of state power would not have been possible without both patriotism and nationalism.

FOUR ATTRIBUTES OF THE STATE: FACT OR FICTION?

Traditional theories of international politics attribute four characteristics to the state: a fixed territory, a specific population, a government recognized as legitimate, and sovereignty over its territory and population. According to such theories, these attributes constitute the very essence of statehood, and the modern era of international relations began when states possessing these elements formed in Western Europe. Some students of international relations believe that it is a mistake to view the state as a "static" or "fixed" institution. They point out that the four attributes are at best a model or "ideal type" to which few states actually correspond. No state possesses all four of these attributes, and some recently formed states in the Third World lack several of them. Nevertheless, the four attritubes offer a useful starting point in the study of states because they help us to understand the dynamics of the modern state system.

Territory

The existence of a distinct territory within fixed borders is the basic element of the state. States first developed in Western Europe in the seventeenth century when defensive fortifications were erected to delineate and defend their new boundaries. Today nearly the whole land portion of the world, including inland lakes and rivers, is claimed by states. The only major exception is Antarctica where, despite the existence of major claims by Argentina, Australia, Chile, France, New Zealand, Norway, and Great Britain, no state has actually attempted to take possession of territory. State boundaries are intended to be as clear as possible; surveyors plot out exact lines not only on the land, but also through inland waters that form part of the border.

Under contemporary international law the territory of the state is considered to extend to the oceans, air space, and underground. The old 3-nautical-mile limit for territorial waters under the complete sovereignty of the state has given way to a 12 nautical-mile limit, which is now accepted by a majority of states. In the past several decades fishing rights have become an important problem and a 200 nautical-mile economic zone is now generally accepted. The contiguous state has the right to set amounts of the fishing catch in this area and to enforce these limits. Nonfishing ships have the right of passage without hindrance. Underwater territory has also become significant with the advent of offshore oil drilling rigs and the possibility of mining other raw materials under the oceans. The continental shelf (flooded edges of the continents) which falls off sharply into the ocean basin at approximately the 200 fathom point is open to exploitation by the contiguous state alone.

The states' jurisdiction also extends above and beneath the state. The state controls the air space (atmosphere) above its territory; airplanes that intrude without permission are often turned away, forced down, or shot down. In practice, space vehicles and earth satellites above the earth's atmosphere are not disturbed, although both the United States and the USSR possess the means to prevent such passage. Finally, the state is also considered to control the resources beneath its soil, and it may be supposed that these boundaries extend to the center of the earth.

Population

The state also possesses a distinct population over which it has legal jurisdiction. The population of the state consists of two groups, citizens and aliens. Citizens are persons formally recognized under law as having membership in the state. In theory, the concept of citizenship implies obligations on the part of both the state and the citizens. The state affords its citizens the rights, privileges, and protection of the state in exchange for their permanent allegiance. Under international law each state has the right to designate who is a citizen and to specify the method by which citizenship may be acquired or lost. In general the criteria for citizenship have been based on one of two rival conceptions, *jus soli* (law of the soil) or *jus sanguinis* (law of the blood). Under *jus soli* any person born on the soil of the state (including its air space and territorial waters) is automatically entitled to citizenship. Most English-speaking countries and the states of Latin America subscribe to the "law of the soil." Under *jus sanguinis* citizenship is considered an inheritance, and at birth a person acquires the citizenship of his or her parents. Most of the states of continental Europe adhere to the "law of the blood." Individual states also establish the rules for naturalization, the legal process by which a person not originally entitled to citizenship may become a citizen. The population of a state may also include aliens, inhabitants who are not citizens of the state. According to international law, states are entitled to admit or exclude aliens, but must observe standards of decent treatment toward those who are admitted.

Government

The third attribute of statehood is the possession of an effective government capable of extending its authority throughout the territory of the state. In the words of the German sociologist Max Weber, a government is an agency that has a "monopoly of the legitimate use of physical force within a given territory."[6] Governments employ their coercive power (or threaten to employ it) to ensure domestic order, maintain external security, and promote the collective welfare of the population. Karl Deutsch argues that governments constitute the "steering mechanism" of the state and the means by which the population expresses itself politically.[7] In the next two chapters, which discuss the government structures of specific states, it is important to keep in mind that all governments derive their authority from the state. Traditional theories of the state emphasize that the government must be effective, capable of exercising real control over the territory and population, and must be viewed by the majority of the population as legitimate. Legitimacy requires that the government be considered morally acceptable according to prevailing political norms.

Sovereignty

Central to the traditional conception of the state is the theory of sovereignty. According to the theory of sovereignty, there is no higher authority above that of the government of the state, and the state posseses supreme decision-making power within its territory. The theory of sovereignty was first advanced by Jean Bodin in the work *Six Books on the State* written in 1576. Bodin sought to justify the claims of the monarch to complete territorial jurisdiction against the claims of local princes, the papacy, and the Holy Roman Empire.[8] In theory states have claimed a monopoly of power since the end of the Thirty Years War in 1648. Critics of the concept of state sovereignty argue that states have always recognized the existence of some authority above them. Historically, the Church, international organizations, and international law have been recognized as above the state, and today the states of Western Europe recognize the institutions of the European Community as constituting a supranational authority in some policy areas.

STATE-BUILDING AND NATION-BUILDING IN THREE WORLDS

Modern states are the result of two processes, state-building and nation-building.[9] State-building is the process by which a state extends its political authority throughout the territory and establishes and defends its borders. State-building activities are carried out by police and military bureaucracies within the government. Nation-building is the process by which loyalty to the state is developed within the general population. Nation-building tasks are undertaken by a wide variety of agencies ranging from the executive branch of government to public school systems. Historically, state-building and nation-building tasks have been the work of state elites whose careers, power, and prestige have depended on the maintenance of a strong state. The origin of the modern state is generally traced to Western Europe in the seventeenth century. European state-building and nation-building tasks were accomplished slowly over a period of more than three centuries. The development of the states of the Second and Third Worlds occurred in a much shorter period of time. The states of the Communist World emerged in the period since 1917 as the result of either domestic revolutions or foreign conquests. Their development has been characterized by intense efforts at state-building and nation-building by ruling Communist party elites. Most states of the Third World formed in the period since 1945 as a result of the decolonization movement. Third World leaders have been subject to extreme pressure to accomplish state-building and nation-building tasks quickly in order to "catch up" with the states of the First and Second Worlds. In much of the Third World state-building and nation-building tasks are only partly completed.

THE FIRST WORLD

The origin and development of the nation-state in Europe was the result of complex processes that occurred between the tenth and nineteenth centuries. Our discussion will focus on two landmark historical events, the signing of the Treaty of Westphalia in 1648 and the French Revolution of 1789, each of which marked the beginning of a new period in the formation of states. The Treaty of Westphalia began the era of the territorial state in which people shifted their loyalties from the ideal of a universal Christian commonwealth (Christendom) to the fatherland. The French Revolution began the era of the national state in which the state became identified with a particular nationality group and nationalism became the dominant belief system in the world. In both phases state-building and nation-building tasks were undertaken by elite groups that owed their power, status, and wealth to the existence of the sovereign state. By the latter half of the nineteenth century the formation of the states of Europe in their modern form was complete except for the changes brought by the two world wars. In the eighteenth and nineteenth centuries, states modeled after those in Europe were transplanted overseas, beginning first as colonial settlements and later becoming independent states.[10] The development of the state in the West took several centuries, and Western state builders were free of the pressures to develop quickly, which now confront Third World elites.

1648: Birth of the Modern State

The modern state emerged in Western Europe in the two centuries between the mid-1600s and the mid-1800s. The year 1648, the date of the signing of the Treaty of Westphalia, is often cited as the beginning of the state era. The Treaty of Westphalia ended the Thirty Years War (1618–1648), marking a turning point in European history. The war began as a struggle between the Catholic kings of Europe united symbolically under the banner of the Holy Roman Empire and the Protestant Kingdom of Bohemia (now the Czech portion of Czechoslovakia). In the first two phases of the war, until 1630, the fighting conformed to the model of a religious conflict with Catholic armies opposing Protestant armies, but in the final two stages, Catholic and Protestant kings fought one another over the spoils of war. This development shattered the illusion of the unity of the Christian world under the leadership of the Roman Catholic Pope and the notion that the Holy Roman Empire constituted a unified Christian commonwealth. Such concepts had been promoted in theological writings throughout the Middle Ages. If heaven was unified under the authority of God, then the faithful must duplicate this unity on Earth under the leadership of the Roman Catholic Church.[11] Church leaders envisioned an imperial structure similar to what had existed under the Roman Empire, but with the Church playing the dominant role. Unlike the Roman Empire, which was maintained by the physical power of the secular state, the Christian empire would be held together by the cohesive power of the common faith.[12] The Church and the Pope, God's representative on Earth, would be the dominant authority. In the Holy Roman Empire there was to be no separation of church and state, but rather the state was to be servant of the Church, helping the latter to realize its aims. Robert Ergang effectively summarized this conception of the proper relationship between Church and state:

> In Roman times religion had been subordinated to the state and the temporal welfare of its citizens, but during the high Middle Ages, it was the Church which prescribed the duties of the state. As the Roman Empire declined, the state had gradually lost the dominant position it had held in classical times and its status

was reduced to that of an ecclesiastical agency. . . . The nation-state with its self-assertive monarch was still in the womb of history.[13]

The Holy Roman Empire never achieved the degree of unity or the position of prominence that Church authorities sought. Although the Holy Roman Empire extended on paper from France on the west to Poland and Hungary on the east, its authority was confined to the areas of present-day Germany and Italy. Much of Europe remained under the control of independent leaders. Most important, within a century after Otto the Great first assumed the title of Holy Roman Emperor in 962, open conflict erupted between the Church and secular political authorities. This conflict dominated international relations between the eleventh and fourteenth centuries and made a unified Christian commonwealth an unfulfilled aspiration rather than an actual political fact. The nature of the Holy Roman Empire precluded the emergence of the state in its modern form.

The Treaty of Westphalia was one of those events in which political and legal thought caught up to reality. The dissolution of the empire was confirmed: 355 separate units were created in the German Empire and Calvinism and Lutheranism were recognized as acceptable religions, the Dutch and Swiss states were recognized as sovereign and independent, and France and Sweden annexed lands that had previously been part of the empire.[14] A new conception of law was advanced when specific rules governing relations between the new units were developed. Law was now seen as a set of rules among or between states rather than above states, and modern international law was born. After the Treaty of Westphalia, the Christian population of Europe was permanently divided into sovereign, independent political units. At the time of its presentation by Jean Bodin in 1576, the concept of state sovereignty was a radical theory. After 1648 it was accepted in every part of Europe that the state was supreme within its own territory and that it recognized no higher authority.

After Westphalia: Patriotism and Dynastic Nationalism

After the Treaty of Westphalia, states entered the phase of patriotism or solidarity by territory.[15] Donald Puchala has noted that identification with and loyalty to the state develop slowly and that political units can be made to look like states long before common people feel profound political identification.[16] This description summarizes the political situation that confronted the states of Europe after 1648. State elites faced the need to accomplish both state-building and nation-building tasks. These tasks were undertaken by elite groups that controlled the political and economic institutions of the state (e.g., kings, nobles, government ministers, military leaders, and prominent merchants). Such groups owed their wealth and power to the state and had a vested interest in its survival and growth. After the Treaty of Westphalia, the various political units were rivals in international competition ranging from diplomatic confrontations to war. Each elite sought to increase its state's ability to compete, its capability-in-action,[17] by fortifying the national borders and promoting popular loyalty to the state. The efforts of elites at state-building and nation-building met with varying degrees of success.

Several factors determined the success of such state-building tasks as the establishment of permanent borders and the creation of law enforcement agencies. Permanent borders were established first in states that were geographically separated from the units around them by oceans or other natural barriers such as mountains and rivers. The borders of England were established by the end of the fifteenth century, even before the Treaty of Westphalia, because of its separation from the continent. The Pyrenees Mountains between France and Spain, and the fact that they bordered the sea on several sides, helped those two countries to establish their borders at an early date, although the eastern border of France (its border with Germany in the area of Alsace-Lorraine) was not finally set until after World War II. Joseph Strayer has noted that the formation of borders was also accomplished more easily in "unitary states," which had remained single territorial units throughout the entire period from the fall of the Roman Empire to 1648, than in "mosaic states" whose territories included conquered lands that had previously been part of other political units.[18] The difficulty in determining the eastern border of France resulted from the fact that France was a mosaic state and that its eastern territory had been gained through military conquests. Germany (that is, the states of the German Empire) and Austria were also mosaic states whose borders were not finally delineated until the twentieth century. The creation of effective law enforcement agencies was accomplished first in Spain, France, and Sweden, which had established centralized military bureaucracies to fight the religious wars before 1648. The demand for "law and order" and an end to anarchy had been part of the politics of Western Europe since the twelfth century and courts were slowly developed to meet that need.

The most difficult task after Westphalia was the development of patriotism, loyalty to the territorial state and its inhabitants. The term patriotism is derived from the Latin word *patria* meaning fatherland. As Karl Deutsch has noted, a patriot is one who identifies the positive and valued experiences in life with the land of one's birth and who believes that the interests of one's compatriots, the fellow inhabitants of the fatherland, should take precedence over the interests of other groups.[19] Patriotism means giving preference to the inhabitants of one's country regardless of their race, language, nationality, or religion.[20] After 1648 the territorial states had to compete for the loyalty of its people with tribes and other local groups within the state as well as with religious institutions which claimed to be above the state. To compete with the Church, state elites developed national flags, crests, and other political symbols that emphasized the uniqueness of the state against the claims of the universality of religious institutions. They also sought to develop an awareness and respect for local achievements. Between the ninth and twelfth centuries, pride in local military heroes, saints, and political leaders had developed in many areas of Western Europe.[21] Aided by the new political mentality after Westphalia, state elites sought to intensify local pride and promote identification with local political and military leaders, songs, literature, political symbols, and most important, the objectives of the state. During this era the state became identified with the royal family and the person of the king or queen who was seen as the living embodiment of the state. Some sources have referred to this period as the age of *dynastic nationalism*. The authority of the government of the state was seen as legitimate as long as it was exercised by the king or queen or proper heir. In France, Spain, and the states of the German Empire, absolute monarchs ruled and were welcomed with relief by the great mass of people, especially by the new middle class, as a deliverance from domestic feuds.[22] In other states (e.g., England, the Netherlands, and Sweden), by the early 1700s the monarch shared power with such groups as the clergy, nobility, or the bourgeoisie.[23]

In the competition with tribes and other local groups within the state, elites stressed the fact that the new territorial state promised protection from the anarchy of the old feudal systems. John Herz has argued that the rise of the territorial state was only possible because people perceived it as having "a hard shell of fortification"—defensible and impenetrable—behind which they were safe.[24] Herz summarized his argument as follows:

> The fact that it [the state] was surrounded by a hard shell rendered it to some extent secure from foreign penetration, and thus made it an ultimate unit of protection for those within its boundaries. Throughout history, that unit which affords protection and security to human beings has tended to become the basic political unit; people, in the long run will recognize that authority which possesses the power of protection.[25]

The state also offered the hope for economic order and economic opportunity which were not possible as long as people identified with local, smaller political units. The transferral of loyalties from tribal units to the state also occurred more easily in the unitary states than in the mosaic states.

The French Revolution: Rise of the National State

The most important and dynamic era in the growth of state power occurred with the development of nationalism, the identification of the state with the nationality group. The development of nationalism created an intense emotional bond between the citizens and the nation-state, which did more than any other factor to increase the state's capability-in-action. As Karl Deutsch has noted, the bloodlines of mankind have been mixed, and many nationalists were misinformed about their perceived common ancestory or descent.[26] In some states (e.g., England, the United States, and Australia), nationalism developed around perceptions of a unique destiny and support for specific political beliefs rather than the usual perceptions of a common language, culture, religion, or biological descent. Regardless of the objective validity of the nationalist claims, the perceptions of the uniqueness of the nationality group created a new and dynamic bond among its members and with the state. In socially homogeneous states, such as France, Germany, and Sweden where one nationality group dominated, national solidarity reinforced the earlier patriotism or territorial solidarity. In other states, such as the Austrian Empire inhabited by several nationality groups, patriotism and nationalism were at odds. In such cases each nationality group ultimately developed its own nationalism and sought the creation of a separate state through which the political will of the group could be expressed.

England must be considered the first modern nation-state because nationalism developed there before it did on the continent. English nationalism grew out of the Reformation of the sixteenth century and culminated in the Glorious Revolution of 1688 to 1689. English national thought stressed support for the concepts of individual liberty, freedom of conscience in matters of religion, and the belief that the English were the chosen people to present these concepts to the world.[27] The development of French nationalism during the Revolution of 1789 proved to be one of the major events in modern history because it stimulated the growth of nationalism in Germany, Spain, and Italy, as well as other European states. French nationalism taught that the entire nation was united in support of the democratic ideals of liberty, equality, and fraternity. It attacked class privileges and the old monarchy and advocated the future development of a nation composed of free individuals protected by law and under the political authority of a national assembly that would represent the entire nation.[28] For the first ten years French nationalism was concerned with the "nationalization" of domestic life, including the creation of a centralized national bureaucracy, a national army, national holidays, and greater use of the French language in education. However, with the ascension to power of Napoleon Bonaparte, French nationalists sought the export of their political principles to other parts of Europe through military conquest. French imperialism acted as a catalyst for the development of national awareness in Germany, Spain, and Italy, which were attacked by French armies. Nationalists in these areas stressed the unique elements that united their populations and sought the development of a nation-state through which the political values of their nationality group could be expressed. A unified national state was achieved in Spain immediately following the expulsion of Napoleon, but it was not realized in Germany and Italy until the completion of unification in 1871. Nationalists in these countries rejected the democratic principles of England and France and instead developed a nationalism based on authoritarianism, discipline, romanticism, expansionism, and an organic theory of the state.*

Integral Nationalism. The nationalism that developed in Europe at the time of the French Revolution was heavily influenced by the principles of liberty, equality, and fraternity. It has been called liberal or *humanitarian national-ism* because it asserted the right of all nationality groups to form their own nation-states (called the right to national self-determination). Liberal nation-alists tolerated other nationality groups with identities as strong as their own and acknowledged the right of all nationalities to develop and express themselves through the nation-state. In the nineteenth century, liberal nationalism gave way to *integral nationalism*. Integral nationalism preached the superiority of the nation's biological inheritance, culture, and institutions over those of other nationality groups. Integral nationalists frequently fostered hatred of other groups and accepted the likelihood of violent conflict between nation states. In the long run the development of integral nationalism proved to be an underlying cause of both World War I and World War II. Its short-term effect on the nation-state was to greatly increase its capability-in-action as citizens fearful of other nations and expecting conflict were prepared for the sacrifices necessary in war. Al-though integral nationalism served to increase the power of most of the states of Europe, in the multinational Austro-Hungarian Empire (established in 1867) it provided the force for the dissolution of the state. Austria-Hungary entered World War I as one of the major powers of Europe, but ended the war as five separate nation states: Poland, Czechoslovakia, Hungary, Yugoslavia, and Austria.

Nationalism in the United States, Canada, and Japan. The development of the nation-state in the areas outside Europe occurred in approximately the same time as in Europe. The development of nationalism in the United States

---

*It was not until after World War II that the nationalism of the Federal Republic of Germany and Italy came to include the liberal–democratic political values of the American, British, and French victors.

Proponents of integral nationalism: Adolf Hitler and leaders of the National Socialist German Workers Party (NSDAP) at a rally in Nuremberg.

began in the eighteenth century and focused on support for the liberal–democratic political values inherited from England. The geographic separation from Europe and the Revolutionary War prompted the development of a new and unique American identity. By the beginning of the twentieth century American nationalism stressed the uniqueness of the United States as a "melting pot" nation (sometimes called "a nation of many nations")[29] and a nation destined to demonstrate the viability of democratic institutions to the rest of the world. American nationalism developed without the common religion or common descent as was the case in many areas of Europe.[30] However, the fact that American support for the nation-state equaled that found in Europe demonstrates that national identity is a matter of subjective perception, not objective ethnic, linguistic, and religious factors.

The development of a nation-state in Canada was shaped by the existence of two nationality groups with separate languages, cultures, and political traditions. The majority and politically dominant English-Canadian group formed its national identity around the political concept of liberal democracy and its historical ties with Great Britain. French-Canadian nationalism developed in reaction to English Canada and stressed the need for loyalty to the French language and support for French-Canadian cultural and political values.[31] Despite the fact that Canada is presently one of the most affluent countries in the world with a well-established democratic tradition, the development of a "Canadian Nationalism" capable of uniting both groups is, at best, incomplete. Although many French-Canadians identify with the "Canadian nation," significant groups within the Province of Quebec advocate the creation of a separate French-Canadian nation-state. The future of Canada may well depend on whether French-Canadian separatism or Canadian nationalism has the greatest popular appeal.

The development of nationalism in Japan was aided by the fact that Japan has one of the most homogeneous populations in the world. Modern Japanese nationalism developed in reaction to the threat to Japan's territorial integrity (and self-imposed isolation) posed by various Western states in the nineteenth century. It is summarized in the nationalist slogan "Honor the Emperor, expel the Barbarians."[32] The Meiji Restoration in 1869 brought the creation of a modern state similar to those of Western Europe, complete with a national bureaucracy, army, tax structure, and school system.[33]

Supranationalism in Europe. After World War II widespread disillusionment set in about the competitive nationalism that had produced two world wars between 1914 and 1939. The expensive physical devastation and the disruption of economic life led important elite groups to conclude that national recovery programs undertaken by individual states would be inadequate for the reconstruction of Europe. With the support of the United States, six Western European states began planning for the regional recovery of the continent. They were Germany, France, Italy, Belgium, the Netherlands, and Luxembourg. Elites in these states were influenced by the principles of *supranationalism*, the belief that it was necessary to create institutions above the state. Between 1952 and 1958 three institutions were created with supranational characteristics, the European Coal and Steel Community (ECSC, 1952), the European Economic Community (EEC, 1957), and the European Atomic Energy Commission (Euratom, 1957). These organizations assumed control over important areas of policy making that previously had been under the control of individual states, including the levying of customs taxes, the establishment of subsidies, and the establishment of a minimum wage. Within these institutions decision-making power rests with a council of ministers composed of the representatives of each state. Decisions are by a modified majority rule and on certain issues individual states can be bound by decisions that they oppose. The day-to-day admin-

Ceremony at the City Hall of Rome on the twentieth anniversary of the founding of the European Economic Community.

istration is in the hands of professionals who are uninstructed by their governments and are "European" rather than "national" civil servants. In a very real sense these organizations place limits on the sovereignty of member states because they have removed important areas of economic and social policy from their control. The organizations of the European Community proved successful in accomplishing economic recovery, and this success led to calls for the total integration of the states into a single political unit or "United States of Europe."

The movement toward European integration stalled in the 1960s when nationalism reasserted itself in France and to a lesser extent in Germany. In the short run, the "United States of Europe" was not to be. In 1954 the French legislature rejected the proposed European Defense Community (EDC) which would have created a European army under the authority of a European minister of defense. Under the leadership of Charles de Gaulle France vetoed British entry in the EEC in 1963 and again in 1967. De Gaulle also opposed any extension of supranational authority within the European Community. In the 1970s (after de Gaulle's death) Great Britain, Denmark, and Ireland, and later (in 1981) Greece were accepted into the EEC. Subsequently, Spain and Portugal were also accepted for membership.

However, the world economic crisis of 1973-1974 prevented any new movement toward supranationalism in that decade.[34] Richard Mansbach and Yale Ferguson have described the present political condition as the "Half-way House of Europe" in which the states of Europe are somewhere between national sovereignty and supranational authority.[35]

THE SECOND WORLD

Attributes of Statehood in the Second World

The basic political philosophy of the Second World is Marxism–Leninism, which boasts a coherent and comprehensive theory of the state. Understanding this theory is vital to understanding the Communist system. As previously mentioned, Communists believe that human society is progressing through five stages of development. This development occurs not in a linear fashion, but rather in dialectical leaps—revolutionary changes—which are major upheavals in the economic, political, and social structure of human society.

Communist politicians in the 17 ruling Communist party states (see Chapter 9) and other Communists worldwide of whatever persuasion (Soviet or independent orientation), specifically reject theories of the origin of the state involving: intervention of God or supernatural forces; social contract (a freely entered agreement between rulers and ruled); force and violence (force may occur but states do not come into existence because of coercion alone); and charismatic leadership (which may explain why a particular individual is in power but is not the reason for the foundation of the state). Rather, they see the state as the necessary "product of society at a definite stage of its development."[36]

Basically, humanity is bound by "laws" of social development which determine the *five stages (epochs) of history*. The determinant for each stage is the way in which production is organized and in what form production takes place—production need not be thought of as only modern manufacturing but as any activity that serves to feed and maintain human life; thus, "production" could include the most primitive of hunting, fishing, and agricultural activities. This approach is called *historical materialism* or the materialist approach to history. In going through change humans move from a lesser to a higher level of development within the limits of the social–historical laws. The basis for social life in any given epoch of history is found in the way production takes place and who controls the productive forces. Thus, the basis of society is its economic foundation. Everything else is said to be the superstructure of society, that is, its political, legal, philosophical, religious, class, and social aspects. Once one determines the economic foundation of society, the rest of it can be understood.

Marxist–Leninists believe that when humans began to develop separately from other primates they were in the *primitive–communal epoch*. Production was communal; that is, all shared in hunting, fishing, animal husbandry, and agricultural activities. Simple stone implements, digging sticks, and bows and arrows were the tools of production. In this period there was no state; people lived at a bare subsistence level without the nuclear family and society was matriarchal.

Metal implements began to be forged and used in the late primitive–communal period and this caused such an expansion in production capacity that communal labor was no longer needed. Individuals could now produce not only the basic amount of consumables to keep themselves and their families alive but also a little bit more. This "little bit more," the surplus value of production, now became available for seizure by others. It became possible for some to dominate others to take away the surplus (to appropriate to themselves part of someone else's product). This situation created the conditions wherein farmers, herders, fishers began to come under the control of stronger elements. Women, too, were forced into subservience. Marxist–Leninists assume that this occurred in prehistory, before written records.[37] What came out of all of this was the rise of classes, the exploitation of one group by another. These classes were at odds with each other and humanity moved into a period of use of slavery.

The slave epoch marks the beginning of history and civilization. The economic base of society in this era is slavery. The simple metal tools and the muscle power needed to wield them come under the private property ownership of a ruling class—the slave-holders. These people claimed and enforced control over persons and property. As a natural result of this the *state* came into existence. The state appears, according to Lenin, "when and in so far as class antagonisms cannot be reconciled."[38] Thus, there is the rise of class-based society. Classes, in the Marxist–Leninist sense, are based on a group's relationship with economic and, thus, political, power. Classes are social strata

> that are "grouped" as a result of the relationship they have to the possession or non-possession of the means of production as private property . . . however, [this] is not merely a legal relationship, but also an economic relationship between men. Class relationships allow the surplus product to be appropriated by the possessing class, which thus stands in an exploitive relationship to the producers.[39]

The state is the mechanism used to forcibly but temporarily reconcile a struggle between classes, which in the long run is irreconcilable. We must mention here that Marxist–Leninists divide class conflicts into reconcilable contradictions (ones that can be overcome short of open struggle) and irreconcilable contradictions (ones that are resolved only by a clash, with the destruction of one class by another). As Lenin emphasized in his *State and Revolution,* the ruling class needed the state to maintain its power.[40] In the slave period the slave's desire for freedom cannot be amicably reconciled with the owner's need for control. Thus armed groups of men are needed to keep the slaves in their place. An army is used, first, to control major outbreaks of resistance among the slaves; second, to fend off predatory raids of neighboring slave states that wish to acquire additional laborers, land, and booty; and third, to raid neighbors for the same reasons. A police force is established to maintain everyday order and to enforce the law. Prisons and punishments are established to intimidate those who do not accept their place in society. Rules and regulations legally formulating the class structure of society are drawn up and recorded in the writing system created for that purpose. Law courts and scribes are the start of an administrative class that runs the state on behalf of the rulers. Geometry and arithmetic come into existence for use in defining land and the obligations of the slaves to their masters. Religion is invented to give a divine blessing to society as it exists and to convince the downtrodden that God or the gods sanction the class relationships found in the state and that resistence is sinful. The state is the "dictatorship of the dominant class and is its political arm."[41] In every stage of history in which the state exists there are two essential classes, the classes which define the epoch: slaves–slave-holders, serfs–feudal lords, capitalists–proletarians. There also exist ancillary classes such as civil servants, a priest class, professionals (doctors, teachers), merchants and, of course, criminal elements. These other classes, however, do not determine whom the state serves, but rather these classes service the existing relationships. When the contradictions between the two essential classes can no longer be maintained in balance, then a revolution occurs and a new society forms. Marxist–Leninists claim that revolutions have occurred in the transition from primitive–communal to the slave system, from the slave to the feudal stage, and feudal to capitalist, and that now the world is undergoing the change to socialism.

The feudal epoch occurs when the slave system collapses along with its state and a new situation arises in which ownership of land is paramount. The feudal lord is in control because he owns the productive land and the tools to work it. The serf must acquiesce to the landlord in order to gain access to the land to feed himself and maintain a family. Marxist–Leninists are little concerned with this epoch itself but rather concentrate on the growth of capitalism within it and the subsequent overthrow of the feudal order in favor of capitalism.[42]

The capitalist epoch (and its state) is the result of new property relationships. The capitalist bourgeoisie (the entrepreneurial class) has risen to the top because it controls the new manufacturing methods that began to be used in the preceding feudal period.

> The bourgeoisie has at last conquered for itself, in the modern representative state, exclusive political sway. The executive of the modern state is but a committee for managing the common affairs of the whole bourgeoisie. . . .

> The bourgeoisie . . . has put an end to all feudal . . . relations. It has pitilessly torn asunder the motley feudal ties that bound man to his "natural superiors" and has left remaining no other nexus between man and man than naked self-interest, than callous "cash payment."[43]

Capitalists control society and its economic base because if the industrial workers (the proletariat) want to live, they must contract for work with the exploiting owners of the means of production. Karl Marx was principally involved in analyzing nineteenth-century capitalism and he spent relatively little time worrying about exactly what would happen when capitalists and their states (the state governments of the First World) were overthrown. Nevertheless, Marx did mention some fundamental notions.

The capitalist system would end when the majority working class (all those who need to work for pay) led by the proletariat (the politically active industrial workers) realized its power and began to act as a class, first philosophically (understanding itself and its role in capitalist society), then politically (organizing working-class political parties), and finally in a revolutionary fashion (overthrowing the ruling class and seizing power).

States that existed prior to the working-class seizure of power were always exploitive and always served the ruling class, whether they were the Athenian democracy, oriental tyranny, the Roman Republic or the Roman Empire (of the Slave Epoch). In the feudal epoch, authoritarian states, monarchies, empires, and republics also served their masters. British-type parliaments, presidential systems of the U. S. style, military dictatorships, and Fascist regimes were and are subservient to the capitalist class. When the working class seizes power, however, an entirely new situation occurs. For the first time the majority is in power (albeit actual power being in the hands of the Communist party).

This new, unique "socialist" state, the political mechanism in the first part of the *socialist–communist epoch,* is a transitional organization destined to disappear. No longer is a mechanism needed to suppress the majority, and as soon as the small minority of former rulers accepts their loss of power, the state can begin to erode away as classes disappear. In full-scale Communism (the second half of the socialist–communist epoch) the state will be gone, leaving behind an economic exchange mechanism and public self-government.[44]

> The classics of Marxism believe that the society which organizes production on new lines—free and equal association of producers—will consign the state mechanism to its proper place, namely the museum of antiquities alongside the distaff and the bronze axe.[45]

With this very broad statement it would appear we could draw to a close our discussion of the Marxist theory of the state. However, this is not the case because the attainment of the goal of full-scale Communist society, although originally thought to be reachable in relatively short order (see, for example, Lenin's writings after the seizure of power or the thinking behind China's Great Leap Forward), has been relegated to the far and undefined future in all Communist party states and, except for ritual slogans used at party congresses, all discussion of it has been left to utopian speculations.

Today the Second World has an extremely powerful state system—a state mechanism frequently referred to as totalitarian (seeking as much control as possible over all aspects of society). The reasons put forward for the existence and continuation of powerful socialist states are outlined in the following paragraphs.

First, Lenin specifically said the old ruling classes would not just go away nor would the old state just disappear. Rather the "revolution [will] . . . set itself the aim, not of improving the state machine, but of smashing and destroying it."[46] The class struggle, the struggle for power, would continue for a period of time until the Communist revolution was triumphant more or less worldwide. Lenin had an apocalyptic view of the world. He foresaw a series of "frightful clashes" between the retreating but still potent capitalist system and the advancing Communist one. Although in its death throes, capitalism still has one final period to live through, the "imperialist" one, when capitalism would break out of national frontiers to seize control of laborers, markets, and raw materials on a worldwide scale. The threat of the new socialist states to imperialism would be too great to be ignored. So, in between periods of fighting among themselves for markets, the capitalist–imperialists would periodically throw their forces against socialism in an attempt to crush it. Hence, the proletariat would have to keep up its guard over long periods of time and, because full-scale Communism was possible only when there was at least a worldwide socialist system, there is a necessity to create and maintain a new, powerful state to fend off capitalist attacks.[47] This "siege mentality" is a mainspring of many Second World states' foreign and domestic policies.

Thus, the fifth historical epoch, the socialist–communist, is now divided by Marxist–Leninists into three distinct evolutionary phases. (The last, full-scale Communism, need not concern us here as it lies, as mentioned, in the realm of the far future.) The first phase, the actual seizure of power, and its immediate aftermath, is called the period of the *Dictatorship of the Proletariat*, a term used several times by Marx but only fully developed by Lenin. This is the phase of savage class warfare in which the old rulers strike back at the proletariat while calling on international capitalism (imperialism) for support. The proletariat, on the other hand, forms a working-class army and a revolutionary police force in order to destroy foreign enemies and to ruthlessly suppress internal class opponents. Lenin formulated a five-point program for the Dictatorship of the Proletariat:

1. Suppression of the exploiters' resistance.
2. Fighting a civil war and perhaps foreign imperialist intervention.
3. Neutralization of the lower-level bourgeoisie—small shopkeepers, minor officials, professionals, and small-scale manufacturers.
4. Utilization of bourgeois specialists (engineers, mechanics, administrators, army officers), compelling them to serve the proletariat.
5. Introduction of new discipline and development of a Communist attitude to work.[48]

When finally the external opponent can be kept at permanent bay and the internal foes cease to be a threat, the system would evolve into a socialist state of "all the people." This phase was not to be seen by Lenin, however, for he fell ill during the Dictatorship of the Proletariat in 1922 and died in 1924. It remained for his successor, Josif Stalin, to give form to the socialist state, a formulation now used by 17 countries.

Stalin had already noted in 1918 that "the world has definitely and irrevocably split into two camps: the camp of imperialism and the camp of socialism."[49] In developing and systematizing Lenin's ideas, Stalin formulated tactics and strategy for socialist success in Russia. He constructed a so-called dialectical paradox in stating that the socialist state must become the strongest and most powerful state to ever exist in order to destroy its enemies and then and only then would it begin to wither away.[50] Along with Lenin, Stalin saw the Communist party as the leading and guiding force that would direct the socialist states in their advances. The formula for Communist party control is the following: the Communist party is the only political party that is able to comprehend the forces of history and to direct society onto the path to Communism. Communists are the most advanced thinkers of the industrial proletariat—the only segment of the working class with enough political understanding to recognize working-class interests. The rest of the working class (peasants, shop clerks, minor state workers, soldiers) would look to the proletariat and its party for guidance. The Communist party would lead the workers to power and the new workers' state would assist workers in other states to gain power. Over a long period of time the workers would gain control worldwide and the socialist–Communist system would be the world's system.

However, in the 1920s and 1930s Stalin pressed the idea that it was possible to develop socialism in one state while awaiting the next revolutionary wave. The first wave had included Russia, Belorus, Ukraine (which formed the Soviet Union in 1923), and Mongolia. While awaiting the expected second wave Stalin postulated that the USSR was the fortress of socialism and that it needed to become extremely strong, with all the trappings of power found in capitalist countries.[51] This model of a powerful state is used in all Communist party states today. The state mechanism under the control of the Communist party is dominant in all spheres of life. (There is a strong argument to be made that Karl Marx did not anticipate the Dictatorship of the Proletariat or a state of the Leninist–Stalinist variety, because of his explicit praise of the Paris Commune of 1871.[52])

The contemporary socialist state is said not to have classes as such but strata of proletarians, intellectuals, and farmers. Any conflicts that occur within socialist states are said to be reconcilable. The first state to claim to have achieved Marxist socialism was the USSR, in 1936, when the so-called Stalin Constitution was promulgated, which eliminated the legal distinctions between classes that had been contained in the 1918 and 1923 constitutions.

It should be added that the revolution must come internally by efforts of the proletariat and its party; Communists explicitly condemn the idea that revolution can be exported. Revolution must be based on existing internal conditions.[53] States that went through a revolution on the Soviet model include Yugoslavia, Albania, Cuba, China, and Vietnam; but the "assisted" revolutions that took place in Afghanistan, Poland, East Germany, Czechoslovakia, Romania, Hungary, Bulgaria, Mongolia, and North Korea where force or threat of force by the Red Army played a decisive role (and Laos and Kampuchea where Vietnamese armed forces settled the matter) do not fit the theoretical framework. For this latter group the term "People's Democracies" was invented, which indicates that military forces of a fraternal Communist regime, while performing their duties according to the doctrine of Proletarian Internationalism, assisted local Communists in seizing power.

Nationalism and Patriotism

It is interesting to note that Marxist–Leninists are ambivalent about nationalism and patriotism. On the one hand, nationality is considered to be an invention of the bourgeoisie (property owners in capitalism) by which a

Prague, Czechoslovakia—mass demonstration of Communists calls for seizure of full power in February, 1948.

group of people is convinced that they are a unique nation and that their support should be given to their national bourgeois leaders. The capitalists do this for two reasons: (1) to create a national market for their goods, and (2) to prevent coalitions of the exploited across national frontiers which would be detrimental to the capitalist cause. On the other hand, ruling Communist parties have been forced, in practice, to recognize that national feelings are not simply inventions of market-builders but rather are an important part of a state's political culture. It is true that the disappearance of nationality as it is now known is still projected, but only in the nebulous future of full-scale Communism. In the meantime the Soviet Union's main divisions, the 15 constituent republics, are based on nationality, as are many of the republics' subdivisions. The only concrete result of Czechoslovakia's upheaval in 1968 was the creation of a federal state consisting of the Czechlands (Bohemia and Moravia) and Slovakia.[54] Yugoslavia also has formed a socialist state of the Soviet federal variety because of nationality problems. It consists of six republics—Slovenia, Croatia, Bosnia-Herzegovina, Crna Gora (Montenegro), Serbia, and Macedona, and two autonomous districts attached to Serbia—Vojvodina and Kosovo-Metohija.[55]

Other Communist party states have opted for a unitary organization. Poland, East Germany, Hungary, Romania, Bulgaria, Albania, North Korea, Vietnam, Laos, Kampuchea, and China are based mainly on one nationality. However, despite official Marxist–Leninist views about nationality and its declining significance, dominant nationalities have not shrunk from expulsion, encouragement to leave, or repression of minorities in these states. Romania has treated its Hungarians and German minorities poorly; as has Poland its Germans, Jews, and Ukrainians; Vietnam its Chinese; and China its non-Han population.[56] In regard to the latter, 93% of the over 1 billion population of China is Han Chinese but some 67 million are other minorities divided into 55 recognized groups. It appears, though, that there is a less rigorous treatment of the Chinese minorities today.[57] In the case of a divided country (that is, a Communist and a non-Communist part, for example North and South Korea, East and West Germany, and Taiwan and Mainland China) neither side is above calling on naked nationalism to rally support to its banner in opposition to the other side. Patriotism in the Second World is condemned when it refers to support by the working class of its state in the First or Third Worlds, but it is encouraged when it means support for the "proletarian" states of the Second World. The USSR is especially noted for its fostering of "Soviet" patriotism.

Sovereignty and Supranationalism

All Marxist–Leninist states affirm the doctrine of sovereignty. Orientation (either pro-Soviet, or independent) determines the meaning of the term sovereignty, however. The Soviet Union and its bloc of direct supporters clearly affirm a limited sovereignty doctrine. Although the Soviet Union and its allies use classical terms to define sovereignty, they nevertheless put forth the notion that support of the "Socialist camp" supersedes specific national interests. Thus, threat of force or force itself has been used to put down resistance in Eastern Europe. On the other hand, Yugoslavia and China, feeling threatened by Soviet aggression, have condemned "hegemonism," and China has fought border clashes with the Soviet Union and the Soviet ally, Vietnam, to indicate China's willingness to resist Soviet pressure. The Soviet invasion of Afghanistan has strengthened considerably Yugoslav and Chinese suspicions about the Soviet Union.

To conclude, the state in the Second World is an extremely strong mechanism, earlier Marxist theory to the contrary, used to carry out the will of the "New [ruling] Class."[58]

THE THIRD WORLD

A majority of states are in the Third World, with almost one-third in Africa. The state era began with the signing of the Treaty of Westphalia in 1648, but it was not until the twentieth century that a large number of sovereign states emerged. Europe "consisted altogether of about 15 sovereign states in 1871, approximately 25 before World War I, and over 30 by the 1930s."[59] It took more than two centuries for the number of sovereign states in Europe to reach 15, but that number more than doubled in the next 50 to 60 years. In the Third World most sovereign states emerged after the Second World War, and most African states gained sovereignty within the last three decades. When the United Nations was established in 1945, of the 51 original members, only 3 (not counting South Africa) were African states—Egypt, Ethiopia, and Liberia. The number of African member states of the United Nations is now approximately 50.

The end of the colonial rule of the Western powers led to the enormous increase in the number of sovereign states in the Third World. In Latin America the Spanish Empire began crumbling in the early nineteenth century with a successful revolution in Argentina and the formation of an independent state in that country. As many as 18 independent states resulted from the end of the Spanish rule in Latin America. Brazil, the sole but vast colony of Portugal in that region, declared independence in 1822. The lesser colonial powers in Latin America held on to their possessions much longer. Guyana, a former British colony in South America, gained limited representative government in 1928, but had to wait until 1966 for independence. Suriname, a former Dutch colony east of Guyana, became free in 1975. Several British colonies in the Caribbean (such as Barbados, Jamaica, and Trinidad and Tobago) also gained independence after the Second World War. The Western powers still control a few islands in the Caribbean; in South America the last colony is French Guiana in the northeastern part of the continent.

By engulfing principalities, territories controlled by tribes, and existing states in Africa and Asia, the colonial powers reduced the number of states. It is sometimes argued that colonial rule inhibited the development of states in these two continents. However, it is more accurate to say that colonialism delayed rather than inhibited such development and in a sense actually contributed to it. By determining the boundaries of the areas under their control and by introducing governmental and administrative structures in these areas, the colonial powers made political units out of disparate territories in Africa and Asia. A prominent example is that of India. Although several states rose and fell through the long history of this subcontinent, India was divided into many principalities and kingdoms until

Declaration of independence of
Mozambique and proclamation of
Samora Machel as President of the
country, June 25, 1975.

the British brought its various parts under their control in the nineteenth century. India was made a single political unit under British rule and that situation helped to shape it into a state. Similar developments took place in other parts of Asia and Africa.

A few countries in Africa and Asia that escaped being colonized developed into states earlier than did the colonies. Saudi Arabia in the Middle East and Thailand in Asia became consolidated political units in the eighteenth century. Liberia in West Africa, settled by freed slaves from the United States, developed as an independent state by the middle of the nineteenth century. Ethiopia (in Eastern Africa) was the first independent state to emerge in black Africa. Hugh Seton-Watson writes: "In Africa south of Egypt one civilized state maintained itself, with changing fortunes and frontier, for two thousand years: Ethiopia."[60] To say that Ethiopia has been a state for 2000 years in the sense of possession of attributes of statehood to any significant extent is clearly an exaggeration. There is no doubt, however, that except for a brief period of occupation by Italian forces under Mussolini (1935–1941), Ethiopia has enjoyed independence for several centuries.

Attributes of Statehood in the Third World

A state is considered to have a fixed territory accepted by other states. Yet several border disputes continue unresolved in the Third World, especially in Africa. Even in the First or the Second World, border disputes are present. One of the most notable of such disputes is between the Soviet Union and China. Another prominent border dispute involves China and India. However, there are far more border disputes in the Third World than in the First or the Second World, largely because of the history of the creation of states in the Third World. Although the colonial powers contributed to the development of states in the Third World by bringing different areas together and making them into political units, they demarcated artificial boundaries between colonies to distinguish the jurisdiction of one colonial power from that of another. Even when they drew boundaries within their own spheres of control for creating units for administrative convenience, they often ignored natural boundaries. Nowhere is this so apparent as in Africa. Seton-Watson remarks that

> the frontiers drawn by European colonial governments in the nineteenth century [in Africa], both between their territories and those of another colonial power, and within their vast domains, were often quite artificial—mere lines on the map, sometimes taking account of river valleys, sometimes not even that. They cut across regions which might have formed natural units, and they divided peoples and language groups.[61]

Dividing peoples and language groups was even more serious than ignoring natural boundaries. This division created problems for nation-building in African states, as discussed later. Because of artificial boundaries border disputes exist in Africa and show little sign of being resolved. (Border disputes occur in Asia and Latin America also, but they are not as numerous as in Africa.) Clearly the attribute of a fixed territory, expected of a state, has not been achieved by a substantial majority of the African states.

Notwithstanding border disputes, legal jurisdiction is exercised over the population under the control of a state. Like the states in the First and the Second Worlds, Third World states also prescribe rules governing citizens and aliens under their jurisdiction. The records of citizens and aliens and even of total populations are not as precise in the Third World as in the First and the Second Worlds. In some Third World states a census is not taken at regular intervals. In Nigeria, for example, which became independent in 1960 and is the most populous state in Africa, a census has not yet been taken. Birth and death records in the Third World, especially in Africa and Asia, are also incomplete. In several African and Asian states, therefore, population figures are considered estimates rather than actual counted numbers.

During the last 30 to 40 years large numbers of citizens from the Third World states have emigrated to other states. Some have gone to Europe, particularly Britain and France; others have gone to the United States and Canada; still others, especially since the early 1970s have landed jobs in the oil-rich states of the Middle East. Many of these immigrants have become citizens of the states that are their new homes. Unless dual citizenship is permitted, this results in the giving up of allegiance to the old country. Of course, the acceptance of an alien as a citizen is governed by the rules prescribed by a state's government. These rules vary in different states. The oil-exporting Middle Eastern countries are very reluctant to accept aliens as citizens. The United States and Canada have rather liberal rules on naturalization, but they prefer professionally trained or skilled workers. In Britain, France, and other West European states, rules governing naturalization have been made quite strict with a view to discouraging immigrants from the Third World.

Another form of mobility of people from the Third World is that of refugees, displaced because of internal conflicts or wars or food shortages. The United States has accepted refugees from countries such as Kampuchea, Cuba, Hungary, and Vietnam. A large number of refugees move to neighboring states, hoping to return when the situation improves. Millions of such refugees are in Africa and Asia. To give just one example, almost 10 million refugees from East Pakistan, which became Bangladesh, fled to India in 1971 to escape civil war at home. Most of these refugees returned to their homes in a few months at the end of the civil war. Since the Soviet invasion of Afghanistan in 1979, 3 million refugees (out of a population of 14 million) have moved to neighboring Pakistan.

It is the government (the third attribute of statehood) that exercises legal jurisdiction over a state's population within a fixed territory. The governments in Third World states are less effective than those in the First and Second World states. In many Third World states, people abide by the rules of groups such as tribes or castes more diligently than by the laws passed by governments. Governments in several Third World states lack legitimacy. The lack of legitimacy is evident from the frequency of government changes by military coups in the Third World. According to *Time* magazine, "In the past 25 years, more than 70 leaders in 29 African nations have been deposed by assassinations, purges or coups."[62] It is important to note here that in order to be legitimate, a government does not have to be democratic; as explained earlier in this chapter, it must be considered morally acceptable by a majority of the population according to the prevailing political norms. Even a military government that comes to power by means of a coup can enjoy legitimacy. Evidence, however, indicates that such governments do not enjoy legitimacy for long.

Governments in Third World states have tried various methods for ensuring legitimacy. In a study of the Third World, J. D. B. Miller mentions four such methods:

[1] the combination of tight coercive control with indigenous symbols of authority; . . . [2] the combination of tight control with a local modernizing leader; . . . [3] a variant of the second [method], often to be found in states in which the conditions for tight efficient control do not exist, but in which a mesmeric leader imposes his personality for a time upon those around him; . . . [4] a system of loose control with intermittent severity, perhaps with a notable leader to provide unifying direction.[63]

The first method has so far succeeded in Saudi Arabia and some other oil-producing states in the Middle East. The second method was successfully used by President Nasser of Egypt (in power 1954–1970) and to a lesser extent by his successor Sadat (in power 1970–1981). The major examples of the use of the third method are Ghana under Nkrumah (in power 1952–1966) and Indonesia under Sukarno (in power 1949–1968). Miller considers India under Nehru (in power 1947–1964),[64] Tanzania under Nyerere (in power 1961–present), and Tunisia under Bourguiba (in power 1956–present) as the examples of the fourth method. Miller accepts that "none of these is a reliable solution" and that "each may be upset by bad luck, external pressures, or internal disturbances."[65] It is not uncommon for the government of a Third World state to enjoy legitimacy for some time by using one of these methods and then to lose legitimacy.

Sovereignty—supreme decision-making and decision-enforcing authority in domestic and foreign affairs—is claimed by all independent states, including the Third World states. Most Third World states do not consider international organizations, especially the United Nations, as limiting their sovereignty. The United Nations is perceived by them as an expression of, rather than a limitation on, their sovereign status. The limitations on the Third World states' sovereignty stem from their economic and military dependence on the states of the First and the Second Worlds. Major powers such as the United States and the Soviet Union expect economic as well as political returns for foreign aid and trade concessions. Support of policies acceptable to the aid-donors is considered a political return for aid and trade. It is debatable, however, to what an extent trade or aid constrains Third World states' sovereignty. Dependence on oil controlled by a few states, a majority of them in the Third World, has perhaps placed greater limits on the sovereignty of the oil-importing states than has aid or trade.

The violation of human rights is more common in the Third World than in the First World. The United States under President Jimmy Carter attempted to tie aid to the observance of human rights in aid-recipient states in the Third World—a policy inconsistently pursued under Carter and virtually given up by his successor, President Ronald Reagan. This issue was, however, seriously debated by Reagan's administration. A presidential

commission headed by former Secretary of State Henry Kissinger advocated, in early 1984, tying of American aid to the observance of human rights
in Central America. If such a policy is adopted, it can be construed as an
American attempt to limit the sovereignty of the aid-recipients.

Nationalism in the Third World

State-building—the process by which a state extends its authority throughout its territory—has been hindered in the Third World by the lack of a
feeling of nationalism. Nationalism is interpreted by the elites of the Third
World to mean a feeling of togetherness and a sense of loyalty to the state
felt by the people. As most Third World states are beset with tribal and other
group-related differences in the populations, loyalty to the state rather than
to tribal or other groups is stressed. The governments of the Third World
states have attempted to inculcate such a feeling of togetherness and a sense
of loyalty among their populations through policies and symbols. The
process of urbanization, which has been a feature of virtually every Third
World state since independence, has undermined somewhat the loyalty to
smaller groups, because those leaving villages for cities are more distant
from such groups. Despite the governments' efforts and urbanization, a
substantial majority of the people in the Third World still continue to think
in terms of belonging to smaller groups instead of to the state. This is much
more true of states in Africa and Asia than in Latin America.

An even more serious hindrance to the development of nationalism in
Third World states is the lack of a common language within a state. In most
cases the language of the former colonial power is used as the official
language, but only a minority of the people can speak this language. People
in the Third World often speak languages or dialects used by their tribes or
confined to their particular regions and are unable to communicate with
those who live within the boundaries of the same state but speak a different
language. The variety of these languages and dialects is enormous indeed.
To give some examples, in former French African colonies, over 125
languages are spoken;[66] in Zaire, 75 languages are used;[67] and in India, 1652
"mother tongues," including 14 major languages, exist.[68] Several states
(including India, Indonesia, Kenya, Somalia, Sudan, and Tanzania) have
adopted indigenous languages as official languages and encourage people
from different groups to learn those languages. Most of these attempts have
not been successful, with the result that the languages of the former colonial
powers continue to be used.

In comparison with Western states, Third World states have had very
little time to develop a sense of nationalism. Robert Bone states that "it took
a period of several centuries for Westerners to grow accustomed to think of

themselves as Englishmen, Frenchmen, Italians, or Germans, but for the non-Westerner there was no such time span involved."[69] In Africa the development of such nationalism was further hindered by the map imposed on this continent by the Western powers in the Berlin Colonial Conference of 1884-1885. In drawing up the map of Africa, the European powers paid no attention to the tribal structure of Africa. As a result, a tribe was often divided between different colonies and antagonistic tribes were placed together within the borders of the same colony.

Miller points out that

> whereas classical European nationalism of the nineteenth century was *linguistic*, that of Asia and Africa has been essentially *administrative*. Both showed a similar stimulation of feeling against the imperial power, but there is a contrast between the strong emphasis of the former on local culture and social forms and of the latter on the taking over of an administrative machine and existing frontiers.[70]

In African and Asian states the administrative nationalism changed after independence (from the colonial rule) and the emphasis shifted to unity, togetherness, and loyalty to the state. It is possible that unity, togetherness, and loyalty to the state might gradually develop in Africa and Asia, yet the obstacles against such a development are quite serious.

Supranationalism in the Third World

Supranationalism in the Third World has been motivated not by the objective of avoiding wars caused by competitive nationalism, but by the hope of achieving economic progress. A number of organizations similar in some ways to the European Community have been formed in Africa, Asia, and Latin America. Some examples of such organizations are (dates of formation and membership are indicated in parentheses) the Andean Group (1969; Bolivia, Colombia, Ecuador, Peru, and Venezuela), Association of Southeast Asian Nations (1967; Indonesia, Malaysia, the Philippines, Singapore, and Thailand), and Central African Economic and Customs Union (1966; Cameroon, Central African Republic, Congo, and Gabon). The Third World organizations have been far less successful than the European Community. The reasons for their lack of success lie in the gap within these organizations between their relatively developed and less-developed states, causing dissension among the members, paucity of necessary talent, and perhaps in the very nature of their economies.[71]

An ambitious attempt at supranationalism not restricted to economic goals alone was made by Ghana's leader Nkrumah in the 1950s and 1960s. Nkrumah's dream was to establish a united Africa. The other African leaders were not willing to give up their states' sovereignty. A compromise was reached with the establishment of the Organization of African Unity in 1963. This organization includes every independent African state except the white-dominated South Africa. Established to achieve the objectives of promoting unity, defending member states' sovereignty, stimulating economic progress, and ending colonial rule, it has succeeded in realizing only the last of these goals. The Organization of African Unity has often been divided on the major African issues it has faced.

NOTES

1. Donald James Puchala, *International Politics Today* (New York: Dodd, Mead, 1971), p. 198.
2. Ibid.
3. Of course, languages such as English, French, and Spanish are spoken in numerous states and are not unique to any one state.
4. Hans Kohn, *Nationalism: Its Meaning and History* (Princeton, N.J.: Van Nostrand, 1965), p. 9.
5. Puchala, p. 208.
6. Quoted in Ivo D. Duchacek, *Nations and Men: International Politics Today* (New York: Holt, Rinehart and Winston, 1966), p. 37.
7. Karl W. Deutsch, *Politics and Government: How People Decide Their Fate,* 3d ed. (Boston: Houghton Mifflin, 1980), pp. 152–153.
8. Jack C. Plano and Roy Olton, *The International Relations Dictionary,* 3d ed. (Santa Barbara, Calif.: ABC-Clio, 1982), pp. 285–286.
9. For a discussion of state-building and nation-building see Karl W. Deutsch and William J. Foltz, eds., *Nation-Building* (New York: Atherton Press, 1966); and Charles Tilly, ed., *The Formation of National States in Western Europe* (Princeton, N.J.: Princeton University Press, 1975).
10. Hugh Seton-Watson, *Nations and States: An Inquiry into the Origins of Nations and the Politics of Nationalism* (Boulder, Colo.: Westview Press, 1977), p. 193. See also Alfred Coban, *The Nation State and National Self-Determination* (New York: Crowell, 1970), pp. 153–183, 219–244.
11. Richard W. Mansbach, Yale H. Ferguson, and Donald E. Lampert, *The Web of Politics: Nonstate Actors in the Global System* (Englewood Cliffs, N.J.: Prentice-Hall, 1976), p. 9.
12. Robert Ergang, *Emergence of the National State* (New York: Van Nostrand, 1971), p. 14.
13. Ibid., pp. 5–6.
14. R. R. Palmer and Joel Colton, *A History of the Modern State* (New York: Knopf, 1956), p. 127.
15. Deutsch, p. 118.

16. Puchala, p. 203.
17. Ibid., pp. 197–217.
18. Joseph R. Strayer, "The Historical Experience of Nation-Building in Europe," in Karl W. Deutsch and William J. Foltz, p. 23.
19. Deutsch, pp. 118–119.
20. Ibid., p. 119.
21. See Haldan Koht, "The Dawn of Nationalism in Europe," in Louis L. Snyder, ed., *The Dynamics of Nationalism: Readings in its Meaning and Development* (Princeton, N.J.: Van Nostrand, 1964), pp. 30–31.
22. Gerhard Ritter, "Origins of the Modern States," in Heinz Lubasz, ed., *The Development of the Modern State* (New York: Macmillan, 1964), p. 23.
23. See Emile Lousse, "Absolutism," in Lubasz, p. 46.
24. See John Herz, "The Rise and Demise of the Territorial State," in Lubasz, pp. 130–151.
25. Ibid., p. 131.
26. Deutsch, p. 119.
27. Hans Kohn, "The Genesis of English Nationalism," in Snyder, pp. 77–78; and Kohn, pp. 16–17.
28. Snyder, p. 104.
29. Ibid., p. 253.
30. Ibid.
31. For a discussion of French-Canadian nationalism see Donald V. Smiley, *The Canadian Political Nationality* (Toronto: Methuen, 1967); and Dale Posgate and Kenneth McRoberts, *Quebec: Social Change and Political Crisis* (Toronto: McClelland and Stewart, 1976).
32. See Seton-Watson, pp. 287–290.
33. Ibid., p. 289.
34. For a discussion of these applications, see Anne Daltrop, *Political Realities: Politics and the European Community* (Burnt Mill, England: Longman, 1982), pp. 129–132.
35. See Mansbach, pp. 254–270.
36. V. M. Chkhikvadze, ed., *The Soviet State and Law* (Moscow: Progress Publishers, 1969), p. 11.
37. See Friedrich Engels, *The Origin of the Family, Private Property and the State,* in any of the many editions of Marxist writings.
38. Quoted in Chkhikvadze, p. 12.
39. M. C. Howard and J. E. King, *The Political Economy of Marx* (London: Longman, 1975), p. 6.
40. Vladimir Ilych Ulyanov (Lenin), *The State and Revolution,* first published in Russian in 1917. Many translations are available to the interested student.
41. Chkhikvadze, p. 13.
42. See Clemens Dutt, trans., *Fundamentals of Marxism-Leninism: Manual,* 2d rev. ed. (Moscow: Foreign Languages Publishing House, 1963), pp. 125–134.
43. "The Communist Manifesto," in Robert C. Tucker, ed., *The Marx-Engels Reader,* 2d ed. (New York: Norton, 1978), p. 475.

44. Stanislaw G. Strumilin, *Man, Society and the Future* (New York: Crosscurrents Press, 1964), pp. 108–111.
45. Chkhikvadze, p. 23.
46. "The State and Revolution," in Robert C. Tucker, ed., *The Lenin Anthology* (New York: Norton, 1975), p. 331.
47. For an interesting discussion of the problem see Elliot R. Goodman, *The Soviet Design for a World State* (New York: Columbia University Press, 1957).
48. "The Dictatorship of the Proletariat," in Tucker, *The Lenin Anthology,* pp. 489–490.
49. Bruce Franklin, ed., *The Essential Stalin* (Garden City, N.Y.: Doubleday, 1972), p. 85.
50. Herbert Marcuse, *Soviet Marxism: A Critical Analysis* (New York: Vintage Books, 1961), pp. 85–86, quotes Stalin's political reports to the sixteenth and eighteenth Communist Party of the Soviet Union congresses.
51. Robert C. Tucker, *Stalin as Revolutionary: 1879–1929* (New York: Norton, 1973), pp. 317–329; "Foundations of Leninism," in Joseph Stalin, *Leninism* (New York: International Publishers, 1935[?]), pp. 11–101.
52. See Irving Zeitlin, *Marxism: A Re-Examination* (Princeton, N.J.: Van Nostrand, 1967); and Karl Kautsky, *The Dictatorship of the Proletariat* (Ann Arbor: University of Michigan Press, 1964).
53. See selected quotes from Marx, Engels, Lenin, and Romain Rolland in Henry B. Mayo, *Introduction to Marxist Theory* (New York: Oxford University Press, 1960), pp. 142–143; and Chkhikvadze, pp. 26–27.
54. Otto Ulč , *Politics in Czechoslovakia* (San Francisco: Freeman, 1974), pp. 14–18.
55. Jack C. Fisher, *Yugoslavia—A Multinational State* (San Francisco: Chandler, 1966), p. 118, figure 1.
56. Yung Wei, ed., *Communist China: A System—Functional Reader* (Columbus, Ohio: Merrill, 1972), pp. 48–55.
57. Wang How-Man, "People's Republic of China's Far Provinces," *National Geographic* 165 (March 1984): 283–333.
58. See Milovan Djilas, *The New Class: An Analysis of the Communist System* (New York: Praeger, 1957).
59. Deutsch, p. 112.
60. Seton-Watson, p. 323.
61. Ibid., p. 339.
62. *Time,* January 16, 1984, p. 26.
63. See J. D. B. Miller, *The Politics of the Third World* (New York: Oxford University Press, 1967), p. 6.
64. India under Nehru's daughter Indira Gandhi (in power, 1966–1977, 1980–1984), also comes under the same category.
65. Miller, p. 6.
66. Rupert Emerson, *From Empire to Nation* (Cambridge, Mass: Harvard University Press, 1967), p. 146.
67. *Time,* January 16, 1984, p. 29.

68. Robert L. Hardgrave, Jr., *India: Government and Politics in a Developing Nation,* 3d ed. (New York: Harcourt Brace Jovanovich, 1980), p. 98.

69. Robert C. Bone, *Action and Organization* (New York: Harper & Row, 1972), p. 258.

70. Miller, p. 4.

71. See James Lee Ray, *Global Politics,* 2d ed. (Boston, Houghton Mifflin, 1983), pp. 312–313.

CHAPTER 6

Government Structures in the First World

Government structures play a critical role in the authoritative allocation of values in a society and in the resolution of domestic political conflict. Specifically, legislative structures perform the function of rule making, executive structures the function of rule application, and courts the function of rule adjudication. Government structures consist of people interacting on the basis of patterned roles. For this reason they should be viewed as dynamic and changing rather than static or fixed. Government structures in the three worlds are the products of the political problems with which they are confronted and the dominant values of the political culture.

Government structures in the West reflect the influence of liberal political beliefs and an advanced level of development. They are highly specialized bureaucracies, which form complex governmental systems. Despite the similarity of Western political structures, factors unique to certain states have produced distinct variants.

In the area of executive–legislative relations, two basic varieties of governmental systems exist: presidential systems and parliamentary systems. Unitary and federal states display differing degrees of system centralization. Despite some notable exceptions, the majority of European states are unitary parliamentary systems, whereas the United States has a federal presidential system. Judicial structures and administrative agencies are also important parts of the governmental system. Two basic types of legal systems exist in the West, common law systems and code law systems. In several Western states courts possess the power of judicial review, which gives them added importance in the governmental system.

Government structures are the most visible institutions in the political process. In every state the daily lives of citizens are shaped by rules and regulations made and enforced by government structures. In the twentieth century, acts of repression undertaken by police and military agencies have demonstrated that in certain situations governments hold the power of life and death over the citizenry. Other government actions, including the development of social welfare programs, civil rights legislation, and regulations to improve working conditions, have revealed the power of governments to improve the quality of life. In every state, political activities revolve around governmental structures and the political actors who work within them. Chief executives such as presidents and prime ministers are viewed as both the moral and political leaders of society. In addition, on a daily basis legislatures are the focal point of a wide range of political activities ranging from lobbying by organized interest groups to public protests and demonstrations.

FUNCTIONS OF GOVERNMENT STRUCTURES

Government structures, political parties, and interest groups are political institutions that collectively make up the political system. In every society the political system performs the function of resolving conflicts that arise among groups in the general population. Political institutions participate in the process by which public policies or authoritative decisions are made concerning how the scarce values (resources) of society will be distributed to those groups. The values that groups seek in political competition include power, respect, rectitude (the ability to live according to one's own moral code), health, wealth, education, rights, privileges, benefits, and opportunities.[1] The American political scientist David Easton has called the political process "the authoritative allocation of values in a society."[2] The policies or decisions made by political institutions are authoritative in that they are imposed on the citizenry and are backed by the full force of the law and the possible use of force. Many political thinkers have argued that the modern state rests on two basic principles: (1) that citizens have the obligation of obedience to the decisions made by legally constituted political structures, and (2) that government structures have a monopoly over the legitimate use of force in the society—that government alone has the legal right to use force against citizens of the state. No political system could exist for any length of time without political institutions and the functions they perform. Resolving conflict among group members is an absolute prerequisite to the continuation of the political unit.

The tasks performed by political institutions can best be understood through reference to the model of the political process offered by David Easton (see Figure 6.1). The population of every state consists of groups that have distinct characteristics setting them off from the rest of the population.

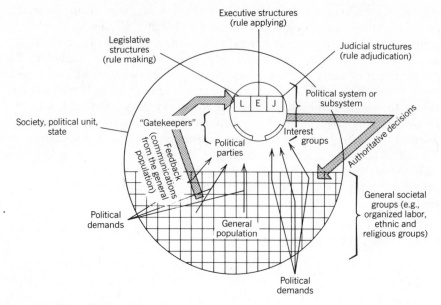

Figure 6.1. The political system and society.

These groups, which we call general societal groups, include such categories as men, women, the elderly, individual ethnic and racial groups, unionized labor, nonunionized labor, big business, small business, and so on. Conflict in society develops from the fact that each of these general societal groups constantly demands increased rights, privileges, benefits, and opportunities. In addition, the special characteristics of certain general societal groups may lead to direct conflict. For example, in the United States minority groups have demanded the establishment of quotas in hiring and education as a way of attaining greater opportunity in employment. These demands have been resisted by labor unions that represent the interests of nonminority members and by students who are not members of minority groups on the grounds that quotas are discriminatory. The result has been several political and legal conflicts. One example is the heralded Bakke case in which a white student challenged a university admissions policy reserving a certain number of spaces for minority applicants. At any given time the number of conflicting demands in society will be so large as to be almost incalculable. However, if the political unit is to survive, the most serious conflicts, those with the greatest potential for disruption or violence, must be identified and resolved. Resolution of a political conflict consists of the development of a law or public policy stating which groups have won or lost values in an individual instance, as well as the enforcement of the law or policy.

In order to resolve conflicts, government institutions, political parties and interest groups perform different functions. Political parties and interest groups indentify or select those conflicts that require attention. David Easton calls political parties and interest groups the "gate keepers" to the political system because if they do not identify a particular demand or political conflict as important and communicate its importance to the government structures, it will usually be ignored. Political parties communicate the importance of political demands by combining a number of these demands into party platforms or programs, whereas interest groups lobby or communicate directly with government structures. (More will be said about political parties and interest groups in Chapters 8 and 9.) Once a political demand or conflict has been selected for resolution, government structures perform three functions: rule making, rule application, and rule adjudication. Rule making is carried out by the legislative structures of the state which develop laws that are statements concerning the distribution of rights, privileges, benefits, and opportunities. Rule application is undertaken by the executive structure of the state. Executive structures such as police and regulatory agencies perform the function of applying and enforcing laws. Rule adjudication or interpretation is the function of judicial structures (courts and tribunals) that must decide the precise meaning of the law in a particular circumstance or which law applies to a given problem. The three functions of rule making, rule application, and rule adjudication are critically important in every society, and it is the performance of these functions that gives government structures a central role in the political process.

GOVERNMENT STRUCTURES: THEIR NUMBER AND NATURE

In order to understand the way government structures actually function in the three political worlds, two important qualifications must be made to our model of the political process. First, although the functions of government consist of three separate actions—legislative, executive, and judicial—they are not necessarily performed by separate government structures. In the United States people are accustomed to a legal and formal threefold separation of government functions, but in some political systems a lesser number of government structures may perform all three functions. For example, in a primitive political system such as a tribe a single political actor, the chief, may function simultaneously as a legislator, executive, and judge. In several postindustrial states of Western Europe, the legislative and executive powers are fused or combined in such a way that the members of the executive branch perform the tasks of both rule making and rule application. In every society the political structures must perform the legislative, executive, and judicial functions, but these functions need not be performed by separate political structures. In many political systems the number of political structures and the functions of each are specified in legal documents called constitutions. Constitutions have been called "basic" or "first" laws because they establish the institutional framework for the resolution of conflict in society. Constitutions tell the members of a society how to engage in political conflict with one another and identify the institutions that will decide which groups win and which groups lose.

The second qualification concerns the nature of political structures. It is important that we view government structures as dynamic and changing rather than as static and fixed. In discussing governments we have chosen to use the word "structures" rather than the older term "institutions" because "structure" correctly conveys the understanding that government bodies are composed of people interacting on the basis of patterned or structured roles. The U.S. House of Representatives has functioned for nearly 200 years in the American political process in much the same way because successive generations of representatives have accepted certain role expectations as first term legislators, committee chairpersons, or Speaker of the House. It has been their behavior that has given consistency and structure to the House. However, as political actors, people can refuse to accept roles and can seek to create new and expanded ones. There is little doubt that today younger representatives feel less compelled to conform to the wishes of the Speaker of the House than did their predecessors, and after the war in Vietnam most representatives sought an expanded role at the expense of the president in the foreign policy-making process. These are but two examples of the fact that government structures are constantly subject to the process of change which may be accelerated by shifts in the pattern of beliefs in the society, negative feedback (communication) from the general population, and human ambition.

In considering the human factor it is also important to keep in mind that government structures are themselves arenas of conflict and not merely the "machinery of government" as described in older books on the subject. Although the structures of government collectively perform the three functions necessary to resolve conflict, the political actors within the various legislative, executive, and judicial structures are constantly in competition to increase their power over the decision-making process. Power has been defined by Robert Dahl as "the capacity to change the probability of outcome," and by Harold Lasswell as "the ability to make decisions about major rewards and deprivations." Power has also been used more or less interchangeably with such terms as influence, coercion, compulsion, control, force, inducement, and persuasion.[3] Although social scientists have been unable to agree on a single definition of power, it is generally agreed that the struggle for power goes on both within government structures and among government structures. Most schemes for classifying political systems are based on the distribution of power within the various government structures, and the political world contains examples of dominance by legislatures, executives, and even political parties.

GOVERNMENT STRUCTURES IN THREE POLITICAL WORLDS

Government structures are the product of the two main factors of political life, the level of development and the element of human choice. Political structures in the Western and Communist Worlds are large-scale, highly specialized bureaucracies that reflect advanced industrial and postindustrial development. Government structures develop in response to political problems, and the states of the West have encountered and overcome to some extent the four great problems of political development: state-building, nation-building, the demand for distribution, and the demand for participation (see Chapter 2). The industrialized states of the Communist World have also encountered the four problems, but their political beliefs cause them to respond to the last two problems in different and limited ways. Both the states of the West and the industrialized Communist states contain large-scale military, police, and regulatory agencies that were developed in response to the four problems. The differences between Western and Communist structures are the result of the commitment to the rival political beliefs of liberalism and Marxism–Leninism. Western government structures reflect a concern for popular control and the need to confine and limit government power. Communist political systems are examples of party dominance by which members of the Communist party attempt to control the direction and development of society.

Political structures in the Third World tend to be less specialized and fewer in number. Many of these states have yet to overcome the four problems of development, and education and bureaucratic expertise are less available in the Third World. Like Third World political beliefs, the political structures have been borrowed from the Western and Communist Worlds and are sometimes combinations of both. In some states present political structures are based on traditional and precolonial institutions.

WESTERN GOVERNMENT STRUCTURES

Western government structures are products of three factors: (1) liberal political beliefs, (2) an advanced level of development, and (3) the particular historical experiences of the individual Western states. Beginning in the seventeenth century modern liberal thinkers sought to protect individual freedom by limiting the power of government and making government institutions responsible to the electorate. This effort produced a number of specific devices and procedures that have shaped the government process in the states of the West: separation of powers, cabinet responsibility to the legislature, bicameral legislatures, independent judges, judicial review, federalism, and frequent elections. One of the most important devices was the principle of separation of powers advocated by the French liberal, the Baron de Montesquieu, and the English theorist, John Locke. Under the separation of powers scheme the legislative, executive, and judicial powers are separate and independent, creating a system of checks and balances in which the power of one part of the government counters the power of the other parts. Karl Deutsch points out that liberal principles helped to create a conception of government legitimacy that required that all government decisions be made through an open, orderly, and continuous process of debate.[4] Such a deliberative process is at the heart of democratic politics, and it is this process that is detailed in the constitutions of the various Western states.

Government structures have also been influenced by the advanced level of development of Western society. Like political structures in the industrial states of the Communist World, government structures in the West are highly specialized bureaucracies. The growth in the size and complexity of government is most apparent in the executive agencies (ministries, departments, and regulatory agencies) that have been developed to implement the many programs of the welfare state. The ranks of the permanent civil servants who staff these administrative agencies have come to include an increasing number of highly trained "experts" possessing advanced technical and scientific knowledge. Since World War II the role of civil servants in the policy-making process has increased in all of the states of the West, and the presence of experts within the civil service has contributed to both the bureaucratic style of Western politics and to the development of political issues based on scientific knowledge (environmental issues, quality-of-life issues, and so on).

Although liberal political beliefs and a high level of societal development have determined the general nature of government institutions in the West, the unique historical experiences of several states have also had an important effect in shaping the governmental process. The presence of a large and politically well-organized French language group in Canada led to the development of a federal system (a system of dual jurisdictions, one at the national level and one at the subnational or provincial level) in which the Canadian provinces exercise considerable power over public policy. Both the German Federal Republic and France experienced prolonged periods of governmental immobility during the interwar period which resulted from excessive competition between political parties. In the German Weimar

Republic (1919–1933) this immobility contributed to the rise of Adolf Hitler and Nazism. In France it was a major factor in the inability of successive French governments to deal effectively with the growing external threat posed by the Nazis. Given the catastrophic effects of this immobility, the German Basic Law of 1949 (the German Constitution) included several devices making it more difficult for a government in power to be defeated on a vote of no confidence in the legislature, and in 1958 the Constitution of the French Fifth Republic included provisions for a strong president who could assume extraordinary powers during periods of crisis. As a result of another historical experience, defeat in World Ward II, the liberal beliefs that form the foundations of the present constitutions in the German Federal Republic and Japan were brought to those states by Anglo-American occupation forces.

Government Systems

In every country individual political structures such as courts and legislatures are part of the government system. The governmental system, like any system, is composed of parts that are related to one another in a patterned way and perform particular functions. The system performs two functions at the heart of the process by which public policies are made. First, it establishes a process of deliberation by establishing the stages of debate that must occur before a public policy can be developed. For example, in the U.S. governmental system, a bill must pass both houses of the legislature and be signed by the president before it becomes a law. After passage, a law may also be subject to judicial review by the courts to assure that it is consistent with the Constitution. Each of these stages provides an opportunity for interest groups and other concerned parties to affect the content of the bill. Second, the system also establishes a system of power in which each of the governmental structures is assigned a varying degree of authority over the decision-making process. The power possessed by identical political structures may vary from one system to the next. In the U.S. political system, the upper house of the legislature, the Senate, can initiate bills (except for money-making bills) and has co-equal power with the lower house; in Great Britain the upper house of the legislature, the House of Lords, has the power only to delay passage of a bill passed by the lower house. In this discussion primary emphasis will be on the formal power relationship among government structures as stipulated in constitutions and related documents. However, in some cases it will also be necessary to discuss the informal factors that affect the distribution of power among governmental structures, including informal political practices and the political party system.[5] The variety of governmental systems in the West precludes the consideration of all of the arrangements, but the United States, Canada, Great Britain, the German Federal Republic, Italy, and Sweden are used as examples of the major types of systems.

Executive–Legislative Relations: Presidential and Parliamentary Systems

In the area of executive–legislative relations two basic arrangements exist in the West, *parliamentarianism* and *presidentialism*. In the United States, which is a presidential system, a separation of powers exists between the executive and legislative branches. Canada and most of the states of Western Europe have parliamentary systems in which a fusion occurs between the executive and the legislature. The present governmental system of France, established under the Constitution of the Fifth Republic, is a mixed system combining elements of both parliamentarianism and presidentialism. Because this discussion is meant to be an introduction to the governmental systems of the West, consideration of executive–legislative relations in France will be undertaken separately.

The U.S. Presidential System. The U.S. system is based on separation of powers. Executive power is vested in the president, legislative power in the Congress, and primary judicial power in the federal court system at the pinnacle of which is the Supreme Court. The president is independently elected for a period of four years and is limited to two terms in office. Under the terms of the U.S. Constitution the president is indirectly elected by an electoral college composed of electors from each state equal to the sum total of representatives and senators. In actual practice, however, the electoral college reflects the popular vote and has rarely acted to thwart the will of the majority. The president appoints all officials of the executive branch subject to the consent of the Senate. The Congress is a bicameral legislature composed of the House of Representatives and the Senate. The House of Representatives, the lower house, consists of 435 members who represent the population of each state based on a ratio of one representative for approximately 500,000 inhabitants.[6] The Senate, the upper house, consists of 100 members and provides territorial representation with each state receiving two senators. The House and the Senate are roughly equal in legislative power, and most legislation can be initiated by either body. Judges of the Supreme Court as well as of lower federal courts have greater power in the American political system than in most other Western states where their functions are usually narrow and circumscribed.[7] (Judicial power in the United States will be discussed later.)

A system of checks and balances exists because each of the branches has some powers in the areas of the other two. This system has been summarized by Herbert Levine:

> Because of checks and balances, Congress has some executive power (such as the power of the Senate to confirm appointments by the President) and some judicial power (such as the power to create new courts and to enlarge the size of the Supreme Court membership). The President has legislative power (such as the power to veto bills passed by Congress) and judicial power (such as the power to nominate justices to the court). The court has legislative power (the power to declare a statute unconstitutional) and executive power (the power to administer court rulings). By establishing a system of checks and balances, the Founding Fathers deliberately made government cumbersome.[8]

The existence of separate branches creates a fragmentation of power in both the deliberative and decision-making processes. For example, in order for a bill to become a law it must pass both houses of Congress and be signed into law by the president. This is not easily accomplished as there are opportunities for a minority to defeat the bill at every stage in the process. The real work of both houses of Congress is carried out by committees that function as "little legislatures." In order for a bill to reach the floor of either house for a vote by the full membership, it must first receive approval from the relevant committee or committees. There are 20 standing committees in the House, each having approximately 30 members, and 16 standing committees in the Senate with between 7 and 27 members. Committee chairpersons, selected primarily on the basis of seniority, have inordinate power over the work of the committees, and the opposition of a chairperson is usually enough to prevent further consideration of a bill. A further stumbling block to legislation may occur if a bill passes the Senate and the House in a different form. In such cases a compromise version must be worked out in a joint conference committee and it then must be resubmitted to both houses for final approval before the bill can be sent to the president. The president's signature is needed before a bill can become law, but the president may also refuse to sign it, an action known as a *veto*. A presidential veto can be overridden by a two-thirds majority of both houses of Congress.

Advocates of the American presidential system of government argue that it is democratic because it permits every interested group an opportunity to influence the content of legislation. The main problem confronting interest groups is not how to gain access to the decision-making process, but at which point in the process (individual committees, committee chairperson, the House of Representatives, the Senate, or the president) to direct their lobbying efforts. As will be discussed shortly, it is even possible for interest groups to seek to have an existing law declared invalid by the judicial branch. Because representatives are elected by local constituencies (the president and the vice-president are the only nationally elected officials), they are responsive to interest group pressure from within their congressional districts. Critics of the separation of powers maintain that the collective political authority in the American government is too weak to permit it to make effective political decisions. Richard Rose, a British political scientist, argues that the American political system is not a government but a system of subgovernments having no single locus of authority, no hierarchical relationship between its parts, and no stable pattern of power.[9] In order for a major program of legislation to be enacted, it is necessary for presidents to "lasso" and "create" government by influencing the various branches and parts of the system, as well as the interest groups, to accept their direction. As Rose points out, recent American presidents have found this task generally difficult. The task of the president is especially difficult when one or both of the houses of Congress are controlled by the opposition party. When the president's party controls both houses of Congress, party membership provides a linkage between the members of the legislative and executive branches. In this way, an informal power factor, the party system, influences the performance of the government structures.

Parliamentary Systems: Canada and Western Europe. Canada and most states of Western Europe are parliamentary systems. A fusion of power exists between the legislature and the executive in which the executive is not independently elected as in a presidential system, but instead is elected by the members of the majority party or parties in the legislature. In Britain and Canada the head of government is called the prime minister; in Italy and Sweden the premier; and in Germany the chancellor. With the exception of Sweden, the states under discussion have bicameral legislatures, and the chief of government is elected by the members of the lower house. In Britain and Canada the lower house is the House of Commons, in Italy the Chamber of Deputies, and in Germany the *Bundestag*. The unicameral legislature of Sweden is the *Riksdag*. In multiparty systems it is common for the head of government to require the support of members of several political parties (a coalition government) in order to gain the needed majority in the legislature. Once elected the head of government selects the members of the *cabinet*, the group of top ministers who direct the various departments (ministries) of the government bureaucracy. Ministers not only administer their departments but also take responsibility for the development of policies within the scope of their ministries.

At the heart of the parliamentary system is the concept of responsible government, cabinet responsibility to the legislature. The prime minister and the cabinet are accountable to the full house of the legislature for all their

Ottawa, Canada—the Canadian House of Commons votes concerning the Constitution.

political and administrative actions. The cabinet serves only as long as it has the confidence (majority support) of the legislature or until a general election produces a new majority in the lower house. General elections for the lower house must be held within five years in Britain, Canada, Italy, and within three years in Sweden. A vote of "no confidence" by a majority of the legislature can terminate a government at any time. One of the major questions confronting parliamentary systems is the issue of what constitutes a vote of no confidence. In Britain in the 1960s the "100 per cent" rule was advanced by some observers of British government.[10] According to this rule, every defeat for a government is a matter of confidence regardless of the nature of the issue being voted on. If a government suffers a defeat, it must seek to reverse it in a subsequent vote or else seek a formal vote of confidence on the basis of the specific issue on which it has already been defeated, or resign. In actual practice, British parliamentary behavior has never conformed to this rule, and British governments in the 1970s suffered several defeats on individual pieces of legislation but did not resign. The prevailing conception of no confidence in Britain today is that it must come on a formal vote requested by the opposition or as a result of a defeat on a major bill. Because of strong party discipline, such votes have rarely occurred in this century, although the minority government of Prime Minister James Callaghan was defeated on a confidence vote in 1979. Other systems have also operationalized the concept of confidence in ways which make it difficult to defeat the government. Under the German Constitution (the Basic Law of 1949), the chancellor and his cabinet can only be defeated if the vote of no confidence has been on an opposition motion that names a new chancellor and passes by a majority vote.[11] Such a vote, sometimes called a "constructive vote of no confidence," has occurred only once since the creation of the German Federal Republic when Helmut Kohl defeated and replaced Helmut Schmidt as chancellor in 1982. The Constitution of the French Fifth Republic (established in 1958) places limits on the number of votes of confidence that can be held in a single session of the legislature and stipulates that such a vote must be supported by an absolute majority of the members (abstentions count for the government).

Students of the British parliamentary system have long noted that it has two elements: an initiating, directing, energizing element—the cabinet; and a checking, criticizing element—Parliament (the legislature).[12] The same observation can be made of the other parliamentary systems of Western Europe. The prime ministers and the cabinets collectively decide the major pieces of legislation that will be introduced, and most of the work of the legislature is devoted to the consideration and discussion of the programs and actions of the government. The dominant role of the cabinet develops from the fact that it is the steering committee of the legislature, that its members are ministers (heads of departments), and that its members are leaders of the majority party. If the other members of the majority party (those not in the cabinet) vote to bring down the government and for dissolution of the legislature, they are voting against their own seats in Parliament which they may lose in the new election.

No discussion of the parliamentary systems of Western Europe would be complete without reference to the party systems. Various students of parliamentarianism have referred to political parties as the "cement" that holds the cabinet and the Parliament together. Strict party discipline and party line voting in the legislature are far more common in Western Europe than in the United States. Until the 1970s, party line voting was almost total in Great Britain, producing a system of party government. Successive governments of both major parties (Labour and Conservative) were able to implement their entire legislative programs into law with virtual 100% support of the party's members in the House of Commons. Since the 1970s, cross-voting (voting with the opposition) has been on the increase, especially among younger members of Parliament, but with the exception of one case, it has not been widespread enough to threaten the tenure of any government. Legislators in Canada, Italy, Sweden, and Germany also desire to keep their leaders in power, and there is a high degree of party cohesion in these systems as well. Party line voting is the norm in the legislatures of all of these states, and governments do not usually have to be concerned that they will be defeated on a vote of no confidence because of defections within their own party. However, some votes of no confidence have occurred. As mentioned, earlier in Germany the coalition government of Helmut Schmidt (Social Democratic party and Free Democratic party) was terminated on a vote of no confidence in 1982. Numerous Italian coalition governments (Christian Democratic party and its allies) have been similarly defeated. These votes of no confidence resulted from interparty conflicts (conflicts between two parties within the same coalition) rather than from intraparty conflicts (conflicts involving members of the same party).[13]

France: A Mixed System. The current French system of government was established by the Constitution of the Fifth Republic of 1958. It departed from the parliamentary model of states like Italy and Germany in two respects: (1) it imposes a strong president above the parliamentary system with powers sufficient to make the office the center of political power, and (2) it strengthens the role of the prime minister and the cabinet in the law-making process and weakens the role of the legislature. Both developments were deliberately undertaken by the founders of the Fifth Republic to overcome the problem of parliamentary instability that had plagued France in the periods of both the Third Republic (1870–1940) and the Fourth Republic (1946–1958). Before the Fifth Republic the fragmented party system had required the formation of coalition governments composed of several parties. Such governments often dissolved in times of crisis when one or more of the parties left the coalition and voted in the legislature against the cabinet (government). Even when votes of no confidence did not occur, cabinets were reluctant to undertake strong leadership or decisive actions in fear of alienating one of the coalition members. The current Constitution strengthens the role of the prime minister and the cabinet and does much to insulate them from the control of the National Assembly, the lower house of the French legislature. In the Fifth Republic the prime minister is chosen by the president and not by parliament. The number of votes of no confidence against the government is limited by the requirement that such motions must be signed by one-tenth of the National Assembly and receive the support of an absolute majority of the membership (not just a majority of those present and actually voting). If the censure (no confidence) measure fails, those members who signed it may not sign another during that

French President Francois Mitterrand accompanies Crown Prince Abdullah of Saudi Arabia from the Elysee Palace in January, 1985.

session. The constitution also restricts the law making power of Parliament to certain matters defined in the Constitution and allows the cabinet to legislate in all other matters by simple decree. In addition, through one of the most controversial constitutional measures, the prime minister can declare that a pending bill is a matter of confidence in the government, in which case the bill passes without a vote in the legislature unless the opposition can meet the stringent requirements for a censure vote (the signatures of one-tenth of the membership plus an absolute majority vote). Roy Macridis has noted that in the Fifth Republic "assembly government" has been replaced by a government dominated by the prime minister and the cabinet.[14]

The strong powers given to the president of the Fifth Republic were intended to place the office above parliamentary politics and to allow the president to assume a leadership position vis-a-vis the cabinet and the legislature. In addition to the power to appoint the prime minister, the president presides over cabinet meetings and is able to control discussion within the government. The president can also force the National Assembly to reconsider legislation it has passed and dissolve it if faced with a hostile majority.[15] Such an action, however, can be undertaken only once a year and requires prior consultation with the prime minister. Articles 11 and 16 of the French Constitution provide the presidency with its most sweeping powers. Article 11 permits the president to submit pending bills directly to the electorate through a national referendum, thus bypassing the normal legislative process. Most important, Article 16 grants the president the right to declare a state of emergency or national crisis and rule by presidential decree for a period up to six months. During such a crisis the Constitutional Council* must be consulted and the National Assembly must remain in session, but the normal legislative process is suspended. In the history of the Fifth Republic, Article 16 has been invoked only once—in 1961—by Charles de Gaulle during the Algerian crisis. The Constitution of the Fifth Republic has made the president a national mediator of political disputes, and in this respect, the current French system more nearly resembles a presidential system than a parliamentary one.

Administrative Agencies: Ministries and Departments

In every political system, administrative agencies, ministries, and departments exist to carry out the laws made by the legislasture. The traditional conception of these agencies is that they are staffed by politically neutral civil servants and play only a minor role in the political process. Recent studies of public policy making in the United States and Western Europe, however, have shown that civil servants play an active role in the political process. Although their role is far less significant than that of the elected officials, the importance of civil servants comes from two factors: (1) the general nature of most laws, and (2) the degree of knowledge and expertise possessed by upper-level civil servants. Most laws passed by legislatures are general framework laws. Administrative agencies have considerable discretion in the manner in which laws are implemented. Individual pieces of legislation also empower administrative agencies to regulate important areas of life such as commerce, labor relations, transportation, and the licensing of professionals. In these areas as well, administrative agencies have considerable latitude in the timing, style, and strictness of enforcement. The influence and size of government agencies have also increased as a result of their involvement in the many social welfare programs that have been developed in the West. Such programs as unemployment compensation, housing, retirement pensions, aid to families, national health services, general welfare, and aid to the arts are administered and delivered to the

*The Council consists of three members chosen by the president of the Republic, three by the president of the Senate, and three by the president of the National Assembly. Former presidents of France are also members.

public by employees of the civil service. Involvement in such programs has led to a steady increase in the size of government ministries. Britain presently has 547,000 nonindustrial civil servants (those outside of nationalized industries),[16] France approximately 1 million (including teachers and manual workers), and the United States 3 million. By the end of the 1970s, 1 out of every 8 Germans was employed by the government, although only about 20,000 worked in federal (national) ministries.[17]

Civil servants also have a role in the process by which laws and executive policies are made. In each of the Western states, high-level civil servants possess experience and knowledge about the areas controlled by their ministries, skills that are needed by elected officials who are often inexperienced generalists. In parliamentary systems, ministers come into daily contact with career civil servants in their ministries who recommend to them possible areas of future legislation. These recommendations are then taken to the prime minister and the rest of the cabinet for consideration. Civil servants also directly propose legislation during testimony before legislative committees. The number of high-level civil servants involved in the development stage of policy making may number from a few hundred to a few thousand. They correspond to the old administrative class in the British civil service. They are hired and promoted on the basis of competitive examinations and other professional assessments, and are all career employees. Despite this merit system of hiring, however, political professionals are not value-free in their recommendations to elected officials. This fact has led some observers of the U.S. political system to call the federal bureaucracy the "fourth branch of government."

Judicial Structures

In every political system courts perform three basic functions: interpreting the law (determining its meanings), applying the law in individual cases, and settling disputes between individuals and groups. In some political systems judicial structures perform additional tasks and may take on greater importance within the governmental system. The role of judicial structures is determined by the general legal culture that prevails within the political system. The *legal culture* is the set of attitudes and values about law, including ideas about the role of law in the society, the way the law should be applied, the manner in which legal professionals should be trained, and when it is appropriate to refer conflicts to legal institutions.[18] The legal culture of the United States provides a greater role for the courts than is the case in Europe, and this role is further strengthened by certain judicial practices that originated early in the country's history. American law is derived from the British system of common law in which precedents based on long-standing customs and previous court decisions are applied by judges. Judges in common law systems assume special importance because in cases for which past precedents do not exist, their decisions create precedents that will be applied in future cases. In such cases judges actually perform the legislative function of establishing law in addition to the judicial function of interpreting the law. Because of the importance of such court decisions, U.S. judges have always been appointed with political considerations in mind. Federal (national) judges are appointed by the president with the consent of the Senate and serve for the "tenure of good behavior." As a work on the subject has recently noted, such judges are appointed because of their "attachment to particular economic, social, political, and religious values and their full knowledge of the important political implications of judicial decisions."[19]

An important role for the judiciary in the United States was established early in the country's history. The U.S. Constitution established only one federal court, a Supreme Court of five judges, but authorized Congress to establish inferior courts and to determine the size of all federal courts.[20] Congress subsequently established district courts and courts of appeal beneath the Supreme Court. The Supreme Court has also been increased from five judges to the present nine. Most important, the power of *judicial review* was recognized in giving the courts the right to decide whether laws and acts are valid under the Constitution. The power of judicial review was not stated in the Constitution but was established as an interpretation of the Constitution in the famous case of *Marbury* v. *Madison* (1803). In this case the Supreme Court declared an act of Congress unconstitutional for the first time, and when this action of the Supreme Court went unchallenged by the other branches, the precedent of judicial review was established.

The British judicial system is also a common law system, and, like the United States, judges are appointed for the term of good behavior. A strong tradition of independence exists within the British judiciary and judges enjoy considerable prestige. Unlike U.S. courts, British courts do not claim the power of judicial review, and no court can declare an act of Parliament unconstitutional. British courts, however, decide whether an act of government is *ultra vires* (outside the statutory powers granted to it under a specific law). If the courts find that a government has exceeded its authority, it can order the government to desist. Two separate judicial hierarchies exist, one civil and the other criminal. The upper house of the legislature, the House of Lords, serves as the final court of appeal for both criminal and civil cases. Appeals to the House of Lords are handled by the Law Lords, a group of legally trained professionals within its membership, but appeals are not common and all appeals in Britain require the permission of the higher court.

The role of the judiciary is more narrow and circumscribed in Germany,

British jurists outside Old Bailey court house, London.

Italy, France, and Sweden. In these states, systems of code law, called the continental European system, rather than common law, prevail. In Germany, Sweden, and Italy the codes are derived from the Roman law tradition, and in France they are based on the Napoleonic Code (which was in turn derived from Roman Law). In these legal systems, laws have been codified into complex categories and subcategories. The codes are very specific and courts have limited discretion in applying them.[21] Swedish law also uses some elements of common law.[22] In these countries judges are civil servants, employees of the ministries of justice, and even justices at the highest levels are appointed by the ministry. Although the court systems are not identical in every detail, they consist of two hierarchies, one criminal and civil, and one administrative. Each is headed by a separate appellate court. Swedish courts, like those of Britain, lack the power of judicial review. Italy, France, and Germany currently do have constitutional courts that have the theoretical power of judicial review, but this power is much less important than that of the Supreme Court of the United States.

Territorial Dimension of Government: Federalism

So far we have discussed the separation or fusion of powers within the national governments of several Western states. In the United States,

Canada, the German Federal Republic, Austria, and Switzerland there is also a division of powers between the national government and the governments of various subunits. These countries are *federal systems* in which dual jurisdictions and dual systems of government exist. William Riker has identified three conditions that prevail in all federal systems: (1) two levels of government exist for the same land and people, (2) each level has at least one area of action in which it is autonomous, and (3) there is some guarantee (even merely a statement in the constitution) of the autonomy of each government in its own sphere.[23] In a federal system certain powers are assigned to the legislature of the national government (also called the central government) and certain other powers to the legislatures of the subunits. In the federal states of the West, the national governments have jurisdiction over such areas as defense, the conduct of foreign affairs, the coining of money, commerce, and communications; whereas the subunits have power over education, municipal governments, and police. Concurrent powers may also exist in which both the national government and the subunits have jurisdiction. The division of powers is set down in a written constitution and a constitutional court exists to settle disputes between the two levels of government. In the United States the subunits are called states (of which there are 50), in Germany *Länder* (10), in Austria also *Länder* (9), in Canada provinces (10), and in Switzerland cantons (26). Countries in which the national government retains full jurisdiction are called *unitary systems*. These systems may have regional and local governments, but they are merely administrative units that may be reorganized or terminated at any time by the national government. Subunits such as states and cantons in federal systems are legally recognized, fixed units and cannot be changed except through the constitutional amendment process. Great Britain, Sweden, Italy, France, and most states of Western Europe are unitary systems.

Federal systems are usually the result of historical circumstances that created special needs among segments of the population. Federalism was necessitated in Canada by the existence of the French-Canadian community, which accounted for about one-third of the population at the time the first federal constitution was written in 1867 (the British North America Act). French-Canadians feared that their language rights might be violated by a national government controlled by English-speaking Canadians. Under the Canadian Constitution the provinces have control over such areas as education and the licensing of professionals, which has enabled the government of the Province of Quebec to advance the interests of French-speaking groups in that province. The federal arrangement in the German Federal Republic was both a reaction to the extreme centralization of power during the Nazi period and a recognition of the fact that the old German states (now *Länder*) had unique interests and traditions that they wished to protect. In the United States, a federal system of government was necessary in 1787 to overcome the fear of many that the national government might deny citizens their rights and infringe upon their liberty the way the British had. In the United States, enumerated powers (those explicitly listed in the Constitution) are assigned to the national government, whereas all other, residual powers remain with the states. In Canada the reverse is true; the provinces have the enumerated powers and the central government retains the residual ones.

The existence of two levels of government within a state creates the potential for both federal–state cooperation and federal–state conflict. It also alters the process by which public policies are made and implemented because consultation between the two levels is often required. In the United States and Germany it is common for the national government to establish general guidelines for social programs but to leave the details and actual administration to the states and *Länder*. In most cases federal–state relations are cooperative in nature, but the existence of two levels of government also produces jurisdictional disputes, disagreements over the sharing of tax revenues, and status conflicts between federal and state governmental elites.

NOTES

1. Karl Deutsch, *Politics and Government: How People Decide Their Fate* (Boston: Houghton Mifflin, 1980), pp. 32–39.
2. David Easton, *The Political System* (New York: Knopf, 1953), p. 129.
3. Deutsch, p. 27.
4. Ibid., p. 174.
5. David Wood, *Power and Policy in Western European Democracies*, 2nd ed. (New York: Wiley, 1982), p. 102.
6. Deutsch, p. 276.
7. Alex N. Dragnich, John T. Dorsey, Jr., and Taketsugu Tsurutani, *Politics and Government: A Brief Introduction* (Chatham, N.J.: Chatham House, 1982), pp. 38–39.
8. Herbert M. Levine, *Political Issues Debated: An Introduction to Politics* (Englewood Cliffs, N.J.: Prentice-Hall, 1982), p. 228.
9. Richard Rose and Ezra N. Suleiman, eds., *Presidents and Prime Ministers* (Washington, D.C.: American Enterprise Institute for Public Policy Research, 1981), pp. 285–299.
10. Samuel H. Beer, *Britain Against Itself: The Political Contradictions of Collectivism* (New York: Norton, 1982), p. 187.
11. Wood, p. 108.
12. Beer, p. 191.
13. For a discussion of coalition governments see Eric Brown and John Dreijimanis, eds., *Government Coalitions in Western Democracies* (New York: Longman, 1982); and Michael Roskin, *Other Governments of Europe: Sweden, Spain, Italy, Yugoslavia, and East Germany* (Englewood Cliffs, N.J.: Prentice-Hall, 1977).

14. Roy C. Macridis, ed., *Modern Political Systems: Europe*, 5th ed. (Englewood Cliffs, N.J.: Prentice-Hall, 1983), p. 109.

15. David F. Roth and Frank L. Wilson, *The Comparative Study of Politics*, 2d ed. (Englewood Cliffs, N.J.: Prentice-Hall, 1980), p. 116.

16. Macridis, p. 62.

17. David P. Conradt, *The German Polity* (New York: Longman, 1978), p. 165.

18. For an excellent introduction to the concept of a legal culture, see Henry W. Ehrmann, *Comparative Legal Cultures* (Englewood Cliffs, N.J.: Prentice-Hall, 1976), pp. 6–11.

19. Dragnich et al., p. 39.

20. Ibid., p. 39.

21. Wood, p. 153.

22. M. Donald Hancock, *Sweden: The Politics of Postindustrial Change* (Hinsdale, Ill.: Dryden Press, 1972), p. 230.

23. William H. Riker, *Federalism: Origin, Operation, Significance* (Boston: Little, Brown, 1964), p. 11.

CHAPTER 7

Government Structures in the Second and Third Worlds

Western governments closely follow the constitutions and laws of their particular states. That is not the case in the Second and Third World states. Although the Communist states have extensive governmental systems, most important policy decisions are made within the organs of the Communist party, not within the branches of the government.

Lenin's ideas of the primacy of the Communist party are clearly articulated in the rules of the Communist party of the Soviet Union as well as in the Soviet Constitution. The principal structures making up the Soviet governmental system at the national level are three: (1) the Supreme Soviet, (2) the Presidium, and (3) the Council of Ministers. These are supplemented by a system of elective legislative bodies called soviets (councils), which exist at all administrative levels. The Communist party, however, holds the primary position in the public policy process at all levels. Most Communist party states have governmental structures similar to those of the Soviet Union.

In a majority of Third World states power is concentrated in the executive. These executives are of three types: (1) military leaders, (2) traditional monarchs, and (3) executives in one-party civilian governments. Another important feature of Third World governments is that they are predominantly authoritarian in nature. The most common form of authoritarian government in the Third World is military government. In some Latin American countries, however, democracy is reemerging. Military rule also is being challenged in some countries in Africa, Asia, and the Middle East. Traditional monarchies, also authoritarian in nature, exist in a few countries in Africa, Asia, and the Middle East. Three major examples of one-party civilian government are India, Mexico, and Tanzania. Tanzania, a one-party state since 1965, does not permit other parties. India and Mexico do permit other parties, but these parties are weak and divided.

In the preceding chapter we discussed the general theory of government and in particular examined First World government structures. In this chapter we consider governments that are probably less familiar to students. Western governments closely follow the constitutions and laws of their particular states. An analysis based on structures and functions is thus a useful tool for understanding these governments. The governments of Second and Third World states are not, however, so easily understood. The examination of the formal government structures of Second World states would merely indicate to the student the shape of the administrative apparatus of the state without revealing the real source of power, which is the Communist party.

> It is . . . a major distinguishing trait of Communist societies that the party, ceasing to be a mere party of the Western sense, keeps to itself major decision-making and policy direction. It does not organize and staff a government in the framework of which policy is consulted and decided, as in Western political systems, but sets itself up as a supreme authority, a sort of super-government for which the official state serves as administrative agency.[1]

Third World governments are less developed than First and Second World ones in the sense that most of them have existed for shorter periods of time and are found in relatively new states. These governments tend to be less stable because of weak economic and philosophical bases. Coups are frequent in the Third World; military and/or authoritarian regimes tend to be more the rule than the exception. Third World governments must also perform the task, which is mostly completed in the other two worlds, of overcoming tradition and initiating mobilization and modernization. Also, because government structures usually are derivative of First and Second World sources or a combination of them, the situation is such that these government structures are rather alien to the governed.

In the past some Third World politicians attempted to establish "native" regimes, thus resisting both Western and Communist influence, for example Sukarno's "Guided Democracy" in Indonesia, Kwame Nkrumah's "Consciencism" in Ghana, or General Ayub Khan's "Basic Democracy" in Pakistan.[2] Presently, General Muhammed Zia ul-Haq in Pakistan and Ayatollah Ruhollah Khomeini in Iran[3] are attempting to establish Islamic regimes in their countries, based on their understanding of seventh-century A.D. Koranic ideas of government. A rather different sort of regime can be found in Libya where, under Muammar Qaddafi, a type of "Arab Socialism" called "The Socialist People's Libyan Arab Jamahiriya" exists.[4]

Let us now look at Communist regimes and Third World governments. In this discussion we give special attention to the Soviet Union, the German

Democratic Republic, and the People's Republic of China in the Second World and to India, Mexico, and Tanzania in the Third World.

THE SECOND WORLD

Analysts studying the Soviet Union have sometimes described the formulation and content of Soviet foreign policy as being enigmatic. A similar sense of bewilderment may confront students of politics when they attempt to understand the internal functioning of Communist governmental structures—especially when Western standards and concepts are employed. Although the Communist states have extensive governmental systems, most important policy decisions are made within the organs of the Communist party, not within the government. Government structures perform the tasks of legitimating and implementing the decisions of the Communist party. In addition, although the states of the Second World have elaborately written constitutions that assign specific tasks to individual government agencies, in practice these functions are fluid and subject to change and control by the Communist party leadership. Communist governmental systems also seem to resemble Western parliamentary systems; most have an elective legislature or assembly and a council of ministers similar to a Western cabinet. In practice, however, the ministers are not responsible to the legislature and may, as in the Soviet Union, enact more laws than the assembly as a whole. Finally, some Communist systems, the most important of which is the Soviet Union, are federal systems according to their constitutions, but students of federalism have classified such systems as "quasi-federal" rather than true federations because the Communist party creates a channel of communications and a network of authority that renders the federal subunits irrelevant.[5] The governmental structures of the Soviet Union have provided the basic model for the states of the Second World. Government in the Communist World becomes intelligible only when the historical and ideological factors that influenced the development of the Soviet system are understood.

Development of Government in the Soviet Union

Karl Deutsch has noted that Soviet politics has been shaped by a unique combination of historical development and deliberate political design.[6] This statement is consistent with our general interpretation that politics in the three worlds is the product of the level of political development and the element of human choice. In the case of the Soviet Union, the political process was shaped by many factors, including traditional Russian attitudes of authoritarianism, the atmosphere of violence and conspiracy that prevailed before and during the Bolshevik Revolution, and the messianic goal of world revolution established in Marxist theory. These factors favored the development of a highly centralized political system in which the values of obedience to authority and discipline would be emphasized. All of these factors found expression in the political and organizational thought of the Bolshevik leader Lenin. Although Karl Marx and Friedrich Engels were the intellectual founders of the Communist movement and its chief theoreticians, it was Lenin, the master of tactics and organization, who brought to power the first Communist regime. As a macrotheory of history, the theory of Marx and Engels said very little about tactical and organizational matters. According to Marx, socialism-communism, the final stage of history, would develop inevitably from the contradictions of advanced capitalist society. In the midst of increasing industrialization and production, the continued decline in the material condition of the working class would trigger a violent class struggle in which industrial workers (the proletariat, the most advanced segment of the working class), leading the working class as a whole, would establish a dictatorship over the defeated bourgeois class.[7] ("Proletarians" are the industrial workers in the capitalist system. The "working class" includes all who need to work for a living because they do not own the means of production; that is, not only factory workers but also clerks, minor government workers, soldiers, teachers, and so on. Some, especially Asian Communists, included poor farmers and landless peasants as part of the working class.) This revolution was perceived as an historical inevitability and proletarians would move spontaneously toward revolution and dictatorship.[8] The Dictatorship of the Proletariat would last only a short time and it would lead to the final historical epoch which would have two separate periods, socialism and then Communism.

The first period would have an economy of scarcity and the second, an economy of plenty. In this socialist period, inequality and deprivation resulting from previous uneven development would continue to exist and it would be necessary for the state (under the control of the proletariat) to continue to exist in order to defend revolutionary gains.[9]

The second period, full-scale Communism, would emerge at some point in the future. Marx was ambiguous about how long the socialist period would last and about what specific form the state would have during this time. Before 1917, Lenin faced political realities that differed from the conditions theorized by Marx and Engels, and after 1917 it was left to Lenin to determine the specific form the Dictatorship of the Proletariat and socialist state would take.

The Contributions of Lenin. Lenin's thought represented an adjustment to the prevailing political conditions in Russia and throughout Europe. The expected revolutions by factory workers in the two most advanced capitalist states, Germany and England, failed to develop. In the absence of such revolutions, and given the fact that there were relatively few factory workers in agrarian Russia, Lenin had to include in his thinking the revolutionary potential of the peasants and other working class groups, such as civil servants and shop clerks. He argued that a worker-peasant alliance was a prerequisite to proletarian revolution. In addition, Lenin did not believe that the tendency toward socialism would be inevitable and automatic, or that the spontaneous actions of the proletarians leading the whole working class would be sufficient to produce revolution. Instead, he argued that the alliance between the peasants (the rural working class) and the urban working class, led by the proletariat, must be forged by a small group within the proletariat itself, consisting of its most politically experienced and astute members. Such a group was needed to give guidance and to supply a proper sense of historical mission. Once the proletarian dictatorship was achieved, this group would be necessary to direct the activities of the workers in order to bring about rapid economic development. Lenin also favored elite rule for practical reasons; only a tightly knit, disciplined group could survive in the repressive political atmosphere of prerevolutionary Russia.

Three principles of Lenin were especially important in the development of the Soviet governmental system. First, Lenin advocated the notion of the "Vanguard of the Proletariat," presented for the first time in the 1902 political tract *What is to be Done?* According to this principle, which legitimized elite rule, the proletariat could achieve final victory only if it were led by a small, disciplined political party possessing an advanced theory (Marxism). This party would combine in itself the experience, political wisdom, and leadership skills necessary to the proletariat. Leadership by the vanguard was also necessary because Lenin believed that Marxist theory could be understood only by the most advanced elements of the proletariat and not by all proletarians, much less all workers, whether rural or urban. Since the time of Lenin, the Communist party membership has been considered to constitute the vanguard of the proletariat, and the principle has provided the theoretical justification for a dominant role by the Communist party leadership in the political system.

Second, Lenin advocated the principle of "democratic centralism" as the proper mode of organization within the organs of both the Communist party and the Soviet government. The democratic element required that the membership of higher units be selected by lower, subordinate units under their authority. The centralist element called for strict discipline and absolute obedience by lower units to policy decisions made by higher units. In actual practice the democratic element has been ignored, and individuals are appointed to positions in both the party and government by leaders at the top level of the Communist party. The requirements of discipline and centralized control have been rigorously enforced, however, and the principle of democratic centralism established the basis for dictatorial control by the Communist party leadership.[10]

Finally, Lenin advocated the principle of qualitative rather than quantitative decision making. Since the time of Lenin it has become custom that decisions within the organs of the party and the government be made not on the basis of majority rule but rather on the basis of qualitative assessments of the protagonists. In several important policy disputes, Lenin was able to override the objections of most of the rest of party leadership and impose his policy choices based on the claim, apparently accepted by the other leaders, that his political judgment was superior to the collective judgment of the rest of the leadership. Since that time support for a policy by a few of the top leaders (or, as during the period of Stalin, by *the* top leader) has been sufficient to guarantee its acceptance. In the Soviet Union as well as the other states of the Second World, Communist party leaders exercise great discretionary power over the operation of the political system. Governmental forms and constitutional requirements are secondary to the goals of the revolution, and the direction of the revolution is in the hands of the leaders of the Communist party.[11]

Leninism in the USSR Today. Lenin's organizational principles are clearly articulated in both the rules of the Communist party and the Soviet Constitution. Article 6 of the Constitution of 1977 establishes the principle of the primacy of the Communist party in both domestic and foreign policy decision making. It states:

> The Communist Party of the Soviet Union is the leading and guiding force of Soviet society, the nucleus of its political system and of (all) state and public organizations. The CPSU exists for the people and serves the people.

> Armed with the Marxist–Leninist teaching, the Communist Party determines general prospects for the development of society and the lines of the USSR's domestic and foreign policy, directs the great creative activity of the Soviet people, and gives their struggle for the victory of communism a planned, scientifically substantiated nature.[12]

Article 3 establishes the principle of democratic centralism:

> The organization and activity of the Soviet state are constructed in accordance with the principle of democratic centralism: the elective nature of all bodies of state power, from top to bottom, their accountability to the people, and the binding nature of the decisions of higher bodies on lower. Democratic centralism combines single leadership with local initiative and creative activeness, with the responsibility of every state agency and official for the assigned task.[13]

Article 19 of the 1961 party statutes also articulates the principle of democratic centralism:

> The guiding principle of party organizational structures is democratic centralism, which means:
>
> **a.** Election of all leading party organs, from the lowest to the highest.
>
> **b.** Periodic accountability of party organs to their party organizations and higher organs.
>
> **c.** Strict party discipline and subordination of the minority to the majority.
>
> **d.** The decision of the higher organs are absolutely binding on lower organs.[14]

The power relationship between the party and the government is the subject of extensive discussion in official literature. Citing official texts, Darrell Hammer has argued that two principles govern party–government relations: (1) "No important decision is ever taken by an organ of government, or by an administrative organ, without corresponding instructions from the party." (2) "The central party organs give guiding instructions to the ministries . . . while not restricting their operational independence."[15] Taken together these two principles create an institutional arrangement in which the party is the sole, legitimate source of ideas and policy initiatives. The party guides and controls the government, which serves as the party's administrative agent by implementing party policies and enforcing them in the general population.

　　In actual practice, the party seeks to exercise control over the government in three ways. First, the Communist party maintains structures that parallel those of the government at every level from village and city to the highest national level (see Figure 7.1). At each level Communist party personnel are assigned to oversee the activities of the government to assure conformity to party policies. Second, the Communist party recruits and supplies personnel for all important government positions (a system called *nomenklatura*), thus placing government operations directly in the hands of party bureaucrats. There is a far greater proportion of party members at the higher levels of government than at the lower levels. Third, the party draws into its ranks government bureaucrats, scientists, technicians, and military personnel who wish to further their careers. In most cases, advancement is not possible without party membership.

Soviet Governmental Structures

Three principal structures make up the Soviet governmental system at the national level: (1) the *Supreme Soviet*, (2) the *Presidium*, and (3) the *Council of Ministers*. These are supplemented by a system of elective legislative

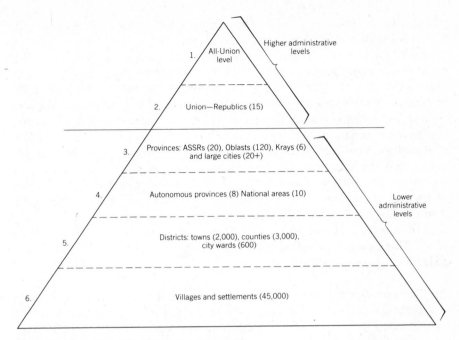

Figure 7.1. Administrative Structure of the USSR.

bodies called soviets (councils) which exist at all administrative levels. The Soviet Union has a very complex administrative structure and there is no satisfactory way to represent this complexity. One of the simplest ways is to recognize 6 levels of administration in two groups (see Figure 7.1). The first group is the higher levels: (1) the national or all-union level; and (2) the union-republic level (15 republics). The second group contains the lower levels of state administration: (3) the provincial level containing (a) the Autonomous Soviet Socialistic Republics (called ASSRs—there are 20 of them), (b) the administrative province (called *oblasts*—120), (c) administrative territories (*krays*—6), and (d) large cities (called *gorods*—20+); (4) autonomous provinces (APs—8), and national areas (*okrugs*—10); (5) the district level containing (a) towns—2,000+, (b) counties (rural *rayons*—3,000+), and (c) urban wards (also *rayons*—about 600); and (6) villages and settlements—about 45,000.[16] According to the constitution, the soviets are the ultimate repositories of "state power" for the territories they administer and have control over the judicial, executive, legislative, and administrative activities of the local governments.[17] Soviets at all levels are elective and all citizens over the age of 18 are eligible to vote. Officially the Soviet Union is a federal system with the republics based on nationality distinctions and their subunits based on geographic or ethnic divisions. The nationality units include the 15 union republics, the ethnic units include 20 autonomous Soviet Socialistic Republics, 8 autonomous provinces, and 10 national areas (*okrugs*). These units do not possess the same degree of autonomy. The greatest autonomy is reserved for the union republics, the largest units and those in which the nationalities are theoretically the most "culturally advanced."[18] On paper the powers of the union republics are impressive and include the right to conduct diplomatic relations, maintain separate troops, and develop separate flags and constitutions. These powers are actually meaningless, however, because the Soviet constitutions have always required that the subunits carry out the decisions of political bodies at the national or all-union level and deprived the subunits of independent sources of revenue.[19] Of course, the existence of the Communist party is the most important factor in limiting federal decentralization. The Constitution presently in effect is that of 1977, sometimes called the "Brezhnev Constitution." Three earlier versions existed, dated 1918, 1924, and 1936, the latter called the "Stalin Constitution."

The Supreme Soviet. The three structures at the national level establish a governmental system that superficially resembles a Western parliamentary system (see Figure 7.2). The Supreme Soviet is comparable to a legislature or parliament having two houses and consists of the Soviet of the Union and the Soviet of Nationalities. At present each house has about 750 members and the two houses possess equal powers. Deputies to the Soviet of the Union are elected from districts of equal population and serve for a period of five years. Deputies to the Soviet of Nationalities are elected from the nationality and ethnic subunits (union republics, autonomous republics, and so on) with each of the subunits entitled to a specific but different number of representatives (see Figure 7.2). Deputies to the Soviet of Nationalities also serve for five years. The significance of the Soviet of Nationalities is that its deputies are not just territorial representatives like American senators who represent states, but are representatives of the ethnic and nationality groups on which some of the various units of the Soviet federal system are based. According to the 1977 Constitution, the Supreme Soviet is the highest body of state power in the USSR. It is empowered to enact statutes that take precedence over all other laws and regulations passed at all lower administrative levels. The Supreme Soviet is also responsible for electing the personnel of four other higher organs of the state: the Presidium of the Soviet Union, the Council of Ministers, the Supreme Court and the Prosecutor General. The Supreme Soviet convenes several times a year with each session usually lasting less than two weeks.

    Although the Constitution established the Supreme Soviet as the highest organ of state power, its powers are actually minimal. The large size of the

Supreme Soviet—meets twice a year, composed of two chambers:
  Soviet of the Union—one representative for every 300,000+ people.
  Soviet of the Nationalities

   Union Republic (32 deputies)
   Autonomous Soviet Socialist Republic (11 deputies)
   Autonomous Province (5 deputies)
   National area (1 deputy)

The Supreme Soviet appoints the Presidium of the Soviet, which operates when the Supreme Soviet is not in session, the head of which (the Chairman) is the head of state (often called president in English).

Council of Ministers, the highest administrative organ of the Soviet State, the chairman of which is the head of government.
  Supreme Court of the USSR.
  Prosecutor-General of the USSR.

Figure 7.2. Organs of state power of the USSR.

membership (1500) and the short duration of its sessions clearly indicate that it is not an important or independent policy-making body. In addition, although the Supreme Soviet "elects" both the Presidium and the Council of Ministers, these bodies are largely autonomous and are not responsible to the Supreme Soviet the way cabinet bodies are responsible to legislatures in true parliamentary systems. Most important, the Communist party exercises actual political control over the Supreme Soviet. Approximately 75% of its deputies are Communist party members, 40% of whom are professional party bureaucrats.[20] Only one slate of candidates appears on the ballot for election to the Supreme Soviet, and all of the candidates are approved by the Communist party. The deputies accept the party's claim that it is the only legitimate voice of the Soviet people and assume that the party has already reached the correct decision in all policy deliberations.[21] It is also accepted that the chief function of the Supreme Soviet is to ratify and legitimate the policies and actions of the Communist party.

The Presidium of the Supreme Soviet. The Soviet of the Union and the Soviet of Nationalities jointly elect the 39-member Presidium of the Supreme Soviet. The Presidium is the collegial (plural) head of state of the Soviet Union which, according to Soviet sources, eliminates the danger of one-person rule common to presidential systems.[22] The Constitution grants broad powers to the Presidium of the Supreme Soviet, including the power to ratify treaties, confirm actions of the Council of Ministers, exercise full legislative powers when the Supreme Soviet is not in session (it issues about 75% of all laws as decrees, later to be confirmed by a regular meeting of the Supreme Soviet), and interpret the meaning of statutes—a power reserved for the Supreme Court in the United States.[23] The Presidium of the Supreme Soviet also has the power to grant pardons, appoint commissions to investigate special problems, name the heads of the army and navy, mobilize the armed forces, and declare war. The Presidium is headed by a Chairman who is sometimes referred to, in English, as the president of the Soviet Union.

Several factors give the Presidium greater significance in the political process than its parent body, the Supreme Soviet. Because of the size of the Supreme Soviet and the long intervals during which it is not in session, most legislative work is undertaken by the smaller Presidium whose members are said to possess greater governmental expertise and experience. In addition, important policy decisions endorsing and legitimizing Communist party policies are likely to be made in the sessions of the Presidium. Furthermore, recent actions by the Communist party leadership have given the Presidium added importance. In 1977 the party General Secretary, Leonid Brezhnev, removed Nikolai Podgorny as Chairman of the Presidium and personally assumed the position, which he held until his death in 1982. The next leader of the Communist party, Yuri Andropov, also assumed the chairmanship of the Presidium as did Konstantin Chernenko, his sucessor. As one source noted, in assuming this position, Brezhnev (and Andropov and Chernenko) "ended the anomaly of the all-powerful party leader lacking any major governmental position."[24]

All members of the Presidium are selected by the Communist party leadership, and the Supreme Soviet merely endorses the party's choices. When Leonid Brezhnev replaced Nikolai Podgorny as Chairman in 1977 the Supreme Soviet had no prior knowledge of the action and played no formal role in the ouster.[25]

Council of Ministers. Executive power is vested in the Council of Ministers, which is superficially analogous to a cabinet in a true parliamentary system. Under the constitution, ministers are elected by both houses of the Supreme Soviet to which they are responsible. In actual practice, however, they are selected by the leadership of the Communist party, automatically confirmed by the Supreme Soviet, and operate independently of the legislative body. The Council of Ministers is headed by a Chairman whose functions roughly correspond to those of a prime minister in a parliamentary system. Vernon Aspaturian has noted that the Council of Ministers functions more nearly as the administrative arm of the Politburo of the Communist party than as the administrative arm of the Supreme Soviet.[26] Presently there are 116 members of the Council of Ministers. The membership includes 64 ministers, representatives of 18 state committees, representatives of 4 specialized agencies, 15 premiers of the union republics, and 15 members of the Presidium of the Council of Ministers (a group consisting of the most important administrators).[27] It is important to realize that the Council of Ministers includes the top administrators of the republics as well as those at the national level. Ministers at both levels are the heads of functional departments that correspond to Western ministries of foreign affairs, health, education, agriculture, and so on.

Although the Council of Ministers is not a significant policy-making group, it is important in the process by which policy is formulated and executed. The Council of Ministers is responsible for overseeing and coordinating the work of all administrative bodies at the national and union–republic levels. This includes the implementation of all economic programs. Individual ministers have control over departments with thousands of employees whose activities touch the lives of most Soviet citizens on a daily basis. In addition, the Council of Ministers performs an important legislative function. Under the Soviet Constitution, ministries are able to issue regulations which have the force of law unless explicitly annulled by the Supreme Soviet or its Presidium. Studies have shown that the Council and its ministers are the main source of legislation in the Soviet system and that they issue regulations governing all areas of economic and social life.[28] Finally, ministers are drawn from the top level of the Communist party. In such cases the information that they communicate to the party's decision-making bodies will be important in the development of future policy, and in cases where the party's decisions are formulated in broad terms, such ministers may have considerable latitude in the interpretation and implementation of policies.

The Quasi-Federal System. The Communist party also dominates the soviets or councils in the union republics, autonomous republics, and other subunits of the federal system in the same fashion that it dominates the Supreme Soviet of the USSR. The presence of the Communist party creates a centralized channel of communications and authority that negates the federal structure. In the Soviet federal system the nationality units do not enjoy any real autonomy and do not have jurisdiction or control over specific governmental activities. Because the nationality units do not possess the attributes of other federal subunits, students of federalism have classified the Soviet Union as a quasi-federal system rather than a true federation (see Figure 7.3).[29]

1. Armenian Soviet Socialist Republic (SSR)
2. Azerbaidjan SSR
     Nakhichevan Autonomous Soviet Socialist Republic (ASSR)
     Nagorno–Karabakh Autonomous Province (AP)
3. Belorus SSR
4. Estonian SSR
5. Georgian SSR
     Abkhazian ASSR
     Adjar ASSR
         South Ossetian
6. Kazakh SSR
7. Kirghiz SSR
8. Latvian SSR
9. Lithuanian SSR
10. Moldavian SSR
11. Russian Soviet Federative Socialist Republic
     16 ASSRs—Baskir, Buryat, Daghestan, Kabardinian–Balkar, Kalmyk Karelian, Komi, Mari, Mordvinian, North Ossetian, Tatar, Tuva, Udmurt, Chechen–Ingush, Chuvash, Yakut
     5 APs—Adyei, Gorno–Altai, Jewish, Karachayevo–Cherkess, Khakass
     10 national areas
12. Tadzhik SSR
     Gorno–Badakhshan AP
13. Turkmen SSR
14. Ukrainian SSR
15. Uzbek SSR
     Kara–Kalpak ASSR

Figure 7.3. State structure of the USSR.

Party–Government Relations in Historical Perspective

In the 1960s, Jacobs and Zink made the following observation about the relationship between the Communist party and the governmental system in the Soviet Union:

> The governmental system in the Soviet Union is merely a tool in the hands of the Communist Party dictatorship. The government has no existence and no legitimacy outside that given to it by the party. The government is not a policy determining body but is a network for the implementation of decisions made by the party leadership.
>
> These decisions of the party leadership are in no way restricted by the

constitution. The constitution is expendable in the name of the revolution. It can be changed, or ignored, by the party. . . . The constitution and, indeed, all governmental institutions in the Soviet Union are simple administrative conveniences to be manipulated, changed, or abolished as party leaders see fit.[30]

Although this explanation still represents a good starting point for the study of Soviet institutions, recent scholarship has revealed that the contemporary relationship between the party and government is more complex. In assessing the changes that have occurred in the Soviet Union since the rule of Josif Stalin (1928–1953), Zbigniew Brzezinski cites several factors that may be leading to an increase in the autonomy and importance of the state bureaucracy.[31] First, since the death of Stalin in 1953, the Communist party leadership has refrained from using terror tactics and violence against high-level members of the party and government. This development has reduced the personal danger involved in opposing or questioning official party policies. Such opponents now face bureaucratic discipline, demotion, or expulsion from the Communist party, but not torture, internal exile, or death. By the beginning of the 1970s a significant number of persons had demonstrated a willingness to question official policies. Second, the present generation of Communist party leaders was trained in the bureaucratic tradition and favor bureaucratic solutions to political problems. Unlike Lenin, Stalin, and Khrushchev, the present leadership did not directly experience the Russian Revolution, and they have been more restrained in their personal manipulations of party and government agencies. Brzezinski notes that "to the new generation of clerks, bureaucratic stability—indeed, bureaucratic dictatorship—must seem to be the only solid foundation for effective government."[32] Finally, certain groups within the government, including the military, the police, the scientific community, the managers of state industry, and the leaders of the collective farm system, have developed special political and institutional interests. Recognizing that the functions they perform are indispensable if the Soviet system is to maintain and enhance its superpower status, these groups have sought increased resource support for their activities from the Communist party. There is evidence to suggest that these "interest groups" have experienced some degree of acceptance and success.[33] As an example, the Central Committee of the Communist party has been altered and expanded in order to function as a forum for the interaction between these groups and the party leadership. In addition, party leaders have usually given all the various departments an incremental budgetary increase each year.[34]

The role of the government has also been enhanced by the general socioeconomic development that has occurred in the Soviet Union and the resulting increase in the scope of governmental activity.[35] Today, like its counterparts in the United States and Western Europe, the Soviet government is involved in a vast array of activities such as disease eradication, space exploration, education, urban redevelopment, conservation, and natural resource exploitation, to name just a few. Involvement in such activities requires the possession of advanced scientific and technological expertise. Although groups of experts within the Communist party are designated to oversee individual ministries of the government, no leadership group, including that of the Communist party, possesses the specialized knowledge necessary to regulate all of the programs and operations of modern government. In areas where the knowledge of the party group is lacking, government agencies gain increased freedom of action.

Studies undertaken since the early 1970s also report a larger role for government officials in the public policy process. In discussing foreign policy decision making in the USSR, Morton Schwartz notes that Communist party leaders have been "according greater weight and authority to those groups in society which possess the knowledge and skills necessary to make the increasingly complex Soviet system work."[36] He cites leading scientists, engineers, plant managers, and government officials—all state bureaucrats—as the chief beneficiaries of this development. Jerry Hough argues that since the term of Nikita Khrushchev as Communist party leader (1953–1964), "devolution of power to the major institutional centers" has taken place.[37] As a result of this development, Hough notes that many social scientists are now applying models of "institutional pluralism" and "participatory bureaucracy" to the Soviet Union. These models recognize that significant conflict occurs in the policy-making process and that "governmental decisions are most heavily influenced by those affected by them and those especially knowledgeable about them."[38] Summarizing the changes that have occurred in the public policy process in the last two decades, Gary Bertsch notes:

> Changes have definitely occurred in the Communist systems over the last few decades and they have had a major impact on the way policy is made. With the death of Joseph Stalin and the deconcentration of power that Khruschev's rule ushered in, political power has devolved to a certain extent from the highest party bodies to different bureaucratic and state organs.
>
> . . . The post-Khrushchev leadership provided the specialized state, party, and scientific complexes with considerable policy-making autonomy in their fields. . . . Although many terms have been used to describe Soviet politics over the past few decades—institutional pluralism, bureaucratic pluralism, participatory bureaucracy, and so on—all draw attention to a sharing of political power in which ideas and actions flow up as well as down the traditional power hierarchy.[39]

In the Soviet Union today the Communist party still holds the primary position in the public policy process. All Soviet elite groups share in the consensus that a strong party is in their best interest. In addition, the power and prestige of top Soviet leaders still come from their position in the hierarchy of the Communist party rather than from their position in the government. However, the relationship between the party and the government is very different from what it was in the time of Stalin. The end of terror in elite relations, the acceptance of a bureaucratic style of politics by Communist party elites, and the broadened scope of governmental activity have contributed to a new and more complex relationship. A proper understanding of the governmental system of the USSR requires recognition of these developments.

Eastern Europe: Soviet Bloc States

The Eastern European states that are members of the Soviet bloc have governmental structures similar to those of the Soviet Union. Included in this group are the German Democratic Republic, Poland, Hungary, Bulgaria, Czechoslovakia, and Romania. All of these states are called "Socialist Republics" or "People's Democracies," which means that they adhere to Marxist–Leninist political and organizational principles; and all are members of the Soviet-sponsored and directed military pact, the Warsaw Treaty Organization (WTO) and the economic organization, the Council for Mutual Economic Assistance (CMEA). As such, these states are under the ideological, political, and military control of the Soviet Union. After World War II and the Soviet military occupation of Eastern Europe, these states established Communist party-dominated political systems based on the model of the Soviet Union. The governmental systems of Eastern Europe have an elective assembly (similar to the Supreme Soviet of the USSR), a committee of the assembly that functions as the collegial head of state (similar to the Presidium of the Supreme Soviet), and a council of ministers that oversees the implementation of government policy (see Figure 7.4). As in the Soviet Union, the Communist party dominates the policy-making process and holds the primary position in the political process. Party structures parallel those of the government at most levels, and Communist party leaders hold dominant positions at the upper levels of the government.

German Democratic Republic

In many respects the governmental system of the German Democratic Republic (GDR) is typical of the systems of Eastern Europe. In the GDR the legislative assembly is the *Volkskammer* or People's Chamber. It is a

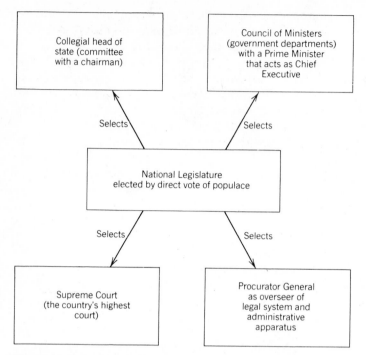

Figure 7.4. National government of a typical Communist state.

unicameral legislature of 500 deputies elected for a five-year term. Because the People's Chamber meets for only about five days a year, the membership elects a permanently sitting 25-member *Staatsrat* or Council of State. Like the Presidium of the Supreme Soviet in the USSR, the Council of State acts for the larger assembly when it is not in session, and its decrees have the force of law. In the period from 1949 to 1971, party leader Walter Ulbricht personally held the position of Chairman of the *Staatsrat* in a fashion similar to Brezhnev's control over the Presidium of the Supreme Soviet after 1977.[40] The *Ministerrat* (Council of Ministers) has 39 members and, like the Soviet Council of Ministers, actually functions as the administrative arm of the dominant party.[41] As in several of the states of Eastern Europe, however, unique historical and political factors have produced some deviations from the Soviet model. The most important deviation in the GDR concerns the dominant party. In the GDR the party is called the Socialist Unity party of Germany (SED) rather than the Communist party. The SED began as a merger in 1949 of two political parties, the *Kommunistische Partei Deutschlands* (KPD), an organization based on Germany's traditional pre–World War II Communist party, and the *Sozialistische Partei*

Deutschlands (SPD), or German Socialist party, dominated in the postwar period by Soviet–German agents trained in the USSR.[42] The merger was dictated by the Soviet occupation authorities and permitted the Soviet-trained elements to dominate the Communist party and create a monolithic structure. There are also several other political parties in existence in the GDR (and in Poland, Czechoslovakia, and Bulgaria, see Chapter 9) which are actually represented in the People's Chamber. These parties are part of a National Front (Nationales Front des demokratischen Deutschlands) dominated by the SED. The parties of the National Front are "obviously and completely dominated by pro-Communist leadership and blindly serve not only the SED's permanent party line, but also its changing day-by-day tactical variations."[43] As Michael Roskin has noted, these parties were created in order to mobilize support for the regime from sectors of the East German population that have a traditional antipathy toward the Communist party.[44] Included are parties for Christians, farmers, small businessmen, and veterans.

The GDR also deviates from the Soviet model in at least one other way. Unlike the Soviet Union which is constitutionally a federal state (although it does not function as a true federal state), the GDR is a unitary state.

People's Republic of China

Government structures in the People's Republic of China (PRC) also parallel those of the Soviet Union and the states of Eastern Europe. As in the other states, there is a national assembly, a collegial body, and a council of ministers. The National People's Congress (NPC), a national assembly, is the highest body of state power. Its membership is elected from the 21 Provincial People's Congresses, which in turn are theoretically elected by congresses or assemblies at the lower, grass-roots level. The National People's Congress has approximately 3500 deputies who serve for a five-year term. Because, like the Supreme Soviet of the USSR, it is too large to function effectively, a Standing Committee of approximately 175 members is elected from its ranks. The Chairman of the Standing Committee functions nominally as China's head of state. At present the Standing Committee's power in the governmental system approaches that of the Presidium of the Supreme Soviet in the USSR. The implementation of government policy is left to the State Council, a body of approximately 45 ministers and vice-premiers.

Government structures in the People's Republic of China have been subject to greater party dominance and greater manipulation by individual Communist leaders than have the structures in the other communist states.[45]

Beijing, China—Premier Zhao Ziyang and President Reagan at the Great Hall of the People in April, 1984.

This reflects two basic facts: (1) that the PRC is a relatively new state, having come into existence in 1949, and (2) that the first generation of revolutionary leaders led by Mao Zedong governed the political system until as recently as 1976. As China's institutional framework was new and not well established, it was susceptible to such manipulation. For example, the National People's Congress is constitutionally the highest state organ, yet the Congress held no meetings between February 1965 and January 1975.[46] In addition, the Constitution of 1954 was rewritten by Mao Zedong in 1975 to incorporate many of the principles of his Cultural Revolution, only to be rewritten again in 1978 (after Mao's death) in a form closer to the 1954 model.[47] Further, at the whim of the party leadership, important government positions went unfilled for several years during the period of Mao Zedong. Communist party dominance is achieved in the PRC in the same way it is in the other states of the Second World. Some form of party organization exists alongside most state organs, and Communist party members are assigned leadership roles in the hierarchies of both the party and government.[48] James Townsend has summarized the role of the Communist party and the government in the public policy process:

> The primary decision maker in the Chinese system is the Chinese Communist Party, which shapes policy on the basis of alternatives made known to it. The decision making structure is therefore narrow, based on party committees acting in closed session. There is no open legislative process and relatively little issuance of public laws. Decisions take the form of general statements on policy or doctrine, or emerge as administrative directives and regulations.[49]

The Chinese Communist party has also sought to control the State Council and the other administrative organs of government by conducting numerous campaigns to limit the size of the government bureaucracy and the scope of its activity. This was a major theme of Mao Zedong's Great Proletarian Cultural Revolution in the mid-1960s when government bureaucrats, both as individuals and as a group, were attacked and criticized for attempting to amass too much power. As in the Soviet Union, the Communist party presently dominates the political system. In the view of the Chinese Communist party, the proper role of the National People's Congress is to endorse and legitimate the decisions of the party, and the appropriate role of the State Council is to implement the party's decisions.

THE THIRD WORLD

A few Third World countries (such as India, Malaysia, and Singapore) have government structures based on the British model of the fusion of power. Some of the countries (Mexico, Nigeria, the Philippines, and Venezuela) have used the U.S. model of separation of powers at least in theory. However, in a majority of Third World countries power is concentrated in the executive. These executives are of three types: (1) military leaders, (2) traditional monarchs (or sheikhs in the Persian Gulf), and (3) executives in one-party civilian governments. Military leaders assume control of the executive by a coup or by a subsequent election in which they determine the role, if any, of the opposition. Military coups are most frequent in Africa, followed by the Middle East, Latin America, and Asia.[50] Elections are held merely to give the appearance of legitimacy to a military coup. Some examples of countries with military leaders in control of the executive are Ethiopia and Zaire in Africa, Algeria and Libya in the Middle East, Chile and Uruguay in Latin America, and Pakistan and Thailand in Asia. In such countries the legislature and judiciary are subordinate to the executive. In some cases legislatures are suspended and laws are made by executive decree.

Saudi Arabian leaders at a public event, Riyadh.

In traditional monarchies (e.g., Swaziland in Africa, Nepal in Asia, and Saudi Arabia in the Middle East) and the Persian Gulf sheikhdoms (such as Bahrain, Kuwait, and United Arab Emirates), either a legislature does not exist or has very limited powers. In the Moslem countries of the Middle East the judiciary is given prominence, as the Koran must be interpreted by the judges, who are religious leaders, to enforce Islamic law. Outside the Middle East, the judiciary is also controlled by the traditional monarchs.

One-party civilian governments are found mostly in Africa (Kenya, Tanzania, and Zambia, for example). Legislatures and judiciaries do exist in these countries, but the executive is the most powerful branch of the government. The legislature works under the direction of the executive. The judiciary is, however, given some independence. A variation of one-party government is a system in which any number of parties are permitted to seek power, but in reality one party always wins. The best-known examples of such a government are in India and Mexico.

Some Third World countries have experimented with military as well as civilian rule. In these countries major changes in the government structure are common. Gary Wynia, an expert on Argentina, writes that "during the past thirty years, the country [Argentina] has experimented with various democratic and authoritarian forms of government."[51] A majority of the regimes in Argentina have been military dictatorships. Whenever the president was popularly elected, as for example in 1958, 1963, and 1983, the executive became less absolute and the powers of the legislature and the judiciary increased. Nigeria and Pakistan are other examples of countries that have been ruled by the military as well as by the popularly elected leaders. After independence from Britain in 1960, Nigeria was governed by a parliamentary form of government (with a fusion of powers) until 1966 when the first military coup occurred in that country. Military rule under different leaders, who came to power by coups, continued in Nigeria until 1979 when a new government based on a U.S. type constitution was elected. However, in early 1984 the military again seized power. Pakistan's postindependence history (since 1947) in this respect is similar to that of Nigeria. After beginning with a democratic (parliamentary) form of government, Pakistan experimented with military rule, went back to democracy, and then returned to military rule.

Third World states' governments are predominantly authoritarian. The most common form of authoritarian government in the Third World is military. According to one scholar, authoritarianism (including military authoritarianism) is "receding" in Latin America.[52] It is true that in several Latin American countries authoritarian rule has been challenged by democratic forces. In some African, Asian, and Middle Eastern countries a similar trend is evident. In general, however, authoritarianism, especially military rule, characterizes the government structures of the Third World states.

When the military comes to power by a coup in a Third World country, it invariably replaces an unpopular civilian government that has lost legitimacy. Inefficiency, corruption, and poor economic performance are the major reasons for the loss of a government's legitimacy in the Third World. In order to gain the confidence of the people the military government promises to bring order and efficiency, eliminate corruption, and improve the economy. Such promises make military governments popular for some time. However, such popularity is often short-lived and military governments seldom last more than a few years. According to one estimate, "military regimes in the Third World have an average life span of approximately five years."[53]

While in power, many Third World military governments introduce constitutions and establish government structures that have the appearance of being democratic. In reality, as Eric Nordlinger remarks, it is a "constitutional–democratic facade."[54] Such a facade may include

a national legislature that can do little more than discuss and approve legislation introduced by the government; elections for national, state, and local offices that are restricted to officially approved candidates; elections for the presidency featuring a single candidate; plebiscites in which the government asks for and "receives" the approval of more than 90 percent of those who cast their ballots; and the "civilianization" of the regime, whereby the head of government sheds his uniform in order to look more like a constitutional president or prime minister.[55]

The power in such a regime remains in the hands of the executive controlled by the military. The facade of democracy makes little impression on the masses, partly because military regimes are unable to develop mobilization parties that Second World states use for maintaining popular support. Military governments do bring some order in the society; however, elimination or reduction of corruption and improvement of economy are seldom achieved. Under such conditions it is virtually impossible for a government to achieve legitimacy. The lack of legitimacy is the underlying cause of the instability of military regimes.

Pakistan is considered a classic example of a country where a military government (under General Ayub Khan) introduced a constitutional–democratic facade and failed to achieve legitimacy.[56] Ayub ruled Pakistan from 1958 to 1969, first by decree, then by a "democratic constitution." The Constitution established a five-tier structure of "elected" councils that were controlled by the government. The most important of these councils were the Basic Democrats of the first tier who elected the president and the legislatures, national as well as provincial. In reality the Basic Democrats and all other "Democrats" existed to serve their military masters. Ayub acquired some popularity in the beginning years of his regime, but resigned in 1969 amidst political turmoil and a national crisis that dismembered Pakistan into two countries, Pakistan and Bangladesh, in 1971.

Although the executives in the military regimes are controlled by the military leaders, they often include civilians as their members. Nordlinger distinguishes "three types of executive arrangements among military regimes: (1) the predominantly military executive in which at least 90 percent of the cabinet positions are held by officers; (2) the mixed military–civilian executive; and (3) an exclusively military council along with a mixed cabinet."[57] The first type of arrangement is the least favored by the military. Including some civilians in leadership positions brings the much-needed expertise to the government and makes the regime acceptable to the people. As a general rule, the civilians holding high positions in military governments are not politicians; instead they are technocrats—experts in industry and other fields. The close relationship between the military and the technocrats in the military regimes of the Third World is well known. The military cannot administer a country without these bureaucrats. Both groups have a somewhat similar orientation to problem solving in that they emphasize efficiency rather than political reconciliations. The military seeks legitimacy through economic progress and order.[58] The bureaucrats are indispensable for achieving these goals.

Brazil's military leaders had utilized the skills of technocrats to a greater extent than is the case in any other Third World military regime. Nordlinger writes that "effective political power clearly resides with the military, but they have depended so heavily upon economists, engineers, agronomists, and urban planners that the Brazilian case has been described as a military–technocratic alliance."[59] (Brazil became democratic in early 1985.) In other military regimes of the Third World technocrats play a crucial role in administering countries. In countries as diverse as Argentina, South Korea, Mali, Nigeria, and Pakistan, technocrats have functioned as loyal allies of the military leaders in power.

In order to achieve a better understanding of the government structures in one party civilian governments in the Third World, we will now discuss governments in three countries—India, Mexico and Tanzania. Except for a brief period from 1977 to 1980, India has been governed by one major political party (the Congress party) since its independence from Britain in 1947. Mexico has been ruled by one party (the Revolutionary Institutional party) since 1929. Tanzania has been a one-party state since 1965. Other parties are permitted in India and Mexico, but not in Tanzania.

India

India promulgated its present Constitution in 1950. It is one of the longest constitutions in the world, in part because it establishes a government structure for the nation as well as for the 22 Indian states. Although India gained independence from Britain in 1947, a constitution had been in effect since 1935. The Constitution of 1950 borrowed heavily from that of 1935. The Constitution of 1950 declares India to be a secular republic (i.e., no preference is given to any religion) and no connection is maintained with the British monarchy. In government structure, although federalism has been adopted because of the diversity of India, India closely follows the British system of parliamentary government and the fusion of power (Britain has a unitary, not a federal system). The parliamentary government has on occasion been questioned in India and other forms of government have been discussed as alternatives. During the 1975 to 1977 Emergency, a French-style presidential system was seriously considered by some,[60] although the debate on the French-style presidential government or any other alternative is virtually nonexistent now. An amendment passed in 1976 centralized power in the hands of the prime minister and reduced the powers of the Parliament and the judiciary. In 1979 this amendment was revised, essentially restoring the Constitution to its pre-1976 status. In other words, India continues to have a government structure similar to what prevails in Britain or other countries with a parliamentary form of government.

The Indian executive branch consists of a president, a vice-president, and the Council of Ministers. The president is the head of state, not of government, and is elected by an electoral college, composed of the elected members of Parliament and the state assemblies. The procedure of election is rather complex; the main object, however, is to ensure parity in votes between Parliament and the state assemblies and to give weight to population, when assigning votes to the latter. The Indian presidency is considered a reward for long years of service to a political party and to the country. In rare circumstances, it is possible for a candidate unaffiliated with any party to be elected to the presidency. In nominating candidates to the Indian presidency, consideration is given to the regional and religious diversity of the country.

The Indian president serves a term of five years and can be reelected. In case of his or her death, resignation, or incapacity, the vice-president (elected by Parliament) assumes the office of the president until a new president is elected which, according to the Constitution, must be done within six months. The vice-president presides over the Council of States (the upper house of the Indian Parliament); otherwise, few official responsibilities have been assigned to the vice-president.

The powers of the president are vast in theory, but limited in practice. The president appoints the prime minister and other members of the Council of Ministers, governors of the states, judges of the national Supreme Court and the states' High Courts, and ambassadors. In actual practice the president appoints the head of the majority party as prime minister, and other ministers are appointed in accordance with the advice of the prime minister. In exercising any power, the general rule is that the president acts on the advice of the Council of Ministers. The tradition in India is well established that the president should not act on his or her own. If no party has a majority in Parliament or the majority party is unable to choose its leader, the president may have some discretion in selecting the prime minister. Even in this case the president must keep in mind that the Council of Ministers needs support of a majority of the members of Parliament in order to function. The president also signs all laws, but has virtually no veto power, as any objections can be overruled by a simple majority in Parliament. On money bills (bills to raise revenue or authorize spending) which the president must also sign, the president cannot object or request reconsideration.

The president has been given extraordinary powers for meeting a national emergency caused by war or external aggression or by internal disturbance. Such an emergency declaration must be approved by Parliament within two months. An important feature of a national emergency is that fundamental rights, guaranteed by the Constitution to the Indian citizens, can be suspended. This was indeed done on three occasions: (1) in 1962 during the Indo-China war, (2) in 1971 during the Indo-Pakistan war, and (3) in 1975 as a response to internal disturbance. The suspension of fundamental rights and jailing of political opponents without trial occurred extensively during the third emergency. It is important to remember, however, that the president acted on the advice of the Council of Ministers and principally the prime minister, Indira Gandhi. Moreover, the powers of the prime minister, not of the president, were increased as a result of the declaration of Emergency. The president can also declare a constitutional emergency in a state if, on the receipt of a report from a state's governor, the president is convinced that government in that state cannot function in accordance with the Constitution. Such an emergency must also be approved by Parliament. Declarations of constitutional emergency have often been politically motivated, because an emergency of this nature replaces a state government with the president's or rather the prime minister's rule.

The real executive branch in India is the prime minister and the Council of Ministers, a body of approximately 45 members. All members of this Council, including its head the prime minister, must be members of Parliament. Though a non-Parliament member can be appointed to the Council of Ministers, he or she must become a Parliament member within six months after joining the Council. The Council of Ministers stays in power as long as it enjoys the support of Parliament. If a no confidence motion is passed in the lower house of Parliament, or a major proposal of the Council of Ministers is defeated in the Parliament's lower house, the Council, including the prime minister, must resign. Then either a new government that commands the support of the lower house of Parliament must be formed or, if that is not possible, new elections to Parliament's lower house must be held.

The Council of Ministers is collectively responsible for all of its decisions. In other words, every member is responsible for the decisions of the Council. This constitutional provision has little significance in practice. A minister can be forced to resign for his or her errors. Moreover, the Council never meets as a body and the policy decisions are made by the more important and politically powerful members of the Council known as the Cabinet.

The Cabinet, headed by the prime minister, has about 20 members and, although not mentioned in the Constitution, is the primary decision-making body of the country. The members of the Cabinet are assigned different departments by the prime minister, and in the performance of their responsibilities they are assisted by lower ranking members of the Council of Ministers called ministers of states. The Cabinet meets regularly and as a general rule makes decisions by consensus, not by vote. The opinions of the prime minister, who presides over these meetings, have the greatest weight in deliberations.

The Cabinet not only makes policy, it is also responsible for the implementation as well as coordination of policy. Major appointments are approved by the Cabinet. In effect, the Cabinet is also the main law-making body, as it is the Cabinet that proposes most of the bills that are enacted as laws by Parliament. The Cabinet works through various committees and is assisted by a Secretariat with civil servants and an intelligence organization (called the Research and Analysis Wing) which is a part of the Cabinet Secretariat.

The prime minister is thus the head of government in India. The members of the Council of Ministers (and of its inner body, the Cabinet) are selected by the prime minister and retain their positions at his or her pleasure. The prime minister receives the credit or the blame for government policies. Although elected by one parliamentary constituency, the prime minister is considered leader of the country.

The Indian Parliament consists of two houses—*Lok Sabha* (House of the People) and *Rajya Sabha* (Council of States). The Indian Constitution also mentions the president as a part of Parliament, thus underscoring the concept of the fusion of power. Members of the *Lok Sabha* are elected by the people (the only exceptions are two members of the Anglo-Indian community who may be appointed by the president if this community has no representation in the *Lok Sabha*). The seats for elected members of the *Lok Sabha* (542) are allocated to the states on the basis of population. *Rajya Sabha* has 250 members, 238 of whom are elected by state assemblies for a six-year term in staggered elections every two years. Twelve members of the upper house are appointed by the president on the basis of their contributions to areas such as literature, science, and the arts.

The *Lok Sabha* is elected every five years unless it is dissolved earlier by the president (on advice of the Council of Ministers or rather the prime minister). During an emergency declared by the president, it can serve for more than five years. It elects a speaker (who, following the British tradition, is expected to be above partisan politics) and operates through a dozen committees. The committees perform vital functions in reviewing the bills presented before the *Lok Sabha,* but do not have the powers enjoyed by the congressional committees in the United States. An important aspect of parliamentary procedure in India (and other countries with a similar government) is the question hour—time set in the beginning of the debate for any member of Parliament to ask questions of the Cabinet members or the Council of Ministers.

In the law-making process the *Lok Sabha* is much more powerful than the *Rajya Sabha*. Most important bills originate in the former. On money bills, which according to the Constitution must originate in the lower house, the *Rajya Sabha* has practically no power. If it disagrees with the *Lok Sabha* on a money bill, the latter can override those objections by merely repassing the bill. On nonmoney bills the differences between the two houses are resolved in joint meetings of Parliament.

As mentioned earlier, the *Lok Sabha* has the power to oust a government by a no confidence vote. Although the Cabinet plays an active role in the law-making process by introducing most bills, Parliament is not a rubber stamp. It does make changes, on occasion substantial, in the bills introduced by the Cabinet. During debates in the Indian Parliament, according to Richard Park and Bruce Bueno de Mesquita, "there is an elevated and dignified quality to much of the activity observable on the floor of the parliament."[61] Another important feature of the Parliament is that over the years the number of its members representing professions, particularly law, has declined and instead, members from other occupations, especially agriculture, have increased.

India has a single, integrated judiciary for the entire country with the Supreme Court at the apex. The Supreme Court has 14 judges appointed by the president who retire at age 65. The judges of the states' highest courts (called High Courts) are also appointed by the president. Legal disputes between the national government and the states and those between states are brought before the Supreme Court. The Supreme Court also hears on appeal those civil and criminal cases which in the judgment of the Court involve constitutional questions.

The powers of the Indian Supreme Court are not as extensive as those of the U.S. Supreme Court, nor are they as limited as those of the British highest court that serves as a part of the House of Lords. The Indian Supreme Court has the power of judicial review and can, therefore, declare the acts of the legislature and of the executive unconstitutional. However, passing a constitutional amendment is relatively easy in India, so Parliament can overrule the Supreme Court. (Parliament alone can amend most provisions of the Constitution and needs ratification by the states only in cases such as changes in the division of powers between the national government and the states.) In India controversy has existed for several years regarding the principles of judicial review and parliamentary supremacy. The Parliament seems to be winning against the Court in this controversy. The Supreme Court, however, is quite powerful and does invalidate acts passed by Parliament. Furthermore, India has developed a judicial tradition in which the decisions of the Supreme Court are given considerable weight and are not reversed by constitutional amendments every time a parliamentary act is declared unconstitutional.

Government structures in the Indian states are patterned after the national government. The state governor is a constitutional head who acts on the advice of the Council of Ministers, headed by a chief minister. In the states the inner bodies of the Council of Ministers are called Cabinets. The relation of the Cabinet to the legislature is similar to that prevailing at the national level.

Within the government structure in India both at the national and the state levels, the civil service plays a very prominent role. The Cabinet members depend on the high-ranking civil servants for advice in law making and law execution. Day-to-day running of government is carried out by the civil service. India has developed one of the finest civil services in the Third World. Civil servants are recruited through written and oral examination and go through training before any assignment. The reputation of the civil service in India is such that as a profession it enjoys the highest social status in the country.

Mexico

The government structure of Mexico is based on the Constitution of 1917 which was adopted following the Revolution of 1910. The 1910 Revolution is considered one of the greatest upheavals of this century.[62] The difference between the theory and practice of this constitution, however, is very great. The Mexican Constitution is based on the U.S. Constitution with emphasis on a bill of rights, federalism, and separation of powers with checks and balances. The Mexican Constitution not only protects rights of the individual and gives to its citizens freedom of speech and assembly, but also provides some guidelines for reformist policies that were the result of the revolutionary fervor of the early twentieth century. Land reform, protection of the rights of the workers by collective bargaining, profit sharing, and national control over the country's resources are among the policy goals mentioned.

The Mexican Constitution establishes federalism; besides the national government, which also controls one federal district, there are 31 states in Mexico with elected governors and legislatures. The principle of separation of powers with checks and balances was adopted by creating three coequal branches of government—the presidency, the Congress, and the Supreme Court. The president is elected for one six-year term. The Congress is bicameral and consists of a Senate representing the states, with 64 members elected for a six-year term, and a Chamber of Deputies with 400 members elected for three years. Mexico's judicial branch is also similar to that of the United States, with the Supreme Court as the highest court of the land. The three branches of the government have checks and balances similar to those provided in the U.S. Constitution.

An important difference between the U.S. and the Mexican constitutions is that the latter places far more limits on the powers of the states. The Mexican Constitution clearly makes the national government dominant over the state governments. The Senate, for example, is empowered to remove elected officials of any state and can request the president to appoint new officials. The Senate can even end all powers of a state.

The reality of Mexican politics is very different from that of the U.S. system. One political party, the Institutional Revolutionary party (PRI), has dominated national as well as state politics in Mexico since its creation in 1929. (From 1929 to 1937, PRI was called the National Revolutionary party; from 1937 to 1945, it was known as the party of the Mexican Revolution.) Other political parties are permitted, particularly as a result of the reforms introduced in 1977. In the presidential elections of 1982, six parties besides PRI nominated candidates. One-fourth of the 400 seats in the Chamber of Deputies are reserved for the opposition parties. The PRI's control over the political machinery in Mexico is, however, so pervasive and firm that the opposition parties have practically no opportunity to wield any real power.

The leader of the PRI is the president who exercises more powers than most executives in the world. As soon as the PRI selects its nominee, it becomes clear who the president will be. Within the party, the incumbent president has a greater influence than anyone else in the selection of the next nominee for the presidency. Often the new president, for example Miguel de la Madrid who was elected in 1982, is the personal choice of the outgoing president. The election of the president is conducted with a great deal of fanfare and the campaign lasts several months. The campaign increases the visibility and popularity of the incoming president in the entire nation.

The Mexican president is the head of state as well as the head of government. Like most other heads of governments, the president has a cabinet with members in charge of different departments (the secretaries). These department heads are completely under the control of the president who can remove them at any time. It is virtually impossible for a Mexican cabinet member to enjoy the kind of power exercised by some members of the U.S. president's Cabinet.

The relation of the Congress to the president is also one of subordination instead of a coequal partner bargaining in the political game. The conflict that takes place on the annual budget between the U.S. president and the Congress is unheard of in Mexico. The Mexican Congress not only obediently approves budget requests of the president, but also any other proposals. Most major bills in Mexico originate with the executive, not the Congress. The president can veto bills passed by Congress but does not need to, because a bill to which the president is opposed cannot get enough votes in Congress to be passed. This situation is somewhat similar to the fusion of power prevailing in the parliamentary governments. In the parliamentary governments, however, the opposition keeps some control over the cabinet by raising questions during the "question hour" in the legislature, and in some countries is in a position to take over the government. Such traditions

Miguel de la Madrid (Hurtado), President
of Mexico.

do not exist in Mexico. With 100 seats now controlled by the opposition in
the lower house, the opposition's voice is often heard, but rarely acted upon
by the party in power. As Pablo Gonzales Casanova writes of the Mexican
Congress: "It seems that the legislative power has a symbolic function: it
sanctions the actions of the Executive."[63]

The Supreme Court is equally docile. In theory the Supreme Court has
been given extensive powers in its relations with the president; in practice,
the Court rarely exercises these powers. Casanova comments, "There is no
doubt that the Supreme Court of Justice is endowed with power; yet it does
generally follow the policy of the Executive, and in fact it serves to make the
Executive more stable."[64] Robert Scott explains that "Mexican courts have
simply carried to its ultimate logical conclusion the United States judicial
practice of refusing to consider 'political questions.' The judges refuse to
attack presidential policies or reject important government programs."[65]

Some critics maintain that the Mexican president exercises authoritarian powers. Kenneth Johnson argues that in the name of protecting internal
security the Mexican president has assumed censorship powers over the
media and the press. "In recent years," according to Johnson, "the
censorship of ideas has become a hallmark of the Mexican Presidency
further underscoring its authoritarian bent."[66]

Tanzania

Tanzania was formed in East Africa in 1964 as a result of a union between Tanganyika and Zanzibar. Tanganyika became free in 1961 (it was a United Nations trust territory administered by Britain) and Zanzibar gained independence (also from Britain) in 1963. Since the formation of the Tanganyika African National Union (TANU) in 1954, Julius Nyerere, its leader, has dominated politics in Tanganyika, and later in Tanzania.[67] Tanganyika is the major partner in Tanzania, and since 1963 TANU has been the only political party in Tanganyika. A constitution adopted in 1965 officially created a single-party state in Tanzania. In Zanzibar, however, a separate party, the Afro-Shirazi party, retained its individual identity. In 1977, TANU and the Afro-Shirazi party merged into a single party, the Revolutionary party.

After achieving independence in 1961, Tanganyika adopted the British-type parliamentary form of government with a cabinet headed by a prime minister. The following year a new constitution replaced the parliamentary government with a different government, giving extensive powers to the president. The Constitution of 1962 retained the ministerial system and a vice-president acted as the prime minister. The real powers were, however, concentrated in the hands of the president. In 1965, as a result of the union of Tanganyika and Zanzibar, another constitution was put into effect. Although subsequently amended, this constitution is the basis of the present-day government structure in Tanzania.

The most important member of Tanzania's government is the president, who is elected by the people for five years after being nominated by an electoral conference of the ruling party. (Note that only one candidate can run for the president's office in Tanzania, as only one party is permitted.) Like the Mexican president, the president of Tanzania is the head of state as well as the head of government. The president appoints two vice-presidents; one is the chief executive of Zanzibar and the other acts as the prime minister. Cabinet members are also appointed by the president. The prime minister and other ministers are members of the National Assembly. The president also makes several other important appointments, including judges of the High Court, regional commissioners, and some members of the legislature. The president signs all bills and has veto power. A presidential veto can be overridden by a two-thirds vote in the Assembly. As Tanzania is a one-party state, veto power is not used. The president has the power to dissolve the National Assembly; in that case, however, the president must also stand for reelection.

The unicameral National Assembly is the law-making body of Tanzania. Its membership is partly elected and partly appointed. The election is held every five years and party nominees, about 107 of them, are easily elected.

The rest, 126 in all (although the actual number may be somewhat less), are either appointed by the president or the executive committee of the party or become members of the Assembly because of some other appointed office that they hold, such as a regional commissioner. The Assembly functions somewhat as the British or the Indian Parliament. Committees are used for reviewing bills and members raise questions on the floor of the Assembly, allowing the ministers to explain government policy. As no opposition is permitted, legislation that originates in the executive branch sails through the Assembly smoothly. Raymond Hopkins argues that "in spite of the open and honest criticisms often voiced in the Assembly, in nearly all cases the Assembly has been concerned with ratifying decisions made by some other group."[68]

The chief court in Tanzania is the High Court. Subordinate and local courts also exist. Conflict between the judiciary and the executive or legislative branches is not expected in a one-party state. The Tanzanian Constitution does not have a formal bill of rights. Instead, the party constitution incorporates such rights which for the most part have been honored in the country and protected by the courts. An unusual feature of the Tanzanian judicial system is a Permanent Commission of Enquiry, which investigates charges of misuse of authority by government officials.

Because *ujamaa* (rural socialism) is the official doctrine practiced in Tanzania, the government's presence is felt all over the country. The system of local government has been completely revamped; now the rural masses often deal directly with the government bureaucracy. Nyerere calls Tanzania a democracy and considering his leadership style, his claim is not totally unjustified.

NOTES

1. Robert G. Wesson, *Communism and Communist Systems* (Englewood Cliffs, N.J.: Prentice-Hall, 1978), p. 6.
2. Robert G. Wesson, *Modern Government: Three Worlds of Politics* (Englewood Cliffs, N.J.: Prentice-Hall, 1981), pp. 199–203.
3. Terence Smith, "Iran: Five Years of Fanaticism," *New York Times Magazine,* February 12, 1984, pp. 21–35.
4. See Muammar Al-Qadhafi, *The Green Book: Part One, The Solution of the Problem of Democracy,* "The Authority of the People" (London: Marten, Brian & O'Keefe, 1976).
5. See K. C. Wheare, *Federal Government* (New York: Oxford University Press, 1964), p. 24.
6. Karl Deutsch, *Politics and Government: How People Decide Their Fate,* 3d ed. (Boston: Houghton Mifflin, 1980), p. 314.
7. Ibid., p. 320.

8. Ibid., p. 317.
9. Ibid., p. 318.
10. Walter Darnell Jacobs and Harold Zink, *Modern Governments,* 3d ed. (New York: Van Nostrand, 1966), p. 527, and Robert C. Tucker, ed., "What Is to Be Done," *The Lenin Anthology* (New York: Norton, 1975), pp. 12–114.
11. Jacobs and Zink, p. 516.
12. Robert Sharlet, ed., *The New Soviet Constitution of 1977: Analysis and Text* (Brunswick, Ohio: King's Court Communications, 1978), p. 78.
13. Ibid., p. 77.
14. Vernon V. Aspaturian, "Soviet Politics," in Roy C. Macridis, ed., *Modern Political Systems: Europe,* 5th ed. (Englewood Cliffs, N.J.: Prentice-Hall, 1983), p. 338.
15. Cited in Gary K. Bertsch, *Power and Policy in Communist Systems,* 2d ed. (New York: Wiley, 1982), p. 129.
16. See the following for some typical ways Western scholars have portrayed the Soviet administrative structure: David Lane, *Politics and Society in the USSR* (New York: Random House, 1971), p. 145; Vadim Medish, *The Soviet Union,* 2d revised ed. (Englewood Cliffs, N.Y.: Prentice-Hall, 1985), p. 117; John Hazard, *The Soviet System of Government,* 4th revised ed. (Chicago: University of Chicago Press, 1968), pp. 216–218; Leonard Schapiro, *The Government and Politics of the Soviet Union* (New York: Random House, 1965), p. 179–181; and Aspaturian, p. 362.
17. Aspaturian, p. 361.
18. Ibid., p. 360.
19. David F. Roth and Frank L. Wilson, *The Comparative Study of Politics,* 2d ed. (Englewood Cliffs, N.J.: Prentice-Hall 1980), p. 123.
20. Bertsch, p. 118.
21. Roth and Wilson, p. 126.
22. Ibid., p. 124.
23. Bertsch, p. 119.
24. Roth and Wilson, p. 125.
25. Bertsch, p. 119.
26. Aspaturian, p. 398.
27. Macridis, p. 369.
28. See Bertsch, p. 120.
29. Wheare, p. 24.
30. Jacobs and Zink, p. 515.
31. Zbigniew Brzezinski, "The Soviet Political System: Transformation or Degeneration?" in Zbigniew Brzezinski, ed., *Dilemmas of Change in Soviet Politics* (New York: Columbia University Press, 1969), pp. 1–34.
32. Ibid., p. 8.
33. Ibid., pp. 19–30.
34. Cited in Bertsch, pp. 138, 139.
35. Karl Deutsch, "Cracks in the Monolith: Possibilities and Patterns of Disintegra-

tion in Totalitarian Systems," in Harry Eckstein and David E. Apter, eds., *Comparative Politics: A Reader* (New York: Free Press, 1968), p. 16.

36. Morton Schwartz, *The Foreign Policy of the U.S.S.R.: Domestic Factors* (Encino, Calif.: Dickenson, 1975), p. 172.

37. Jerry Hough, "The Soviet System: Petrification or Pluralism?" in Lenard J. Cohen and Jane P. Shapiro, eds., *Communist Systems in Comparative Perspective* (New York: Doubleday (Anchor Books), 1974), p. 472.

38. Ibid., p. 456.

39. Bertsch, p. 138.

40. Michael Roskin, *Other Governments of Europe: Sweden, Spain, Italy, Yugoslavia, and East Germany* (Englewood Cliffs, N.J.: Prentice-Hall, 1977), p. 136.

41. Ibid., p. 135.

42. Vaclav Benes, Andrew Gyorgy, and George Stambuk, *Eastern European Government and Politics* (New York: Harper & Row, 1966), p. 103.

43. Ibid., p. 108.

44. Roskin, p. 134.

45. Bertsch, p. 121.

46. James R. Townsend, "Politics in China," in Gabriel A. Almond and G. Bingham Powell, Jr., eds., *Comparative Politics Today: A World View* (Boston: Little, Brown, 1980), p. 402.

47. Ibid., p. 400.

48. Bertsch, p. 131.

49. Townsend, p. 403.

50. See Gary Bertsch, Robert Clark, and David Wood, *Comparing Political Systems: Power and Policy in Three Worlds* (New York: Wiley, 1982), p. 453.

51. Gary W. Wynia, *Argentina in the Postwar Era* (Albuquerque: University of New Mexico Press, 1978), p. 12.

52. David G. Becker, "Development, Democracy and Dependency in Latin America: A Post-Imperalist View," *Third World Quarterly* 6 (April 1984): 418.

53. Eric A. Nordlinger, *Soldiers in Politics: Military Coups and Governments* (Englewood Cliffs, N.J.: Prentice Hall, 1977), p. 139.

54. Ibid., pp. 133–134.

55. Ibid., p. 134.

56. Ibid. Another example is that of Egypt under Nasser. See Edward Feit, *The Armed Bureaucrats* (Boston: Houghton Mifflin, 1973), pp. 132–163, esp. p. 152.

57. Nordlinger, p. 109.

58. Richard A. Falk, *A World Order Perspective on Authoritarian Tendencies* (New York: Institute for World Order, 1980), p. 19.

59. Nordlinger, p. 120.

60. See Robert L. Hardgrave, Jr., *India: Government and Politics in a Developing Nation,* 3d ed. (New York: Harcourt Brace Jovanovich, 1980), p. 47; and Kul B. Rai, "Should India Change Its Parliamentary System?" *Christian Science Monitor,* January 28, 1981, p. 23.

61. Richard L. Park and Bruce Bueno de Mesquita, *India's Political System* (Englewood Cliffs, N.J.: Prentice-Hall, 1979), p. 78.

62. For a brief historical background of the Mexican Revolution, see Robert E. Scott, "Politics in Mexico," in Almond and Powell, pp. 370–371.

63. Pablo Gonzales Casanova, *Democracy in Mexico* (New York: Oxford University Press, 1970), p. 20.

64. Ibid., p. 24.

65. Scott, p. 389.

66. Kenneth E. Johnson, *Mexican Democracy: A Critical View*, rev. ed. (New York: Praeger, 1978), p. 47.

67. For a background on TANU and the Tanzanian political system see Raymond E. Hopkins, *Political Roles in a New State: Tanzania's First Decade* (New Haven, Conn.: Yale University Press, 1971).

68. Ibid., p. 28.

CHAPTER 8

Interest Groups in
Three Worlds

Interest groups exist in all political systems in order to express the needs and demands of particular segments of a country's population. Interest groups hope and expect to get special treatment for themselves and their programs by exerting influence within the political system, not by running candidates for office as political parties do.

First World interest groups are very diverse because Western political systems are open to any group active enough to participate in the political process. Labor unions, professional associations, artisans, scientists, and environmentalists vie for attention and expect to receive consideration from decision makers.

In the Second World, however, interest groups are controlled and directed by the Communist party. In general, they support the existing political structure and its programs. The groups are allowed to point out minor shortcomings, but they cannot attack the leading and guiding role of the Communist party. Those who do not agree with the system are repressed. Within the ruling Communist regime, however, institutional pressure groups struggle for power.

In most of the Third World countries the interest groups are not well organized or effective. The military as a dominant group is particularly evident in several of these countries.

Interest groups are central to the process of politics in all three political worlds. Whether the aim is to promote some form of political cooperation and common problem solving or to compete more effectively for political values, nothing is more common than individuals of a similar persuasion joining together in groups. The reason for this behavior is obvious: groups can more effectively pursue political goals than can isolated individuals. All important political activity occurs at the group level, and in most societies interest group activity is regarded as "politics as usual." Interest groups perform important functions such as political socialization, political communication, and conflict representation (see Chapter 2). Across the three political worlds interest groups exist in a great variety of forms.

SHARED ATTITUDES, EXPECTED REWARDS, AND RESOURCES

Social scientists have given many names to interest groups, for example, special cause groups, intermediary groups, private associations, and lobbying groups. Each of these terms reveals a particular conception of the nature and function of an interest group, but all are in some way misleading.[1] By conceiving of interest groups as *intermediary groups*, attention is given to the fact that interest groups constitute an important link between the government and the rest of the society. It is through interest groups that the general population both communicates political demands to governmental institutions and responds to the previous political decisions of such institutions by demonstrations of support or of protest as in strikes and riots. The concept of an intermediary group, however, conceals the fact that many of the most important modern interest groups consist entirely of elite members within the government or ruling political parties and do not involve the general population at all. The term *lobbying group* implies a formal and highly structured organization of lawyers, public relations specialists, and other professionals like those found in the West, but ignores the informal and intermittent groups found in the Third World. Similarly, the terms *private associations* and *special cause groups* draw attention to the fact that many interest groups consist of a small number of people pursuing limited and specific political goals that will benefit only their own group, but seem to ignore the so-called public interest groups that have recently developed in the West. One such group is Common Cause in the United States.[2] The concept of "special causes" also ignores the fact that some interest groups, like those involved in the fight for women's rights or the preservation of the environment, pursue benefits for a numerical majority of the population. These examples illustrate the fact that in the existing literature interest groups have not been defined precisely and what has passed for a general definition of interest groups is really the enumeration of characteristics and attributes common to some groups but not all.

An adequate definition of an interest group must begin with the identification of the three elements common to all groups: shared attitudes, future expectations of reward, and resources with which the group hopes to influence public policy.[3]

Shared Attitudes

All interest groups consist of persons who presently share a common attitude or attitudes toward some political or social issue. The attitudes may pertain to such diverse issues as taxation and economic policy, human rights, environmental protection, education, foreign policy, and single issues such as abortion, prohibition, or gay rights. Interest groups within government institutions or ruling political parties (e.g., the Communist party of the Soviet Union) often manifest attitudes favoring increased government spending in such fields as military weaponry, industrial development, or social welfare programs. Regardless of the issue, the shared attitude is the cement that holds the members of the interest group together and gives the group a unique identity different from that of other interest groups. It is important to realize, however, that attitudes are not permanent. Attitudinal change is present in every society and may be accelerated by such factors as major historical events, the introduction of foreign ideas, the development of new technology, changes in economic conditions, and generational change. Changing political attitudes often lead to changes in the pattern of interest group activity and to the development of new kinds of interest groups.[4] The effects of attitudinal change on the nature of interest groups are evident in all three political worlds. In Western states, the achievement of economic affluence connected with the development of the welfare state has led to a decline in the popularity of labor unions and the rise of groups concerned with quality-of-life issues such as the environment. In the Second World, new attitudes toward participation and dissent within the Communist party of the Soviet Union have led to the rise of groups representing the military, state industry, and state agriculture. In some Third World countries, attitudinal changes connected with economic and social development have led to the creation of bureaucratically organized business and labor interest groups.

Expectation of Rewards

The second element common to all interest groups is an expectation of future gain or benefit. Interest groups are self-interested groups in which the members act together in the hope of realizing future rewards and benefits for themselves or for client groups on whose behalf they are working. An example of a client relationship is the Children's Welfare League, an interest group in the United States that works to protect the legal rights of its clients, children under the age of majority. The rewards sought by interest groups include increased rights, privileges, benefits, and opportunities. In many societies the majority of interest group activity revolves around the struggle for a larger share of the annual national budget, but the rewards sought may be as diverse as the right of a minority language group to educate its children in its native language rather than in the language of the majority or the opportunity for nonsmokers to enjoy a no smoking area in all public buildings. The rewards sought by interest groups are communicated to the rest of the political system as political demands. The process by which political demands are developed and communicated is called interest articulation, the main function of an interest group. Political demands are commonplace in all three political worlds. In the West, interest groups demand such goals as an Equal Rights Amendment to the U.S. Constitution, reform of the education system in France, and an end to legal restrictions on divorce in Italy. In the Second World, special interest groups inside the Communist party of the Soviet Union seek more funding for agriculture and the development of a foreign policy of global power projection by the USSR. In the Third World, military groups demand more spending for police and defense functions, and left-wing nationalists call for an end to military cooperation with the states of the West.

The creation, growth, and demise of interest groups are often determined by the rate of success in achieving the rewards and benefits sought. Sidney Waldman has noted that an entrepreneurial relationship exists between the organizers and members of interest groups.[5] For the interest group to be sustained, both the organizers and the members must receive benefits. The failure to receive expected rewards may also affect the methods or tactics used by interest groups. Groups may resort to obstructionist tactics, threats, and even violence when peaceful methods fail to achieve results.

Political Resources

All interest groups possess resources with which they hope to influence the political institutions that make decisions about the benefits they seek. The ultimate goal of all interest group activity is to influence the public policy process, the process by which political values are authoritatively allocated.[6] To this end, interest groups employ both direct and indirect methods. Direct methods involve communication and interaction with high-level public policy makers such as that undertaken by lobbyists and other group representatives with elected and appointed officials. Indirect methods involve an intermediary step or objective that the group seeks to achieve as a prerequisite to influencing public policy makers, such as an informational public relations (some would say propaganda) campaign to persuade the general public of the wisdom and necessity of granting the group's demands. Interest groups differ greatly in the resources they possess to influence public policy. Some groups possess a varied and impressive arsenal of resources, whereas others are comparatively resource-poor, although no interest group is totally lacking in resources. Interest group resources include social prestige and respect, membership size, money, group unity, leadership skills, substantive knowledge and expertise, knowledge of the political process and campaign experience, control over jobs, control over votes, the properties of bureaucratic organization, a reputation for effectiveness, and a high level of commitment resulting from acceptance of a common ideology or other factors.[7] Interest groups employ their resources to influence such target organizations as legislatures, administrative agencies, and ruling political parties which make decisions affecting the welfare of the groups. Much of the political process in all three political worlds consists of the competition between interest groups to influence the behavior of government decision makers.

Elites and Parties

Most interest groups also share two other characteristics. First, interest groups are usually elite-led and dominated, and even in the states of the West where a large number of interest groups exist, only a small percentage of the population is involved. The leaders of interest groups consist of high-level members of the elite both inside and outside government, and the general membership is made up of political activists. Second, many interest groups have a special relationship with one or more political parties. A political party consists of a more or less permanent coalition of interest groups that supply votes, financial contributions, and other forms of support in exchange for the party's commitment to work for enactment of their demands into law. Political parties aggregate or bring together the demands of several interest groups in a coherent program which is often presented as a formal party platform. The nature of the relationship of interest group to political party varies from a close one in which the two organizations share common leaders and a common sense of identity, to only informal and intermittent cooperation. In two-party systems and multiparty systems, political parties compete for the support of interest groups. In single-party systems like those found in the Communist states and some countries of the Third World, interest groups must develop a working relationship with the ruling party to participate effectively in the political process.[8]

VARIETIES OF INTEREST GROUPS

Joseph LaPalombara, a long-time student of the subject, has noted that interest groups may be classified in an almost infinite number of ways.[9] Common comparative schemes distinguish between groups on the basis of the attitudes that unite the members, goals, targets, size, wealth, degree of formal organization, membership, and tactics.[10] The use of such factors for comparison reveals the great variety of interest groups in the three political worlds. A comparison of interest groups on the basis of attitudes reveals groups that have formed over such concerns as economics, race, religion, region, ethnicity, foreign policy, and a vast number of philosophical and normative matters such as disarmament, prohibition, antivivisection, and conformity to traditional social values. Comparisons on the basis of group size, membership, wealth, and degree of formal organization also demonstrate the diversity of interest groups. Studies have identified small, well-financed, and highly organized groups in the West such as the British Medical Association, groups in the Second World consisting of high-level government or Communist party bureaucrats, and diffuse and loosely organized groups such as the *Sarvodaya* movement in India in which traveling teachers and holy men seek to organize the traditional population of India's villages. Interest groups also differ in terms of their targets and tactics. Interest group targets vary from chief executives, legislatures, courts, and administrative agencies to ruling political parties and the general public. Tactics include lobbying (direct communication with high-level decision makers), letter-writing campaigns, voter registration drives, strikes, public relations campaigns, direct participation in government decision-making bodies, protests and demonstrations, and violence or the threat of violence.

INTEREST GROUPS IN THREE WORLDS

The purpose in preceding chapters has been to develop a "panoramic view" of politics by identifying the fundamental differences in the political processes of the three political worlds. By employing the same approach in the study of interest groups, their great variety becomes manageable and the basic nature of interest group behavior in each of the political worlds can be understood. Political interest groups develop from the general societies of which they are part. Interest group conflict parallels the basic cleavages or divisions in a society because major social groups will seek to influence the public policy process. The style of interest group behavior also reflects the general style used in economic and social interaction. For example, in societies where a professional and bureaucratic style prevails, interest groups employ lawyers and public relations specialists who utilize specialized information and expertise to influence the public policy process. In general, the social setting is the major determinant of the nature of interest groups. In addition, however, political culture also affects the nature of interest groups because such factors as political values, expectations, laws, and the structure of government shape the tactics and the behavior of group members. Despite similar social settings, differences in political culture have produced unique patterns of interest group activities in the First World and the industrialized states of the Second World.

Western politics occurs in a social setting ranging from advanced industrialization to postindustrialization. *Associational interest groups* dominate at this level of development. Associational interest groups are specialized structures for interest articulation (e.g., trade unions and business organizations).[11] Associational groups are the representatives of the highly differentiated and specialized groups in Western society, including various professions, big and small businesses, and rural and urban populations. The large number of associational groups reflects not only the high degree of specialization in the society, but also a legal and normative emphasis on participation. Associational groups display a high degree of internal organization and are resource-rich. Stable relationships between government and associational groups are common in Western countries, as, for example, in formalized consultation, bargaining, and negotiations.[12]

Politics in the Communist World occurs in a social setting of advanced industrialization in Europe and preindustrialization outside Europe. Despite a level of development similar to many states of the West, institutional interest groups rather than associational groups dominate in the Communist states of Europe. This is the result of the preeminent position of Communist ideology and the Communist party. The most important groups are those within the Communist party or the state bureaucracy (the government), which has the function of implementing the party's policies. Private associational groups like those found in the West are illegal and repressed because the official ideology prescribes collective goals and norms of behavior for all. By definition, *institutional interest groups* are groups that have been created for purposes other than the articulation of interests.[13] In the case of the Communist parties and the state bureaucracies of the Second World, these purposes are the establishment and implementation of public policies. However, these groups act as interest groups by maximizing their own benefits from such policies, especially by seeking larger shares of the national budget or a larger role in the policy making process.[14] Institutional interest groups in the Second World include the military, the scientific community, state industry, and state agriculture. Because of their strategic location inside the ruling Communist party or government, these groups possess a monopoly of influence over the public policy process.

A preindustrial social setting exists in the states of the Third World. In such societies the specialization and differentiation that gave rise to the growth of associational groups in the West has not yet occurred. Although some associational groups (unions and business groups) and some institutional groups (military cliques) do exist in the modern sectors of society, nonassociational groups dominate in the Third World. *Nonassociational groups* include kinship, lineage, ethnic, regional, and class groups. They articulate interests intermittently or irregularly, lack an organized procedure for processing and assigning priorities to demands, and demonstrate a lower level of internal organization than associational or institutional groups.[15] Although some nonassociational groups may not organize for direct political activity, these groups are important because of the strong sense of identity shared by their members. Not only do these groups tend to persist in preindustrial societies, but they also form the basis of strong, politically relevant subcultures.[16] In many cases nonassociational groups are represented by self-appointed leaders and it is not easy to distinguish the demands of such individuals from the demands of the group.[17] The simultaneous existence of associational and nonassociational interests, as well as of protest groups, contributes to the intensity of political conflict in much of the Third World.

Political reality is complex and two qualifications must be made to the preceding classification of interest groups. First, all political systems occasionally experience a fourth type of interest group, anomic or protest groups. *Anomic groups* are usually poorly organized, often spontaneous, and always short-lived. They develop around attitudes of frustration when expectations of reward are not realized or when adequate channels for the communication of demands to political decision makers do not exist. Anomic groups often employ such tactics as mass demonstrations, threats, and violence. Such groups can be found in all three political worlds and range from student protestors in France, to Russian Jews who chain themselves to public buildings (in protest against policies restricting emigration to Israel), to mobs of Islamic fundamentalists in Iran. Anomic groups are most common in the Third World states. Second, although one type of interest group dominates in each of the three political worlds, it is important to remember that some examples of the other types of groups are also present. In the West, private associational groups dominate but institutional groups consisting of persons within the government are also important. In the Second World the domination of the political process by institutional interests has led to the rise of some dissident, anomic groups. In Poland an associational group, the independent labor union, Solidarity, developed only to be quickly repressed. In the Third World some Western-style associational groups exist along with the dominant nonassociational and anomic groups.

THE FIRST WORLD

Interest groups play a prominent and open part in the political process of the Western World. In comparative perspective, Western interest groups are more numerous, better developed, and play a more important role in the public policy process than interest groups in either the Second or the Third World. The number and prominence of Western interest groups are the result of both the level of development of Western society and the political culture. The social setting of the Western states reflects complexity and affluence, two elements conducive to the growth of interest groups. Interest groups duplicate the divisions within the general society, and the complex societies of the West include a wide variety of economic, political, and social attitudes around which groups have formed. For example, Western economies contain such diverse business organizations as giant corporations, small businesses, heavy industries, service firms, unionized industries, nonunionized industries, agricultural firms, multinational corporations, and nationalized or state-owned industries—all having unique political needs and interests. In addition, in the affluent environment of the West the resources needed to establish and maintain interest groups are widely available. In the United States even those interest groups representing prisoners, children below the age of majority, and welfare recipients possess large staffs, public relations specialists, lawyers, and professional lobbyists. Western political culture has also contributed to the rise of interest groups. The constitutions and laws of the Western states grant all citizens important political and legal rights, such as the freedom of speech and the freedom of assembly which are prerequisites to interest group formation. In addition, Western political values place great emphasis on political participation, the pursuit of self-interest, political organization, and competition (see the discussion of liberalism and social liberalism in Chapter 4).

Despite the importance of cultural and developmental factors, these factors alone do not explain the proliferation of Western interest groups. The growth of government programs associated with the rise of the welfare state has also had an important effect. Government programs have stimulated the development of new interest groups by providing their beneficiaries with an incentive for political organization. Groups receiving government grants such as pensions, medical payments, or housing subsidies have sought to preserve and increase their benefits by creating interest groups to represent them. Such interest groups lobby with both the legislature which enacts the program and the executive agency which implements the program. Interest groups oriented toward specific government programs frequently represent institutions such as universities and hospitals which receive large sums of money from the government. Such interest groups have substantial financial and leadership resources and often develop information and expertise in the relevant area equal to that possessed by the government. The 1960s witnessed a rapid increase in the number of interest groups as government programs in states like Great Britain, Canada, the United States, and Sweden proliferated. The economic problems that beset the West at the end of the 1960s set off an intense competition between interest groups, called by one observer the "benefits scramble,"[18] as the beneficiaries of the various government programs sought to preserve their subsidies in an age of reduced government spending.

Since the 1960s three important trends have emerged in interest group politics in the West. First, there has been a proliferation of both the number and variety of interest groups. Because of the changing nature of Western society, quality-of-life interest groups (e.g., environmental and antinuclear movements) have joined the older economic interest groups. In the Western states today nearly every sector and interest is represented by sophisticated interest groups. Second, interest groups have assumed new functions previously performed by other institutions, particularly political parties.[19] In addition to articulating interests, interest groups now play an important role in shaping public opinion, stimulating political participation, political communication (informing the government of the view of a segment of the population), political finance, and the implementation of government policies. Third, interest groups have achieved an institutionalized role in the process by which government decisions are made. In Western Europe, interest groups participate in hundreds of legally authorized commissions, boards, and councils within both the executive and legislature branches. It is widely accepted by the Western European elites that such participation represents an "indispensable collaboration" in the age of political and economic interdependence. Each of these trends deserves individual attention.

Proliferation of Interest Groups

What factors are responsible for the increase in the number and variety of interest groups in the Western states? To answer this question it is first necessary to survey the nature of Western society, because interest groups duplicate general divisions within a society. The states of the West are divided between industrial societies and postindustrial societies (see Chapter 3). In industrial societies the major divisions include industrial labor, industrial owners and management, and a small number of traditional agricultural groups. In the industrial societies of the West each of these segments of the population is represented by a wide variety of interest groups. For example, industrial labor is represented by national trade unions, which are Communist, socialist, Catholic, and independent, in addition to a myriad of regional and protest groups. The major conflict in industrial society revolves around the issue of how much the government should intervene in the society on behalf of less-advantaged groups. Generally, trade unions and other workers' groups favor an expansion of government programs to aid the less advantaged, whereas business groups seek a reduction of such programs as a way of cutting government spending.

In postindustrial societies new divisions are created within the work force as workers employed in white-collar, service industries outnumber those employed in industrial production. In addition, quality-of-life issues (protection of the environment, civil rights, privacy, and women's equality) divide the population as groups take different positions on the importance of these issues and the speed with which they should be addressed. In theory, the older conflicts of the industrial period, those revolving around the issue of government intervention, should be largely resolved in postindustrial societies. However, because the most affluent states have only recently attained postindustrial development, the new divisions have been added to the older, industrial ones. The proliferation of interest groups in the postindustrial societies of the United States, Great Britain, the German Federal Republic, France, Sweden, and Canada results from the fact that industrial and postindustrial interest groups exist side-by-side.

Industrial Interest Groups. Trade unions and business organizations are the most important economic interest groups. Along with professional associations, labor and business groups are the chief competitors in the effort to influence public policy. Table 8.1 contains a comparison of the trade unions in five major states of Europe. European trade unions share three important characteristics, large memberships, centralized national organizations, and a close relationship with working-class political parties.

Great Britain has nearly 12 million trade unionists and 400 separate unions. Some 85% of the total trade union membership belongs to unions affiliated with the Trade Union Congress (TUC), the largest national labor federation. The British trade union movement has been described as "two parts pressure group and one part political party" because it was labor leaders who founded the British Labour party in 1900.[20] The relationship between the unions and the Labour party today is one of interdependence and direct overlap.[21] Of the 28 seats on the Party's National Executive Council, 12 are filled by unions. In addition, unions supply approximately 80% of the party's general funding, and half of the Labour members of Parliament are directly sponsored (funded) for elections by trade unions.

Although in Sweden representatives of the Swedish Labor Federation (LO) do not sit on the executive board of the Swedish Social Democratic

Table 8.1 European Trade Unions

State	Trade Union	Membership (in millions)	Total Population
Great Britain	Trade Union Congress (TUC) (includes 85% of all trade unionists)	11.5	55,800,000
Germany	German Trade Union Federation (DGB) (includes 16 unions)	17.0	61,350,000
Sweden	Swedish Federation of Labor (LO) (includes 25 blue-collar unions)	2.0	8,300,000
	Swedish Central Organization of Salaried Employees (TCO) (composed of 24 national white-collar unions)	1.0	
France	General Confederation of Labor (CGT)	2.0	53,680,000
	French Confederation of Democratic Labor (CFDT)	0.7	
	French Confederation of Christian Workers (CFTC)	0.4	
	Workers Force (CGT-FO)	0.2	
	French Confederation of Labor (CFT)	0.1	
Italy	General Confederation of Italian Labor (Communist)	3.0	57,100,000
	Italian Confederation of Free Trade Unions (Catholic)	2.0	
	Social Democratic Union of Italian Labor (socialist)	0.8	
	Neo-Fascist CISNAL	0.5	

party, the LO members constitute 60 to 70% of the party's membership and are its chief source of financial support.[22] It is also common for leaders to hold top positions in the LO and Social Democratic party simultaneously.

French trade unions are fragmented along political–ideological lines, and Communist, socialist, Catholic, and white-collar unions exist side-by-side. The most important unions maintain close linkages to French political parties. For example, the Communist General Confederation of Labor (CGT), the nation's largest union with 2 million members, is dominated by the Communist party. Half of the members of the executive branch of the CGT hold high-level positions in the Communist party, and the union has always adhered closely to the party line.[23]

U.S. unions deviate in several respects from the European model. Like governmental institutions, labor unions in the United States are more decentralized than in Europe. Several major unions, the AFL-CIO, United Auto Workers, Teamsters, and United Mine Workers, exist as separate entities and are not affiliated with a single labor federation. In addition, although labor groups have often endorsed Democratic party candidates, the ties between the party and the unions are weaker and less specific than in Europe.

Business interest groups in the Western states fall into three categories; (1) the representatives of big business, especially industry, (2) the representatives of medium-sized and smaller businesses, and (3) protest groups representing shopkeepers and small businessmen. Business organizations (along with professional associations) were the first modern interest groups to form, and trade unions, their chief competitor, developed in reaction to the influence of business in the public policy process. The primary concerns of business groups have always been industrial relations and the development of government policies favorable toward business. Organizations representing the largest industries, such as the Confederation of British Industries (CBI) or the National Association of Manufacturers (NAM) in the United States, wield great influence because their financial resources and leadership skills are vast. The representatives of medium-sized businesses (e.g., the U.S. Chamber of Commerce and the National Association of German Employers) also possess substantial influence because of the number of businesses that they represent. Business organizations do not generally have institutionalized ties with political parties, but they are major contributors to center-right parties (centrist, Catholic, and conservative parties), for example the Conservative party in Britain, the Christian Democratic Union in Germany, and Christian Democratic party in Italy.[24] In France, Italy, and Belgium, groups representing small businessmen and artisans have a tradition of vehement and even violent protest. This trend is perhaps most pronounced in France where in the 1950s the Union for the Defense of Shopkeepers and Artisans, founded by Pierre Poujade, engaged in a series of protests including the symbolic "kidnapping" of tax collectors.[25]

Professional associations and agricultural organizations are other important economic interest groups. The importance of professional associations stems from the fact that they represent affluent and highly educated members of society. Professional associations are primarily interested in issues relating to professional standards and economic matters within their fields. The most important professional associations are those representing physicians, lawyers and teachers. Agricultural organizations represent a small and declining percentage of the population, but they have been among the most successful groups in defending the interests of their members. In Germany where farmers constitute less than 5% of the population and agriculture's contribution to the GNP is less than 3%, farmers receive more government subsidies than any other occupational group.[26] Some observers in Germany have called farmers the "secret rich," and surveys have shown the per capita net worth of farmers to be approximately a half-million marks.[27] Subsidies to farmers are substantial in all of the states of the West. The success of agricultural organizations is the result of several factors, including group cohesiveness, the high percentage of farmers organized, and the overrepresentation of agricultural areas in national legislatures.

Postindustrial Interest Groups. The 1960s and 1970s witnessed the rise of a wide variety of so-called public service or public interest groups. These groups differ from the older, economic interest groups because they pursue goals that will benefit large portions of the population rather than just the narrow interests of their specific membership. Although the distinction between self-interest and public interest groups is somewhat ambiguous, Jeffrey Berry has argued that public interest groups can be identified by the fact that they seek "a collective good, the achievement of which will not selectively and materially benefit the membership or activists of the organization."[28] Organizations generally accepted as public interest groups include those pursuing goals of clean air, clean water, the preservation of wildlife, beautification of the landscape, protection of privacy, children's rights, consumer protection, peace, reduction of noise pollution, and nuclear safety. Although some public interest groups (e.g., the British Society for the Prevention of Cruelty to Animals) date from the nineteenth century, most such groups are the product of postindustrial society. Their formation is dependent on the existence of three factors: (1) an affluent and highly educated population with money to spend on political causes, (2) an "idea-oriented" political style, and (3) a respected scientific community with the means of communicating its concerns to the general population.[29] These factors have been present in the most affluent Western states (the United States, Sweden, the Federal Republic of Germany, Canada, France, and Great Britain) since the 1960s.

In contemporary Western politics, public interest groups frequently find themselves in competition with the older, industrial interests. This can be seen most clearly in the case of environmental groups that demand strict government policies against pollution, which increases the cost of doing business. Such demands are often opposed by businesses fearing the loss of profits and unions fearing that more costly operations may lead to the loss of jobs. For example, in Germany and Austria antinuclear groups have been successful in bringing about a moratorium on the construction of nuclear-generating facilities. This was accomplished despite the fact that major unions and business groups favored their development as a way of lowering the cost of energy and creating new jobs. Consumer groups seeking increased protection in the marketplace have also frequently engaged in conflict with business organizations. Public interest organizations exist in a wide variety of forms, but some have larger memberships with extensive grass-roots organizations. In the United States, the Consumers Union claims 2 million members, Common Cause 275,000, and the Sierra Club 162,000. In the Federal Republic of Germany a number of environmental groups opposed to the development of nuclear energy plants have combined to form the Federal League of Citizen Groups for the Protection of the Environment, popularly known as the "Greens" or "Environmentalists."[30] During the 1983 national election, the Federal League was sufficiently strong to run a slate of "Green" candidates and won 5.7% of the total vote.[31] As postindustrial society continues to develop in the West, public interest organizations will play an even more important role in the political process.

New Functions of Interest Groups

In the 1960s social scientists assumed a threefold division of labor between interest groups, political parties, and governments in the Western political process. The structures were thought to perform the following specialized functions: interest groups articulate (communicate) interests, political parties aggregate interests (combine them into coherent programs), and governments make and implement public policies (make authoritative decisions about political demands). In the division of functions between political parties and interest groups, the role of interest groups was limited to the identification of demands within the general society and the communication of those demands to political parties and government institutions. Interest groups were considered to be organizations with small memberships, limited purposes, and little support within the general population. On the other hand, political parties performed a wide range of functions, including political recruitment, political socialization, political communication, electoral competition, and political accommodation and compromise. Recent studies of Western politics, however, have nearly abandoned the concept of a clear division of functions. Suzanne Berger has written that "there is no longer any conception of a stable division of labor among parties, interest groups, and government, but rather specification of the circumstances under which various configurations emerge."[32] Central to this new outlook is the recognition of the many functions performed by interest groups in Western society. Speaking of interest groups, Berger notes that "the notion of a common function of interest groups—transmitting and articulating the demands of society into the political process—has largely disappeared, and in its stead there is a description of a variety of different roles that interest groups fill in contemporary societies."[33]

The contemporary role of interest groups now includes many of the functions previously performed by political parties. This is even true of the function most often associated with political parties, the aggregation of interests. Many interest groups, such as large national unions with substantial, diverse memberships, are routinely involved in the aggregation of interests. The British TUC is an example of this phenomenon. The TUC is a loose confederation of 100 affiliated unions with over 11 million members. The annual conference at which major policies are developed resembles a political party convention, and the national executive of the TUC must combine and reconcile (aggregate) the demands of the various affiliates each time official union policies are developed.[34] Interest groups have also become important agents of political communication and political socialization, tasks usually attributed to political parties. In contemporary society, interest organizations (e.g., medical societies and environmental groups) often possess information and technical expertise that surpass even that available to government agencies. The communications generated by interest groups have also been important in socializing people to new attitudes and life-styles. Environmentalists have helped to create an awareness of the need to preserve resources, which has created within the attentive public new attitudes toward consumption and conservation. In this sense, interest groups not only articulate preexisting attitudes in society, but also help to introduce new attitudes and create new interests. As the antinuclear movement in Europe demonstrates, once introduced, the new attitudes may be an important force in mobilizing large numbers of people to political action. Interest groups presently perform two other functions previously accomplished by political parties. First, interest groups have become an important source of political recruitment. Since the economic difficulties of the 1960s, the leaders of important lobbies have been recruited to high-level positions within government cabinets and the civil service. Such persons are recruited because of their economic and professional expertise and because of the political effect their appointment will have on the groups that they previously represented. Finally, in the West, interest organizations have assumed an expanded role in campaign activity, especially in the areas of finance and leadership skills. In Europe, labor unions supply up to 80% of the campaign funds for left-wing political parties, and often such parties and unions have overlapping memberships. Furthermore, in a recent study of British politics, Samuel Beer demonstrated a growing independence on the part of interest groups supporting both the Labour and Conservative parties.[35] In the 1970s interest group members demonstrated less support for their traditional party and a greater willingness to support the rival party than at any time since World War II. The trend toward increased interest group independence is present in most states of the West.

The contemporary role of interest groups also includes involvement in policy making and policy implementation, functions previously considered the unique preserve of government institutions. In several states of Western Europe the participation of interest organizations in these two processes has advanced to such a level that the term *neo-corporatism* has been used in describing the political process. Included in this category are Great Britain, France, Italy, Germany, Denmark, Norway, and Sweden. Neo-corporatism refers to a relationship between organized interest groups and government agencies in which a substantial number of interest organizations have a "public or legal status" established by the constitution or individual laws.[36] Because of the importance and complexity of this topic, interest group involvement with government agencies will be discussed separately.

Interest Groups in the Governmental Process

Traditional theories of interest groups assumed a separation between government institutions and interest groups. Interest groups were considered to be private associations within the general society, sometimes providing a link between private citizens and government institutions, but lacking an official or legal status. In the states of Western Europe today, however, an interdependence exists between the government and interest groups, which gives the latter a quasi-governmental status. Many states have laws requiring interest group participation in both policy-making and policy-implementing processes. Interest group representatives are frequently elevated to an official status through participation in national commissions, such as the Royal Commissions of Inquiry common to Great Britain and Canada. In addition, all Western countries, including the United States, grant interest groups the legal power to license, train, and regulate professionals in their field. For example, those wishing to practice law in the United States must be admitted to the Bar by the American Bar Association, and in Great Britain the British Medical Association has the power to discipline a doctor by revoking his or her license to practice. Although the use of interest groups to regulate professions began with the medieval guilds, the present interdependence results from the expanded scope of government activity in the era of the welfare state. As government programs in the social, health, and educational fields proliferated, direct contacts were developed between the civil servants administering the programs and the beneficiary groups. Both groups benefit from such institutionalized contacts. In addition, legislative bodies require the information and technical expertise possessed by economic interest groups and professional organizations to make new laws. By the 1960s, government and interest group leaders alike in the West shared an awareness of the complexity and interdependence of Western society. It is now widely accepted that effective solutions to political and economic problems require the participation of all relevant groups in both policy making and policy implementation.

The institutionalization of interest group participation in the public policy process is the most advanced in Scandinavia. In Sweden and Norway interest groups participate through the *remiss* (consultative) system whereby a ministry considering an administrative action is obliged to consult groups that will be affected.[37] Royal commissions and other consultative committees are also used throughout the Scandinavian states for the discussion of policy alternatives in such areas as economic policy, social policy, trade, and education. M. Donald Hancock has noted that such commissions often effectively "bind" the government to specific policies favored by the largest interest groups.[38] Interest groups also play an important role in policy implementation in Scandinavia. Many of the boards and agencies responsible for program administration are composed of government officials, members of Parliament, and the representatives of interest groups who frequently constitute 50% of the membership.[39] Interest group participation is also advanced in the other states of Western Europe. In France the system of consultation includes 500 councils, 1200 committees, and 3000 commissions at the national level alone.[40] Each of these bodies brings together government officials and the representatives of interest groups for the discussion of policy formulation and implementation. The French Ministry of Finance itself participates in more than 130 such committees, and the Constitution provides for the National Economic and Social Council, an advisory body composed of public and private members which advises the government on national economic policy. In the face of the economic difficulties of the 1970s, several European governments sought the development of an agreement between major interest groups on wages, prices, and economic planning. In Germany this effort was called "Concerted Action"[41] and in Great Britain the "Social Contract." In both states, however, a consensus could not be attained.

Interest Groups and Democracy

Despite their importance, interest groups traditionally have been viewed with suspicion in the West. Writing in *The Federalist* in 1787, the American statesman James Madison called factions (interests) an evil and warned that "the public good is disregarded in the conflict of rival parties."[42] Because he considered factions inevitable in a state of political liberty, Madison sought to control their effects by creating a system in which faction could counter faction so that no one group could dominate political life. In France the influential political theorist Jean Jacques Rousseau (1712–1778) condemned all intermediary groups as detrimental to the development of the "general will" or the common good. During the French Revolution the famous Chapelier Law was enacted which outlawed all private associations.[43] The

Chapelier Law was not formally rescinded until 1901. After World War II many analysts blamed the collapse of the democratic Weimar Republic (1918–1933) and the rise of Adolf Hitler on the excessive conflicts between German interest groups, especially trade unions and business groups.[44] Today many political observers still see interest groups as a threat to the maintenance of democracy. According to this view, interest groups have too much influence over the political process; the satisfaction of interest group demands has replaced the promotion of the collective good as the goal of public policy. Critics of interest groups also believe that they help to perpetuate economic and social inequality because in most political conflicts interest groups representing powerful and wealthy economic groups possess greater resources than organizations representing the less advantaged. As a result, the most powerful interest groups, sometimes referred to collectively as the *Establishment*,[45] perpetuate their dominant position in society.

Theory of Polyarchy. The issue of the role of interest groups in a democracy is a controversial one, and not all political analysts agree with the critics of interest groups. Many students of modern politics believe that extensive interest group activity is compatible with a healthy democracy. The U.S. political scientist Robert Dahl has devoted a lifetime of study to modern democracy and to the role of autonomous groups in the political process. Dahl believes that autonomous interest groups are important elements in the system of modern democracy, which he calls *polyarchy*.[46] In a polyarchy all citizens possess potential political power, but only a minority of the population actually engages in political activity. It is this minority of the population that maintains the autonomous interest groups in society. Dahl believes that interest group competition is an essential characteristic of modern democracy, and that the existence of competition indicates the presence of such favorable conditions as political equality, a wide distribution of political skills, and the opportunity for the expression of political dissent. In modern democracies, political parties and interest groups play an important role in controlling the actions of government and in providing opportunities for influencing government policies. Dahl acknowledges, however, that the existence of autonomous groups poses certain "dilemmas" both for democratic theory and democratic political systems. First, political resources (e.g., wealth, education, information and access to government organizations) are not equally distributed, and the danger exists that the most affluent and powerful groups will use their resources to dominate political life. Second, because private groups (e.g., business corporations and trade unions) make decisions that affect the general public, "an alienation of fine control" may occur in which the majority perceives that it has lost, or actually loses, control of the decisions that affect it.[47]

Despite these dilemmas, Dahl believes that the autonomy of private associations and interest groups is derived from the fundamental rights of their members, including the freedom of choice, the right to participate politically, and the right to use one's property (money) as one chooses.[48] Dahl believes that the solution to the dilemmas lies not in curtailing private associations, but in changing the environment of political ideas in which these groups operate. He calls for the development of a new civic orientation that will help to produce a more responsible interest group behavior. Although the specific contents of the civic orientation may differ from state to state, it should have at its core three elements: (1) increased support for the government institutions and rules which must decide interest group conflicts, (2) a greater awareness of the mutual dependence of groups in modern society, and (3) increased emphasis on the "general good" of society and the long-term interests of the group rather than on short-term gains or the expression of group egoism.[49] At present, most Western interest groups seem preoccupied with short-term gains. Only time will reveal whether a new civic orientation will fundamentally alter the behavior of such groups.

THE SECOND WORLD

Citizens of Western countries are accustomed to freely expressing their demands and are not averse to joining others of like mind in order to gain influence in the political process. Participation in the conflictive process of politics is a choice one may or may not wish to make. In Communist systems, however, becoming involved in politics through anything other than official channels is considered illegal. In this regard Brzezinski and Huntington noted two decades ago that "American popular participation differs from the Soviet by being indirect, segmented and pluralistic, while the Soviet is direct, hierarchical and centralized."[50]

Western political culture accepts the idea that citizens should be involved in government and that it is appropriate for any number of groups to exist and to seek recognition by the government of their special needs and interests. "Soviet political culture," however,

> may be distinguished from politics in liberal–democratic societies in the following ways: the lack of an autonomous public arena in which to mobilize political support; lack of mechanisms by which officials might be held regularly accountable to a public constituency; and freedom of Party officials to decide what constitutes political deviance, and to crack down on those who fall into this category.[51]

In Communist systems only the party may indicate what societal needs are. This creates a system rather the reverse of the one used by Western and some Third World countries. The party rules and influences interest groups to follow the party line; hardly ever do interest groups influence party–government policy.

In Communist regimes three general types of political pressure groups exist.[52] These are "directed" associational groups, institutional pressure groups, and dissenting groups (tolerated or not). Whether any of these groups will be able to influence the regime depends on the following conditions:

1. The issue is not politically or ideologically sensitive.
2. The issue does not threaten the interests or prerogatives of major institutions.
3. The issue can be put forward in such a way as to seem to be advancing the goals of the regime.
4. The source of the issue is not politically suspect or tainted with dissent.
5. Diversity of opinion within the official class provides patrons who will use their power to protect those willing to publish or pass on the ideas involved.
6. Division within the top leadership impels a search for new ideas.[53]

Let us consider how the three identifiable types of pressure groups function within Communist systems.

Directed Associational Groups

"Directed" (controlled) associational groups are organizations officially recognized as system-supportive and therefore legitimate. They are directed in two ways: first, they are under the direct control of the particular country's Communist party which sets policy and supplies leadership; second, though membership may be ostensibly voluntary, there may be an element of coercion involved. It is always more politically healthy to show one's support for the regime by belonging to one or two associations. In some cases membership is officially required to practice one's trade (writers' unions, for instance). These directed organizations are frequently referred to as "Mass organizations" and are part of "mass participation in the political process."

Richard Gripp, in discussing the Communist political system, mentions the existence of the following mass organizations in the German Democratic Republic:

Consumers Cooperatives

Democratic Women's Union

Ernst Thalmann Pioneers (preteens)

Free German Youth (teenagers and young adults)

German Union of Culture

Farmers Mutual Aid Association

Society for Dissemination of Scientific Knowledge (partly an aethestic organization)

League of Nazi Victims

He mentions the following mass organizations in the Democratic People's Republic of Korea:

General Federation of Korean Literature and Arts

General Federation of Trade Unions

Korean Buddhist Federation

Korean Christian Federation

Korean Democratic Lawyers Association

Korean Democratic Women's Union

Korean Journalists Association

Korean Red Cross

Socialist Working Youth League[54]

Generally speaking, if a large enough group exists within a society so that it can be organized, then the party supplies a directed organizational framework. Attempting to establish a noncontrolled organization subjects one to instant repression.

One may classify directed groups under the following headings:

Agriculture. Collective farm workers, state farm workers (for example, in the USSR), private farmers (especially in Poland and Yugoslavia).

Civil defense. Armed forces support organizations and civil defense, for example, the USSR's DOSAAF (voluntary society for assistance to the army, airforce, and navy) or the Czechoslovak Union for Cooperation with the Army.

Culture. There are universal artists, musicians, and theatrical organizations in Communist states.

Peace organizations. Anti-Western, anti-United States, anti-NATO, antihegemonic, antinuclear pro-disarmament (never, however, against the "legitimate," "defensive" military policies of the particular Communist regime).

Religious. Pro-regime Christian, Buddhist, Confucian, or Islamic organizations that are run by patriotic'' priests/ministers/*mullahs*/teachers (for example, the PAX Catholic Organization in Poland).

Sports. Communist regimes provide a full gamut of sports associations plus a national sports federation.

Trade unions. Industrial branches and trades have officially sponsored unions.

Tribal or ethnic associations. If a subgroup is officially recognized, it will be allowed a controlled organization.

Women. Pseudo-feminist, women's peace, motherhood, and working women organizations are universal in Communist states.

Youth. It is usual to provide Communist party-controlled organizations for age groups 7–10, 11–14, 15–26. Communist youth league organizations frequently provide leadership training for later party leaders.

The influence of directed associations cannot be measured and is probably minimal but could be felt if the aforementioned six conditions were met.

Many Communist regimes further organize these associations into groups called "national fronts." A national front is a national-level organization gathering the various allowed groups into one superstructure which, along with the Communist party, selects candidates for elective office. Obviously the top leadership of any group consists of party members and, as there is no likelihood that anyone other than a trusted person would be nominated to office, the actual "weight" of a particular organization within a national front is problematical. National fronts are found in Afghanistan (National Fatherland Front), Albania (Democratic Front), Bulgaria (Fatherland Front), China (Chinese People's Political Consultative Conference), Czechoslovakia (National Front), German Democratic Republic (National Front), Hungary (Patriotic People's Front), Kampuchea (Front of National Construction), Korea (Democratic People's Coalition Front), Laos (Front of National Construction), Poland (Front of National Unity), Romania (Front of Socialist Unity), and Yugoslavia (Socialist Alliance of Working People).[55]

Institutional Groups

Of a more powerful nature is the second variety of Communist state interest groups. Within the system exist subunits that attempt to bring influence to bear within the structure. Little can be discerned about their actual functioning, though their existence can be deduced.[56] These are the so-called institutional pressure groups, parts of the regime itself.

Franklyn Griffiths and H. Gordon Skilling gathered together a group of 11 experts to examine Soviet society. They discovered seven major influence groups, five formally within the regime and two ostensibly outside it: *aparatchiki,* security police, military, managers, policy makers, writers, and jurists.[57] First, full-time workers within the Communist party apparatus, called *aparatchiki,* were identified as a group which, if nothing else, was able to protect its position. For example, the events in Poland surrounding the repression of the Solidarity movement and the elimination of the Alexander Dubcek regime in Czechoslovakia in 1968 show the strength of an entrenched power faction that was willing to go to great lengths, including bloodshed and foreign intervention, to protect its position. A second influential group was identified as the security police. A major feature of a Communist regime is the enormous security apparatus that maintains the system. The ability of the secret police to keep power needs no particular elaboration.

The third powerful unit is the military, which represents itself as the shield against foreign attack and internal subversion. The U.S. Central Intelligence Agency estimates that the USSR expends 12 to 15% of that country's GNP in defense and that the percentage has been increasing.[58] The military gets what it wants, and in the last analysis determines whether the regime will stand or fall—witness the role of the army in China in the 1970s and in Poland in the 1980s.

Because one of the claims to rule of the Communist party is that it alone is able to cope with the problems of the modern industrial state, it stands to reason that industrial managers and economists must play an important role in Communist regimes. John Hardt and Theodore Frankel identified 100,000 top-level management personnel in the Soviet Union in 1970.[59] Another writer, Richard Judy, sees as a distinctive group the economic policy makers gathered in the Academcy of Sciences, the Central Mathematical Economics Institute, the State Planning Commission, the Central Statistical Administration, the various ministries, and higher education.[60]

One group that has occasionally made some headway against the Soviet regime, though not ostensibly part of it—it is technically one of the directed associations—has been the writers' union. Once in a while fights with censors are won.[61] Another outside group identified by Griffiths and Skilling is Soviet jurists. Donald Barry and Harold Berman believe that the legal profession (numbering some 100,000 in 1970) presses for greater regularity and socialist legality.[62]

Certainly the existence of institutional pressure groups can be deduced from the fact that every system has only limited resources available for use by regime units. Any bureaucracy will struggle, using all available means, to ensure that it will not only maintain itself but expand. Communist regimes are even more prone to this internal struggle as the scope of government is much expanded over anything seen in the West. Not only does the government operate all the normal government activities, transportation, defense, welfare, education, and so on, but also all industry, agriculture, mining, woodcutting, consumer trade, foreign trade, and the like. Hence, the ground for struggle is larger and the stakes are higher than in the Western and Third Worlds.

Dissent Groups

The third area of interest group activity is that of dissent. Dissent is of two types, tolerated and nontolerated. The amount of tolerated dissent is very limited. Such dissent has existed for long periods of time in Communist party states with a history of strong religious institutions, but these are found only in a few countries. Poland has the extraordinary situation of having a powerful Roman Catholic church that commands greater loyalty than the state itself. The Polish Communist regime has never felt itself strong enough to move fully against the church, although various levels of repression have been tried. Some political representatives of the church have been allowed an existence in the basically powerless Sejm (legislature) in the so-called Znak Circle but alongside the PAX "patriotic" church movement. Hungary and Yugoslavia also have strong and resilient churches that have accommo-dated to their respective regimes without giving in to them. The churches of Poland, Hungary, and Yugoslavia have been able to exert influence in the political process by modifying or ameliorating certain regime policies. Yugoslavia also has an interesting system of worker self-management, which apparently and occasionally has acted as a tolerated dissent movement by resisting or gaining modification of regime policy.[63]

Beyond the aforementioned groups, dissent is not tolerated and is subject to repression. Dissent in Communist systems is generally unorga-nized as the chances of the security police penetrating an organization are extremely high, inviting direct and rapid repression. One can only talk of vague general groupings or movements. Rudolf Tökés, the editor of *Dissent in the USSR*, and other political scientists identify an intellectual opposition, a democratic movement, an underground of illegal writers of so-called *samizdat* ("self-published") works, religious activists, and individual dis-senters.[64]

It is certain that any dissent outside of the officially allowed limits—if any is allowed at all—is dangerous to the dissenter. What happened to those who attempted to articulate new and different ideas after Mao Zedong's famous "hundred flowers" speech ("Let a hundred schools of thought contend, Let a hundred flowers bloom") is well known—they were "reed-ucated."[65] In the USSR one is liable to end up undergoing "corrective labor" therapy.

> After hearing testimony . . . Orlov's guilt in carrying out subversive anti-Soviet activity aimed at weakening the Soviet system had been fully proved . . . he sent to anti-soviet centers abroad materials of a slanderous nature defaming the Soviet state and social system.
>
> The court sentenced Orlov to seven years deprivation of freedom to be followed by five years of exile.[66]

Orlov had made the mistake of believing Soviet signatures on the final act of the Helsinki Conference on Security and Cooperation in Europe in 1975, which more or less confirmed the results of World War II, were serious, and he was involved in a "Helsinki Watch Group."[67] As this activity was not officially sanctioned, he ended up in prison. Communist regimes only allow system supportive interest groups, as defined by the Communist party itself, to exist.

THE THIRD WORLD

All four types of interest groups—associational, nonassociational, institutional, and anomic—exist in the Third World countries. However, the political function commonly associated with the interest groups (interest articulation) is poorly performed in the Third World. Francis Castles wrote a few years ago:

> To examine the functions of interest articulation and aggregation in the undeveloped system is to look at the reasons why they are not carried out. A similar examination of the developing countries must stress the emergence of groups carrying out these functions, but at the same time emphasize their precariousness and lack of autonomy from each other.[68]

In the present-day world it is virtually impossible to find a political system so undeveloped that the function of interest articulation (or interest aggregation) is not carried out at all. In practically every Third World country some interest groups exist. These groups formulate and articulate the demands of their members less effectively than is done in the West, although there is considerable variation in the degree of effectiveness in Third World States.

The social setting of the Third World countries is preindustrial. Political roles are not as clearly differentiated as in the West and specialization in the performance of economic and political tasks is still at an early stage. Ties of a nonassociational nature such as kinship, caste, or tribe are much more important to people's lives than membership in an association that is organized specifically for the advancement of its members' interests. A major impediment in the development and effectiveness of Third World interest groups, especially of an associational nature, is the low level of industrialization. In countries where literacy rates are below 50%, means of travel are inadequate and slow, telephones are uncommon and inefficient, and computers are nonexistent or rudimentary, it is difficult for associational groups to be organized and to function effectively. Another major reason for the paucity of associational groups in the Third World and their ineffectiveness is that the preindustrial stage does not provide resources needed for the satisfaction of demands of the members of such groups. For example, old-age pensions are virtually nonexistent in the Third World countries because of lack of resources to provide such pensions. The elderly in these countries can gain little by organizing and demanding pensions, because the government would be unable to meet their demand. The emergence of such a demand is also adversely affected by a much lower proportion of the elderly in the populations of the Third World countries than in the Western countries—another feature of the different stages of industrial development.

As is the case in the First and Second Worlds, political culture—political values, expectations, laws, and the structure of government—also affects the nature of interest groups in the Third World. In Third World countries, connections with political leaders based on personal relations or kinship or similar ties are often of greater significance than the organization of a group. In general, the governments are not considered responsive to people's concerns in these countries and a commonly shared political belief is that whatever can be gained from the government is possible only through nonassociational connections. The fierce lobbying for or against important bills that is commonplace in the West does not occur in Third World countries, not only because few such lobbies representing different interest groups exist, but also because there is little rationale for such lobbying. Laws, when passed, are not enforced as diligently in Third World countries as in the First and Second Worlds. Whether a law is passed or not and whatever the provisions of a law are may not be as crucial in a Third World country as it is in the First and Second Worlds.

One-party and military regimes in the Third World discourage the formation and functioning of interest groups. Where such groups exist, the government attempts to control them rather than be influenced by them. In Indonesia, for example, interest groups are permitted; however, "all groups that have political aims are seen as legitimate so long as they support the nationalist elite."[69] The Indonesian situation is typical of one-party or military regimes in the Third World.[70] Before the establishment of one-party government or the military takeover, interest groups were free to function in many of these countries, although their impact on the public policy process was never substantial. The Philippines is an example of a Third World country in which, prior to the declaration of martial law in 1972, the

President of Chile General Pinochet (with hand raised) celebrates the tenth anniversary of the seizure of power.

legislators accepted interest groups as an essential component of the political system. (Although martial law was later lifted and elections were held, the Philippines continues to have an authoritarian government.) Some studies on the Philippines reveal that before 1972 the legislators considered interest groups valuable in the process of political participation and had frequent contacts with them.[71]

In some African countries with one-party governments, new institutional forms of receiving input from the interest groups have developed. In a study of African nations, Donald Rothchild and Robert Curry mention the example of the Ivory Coast (a small country in West Africa) where after demonstrations by students and unemployed youth, the president of the country held "dialogue sessions" with students and certain occupational groups. As a consequence of these sessions he introduced some marginal reforms.[72]

Whether in one-party or military regimes or in relatively open political systems, interest groups in the Third World have a greater influence on the bureaucracy that implements public policy than on the legislature and the executive that make public policy. As the groups are not well organized, they seldom maintain offices in the national capitals for keeping in touch with the legislature and the executive. The bureaucrats are scattered throughout the country and can, therefore, be easily reached. Another important reason for the inability of the interest groups to influence the executive branch or the legislature is that because of insufficient political communication very little is known in these countries regarding the bills and decisions under consideration. After an important law is passed or a major executive decision is made, its impact on those concerned makes its existence known. Repeal of a law or the rescission of an executive decision is much more difficult than influencing its implementation.

Associational Groups

Some of the most visible associational groups in the Third World are labor unions, business groups, and student groups. In several African and Asian countries, labor unions were organized by the leaders of the nationalist movements during the colonial period. The workers, whether on the large plantations growing commodities such as tea and rubber or in factories, were an easy target for mobilizing support against colonial rule. The leaders of such unions were often middle-class professionals, not workers—a tradition that persists in many of these countries. As the African and the Asian colonies gained independence, the political parties sought the support of the labor unions. There is, however, a fundamental difference between a political party in a Western country seeking a labor union's support and a political party in a Third World country seeking such support. In the Western countries the labor unions maintain their independent identities and support parties of their choice; in the Third World the labor unions often become a part of political parties and assume a role subordinate to them. Even when, as in Britain, labor unions have a close relationship with a political party, the party depends on the unions for support. Such is not the case in the Third World. Comparing interest groups, especially labor unions' relationship to parties in Britain and India, Barbara McLennan comments, ". . . in Great Britain, interest groups can sponsor party members and support the party of their choice; in India, the party creates and subsidizes the interest group."[73]

In Latin American countries, which have been free of colonial rule much longer than the African and the Asian countries, labor unions do not display much independence. As Paul Lewis states,

> unlike the labor movements of Western Europe and the United States, . . . the Latin American unions in general did not evolve independently of, and often in opposition to, the state. Rather, the Latin American tendency has been one of government paternalism, in which labor organizations have been created by, nurtured by, and made dependent upon the state.[74]

In a study of trade unionism in Brazil, Christian Tyler explains that "the trade unions depend financially on the state and are so structured as to minimize the likelihood of labor leaders formenting trouble or of the workers mounting organized protest.''[75]

Unlike business groups in the First World, these groups in the Third World do not operate as organized lobbies. Instead, individual businessmen attempt to influence government policy—its implementation rather than formulation—through their personal and family connections with those in positions of power. The businesses have organizations such as chambers of commerce in several Third World countries; however, the deliberations in these organizations seldom have an impact on public policy. The business-men in the Third World, as in the First World, do use the power of their money in order to influence the decisions of the political leaders and the bureaucrats. In countries that permit elections, a large proportion of the campaign money comes from business. Furthermore, bribery is rather common in the Third World, more so than in the First World. However, the influence of business on public policy is quite limited in most Third World countries. In India, for example, businessmen from certain families have had close personal relations with political leaders for years, even decades. The Indian businessmen, like their counterparts in other countries, also use their money for campaign contributions and bribes. Yet, their influence on government policy is considered dubious. Stanley Kochanek, who has studied the relationship between business and politics in India, remarks that business ''has not yet been able to convert its considerable economic power into truly effective political power.''[76]

University students in the Third World appear politicized and are courted by political parties, especially those of the left. Their organizations, however, are quite weak and these organizations represent a minority, often quite small, of the total number of students. Even in Latin American countries, where the stereotyped image of a university student is that of a militant, most students are not ''activists at all.''[77] Paul Lewis contends that student activists in Latin America ''have little positive impact, either on the large society or within the university itself.''[78] This statement is true of student activists in a vast majority of the Third World countries. The discontent of the university students is due to the unsatisfactory conditions at the universities in areas such as curriculum and libraries and the lack of employment opportunities for the educated.

Nonassociational Groups

Third World countries have more nonassociational groups than groups in any other category. This is to be expected, as in the preindustrial social setting people's lives are affected most by membership in social groups such as a clan, a caste, or a tribe. In many Third World countries political parties draw their support from such groups. Some of these parties function as interest groups trying to influence public policy rather than as parties seeking political power directly. The nonassociational groups in the Third World have fewer resources, are less organized, and consequently are less influential than the associational groups.

We will discuss here an unusual nonassociational group—that of ex-untouchables—from a major Third World country, India. This group has a "membership" of well over 100 million, in other words, more than the populations of a majority of the countries in the world. It has achieved some success without sustained efforts. This is not a typical nonassociational interest group in a Third World country; however, its unique nature, large size, and limited success warrant its discussion.

Ex-untouchables in India. Ex-untouchables are considered outside the Indian caste system. The caste system is an integral part of Hinduism, the religion of almost 85% of India's population. The castes evolved centuries ago as occupational groups. The priests were *Brahmins,* the rulers and warriors *Kshatriyas,* the merchants *Vaisyas,* and the ordinary people (those working on farms or in trades) were known as *Sudras.* (These four categories of caste are hierarchical; thus *Brahmins* are considered the highest, *Kshatriyas* the next highest, and so forth.) Those who did menial jobs such as sweeping streets or mending shoes were considered outside the caste system or the *varna* (the Indian word for caste) and the very lowest among the Hindus. These workers came to be known as untouchables, as if the tasks they performed had polluted them. Even today millions of caste Hindus will not eat food handled by the "untouchables."

The Indian caste system is a very rigid social structure. Once born into a caste or outside it, there is absolutely no way by which a person can change it in his or her lifetime. Much of social interaction of the people takes place within their castes. Marrying outside the caste is still frowned upon and is in fact unacceptable to most Hindus. It is virtually impossible for an "untouchable" to marry into a caste. Although there are four major caste groups, there are hundreds of subcastes within each. Crossing subcaste lines for marriage, so long as one remains within the parent caste group, is increasingly acceptable in India.

The Indian Constitution of 1950 abolished untouchability and subsequent legislation declared the practice of untouchability a crime. That is the reason we prefer the term "ex-untouchables." In India, they are known as *Harijans,* which means God's children. They comprise 15% of India's population, which exceeds 750 million.

Being the poorest and the most deprived segment of the population, the ex-untouchables have found it difficult to organize. Some leaders in this group have attempted to establish organizations to promote the interests of its entire membership. Unlike the lobbies of blacks in the United States, these organizations have had little success. One of the best-known of such organizations, Scheduled Castes Federation, was formed by a famous ex-untouchable, Dr. B. R. Ambedkar, in 1942. Although established as a political party, Scheduled Castes Federation, which later became the Republican party, functioned as an interest group rather than a party. As an interest group this "party" has had dubious success. The educated and mostly unemployed ex-untouchable youth of the cities have formed some militant groups. These groups also have been mostly unsuccessful. Over 90% of the ex-untouchables live in villages and it is in the villages, not in the cities, where severe discrimination against them still exists.

Some important changes have been made in India in order to decrease the political and economic helplessness of the ex-untouchables and to make them acceptable to the caste Hindus. Since 1950, 15% of the seats in the Parliament and the state assemblies have been reserved for ex-untouchables. A similar quota system applies for government jobs and seats in the colleges, including professional colleges such as medical schools. These gains were not achieved by the organizational skills of the members of this group. More than any other person, Mahatma Gandhi, a caste Hindu and one of the greatest leaders in the Indian history, who fought the British colonial rule with his unique techniques of nonviolence, was responsible for bringing about these changes for the "untouchables." It is also possible that like white Americans in their relations with the blacks in the United States, the caste Hindus experience guilt feelings about their treatment of the ex-untouchables. As is the case in the United States, reverse discrimination is resented in India, but unlike in the United States, opposition to reverse discrimination is increasingly expressed in the form of violent outbursts.

The newly educated, somewhat affluent, and politically powerful class among the ex-untouchables in India comprises a very small proportion of the total number of ex-untouchables. The vast majority of the ex-untouchables still live in depressing poverty and face discrimination at the hands of the caste Hindus. Some scholars believe that by providing economic benefits and some political power to a small minority of this group, the ruling elites in India are able to control those ex-untouchables who "might otherwise have proved troublesome."[79] It is possible that the ruling Indian elites now perceive the benefits to the ex-untouchables in this light; yet the introduction of these benefits had little to do with such motives. The original motives for the preferential treatment of the ex-untouchables were a combination of altruism and guilt feelings.

Institutional Groups

Although nonassociational groups are most prevalent in the Third World, it is the institutional groups that are most effective. The military is usually the most powerful institutional group not only in the Third World, but also in the First and the Second Worlds. In the United States and in the Soviet Union, the military plays a prominent role in influencing policy concerning the amount allocated to the defense budget. In many Third World countries the military *is* the government; in countries where the military does not exercise power directly, it is an influential interest group. The military and any other institutional groups are not organized the way a labor union and other associational groups are. However, institutional groups are similar to the associational groups in that both types of these groups attempt to influence public policy in the interest of their members.

Paul Lewis writes that "the military may be considered as *the* key pressure group in practically all Latin American countries. It has a virtual monopoly of the means of armed combat and, especially in Latin America, it is often willing to use that power to impose its views on the government."[80] Even in Mexico, "which has developed a tradition of civilian government since 1926, the military there must still be taken into account as a major pressure group."[81] In other Third World countries the military also plays an influential role as a pressure group. In Iran, until early 1979 the Shah had virtually absolute power, and the military played an important role in the country's "political dynamics."[82] This was not entirely unexpected, as the Shah had decided to increase Iran's military power by the purchase of weapons abroad, especially from the United States. The military leaders had to be consulted for their technical expertise in weapons.

What role is the military playing in those Third World countries that aspire to become nuclear powers? India detonated a nuclear device in 1974, and Argentina, Brazil, Iraq, Pakistan, and some other Third World countries have similar ambitions. Evidence suggests that the military played a rather limited role in the Indian government's decision to test a nuclear device.[83] In this case, India presents an exception rather than the general rule in the Third World. Because the military rules in several Third World countries and is a key pressure group in many others, there is little doubt that it would play a crucial role in a government's decision to develop a nuclear capability.

Bureaucrats in the Third World are another example of an institutional interest group. In a study of bureaucrats and higher-education politics in Thailand, India, and China, Richard Kraus, William Maxwell, and Reeve Vanneman point out that the bureaucrats in these countries function as a group and share "similar perceptions of what constitutes a distinctively

A hunger striker being carried by Pakistani students at a demonstration outside Karachi University.

bureaucratic interest in higher education."[84] The authors found through their research that "in conflicts over the bond between degrees and official position, university control, and rates of access to university education, the Thai bureaucrats have prevailed most frequently, Chinese bureaucrats have been least successful, and Indian officials have experienced intermediate results."[85]

Anomic Groups

Anomic groups exist in all three worlds. A major explanation for their being so common in the Third World is that these countries have not yet developed a tradition for resolving conflicts through established political channels. If a group in the United States does not agree with a law or proposed legislation, it attempts to influence the lawmakers through lobbying. In a Third World country serious disagreement with a government policy, whether proposed or in practice, often results in violent outbursts. The Second World governments keep such protests in check by centralized control. Such control does not exist in Third World countries, and a tradition for conflict resolution by established political channels has not yet developed, so violent expression of demands is not unexpected. University students boycotting classes for days or even weeks, members of a minority having violent clashes with police, mobs storming some foreign, generally U.S., embassy are some examples of how anomic groups function in the Third World countries.

Of the four types of interest groups, the anomic groups are the least influential. Sometimes, however, depending on how persistent they are, these groups do wield influence on government policy. Earlier the example of the Ivory Coast was discussed. There demonstrations by students and unemployed youth elicited some response from the government. In India, English was made an associate language largely because of the violent protests of anomic groups against the declaration of Hindi (one of the fourteen major Indian languages spoken by about 40% of the people) as the official language in 1965.

NOTES

1. For a stimulating discussion of various definitions and classificatory schemes employed in the analysis of interest groups see Graham Wootton, *Interest-Groups* (Englewood Cliffs, N.J.: Prentice-Hall, 1970), pp. 1–44.
2. For a discussion of such groups see Andrew McFarland, "Public Interest Lobbies versus Minority Factions," in Allan J. Cigler and Burdett A. Loomis, eds., *Interest Group Politics* (Washington, D.C.: CQ Press, 1983), pp. 324–353.
3. See Joseph LaPalombara, *Politics Within Nations* (Englewood Cliffs, N.J.: Prentice-Hall, 1974), pp. 323–326; Norman J. Ornstein and Shirley Elder, *Interest Groups, Lobbying and Policymaking* (Washington, D.C.: CQ Press, 1978), pp. 69–93; and Wootton, pp. 43–44.
4. For a discussion of such change in the United States see Allan J. Cigler and Burdett A. Loomis, "The Changing Nature of Interest Group Politics," in Cigler and Loomis, pp. 1–31.
5. Sidney R. Waldman, *Foundations of Political Action: An Exchange Theory of Politics* (Boston: Little, Brown, 1972), pp. 159–160.
6. LaPalombara, p. 324.
7. Wootton, p. 83; and LaPalombara, pp. 326–328.
8. Karl W. Deutsch, *Politics and Government: How People Decide Their Fate*, 3d ed. (Boston: Houghton Mifflin, 1980), p. 59.
9. LaPalombara, p. 326.
10. Ibid., p. 327.

11. Gabriel A. Almond and G. Bingham Powell, Jr., *Comparative Politics: A Developmental Approach* (Boston: Little, Brown, 1966), p. 78.
12. Peter H. Merkl, *Modern Comparative Politics,* 2d ed. (Hinsdale, Ill.: Dryden Press, 1977), p. 120.
13. LaPalombara, p. 329.
14. Ibid.
15. Almond and Powell, pp. 76–77.
16. LaPalombara, p. 330.
17. Merkl, p. 116.
18. Samuel H. Beer, *Britain Against Itself: The Contradictions of Collectivism* (New York: Norton, 1982), pp. 15–45.
19. See Suzanne D. Berger, ed., *Organizing Interests in Western Europe* (New York: Cambridge University Press, 1983), pp. 1–26.
20. Richard Rose, *Politics in England* (Boston: Little, Brown, 1980), p. 230.
21. R. M. Punnett, *British Government and Politics,* 4th ed. (London: Heinemann, 1982), p. 143.
22. M. Donald Hancock, *Sweden: The Politics of Postindustrial Change* (Hinsdale, Ill.: Dryden Press, 1972), p. 157.
23. Henry W. Ehrmann, *Politics in France,* 4th ed. (Boston: Little, Brown, 1983), p. 194.
24. See David P. Conradt, "Germany," in Dan N. Jacobs, David P. Conradt, B. Guy Peters, William Safran, eds., *Comparative Politics* (Chatham, N.J.: Chatham House, 1983), p. 202.
25. The *Poujadistes* began as an interest group but later became a political party.
26. Conradt, p. 206.
27. Ibid.
28. Cited in Dennis S. Ippolito and Thomas G. Walker, *Political Parties, Interest Groups, and Public Policy: Group Influence in American Politics* (Englewood Cliffs, N.J.: Prentice-Hall, 1980), p. 302.
29. Cigler and Loomis, pp. 22–23.
30. Conradt, p. 200.
31. Ibid., p. 201.
32. Berger, p. 10.
33. Ibid.
34. See Douglas E. Ashford, *Policy and Politics in Britain: The Limits of Consensus* (Philadelphia: Temple University Press, 1981), pp. 138–150.
35. See Beer, pp. 48–78.
36. For a discussion of neo-corporatism see Claus Offe, "The Functioning of Interest Groups," pp. 136–141; and Gudmund Hernes and Arne Selvik, "Local Corporatism," pp. 102–123, in Berger.
37. Francis G. Castles, "Scandinavia: The Politics of Stability," in Roy C. Macridis, ed., *Modern Political Systems: Europe,* 5th ed. (Englewood Cliffs, N.J.: Prentice-Hall, 1983), p. 409.
38. Hancock, p. 157.
39. Castles, p. 409.

40. Ehrmann, p. 205.

41. David B. Conradt, *The German Polity,* 2d ed. (New York: Longman, 1982), p. 103.

42. *Federalist* no. 10, November 22, 1787. Madison defined a faction as the following: "By a faction I understand a number of citizens, whether amounting to a majority or a minority of the whole who are united and actuated by some common impulse of passion or of interest, adverse to the rights of other citizens, or to the permanent and aggregate interests of the community." *The Federalist* no. 10, November 22, 1787, p. 43.

43. Ehrmann, p. 183.

44. For a discussion of this thesis see David Abraham, *The Collapse of the Weimar Republic: Political Economy and Crisis* (Princeton, N.J.: Princeton University Press, 1981).

45. Deutsch, p. 57.

46. See Robert A. Dahl, *Dilemmas of Pluralist Democracy: Autonomy vs. Control* (New Haven: Yale University Press, 1982).

47. Ibid., p. 195.

48. Ibid., pp. 195–196.

49. Ibid., pp. 161, 186.

50. Zbigniew Brzezinski and Samuel P. Huntington, *Political Power: USA/USSR* (New York: Viking Press, 1963), p. 91.

51. Stanley Rothman and George Breslauer, *Soviet Politics and Society* (St. Paul, Minn.: West, 1978), p. 214.

52. The term *regime* in this text, when referring to Communist-type systems, means the combined party–state apparatus that runs a given country.

53. Adapted from Rothman and Breslauer, p. 214.

54. Richard C. Gripp, *The Political System of Communism* (New York: Dodd, Mead, 1973), p. 127.

55. See Richard F. Staar's 1985, *Yearbook on International Communist Affairs* and *Communist Regimes in Eastern Europe* (4th ed., 1982) put out by the Hoover Institution Press of Stanford, California, for the latest information.

56. H. Gordon Skilling, "Interest Groups and Communist Politics," *World Politics* 18 (April 1966): 435–451, reprinted in Richard Cornell, ed., *The Soviet Political System: A Book of Readings* (Englewood Cliffs, N.J.: Prentice-Hall, 1970), pp. 217–226.

57. Franklyn Griffiths and H. Gordon Skilling, eds., *Interest Groups in Soviet Politics* (Princeton, N.J.: Princeton University Press, 1971).

58. Franklyn Holzman, "Soviet Military Spending: Assessing the Numbers Game," *International Security,* Vol. 6, No. 4, (Spring 1982), p. 78.

59. John P. Hardt and Theodore Frankel, "The Industrial Managers," in Griffiths and Skilling, p. 171.

60. Richard W. Judy, "The Economists," in ibid., pp. 210–216.

61. See Ernest J. Simmons, "The Writers," in ibid., pp. 253–289.

62. Donald D. Barry and Harold J. Berman, "The Jurists," in ibid., pp. 291–333.

63. Bogdan Denitch, "The Relevance of Yugoslav Self-Management," in Gary K.

Bertsch and Thomas W. Ganschow, eds., *Comparative Communism: The Soviet, Chinese and Yugoslav Models* (San Francisco: Freeman, 1976) pp. 268–281.

64. Rudolf L. Tokes, ed., *Dissent in the USSR: Politics, Ideology and People* (Baltimore: Johns Hopkins University Press, 1975).

65. Lucian W. Pye, *China: An Introduction,* 2d ed. (Boston: Little, Brown, 1978), pp. 234–235.

66. Translated and quoted from the Soviet press: "Helsinki Group Founder Yuri Orlov," *The USSR Today: Perspectives from the Soviet Press* (Columbus, Ohio: Current Digest of the Soviet Press, 1981), p. 24.

67. Donald W. Treadgold, *Twentieth Century Russia,* 5th ed. (Boston: Houghton Mifflin, 1981), pp. 485–486.

68. Francis G. Castles, *Pressure Groups and Political Culture: A Comparative Study* (London: Routledge and Kegan Paul, 1967), p. 22. Note that interest aggregation is generally considered the major function of political parties.

69. Barbara N. McLennan, *Comparative Political Systems* (North Scituate, Mass.: Duxbury Press, 1975), p. 159. The interest groups in Indonesia are not any more independent today than they were in 1975.

70. Indonesia is somewhat different in appearance from most other military or one-party regimes. In reality it is both. Elections are held in Indonesia, giving it the appearance of a democracy; however, President General Suharto's party is assured of winning. Suharto rules with the support of the military.

71. See Joseph W. Dodd, "Legislative Adaptability in Developing Areas: The Case of the Philippine Congress," *Asian Survey* 16 (July 1976): 637–653; and Richard A. Styskal, "Philippine Legislators' Reception of Individuals and Interest Groups in the Legislative Process," *Comparative Politics* 1 (April 1969): 405–422.

72. Donald Rothchild and Robert L. Curry, Jr., *Scarcity, Choice, and Public Policy in Middle Africa* (Berkeley: University of California Press, 1978), p. 85.

73. McLennan, p. 147.

74. Paul H. Lewis, *The Governments of Argentina, Brazil and Mexico* (New York: Crowell, 1975), p. 190.

75. Christian Tyler, "Trade Unionism in Brazil," *Third World Quarterly* 4 (April 1982): 314.

76. Stanley A. Kochanek, *Business and Politics in India* (Berkeley: University of California Press, 1974), p. 333.

77. Lewis, p. 255.

78. Ibid., p. 259.

79. See Lelah Dushkin, "Scheduled Caste Politics," in J. Michael Maher, ed., *The Untouchables in Contemporary India* (Tuscon: University of Arizona Press, 1972), p. 165.

80. Lewis, p. 163.

81. Ibid.

82. See David E. Long and Bernard Reich, eds., *The Government and Politics of the Middle East and North Africa* (Boulder, Colo.: Westview Press, 1980), p. 84.

83. See Richard K. Betts, "Incentives for Nuclear Weapons: India, Pakistan, Iran," *Asian Survey* 19 (November 1979): 1053–1072.
84. Richard Kraus, William E. Maxwell, and Reeve D. Vanneman, "The Interests of Bureaucrats: Implications of the Asian Experience for Recent Theories of Development," *American Journal of Sociology* 85 (July 1979): 149.
85. Ibid., pp. 148–149.

CHAPTER 9

Political Parties in Three Worlds

Organizations whose primary goal is obtaining political power in a state are called political parties. These organizations aggregate the interests of certain groups of people, and depending on the particular country, exist alone or in multiple units. The First World is noted for the diversity of political parties that espouse goals ranging from monarchy to anarchy.

The Second World, in contradistinction, has only one political party in power in each country. This party, the Communist party, professes that it has the right and duty to rule because its political philosophy is the only correct one. Further, the Communist party dominates all levels of power, does not allow any opposition, and declares that the world will be just and peaceful only when all countries are ruled by the Communist party.

Third World countries have borrowed political party structures from the First and Second Worlds. For example, Angola, Mozambique, Ethiopia, and Zimbabwe call their single ruling parties "Marxist–Leninist." Like Western countries, India permits any number of political parties. In practice, however, one party has dominated the Indian political scene. The Third World also has some particular features, for example, single-party states and the existence of political facades behind which the reality of military rule stands.

Although political parties are relatively recent developments, they are among the most important political structures today. A study of political parties has noted that they are "the major bodies through which political action occurs in developed and most underdeveloped systems."[1] Another study described political parties as "the institutionalization of important political functions."[2] Indeed, the list of functions attributed to political parties is both extensive and impressive and includes most of the functions necessary for the maintenance of a modern political system. Political parties have also proven to be flexible institutions. They have been associated both with the spread of democracy in the states of the West and with the establishment of totalitarian regimes in the Communist World, Fascist Italy, and Nazi Germany (in the latter two cases in the era between World War I and World War II).

Some critics have expressed mistrust of political parties as divisive and conducive to the rise of demogogues. However, throughout the three political worlds more people identify with the policies and leaders of parties than with any other institution except the state itself. Political parties are found in all major political systems except certain authoritarian regimes in which they have been suppressed by ruling cliques.

WHAT IS A POLITICAL PARTY?

The development of an all-inclusive and universally accepted definition of a political party has proven to be a difficult task. The difficulty results from the fact that parties exist in a wide variety of forms, differing greatly in terms of history, membership, size, recruitment, leadership, internal organization, style, and unifying beliefs. Most definitions begin by trying to clarify the relationship between *interest groups*, *factions*, and *parties*. As discussed in the preceding chapter, an interest group is a body of people united around shared attitudes or beliefs, which seeks to affect the public policy process by influencing policy makers to make decisions compatible with the needs of the group. The areas of concern of most interest groups and the political demands they articulate tend to be narrow and specific, such as lower taxes, increased government spending for individual programs, or protection of the environment. Factions are informal groupings or clubs led by prominent politicians within a single political party.[3] Factions serve as a power base for persons aspiring to the leadership of the party or seeking the adoption of a particular policy by the party as a whole.

Political parties are related to but different from both interest groups and factions. Unlike interest groups, which attempt to affect the public policy process indirectly by influencing government policy makers, political parties seek to gain direct control over the machinery of government through the electoral process. Political parties consist of a number of interest groups brought together in a stable coalition. Party leaders intent on winning elections seek to include enough interest groups to attract a plurality of voters. The party platform, the official statement of the position on key issues, serves as the symbolic vehicle uniting the interest groups. For example, in the U.S. presidential election of 1980, Ronald Reagan sought to create a New Right coalition of economic conservatives, militant anti-Communists, evangelical Christians, and blue-collar workers concerned with the effects of inflation. Consequently, the Republican platform of 1980 included strong statements favoring lower taxes, less government regulation of business, prayer in public schools, less government spending, and "making America great again" in the field of foreign affairs.[4]

Because they bring together a number of different interest groups under the banner of the party, parties are said to perform the function of *aggregating interests*. This is different from the function of articulating or communicating a small number of demands performed by interest groups. Factions are also found in most political parties because it is common for small groups within the party to compete for control of the organization and the party platform. Factions tend to be short-lived and often last no longer than the careers of the party notables around whom they are formed.

Some sources have noted that the distinction between factions, interest groups, and parties is not always clear. In the early years of the nineteenth century, parties developed from groups of political notables within the legislatures of certain Western states. In their infancy these parties had few supporters in the general population and behaved more as factions than real political parties. In addition, it is sometimes difficult to distinguish between an interest group and a small political party. Many political systems contain protest parties or "parties of expression"[5] too small to have any real hope of winning an election and which exist only to express the political beliefs of their members—much the way interest groups articulate the demands of their clients. Notwithstanding these difficulties, a working definition must begin with a distinction between parties and other political groups. Recognizing this fact, Joseph LaPalombara has offerred the following widely accepted definition which we will employ in this chapter:

> A political party is a formal organization whose self-conscious, primary purpose is to place and maintain in public office persons who will control, alone or in coalition, the machinery of government.[6]

HISTORY OF MODERN PARTIES

The development of modern political parties began in the states of the West at the beginning of the nineteenth century. Roy Macridis identified five stages in the evolution of the party which help to explain the diverse forms taken by contemporary parties.[7] In each period the party was shaped by the prevailing political values and institutions. Political parties were "consequences" rather than "causes" of such conditions as representative democracy and totalitarianism, although once in existence they reinforced the prior conditions.[8] In *stage one* the parties emerged as groups within the representative assemblies of England and the United States (Parliament and Congress). The first parties formed around loose ideological principles and assumed labels corresponding to the beliefs of their members—Conservatives, Liberals, Federalists, and Jeffersonian Republicans. In this stage the development of parties was impeded by the fact that party leaders were generally fearful of political involvement by the masses and membership was limited to the aristocracy and the middle class.

Stage two extends from the 1830s to the 1870s. In this stage political parties were influenced by the extension of the franchise, which began in the United States and reached Britain, France, Germany, and the Scandinavian states by the end of the period. As Macrides notes, political parties "resembled a pyramid whose apex is always identified in the representative assemblies but whose base is now broad enough to include most of the people."[9] Central organizations and party symbols were developed to attract voters, but control over the party remained firmly in the hands of elected representatives. The most important limitation to the growth of parties in this period was the failure of the leaders to address major social and economic issues confronting the working classes. As a result, the vast majority of the working class remained outside of the political party system and alienated from parliamentary government.

In *stage three* between 1890 and 1910 a new, extraparliamentary form of party developed. Political organizers replaced legislative notables as leaders, and the party program addressed the specific economic and social needs of the working class. The result was the development of mass political parties displaying a new degree of discipline. Foremost among the new parties were the British Labour party, the German Social Democratic party, and the French Socialists. In this stage party activities came to include strikes, demonstrations, and information campaigns unrelated to the activities of the legislative assembles.

In *stage four,* the period between World War I and World War II, the Communist parties of Western Europe emerged as powerful sources of political power. In this period, Macridis notes, "the Communist party became in essence both an army and a church."[10] It was highly disciplined, exacting in its membership requirements, and often organized into secret cells. Under the influence of the organizational principles developed by Lenin and the Russian Bolsheviks, the party emphasized obedience over debate, and individual work and sacrifice for the cause. Most important, the functions of the political party were redefined to include revolutionary activity. The emergence of the Communist parties in Western Europe provoked strong countermeasures by other groups, which led to a further expansion of the party system. The Catholic church sponsored "Catholic" parties; the socialist parties increasingly accepted parliamentary and democratic methods; and business groups, the middle class, and trade unions became associated with political parties.[11] In addition, the structure and methods of the Communists were adopted by the two revolutionary parties of the right, the Italian Fascist party and the Nazi party.

In *stage five* following World War II, two major developments occurred. First, political parties modeled after both the democratic and Communist variants developed in the states of the Third World. In Africa, Asia, and the Middle East, parties performed the new functions of mobilizing the masses for independence and, with varying degrees of success, integrating diverse tribes, ethnic communities, and regional groups. Second, the political parties in the West became increasingly pragmatic as the achievements of postindustrial society led to a new era described by some as "the end of ideology." Many sources have also commented on the decline of support for political parties in the West.[12] More will be said about this point later.

FUNCTIONS OF POLITICAL PARTIES

Political parties have proven to be flexible structures capable of performing a great variety of functions. Studies have identified and investigated the following functions of political parties: interest aggregation; elite recruitment and candidate selection; political socialization; political communication; electoral brokerage; expression of opposition; political mobilization; political and social integration; revolution, counterorganization, and subversion; public opinion formation; development of voter identity; reconciliation of group demands; and the coordination of government organs.[13] For our purposes this impressive list can be reduced to three basic functions: political mobilization, interest aggregation, and facilitation of legal and orderly opposition.[14]

Political Mobilization

One of the primary tasks confronting every political system is the need to involve the isolated individual in political life. Political parties have proven better able to mobilize citizens for political activity than any other institution. Political mobilization is accomplished through a series of processes including (1) teaching or socializing people to political roles, (2) providing political information, (3) offering symbols with which unsophisticated people can identify, (4) recruiting new members for the political elite, and (5) selecting candidates for electoral competition. In addition to mobilizing people to participate in democratic politics, parties are equally able to accomplish the intense politicization required in totalitarian societies. The achievement of the totalitarian state in the Soviet Union and Nazi Germany was made possible by the existence of the single political party.

Interest Aggregation

In every political system the cleavages in society give rise to a great number of competing political demands. Many of these demands are represented by organized interest groups and forcefully articulated to the political system. The existence of so many diverse and specific demands tends to atomize political life and create a bewildering, complex political agenda that is beyond the comprehension of the average citizen. Political parties aggregate or combine these diverse interests in two ways: (1) the need to win elections facilitates at least temporary cooperation between interest groups, which often results in a stable coalition of interests; and (2) the development of a party platform produces coherent, simplified proposals for dealing with the problems of society which voters may select or reject at election time. By aggregating interests the political party serves as an integrating force in the political system. Interest groups that identify with a national party thereby identify with the entire political system.[15] When this occurs within broad, "catch-all" parties, the intensity of political conflict and the degree of polarization are reduced.[16]

Facilitating Opposition

Conflict is at the center of the political process, and vigorous conflict requires the effective participation of competing groups. Political parties are effective vehicles for the expression of various degrees of opposition. In democratic societies political parties not in power play the role of "the loyal opposition" by overseeing government programs, presenting critiques of policies, and offering an alternative at election time. They also facilitate and legitimize acceptance of defeat in the democratic electoral process and provide an indispensable power base for elites not in control of the machinery of government. In sharply divided societies political parties may be used to mobilize support for extreme forms of opposition including subversion and revolution. Finally, in political systems having only one viable political party (e.g., the Soviet Union and Mexico) conflict occurs between factions within the political party.

TYPES OF POLITICAL PARTIES

Political parties can be classified on the basis of a number of factors, including the nature of their membership, their leadership, their organizational characteristics, or the beliefs professed by them. Parties can also be differentiated on the basis of the interest groups they serve, the political aims they profess, their sources of voter support, or their sources of financial support.[17] Political parties can further be characterized by reference to the party systems of which they are part. Studies recognize three basic types; single-party systems, two-party systems, and multiparty systems.

Single-Party Systems

In single-party systems one political party totally dominates either because it enjoys a legal monopoly and other parties are suppressed as in the Soviet Union, or because it enjoys a controlling position in the electoral competition as in India and Mexico. In the latter case, other small parties may exist, but they are of little practical importance as the dominant party wins all national elections. Although one-party systems exist in some democratic states (India and Mexico), they are more common in authoritarian systems. If a one-party government controls all other political organizations, including unions, educational institutions, and the mass media, the system is totalitarian.[18] In one-party systems all interest groups must accommodate themselves to the structure of the single party.

Two-Party Systems

In two-party systems, only two parties are sufficiently strong to share the majority of the electoral vote, and the major parties alternate as governing parties (in control of the government).[19] It is common for small "third parties" to exist, but they are not capable of seriously challenging the major parties. Examples of third parties include the Liberal party in Great Britain and the New Democratic party in Canada. In two-party systems a great number of interest groups are aggregated within each party. In addition to Britain and Canada, the United States and the Federal Republic of Germany have this type of system. One of the strengths of the two-party system is that the party in power is clearly responsible for its actions, and the party out of power constitutes an equally clear alternative for the electorate.

Multiparty Systems

In multiparty systems three or more political parties exist, and none may be able to achieve majority control in the legislature. It is not uncommon for five, six, or even more parties to exist. In order to form a government in parliamentary systems, several political parties must join together in a coalition whose members total 50% or more of the seats in the legislature.[20] The need for coalition agreements often results in a type of instability characterized by governments of short tenure and prolonged political infighting. However, multiparty systems need not lead to instability, and in some multiparty systems (e.g., Italy) the instability is more the result of political cultural factors than the party system.[21] Parties in this type of system aggregate fewer interests than parties in two-party systems. Most of the countries of Western Europe are multiparty systems.

Parties in Three Political Worlds

Parties are shaped by the general political environments of which they are part. At any point in history, parties will be structured to deal with the major problems or crises confronting the society.[22] The specific style, rhetoric, and tactics of parties reflect the general level of sociopolitical development and follow the general style of economic life. In the states of the Third World, single-party systems dominate in order to mobilize the masses for the monumental tasks of modernization and nation-building. Political parties are the most important force for change and modernization. Party leaders demonstrate a highly ideological, heroic, and charismatic style. With minor modifications, single-party systems also predominate in the states of the Communist World, which seek to mobilize their populations for rapid industrial development and for the achievement of new, revolutionary societies. The single party is effective in facilitating political participation but limits that participation to activities in support of the totalitarian state. Political party leaders in the Communist states of Europe manifest a bureaucratic style typical of industrial states of the West. Leaders in the less-developed Communist states outside Europe display a heroic and charismatic style similar to that of the Third World. The states of the West have both two-party and multiparty systems. Leaders of Western parties reflect a bureaucratic style common to advanced industrial and postindustrial societies. Many large parties in the West adopt pragmatic, nonideological positions and favor compromise and bargaining with other parties.

THE FIRST WORLD

Development and Diversity of Western Parties

A wide variety of parties and party systems exists in the West. This diversity is a result of the fact that Western parties have been shaped by social and political factors unique in each country. Five factors have been important in the development of Western parties: (1) the country's early political history, (2) cleavages or divisions within the general society (such as between classes or ethnic groups), (3) the political culture, (4) the degree of political centralization, and (5) the constitution and laws governing electoral competition. Modern parties and party systems in Europe, North America, and the democratic countries of Asia (Japan, Australia and New Zealand) reflect the cumulative effect of these factors, which one source has called "national circumstances."[23]

National circumstances differ considerably from country to country. The cases of Italy and the United States illustrate this point. Italy's multiparty system has been shaped by the prevailing social and political conditions within that country: a high degree of political centralization, a fragmented society, and an acute class-consciousness. As a result, Italian parties have strong national organizations and employ the language of class politics in their appeals to the public. The two-party system in the United States reflects the influence of the opposite conditions: extreme political decentralization, a largely consensual society, and an absence of acute class-consciousness. American party organization is strongest at the state level, and both major parties appeal to voters of all social classes. All political parties "live off" the conflicts in society. To achieve electoral success, democratic parties must mirror the social and political values of large segments of the population. In addition, as leadership skills and money are important in political campaigns, party leaders must promise, if elected, to enact into law the political demands of important elite groups. In short, political parties must identify and reflect contemporary values of society; they cannot afford to be ahead or behind the contemporary political agenda. As Everett Ladd has noted, political parties respond to social change, they do not initiate social change.[24] The issue of the selection of a woman for the presidency or vice-presidency in the United States illustrates this point. Geraldine Ferraro was nominated as a candidate for vice-president in 1984, when a majority of the public already supported such a development.

The diversity of Western political parties makes their study somewhat difficult. Almost any statement one chooses to make about parties must be qualified to account for exceptions. For example, it is generally assumed that American political parties are "parties of action,"[25] concerned with winning elections rather than expressing particular doctrines. This statement accurately describes the two major parties, but it is not true of many smaller third parties that have historically been "parties of expression" primarily concerned with representing particular ideological viewpoints. (The Socialist Workers' party, the States' Rights party, and the Libertarian party are examples.) Exceptions and qualifications even extend to points that are seemingly obvious. Most studies of Western parties stress that by mobilizing the masses to political action and educating them on political issues, parties have contributed to the maintenance of democracy. In the years between the two World Wars, however, political parties in Italy, Germany, and Austria were used to teach anti-democratic values and to mobilize the general population in support of authoritarian and totalitarian regimes. Even the three functions usually attributed to political parties, aggregating interests, mobilizing the general population, and expressing opposition, are not performed equally throughout the West. In some cases national circumstances create conditions that limit the ability of parties to perform certain functions. In Italy, for example, societal divisions based on class, region, and religious affiliations make it impossible for any two parties to aggregate or unite all of the country's interests in the manner of the Democratic and Republican parties of the United States.

Because of the complexity of party activity in the West, our discussion will focus on four major points. First, we will discuss the general contribution of parties to the maintenance of democratic politics in the West. This discussion will include the role of the Fascist and Nazi parties in the breakdown of democratic regimes in the interwar years. Second, two-party and multiparty systems will be compared. Third, we will compare the parties and party systems in the United States and Europe. Models or "ideal types" will be used in this discussion, but their limitations, especially the inability to account for exceptions, will be made clear. Finally, the decline of political parties will be considered. Special attention will be given to the potential effects of the decline on Western democracy.

Political Parties and Western Democracy

Although political parties frequently are the subject of controversy in the West, it is generally accepted that contemporary political parties are useful instruments for the promotion of democracy. Parties have helped to achieve the conditions cited by traditional democratic theorists as the prerequisites of democracy, and political parties actually developed in response to the problem of achieving these conditions. Foremost among the conditions for democracy are *popular sovereignty, majority rule, popular consultation*, and *political equality*.[26] In the contemporary period, popular sovereignty and majority rule refer to a political process in which decision makers are responsible to the general electorate and acquire the right to make political decisions by winning the competition for votes.[27] Parties and elections provide an effective means of making leaders accountable to the public as well as a means for providing government officials with feedback about public opinion on specific policy questions. Parties also play an important role in the promotion of political consultation (discussion and criticism). As Robert Dahl has noted, the development of a mechanism for representing the opposition was one of the great milestones in the development of democratic institutions.[28] Although in the Second and Third Worlds peaceful and orderly modes of opposition have been rare, political parties in the West are recognized as legitimate and protected by law.[29] They have served as effective instruments for those wishing to scrutinize the actions of groups in control of the government. Finally, political parties have done much to promote political equality by accommodating members of the general population seeking the opportunity to participate in the political process. Many contemporary political parties in the West originated in the early years of the twentieth century when millions of working class men sought inclusion in the political system after acquiring the right to vote. Between the 1920s and the 1960s, parties accommodated and were strengthened by the inclusion of women and young adults in the electoral process. Overall, parties have contributed to the democratic process by promoting the peaceful accommodation of conflict. Parties provide institutions, independent of government authority, through which partisan groups of all persuasion can compete peacefully for political power.

Parties against Democracy: Nazi and Fascist Parties. So far we have focused on the contributions of modern parties to the democratic process. In the period between World War I and World War II, however, political parties in several Western European countries were used to mobilize authoritarian groups against democratic political institutions. These groups sought to replace the democratic political order with a dictatorship that would outlaw opposition parties and place all political, economic, and social institutions under the control of the state.[30] The state, in turn, was to be the servant of the party and its leaders. The Nazi party in Germany led by Adolf Hitler and the Fascist party in Italy headed by Benito Mussolini are the best-known examples, although smaller authoritarian parties based on the German and Italian models were established in most of the states of Europe. In no state did the authoritarian parties achieve a majority electoral victory, and these parties must not be confused with contemporary democratic parties. Despite the fact that only a few Fascists held seats in the Parliament, Mussolini assumed power in 1922 through his "March on Rome," which one source has described as "halfway between a genuine coup and a hopped-up political demonstration."[31] After 1925 the Fascists used violence, intimidation, and even murder in order to consolidate power. Adolf Hitler became chancellor of Germany on January 30, 1933, following complicated parliamentary maneuvering. On February 28, the decree "For the Protection of Nation and State" was promulgated by the Nazi government. It abolished basic democratic rights, including freedom of the press, free speech, and freedom of association; and permitted searches, confiscation, and censorship of mail.[32] Between 1933 and the end of the regime in 1945, the Nazis established a totalitarian system (see Chapter 6) in Germany that employed violence on a

Hitler and Mussolini meet in Venice, 1934.

scale unprecedented in the modern world. This violence culminated in the genocide of European Jews, which claimed more than 6 million victims. Although the Nazis and Fascists demonstrated that parties could mobilize people toward the pursuit of authoritarian as well as democratic objectives, they had nothing else in common with contemporary Western parties. Unlike democratic parties, the authoritarian parties were open only to those recruits who met class, racial, or religious criteria and who passed special membership tests.[33] These parties also demanded absolute obedience to the party leader, operated in an environment of secrecy, and expelled members who deviated from the official party line. In addition, the purpose of the authoritarian party was to abolish the opposition both inside and outside the party, not to participate in a system of free and open competition. These parties represented ideologies that tolerated and even glorified violence and were absolutely incompatible with liberal political values (see Chapter 4). After World War II, the Nazi and Fascist parties were made illegal and many of their leaders were prosecuted for their crimes.

Party Systems in the West

Two major types of party systems exist in the West, two-party systems and multiparty systems. Although single-party systems existed earlier in some European states, all Western states now have competitive party systems. At present, Great Britain, the United States, Canada, Australia, and New Zealand have two-party competition. In a two-party system, each of the major parties has the capacity to gain an electoral majority, and the two alternate in control of the national government. The major parties do not usually share power equally, however, and it is common for one party to dominate for a decade or more. In addition, third parties (e.g., the Liberal party in Britain and the New Democratic party in Canada) may exist. However, in two-party systems the major parties generally receive 80% or more of the vote, and the general expectation exists that they will continue to monopolize political power.

In two-party systems, one party often specializes in initiating change and the other in consolidating it.[34] In the United States, Great Britain, and Canada, the Democratic party, the British Labour party, and the Liberal party, respectively, have been the parties of change, whereas the U.S. Republican party, the British Conservative party, and Progressive-Conservative party of Canada have been the parties associated with slowing or consolidating change. In Australia and New Zealand the Labour parties have been the parties of change and the Liberal party of Australia and the National party of New Zealand have been the parties of consolidation. In two-party systems all the major interest groups are aggregated within the two major parties. Because of this fact, the parties often have the characteristics of "catch-all" parties, being internally heterogeneous and nonprogrammatic (placing little emphasis on programs and doctrines). American parties in particular are often considered to be "issueless parties" devoid of meaningful ideological differences.[35] This view must be qualified, however. Although not programmatic when compared with some European parties, the Democratic and Republican parties in the United States have advocated sharply different programs in several elections, for example, in 1932, 1964, 1972, and 1984. In addition, three major parties in the states under consideration can be classified as programmatic in nature. These are the British Labour party, the Australian Labour party, and the Labour party of New Zealand. Despite their commitment to social democratic programs, however, these parties, like all major parties in two-party systems, are first and foremost "parties of action" (concerned with winning elections) rather than "parties of expression."[36]

The majority of states in the West have multiparty competition. Since World War II, the number of parties in such systems has ranged from 3 to 14.

Prime Minister Margaret Thatcher emerges from the official residence at 10 Downing Street, London.

It is important to realize that all party systems are dynamic, not static, and that the number and nature of parties are constantly subject to change. Such factors as social change, changes in the electoral laws, and revisions in the general constitutional order can affect the number of parties and the nature of party competition. Since the origin of the Fifth Republic in France in 1958, the number of relevant parties has been reduced from 10 to 4. In the 1981 French national elections, the two major parties of the left and the two major parties of the right each combined in an electoral bloc or coalition. This development was in part a response to two important changes in the constitution: (1) the creation of a powerful presidency that could only be won by large parties or coalitions, and (2) the abandonment of proportional representation for a modified plurality system, which allowed only one winner in an electoral district and provided no reward to parties coming in second or third. Parties in multiparty systems aggregate a smaller number of interests than parties in a two-party system. For this reason, parties in such systems are frequently internally homogeneous, and committed to specific doctrines. Most multiparty systems combine "parties of action" with smaller "parties of expression."[37] The parties of expression frequently accept limited electoral success in order to represent a specific minority viewpoint.

Japan represents an interesting variation on the multiparty system. It is sometimes called a one-and-half party state. The Liberal Democratic party

The Emperor of Japan opens a new session of the Japanese Diet.

(LDP), the leading conservative party, has ruled Japan since its founding in 1955. Though it is true its majority in the Japanese Diet has been declining in recent elections, the second major party, the social democratic-oriented Japan Socialist party, has not been able to mount a sufficiently strong opposition to overcome LDP control. The five smaller parties gain seats in the Japanese Diet but are too divided to unite in a common anti-LDP front. Some observers believe, however, that in the near future the LDP will finally lose the majority and Japan will evolve toward coalitions or true two-party democracy.[38]

In much of the literature on political parties, multiparty systems have been equated with political instability. It is argued that such systems are unstable because they require coalition agreements between parties in order to obtain a majority in the lower house of the legislature (see Chapter 6). Italy and France in the Fourth Republic (1947–1958) are often cited to prove that multiparty systems and coalition agreements are unworkable. Studies suggest that multiparty systems are not inherently unstable, however. The Netherlands, Luxembourg, Iceland, Ireland, Denmark, Sweden, and Norway stand as testimony that multiparties working in cabinet coalitions can be stable, in some cases even as stable as single-party cabinets.[39] The main factors in determining stability and instability may be the number of political parties and the ideological distance between them. Giovanni Sartori has argued that the critical differences among multiparty systems occur when the number of parties exceeds five and when there are extreme ideological polarities.[40] The presence of more than five parties indicates severe fragmentation both within the legislature and the society as a whole. On the other hand, several European states demonstrate that multiparty systems with fewer than five parties and possessing one dominant political party around which governing coalitions can form are capable of producing stable government majorities over a period of decades. Such systems are sometimes called "dominant multiparty systems" or "hegemonic multiparty systems."[41] Sweden and Norway are often classified as dominant multiparty systems because the Labour party in Norway and the Social Democratic party in Sweden frequently approach a majority in the legislature.[42] Multiparty systems demonstrate again the danger of generalizations in the study of political parties.

U.S. and European Political Parties: A Comparison

One study has described U.S. political parties as "skeletal, their selection of candidates relatively open, their structure federative, their general character explicitly non-class conscious, their emphasis generally non-programmatic, and their governmental representation fairly individualistic."[43] The same study characterized major European parties as "mass-membership organizations, their candidate selection closed and private, their structure national, their general character explicitly class conscious, their emphasis proudly programmatic, and their governmental representation highly cohesive."[44] The two descriptions point out that political parties in the United States and Europe differ in several respects. The following discussion will compare U.S. and European political parties on the basis of three analytical categories: (1) skeletal parties versus mass parties, (2) organization and style of representation in government, and (3) commitment to programs, doctrines, and class-consciousness.

Skeletal Parties and Mass Parties. The Democratic and Republican parties in the United States are called skeletal or cadre parties because between elections participation in party activities is limited to a small group of party activists who constitute the "skeleton" of the party. Although voters may indicate their preferences as Democrats or Republicans at the time of registration, they perform no special tasks for the party such as paying dues or attending meetings. At election time voters demonstrate their support for a party by voting for it, but there are no other formal membership requirements. When Americans speak of party members, they really mean party supporters.[45] Two important consequences follow from the skeletal nature of U.S. parties and the absence of a permanent mass following. First, candidates who have the personal characteristics to make themselves attractive to voters must be selected. For example, in 1952 both the Democratic and Republican parties sought General Dwight Eisenhower as their presidential candidate, despite the fact that he had not previously been affiliated with either group.[46] Party leaders considered party loyalty secondary to electability. Second, skeletal parties must spend large amounts of money at election time to purchase the campaign staffs and services that they otherwise lack.[47] U.S. elections are the most expensive in the world. In the 1980 national election, for example, the presidential candidates of the two major parties spent in excess of $58.5 million. Studies suggest that the skeletal nature of U.S. political parties is related to the fact that the franchise (the right to vote) has existed in the United States since the first half of the nineteenth century. Mass political parties occur primarily at the stage of history when major segments of the population have only recently received the right to vote for the first time. At the turn of the century newly enfranchised immigrants supplied a substantial mass following for the "party machines in American cities, but since the 1940s these organizations have given way to skeletal parties."[48]

Every West European state has at least one mass-membership party. Such parties have a permanent following of rank and file members who perform acts of commitment such as paying dues and attending meetings.[49] In many cases the members are indirectly affiliated with the party through auxiliary organizations such as trade unions; members of affiliated groups are automatically enrolled in the party and dues are deducted from their paychecks unless they formally "contract out."[50] Most mass parties combine members directly affiliated with the party in constituent groups with larger numbers of members indirectly affiliated through auxiliary organizations. For example, of the present 7 million members of the British Labour party, 6 million are indirect trade union members.[51] The movement toward mass parties in Europe began with the socialist parties. The goal of achieving socialism by means of democratic parliamentary institutions required a mass organization to deliver the working-class vote.[52] The creation of socialist parties in the West later in the nineteenth century was made possible by the extension of the franchise to large segments of the male population earlier in the nineteenth century. By 1914 all states of Western Europe had socialist parties. The possession of a permanent base of supporters has important implications for electoral competition. Rank and file members supply the party with important financial resources. In addition, the leaders of mass parties need not be as concerned with the personal characteristics of their candidates as the leaders of skeletal parties because, at least in theory, their members will vote for candidates out of loyalty to the party.

Several important qualifications must be made to our discussion of mass parties. First, in the contemporary period centrist and conservative parties in Europe are cadre parties and not mass-membership organizations. In some cases the distinction between the two types is difficult to make. The British Labour party stands as an example of this point. In the 1983 general election, the Labour party witnessed huge defections to both the Conservative party and the new Social Democratic party whose leaders broke from the ranks of Labour. Rank and file members are always important as sources of financial support, but they are not always reliable sources of electoral support.

Organization and Style of Representation in Government. The extent of government centralization is the chief determinant of the degree of centralization in a political party. The nature of a country's political institutions is the most important influence on the style of representation adopted by the members of a party elected to office. These facts help to explain the basic differences in the organization and style of U.S. and European political parties. U.S. parties developed in an environment of extreme political decentralization. The U.S. federal system established under the constitution divides the political system into 51 units, the 50 states and the national government (plus territorial governments in Puerto Rico and the Pacific Islands). In addition, separation of powers is imposed on the federal system, whereby the national government is separated by functions into three parts, the executive, legislative, and judicial branches. Both of these "national circumstances" have had a profound effect on the development of U.S. political parties. Since the early history of the United States, political parties have been organized at the level of the state, the level at which all candidates except the president and vice-president are elected. State party organizations were also needed because each state possessed a unique political culture with values and interests different from those of other states. In such a decentralized political system, the establishment of strong state parties was the most effective way to organize for electoral victory. The parties have national conventions that meet every four years to select the two presidential nominees and the Republican and Democratic National Committees, which are each headed by a national chairman. Despite their imposing titles, these national organizations have no real control over state and local organizations. It is interesting to note that political parties in Canada, North America's other federal system, are also decentralized compared with their European counterparts. The ethnic differences in Canada, especially the existence of separate English and French language groups, have also contributed to strong parties at the provincial level. However, the trend toward decentralization has been mitigated to some extent by the need for Canada's two major parties, the Liberal party and the Progressive-Conservative party, to achieve a majority in the Canadian Parliament. (See Chapter 6 for the workings of a parliamentary system.)

In the United States the separation of powers at the national level has also contributed to the development of a highly individualistic style of representation in government. Unlike their European counterparts who must work together in a parliamentary system, U.S. legislators and executives (president, governors of states, and so on) serve in separate branches. The separation of powers permits a degree of independence and intraparty conflict not seen in Europe. In addition, since congressmen and congresswomen are elected by constituencies within individual states, they are not dependent on national party leaders for their positions.

In general, European political parties are highly centralized, national structures. Campaigns are directed by the national leaders of the party, finances are collected and dispensed nationally, and the national party organizations control most nominations. In some cases this control is direct and candidates for office are selected directly by the national leadership, but in a majority of cases the national party only retains the power to veto nominations made by local constituency groups.[53] Political party organizations in Europe reflect the fact that the majority of the European states are unitary political systems having only one level of government. Unitary systems lack the territorial subunits (states, provinces, cantons) necessary for the development of decentralized, federative parties. The centralized political party developed in response to the centralized national polity. Three European states, the German Federal Republic, Austria, and Switzerland, are federal systems. In the cases of Germany and Austria, the development of centralized political parties predated the federal system by nearly half a century. With the exception of the Christian-Social Union in Bavaria (a state in the German Federal Republic), German and Austrian political parties are organized on a national rather than a federal basis.[54] Switzerland represents a unique case: the potential decentralizing influence of the federal system is offset by the fact that Switzerland has a parliamentary system like Canada's rather than a separation of powers system like that of the United States.[55]

The parliamentary system of government has also contributed to the development of centralized political parties in Europe. As one source noted, the imperatives of cabinet government require centralization.[56] In order for any one member of the party to achieve the power available to a governing party, the party must win a majority of seats in the lower house of the Parliament. This means winning a national election, something that strictly regional parties can never hope to do. The parliamentary system also encourages party discipline and cohesion within the party.[57] Every member of the party realizes that an attack on the party is also an attack on one's status as a member of the government. The fusion of the legislative and executive functions in a parliamentary system (see Chapter 6) also eliminates much of the conflict experienced by representatives and presidents of the same party in the United States.

Commitment to Programs and Doctrines. Special care must be exercised in any discussion of the commitment of Western parties to programs and ideologies. Traditional studies stressed that U.S. parties are nonprogrammatic, more concerned with winning elections than representing ideologies, and that they are explicitly not class-conscious. By comparison, European parties were seen as "proudly programmatic," stongly committed to doctrines and ideologies, and explicitly class-conscious.[58] In the contemporary period, many qualifications must be made in these descriptions. First, all political parties claim some program, policy, principle, doctrine, or ideology.[59] Although major U.S. parties have been less committed historically to doctrines and programs than have European parties, many third parties in the United States have been doctrinaire and programmatic. Of course, both the Democratic and Republican parties do develop party platforms for state and national elections, which state the party's positions on the major issues. Second, the description of European parties as programmatic and class-conscious has applied historically to European socialist parties, but it has applied less so to centrist and conservative parties. Since World War II, most European parties of the center and right have been opportunistic rather than programmatic because they have been in competition for votes from the same groups. In their electoral appeals center-right parties have also relied heavily on the personalities of such party leaders as Winston Churchill (Great Britain), Alcide de Gaspari (Italy), Konrad Adenauer (Germany), and Charles de Gaulle (France). Overall, most of the successful center-right parties resemble the two major parties in the United States in their electoral behavior. Finally, since the 1950's even the socialist parties of Europe have demonstrated an increased flexibility in their commitment to programs and doctrines. This new flexibility is a prerequisite to success at the polls in an age of postindustrial affluence in which blue-collar workers no longer perceive themselves as the "exploited proletariat." Studies of socialist parties in Italy, France, and Germany suggest an inverse relationship between doctrinal rigidity and electoral success.[60] Doctrinal moderation and pragmatism have been the price of electoral victory, and socialist leaders in power (e.g., Francois Mitterand in France and Bettino Craxi in Italy) have employed a pragmatic approach to policy making. In short, although

European parties historically were more programmatic and class-conscious than were U.S. parties, some major European parties increasingly resemble the U.S. Democratic and Republican parties.

Decline of Political Parties

Studies of both the United States and the countries of Western Europe report a decline in the support for political parties. This development assumes four major dimensions. First, at the attitudinal level, public opinion surveys show a loss of confidence in the ability of political parties to perform important tasks. Large segments of the general population currently believe that political parties are inadequate to keep elected officials responsive to the wishes of the public.[61] Public perceptions of lost control and responsiveness have grown more intense as the size of government bureaucracies has burgeoned. Second, support within the general population has also declined in the area of voter allegiance. Voters demonstrate growing willingness to switch their votes from parties that they have traditionally supported or to refrain from voting entirely. An example of this trend is Great Britain where both the Labour and Conservative parties have suffered major defections from groups that had previously supported them for most of this century.[62] Large numbers of young adults in Europe have withdrawn their support from the major parties and have given it to the environmental and nuclear freeze movements; new voters in the United States have shown an increasing willingness to register as "unaffiliated" rather than to declare for one of the two major parties. Third, political parties are under attack from interest groups. Traditionally, interest groups were integrated into major political parties and were dependent on party leaders who would enact their programs if elected. Today, interest groups (e.g., unions and rights groups, see Chapter 8) refuse to accept the dictates of party leaders and frequently prefer to undertake direct political action on their own behalf. Finally, parties are less able to impose discipline on their candidates and members in government than in the past. Interest groups provide alternative sources of funding and support for candidates, and, as the commitment of voters to parties weakens, party leaders experience a corresponding loss of control over party members.

Many theories have been advanced to explain the decline of political parties. Most focus on the affluent nature of Western society. In the environment of affluence, interest group members expect full satisfaction of their political demands and prefer to conduct their own national campaigns rather than to compromise those demands within the framework of a national party. Individual citizens in the West also hold high, perhaps unrealistic, expectations concerning the extent to which parties can respond to their demands. Parties cannot be everything to all groups, yet frustrated voters are abandoning parties in record numbers. Most important, the social setting of affluence has deprived the major parties of their traditional base of support. All Western parties, including those in the United States, developed from and were sustained by the class divisions in society that developed during the period of industrialization. Parties became identified in varying degrees with organized labor or the business community and drew their support from those groups. In the current postindustrial period a majority of the population is employed in service industries, and the sharp social distinctions around which parties developed have disappeared. The decline of political parties raises a sobering question for the Western democracies. If the decline of political parties continues, what institution or institutions will perform the functions now performed by parties? So far, no other institution seems capable of performing such functions as effectively (see Chapter 8 on interest groups).

THE SECOND WORLD

The Communist political system cannot be comprehended unless the role of the Communist party is clearly understood. In all Communist states there is only one ruling party. This party claims for itself not only the right but the duty to rule, to the total exclusion of any other political group. The only exception to this statement is the existence of essentially powerless "allied" parties in Poland, the German Democratic Republic, Czechoslovakia, Bulgaria, and North Korea. These "parties" join with the ruling Communist party in a "national front" (see Chapter 8) in which a common policy and a common ballot, with a single list of candidates (usually with only one candidate per electoral position), are presented to the electorate. The allied parties accept permanent subordination to the Communist party, have no autonomy, and are in no sense an opposition. Their actual role is that of transmitting Communist ideas to certain groups (intellectuals, farmers, religious people) that might be less easily reached by the Communist party itself. Allied parties are never allowed to seek support among the proletariat. Thus, in actual fact, there is only one political philosophy and only one political party in the 17 states ruled by Communist parties.

A few words should be said about the term *Communist* before we delve into the party itself. "Communist" is used to identify that political party which projects an ideal future, a utopian society in which each will work according to one's abilities; thus work will be one of the basic motivating forces of life, and at the same time one would draw from society only what one needed.[63] This future society would be without formal political structure (the state will have "withered away") and classless (no one would be exploiting anyone else), leaving an economic system of collectivist nature.[64]

No Communist party-controlled state claims to be Communist now—Communism is a goal. When this goal will be reached is no longer predicted (although Lenin, Mao, and Krushchev made statements that appeared to say that Communist society was close at hand). "Communist" is also used to differentiate this party from other socialist parties. Socialists and Communists share the notion that a cooperative effort is necessary to better society, but whereas most socialists are democratic in nature, Communists are totalitarian (they see politics as absolute and government as all-encompassing). To confuse the issue a bit, Communists sometimes refer to themselves and their countries as socialistic, but they mean that socialism is a stage on the road to Communism and that only they are "true" socialists. Liberal–democratic socialists (social democrats), on the other hand, never call themselves Communists, see socialism as a goal in itself, and do not predict an ideal future society.

Emergence of the Communist Party

What are the origins of the Communist party? On what does this party base its claims that it alone has the right and duty to rule, and that all other political thought is error? The immediate roots of the contemporary Communist party lie in the late eighteenth century. As mentioned before, J. L. Talmon, in his *Origins of Totalitarian Democracy*, examined the source of both liberal and totalitarian democratic thought. He found in the French Revolution (1789–1815) that two schools developed. The liberal school considered politics to be a pragmatic activity, a matter of trial and error. It held that government should be limited, with much human activity taking place outside the scope of politics. The totalitarian democratic school, however, felt there was a single truth in politics. This truth was found in a single philosophy, and this philosophy must be applied to human government. Politics was to be all-embracing, and no human activity could be considered to be nonpolitical. The governing of people was therefore considered a "total" activity.[65]

Interestingly, both the liberal-democratic and the totalitarian-democratic schools affirm liberty. The former sees liberty as the right to individuality, in "doing one's thing," as long as it does not interfere with the needs of society; the latter believes freedom is only consistent with the "attainment of an absolute collective purpose".[66]

A second root of twentieth-century Communism is found in the struggle between competitive capitalism (a conflict system in which private enterprise rules in the economic sphere under conditions of an open and free market) and cooperative socialism (a system in which collective effort and control of the economic system, usually through the state apparatus, are emphasized). Many who recognized human sufferings rife in nineteenth-century capitalist exploitation of industrial workers (the proletariat) turned to the idea of cooperation (socialism) as better suited to human development. One of these socialist thinkers was Karl Marx (1818–1883) who spent his whole adult life dissecting capitalism to reveal the evils within it. He roundly condemned the terrible conditions in which the proletariat worked (see any edition of his *Capital* and the many commentaries on it) and predicted that this relatively new class, decisively important to capitalist society, would recognize its own importance and rise up and seize power from the owners of industry. This would happen as the proletariat, by internal spontaneous development, passed through a stage of economic struggle (better working conditions, more pay, and so on), to ideological development, to a political stage (development of labor-based political parties), and finally to revolutionary struggle in reaching for political power. Political thinkers could assist in this development. Marx and his close collaborator Friedrich Engels (1820–1895) believed that Communists could facilitate this progression. "The Communists" as Marx and Engels said in their famous *Manifesto* of 1848, "are . . . the most advanced and resolute section of the working class parties of every country." However, they "do not form a separate party opposed to other working class parties . . . they do not set up any sectarian principles of their own."[67] They were not advocating the formation of a separate formal political party. Although Marx and Engels stated that revolution was necessary to overthrow the existing order, it is not altogether clear whether they meant the violent, cataclysmic destruction of opposing forces, as more or less espoused by ruling Communist parties today, or a benign "revolution" caused by the mass (majority) coming to power through a democratic process and their making radical changes in government and society.

At least one author, looking at Marx's examination of the Paris Commune (a short-lived revolutionary government in France, September 1870–May 1871) believes that Marx was not a totalitarian and thus can not be blamed for today's Communism (although Communist parties claim to be the direct lineal successors to Marx):

> The Commune was based on the support of the majority as determined by universal suffrage. The acceptance of the people's right to frequent elections of their representatives implies full popular participation in the working of the "dictatorship." The Commune was exercised through the elected body based upon popular choice and subject to public opinion. . . . Marx's praise of the workings of the Commune shows beyond any doubt that nothing could be any more foreign to his view than the suppression of universal suffrage by the rule of a party. It seems inescapable that Marx and Engels did not equate the

dictatorship of the proletariat with the dictatorship of a party over the rest of the community.[68]

Nonetheless, Communist parties place their philosophical superstructure on the foundation of Marx's thought. There are two reasons why one cannot accept this claim completely. First, revolutionary seizures of power have taken place in countries that were not at the stage of fully developed capitalism (the natural jumping-off point to the next historical stage, socialism–communism).

> *Marx:* No social order can ever disappear before all productive forces for which there is room in it have developed; and new higher relations of production never appear before the material conditions of their existence have matured in the womb of the old society itself.

> *Engels:* Revolutions are not made intentionally and arbitrarily, but everywhere and always they have been the necessary consequences of conditions which were wholly independent of the will and direction of individual parties and entire classes.[69]

The other reason for not placing the weight of today's Communism directly on Marx and Engels concerns where the revolutions would take place.

> The Communist revolution will not be merely a national phenomenon but must take place simultaneously in all civilized countries, that is to say, at least England, America, France and Germany.[70]

It should be mentioned here that many Western and Third World economists, sociologists, and political scientists use Marxist ideas in a heuristic way—that is, as a guide or tool for research—without in any way becoming Communists.[71]

The reason today's Communists call upon Marx and Engels lies in the great success of one branch of the followers of Marx and Engels, the Russian branch, and in the successful adaptation, interpretation, and revision of Marxism by Lenin, the leader of that branch.

The Communist Party Seizes Power

Russia in the nineteenth century was a peasant agricultural society suffering under the heavy oppression of a degenerate landowner class and a monarchical system in which the Tsar claimed all power and assigned none to any group other than his immediate entourage. The small Russian revolutionary movement hoped to overthrow the system with the help of the peasant masses but received little support from that quarter.

When large-scale industrialization began in the 1880s, Marxism began to play an increasing role in revolutionary thought. In 1883 George Plekhanov (1857–1918) was instrumental in forming the first Russian Marxist party, Liberation of Labor, while he was in exile in Switzerland.[72]

At the same time, Western Marxism was undergoing a deradicalization because the increasing impoverishment of the workers, predicted by Marx, and the deepening of the chasm between workers and owners, foreseen by Marx, were not taking place. In fact Eduard Bernstein, in his work *Evolutionary Socialism*, maintained that revolution would not occur, that change would be gradual and liberal democratic, and that Marx was obsolete. Bernstein may be considered one of the fathers of the social democratic movement.[73]

The defense of Marx came not from mainstream socialist thinkers but rather from an obscure young lawyer (Vladimir Ilyich Ulyanov, 1870–1924) from the backwoods town of Simbirsk on the Volga River in the Russian Empire. Universally known by his revolutionary name, Lenin, he attacked Bernstein as a revisionist (one who changes, for the worse, revolutionary doctrine) who was objectively playing into the hands of the ruling class. Lenin said that the appearance of modern imperialism, with the advanced industrialized countries seizing colonies around the world, had delayed temporarily the economic decline of the proletariat because capitalists were reaping superprofits from the world's colonial poor. Part of this huge income trickled down to the workers of the capitalist world and actually, though temporarily, bettered their economic conditions. True Marxists, understanding this, should not fall into the trap of revisionism. Lenin concluded that politically astute Marxists should form a revolutionary party untainted by revisionism, which would maintain purity of doctrine (as interpreted by Lenin) and carry forward the revolutionary banner. Basing his ideas on nineteenth-century Russian revolutionary theories, he declared that this new party should be conspiratorial in nature and elite in composition consisting only of tried and true, fully committed members. Lenin maintained that without the leadership of this Communist party (a name adopted in 1918; before that it was called the Bolshevik (majority) faction of the Russian Social Democratic Labor party) workers would never go beyond the economic stage of development. Ideology, political struggle, and revolution had to be brought to the workers by the Leninist party. Only such a party could have a chance of success in the oppressive Imperial Russian state.[74]

The actual majority of Russian Marxists, the so-called Menshevik (minority) faction, in the pre-1917 period opposed Lenin as a dangerous fanatic, and despite his use of the term *majority* (Bolshevik), his amorphous group was regularly in the minority.[75] Lenin was either extremely lucky or a perspicacious politician, for in the second half of World War I the Russian Empire collapsed. Into the ruins stepped a series of basically incompetent provisional governments. Simultaneously, Lenin's faction increased its power in the chaotic and radicalized atmosphere of the period. By gradually gaining control of the workers' councils (soviets), the Bolsheviks placed themselves in a position to seize power, which they finally accomplished on the night of November 7/8, 1917 (October 26/27 of the Julian Calendar then in use in Russia, hence the so-called October Revolution), an event that permanently sundered the socialist camp into totalitarian Communism and social democracy. Marx had explicitly said that revolution would not occur in an incompletely industrialized country:

> If therefore, the proletariat should overthrow the political rule of the bourgeoisie its victory would only be temporary so long as the material conditions which render necessary the abolition of the bourgeois mode of production . . . had not yet been created in the course of historical development.[76]

Lenin rationalized his move by stating that under the new conditions created by a worldwide imperialist system, Russia could be viewed as part of this system. The imperialist chain could be broken in Russia because Russia was its weakest link.[77]

Lenin's bold move and his ability to maintain the Communist party in power at the end of World War I and during civil war and foreign intervention were justification that he was right. With the exception of the period between November 1917 and March 1918, when a few left-wing Social Revolutionaries (agrarian radicals) assisted the new Bolshevik regime, the Bolsheviks did not share power and crushed all opposition.

The claim to rule based on right, duty, and purity of doctrine, by an elite band of dedicated revolutionaries to the exclusion of all others is the hallmark of all ruling Communist parties. All Communist parties claim a Marxist base, but only as interpreted and modified by Lenin. Current basic Communist doctrine may be described as 80 to 90% Lenin and 10 to 20% Marx. Marx's ideas are the base philosophy and Lenin's their practical application, but there remains a little-talked-about third element in the structure and practice of all ruling Communist parties. That third element was provided by Stalin.

Josif Vissarionovich Djugashvili (1879–1953; revolutionary name, Stalin) became the leader in the Soviet Union on the incapacitation and death of Lenin.[78] Stalin structured and regularized the Communist regime in the USSR—the model is used in some form in all Communist party states. The general model is a pyramidical hierarchy along the following lines:

Vertical Structure of the Communist Party

1 Politburo/Presidium
   (15± voting members plus 8± nonvoting candidate members)

2 Secretariat
   (many thousands employed)   national level

3 Central Committee
   (300+ voting members plus 150± nonvoting candidate members)

4 Province–level committees
   (120)

5 Local committees of party
   (4600)

6 Primary party organizations
   (350,000)

The numbers in parentheses refer to number of units or people involved at the respective levels in the Communist party of the Soviet Union. In the USSR, Yugoslavia, and Czechslovakia, between levels 3 and 4 is inserted a republic-level, containing 15, 5, and 2 units, respectively. The base of the pyramid rests on the primary party organizations (PPO), which are organized in the "collective"—the place of work—the factory, farm, school, hospital, government institute, and so on. The PPOs are organized geographically in local units, provincial units, and national units under day-to-day administrative direction of the Secretariat and policy control of the Central Committee and Politburo (called, in some countries, a presidium, not to be confused with the Presidium of the Soviet government).

In Communist party states, the party maintains an extensive professionally staffed bureaucratic apparatus that starts with a full-time secretary (administrator) in many PPOs. On the national level in all the countries many people are employed to run the party. The following chart gives some idea of how the Communist party of the Soviet Union is organized on the national level.

Structure of the Leading Organs of the Communist Party of the Soviet Union

Supreme Organ—*All-Union Party Congress*[a], meeting once every five years, hears reports of party work and elects:

1. *Central Auditing Commission,* which supervises the monetary end of party work.

2. *Central Committee* (CC) of the party[b], which meets in plenary session once every six months and has the right to all power when a congress is not meeting. The CC appoints:

   A. *General Secretary*[c] who is the *de facto* head of the Communist party of the Soviet Union.

   B. *Politburo*[d], the *de jure* collective head of the party which directs party work between sessions of the Central Committee.

   C. *Party Control Commission,* which is a supervisory body and judicial organ for the party.

   D. *Secretariat* of the Central Committee of the Communist party of the Soviet Union. *The Secretariat* consists of 24 departments:

Administration of Affairs	International
Administrative Organs	International Information
Agriculture and Food Industry	Letters
Agriculture Machine Building	Liaison with Bloc Parties
Cadres Abroad	Light Industry and Consumer Goods
Chemical Industry	Machine Building
Construction	Main Political Directorate
Culture	Organizational Party Work
Defense Industry	Propaganda
Economic Affairs	Science and Educational Instutions
General	Trade and Domestic Services
Heavy Industry and Power	Transportation and Communications

Source: Richard F. Staar, *USSR Foreign Policies After Detente* (Stanford, CA: Hoover Institution Press, 1985), Figure 2.1, p. 28; copyright 1985 by the Board of Trustees of Leland Stanford Junior University.

[a] The number of representatives to a given party congress is decided by the Central Committee.

[b] Membership of the CC is also not fixed but runs to more than 300 plus about 150 non voting candidate members.

[c] Political decision-making powers lie with the General Secretary and the Politburo. The General Secretary is always a member of the Politburo.

[d] Membership of the Politburo is not fixed either but is usually around 15 plus about 8 nonvoting candidate members.

Politburo members Mikhail Gorbachev (front right), General Secretary of the Communist Party of the Soviet Union, and Andrei Gromyko (front left), Foreign Minister of the Soviet Union, at a government meeting in Moscow, March, 1985.

There is a radical difference between theory and practice in the operation of the party. First, let us look at the theoretical general structure (*de jure*—according to the rules of a Communist party) and then the practical facts (*de facto*—actual situation). The most important body is the national party congress which meets every four or five years. It consists of delegates sent from lower levels of the party who meet to discuss party operations, develop party policy, and elect the party leadership. To keep the party functioning between congresses, on a nationwide basis the congress elects a several-hundred-member Central Committee, which makes all necessary decisions. These decisions are confirmed or vetoed by the next congress. As the CC meets only several times a year in a Plenum (full meeting), day-to-day operations are assigned to a subcommittee, called the Political Bureau (Politburo) or Presidium, consisting of about 15 people. The administrative staff apparatus—the Secretariat—is run by the General (or First) Secretary assisted by department heads called secretaries. The Central Auditing Commission, which supervises party funds, and the party Control Commission, which is an internal control committee, are not significant.[79] The party operates internally according to the theory of "democratic centralism" which theoretically holds for democracy within the party.[80]

Actually, all ruling Communist parties follow quite a different procedure. The unit at the apex, the Politburo, is a self-perpetuating body that recommends policy, programs, and personnel to the CC and through it to the Party Congress, both of which accept these recommendations with little if any debate, generally by a unanimous vote. Power flows from the top down. Lower units are expected to obey unquestioningly higher authority in order to affirm the unshakable unity and monolithic strength of the party in the face of its enemies.

Outside the party, as all wisdom and knowledge flows from the party and divergent ideas would be dangerous to the less politically aware, the party imposes an iron discipline through censorship and a thorough control of all aspects of society—in the name of freedom. Freedom is defined as working "in accordance with the interests of the people and in order to strengthen and develop the socialist system"[81] and "in accordance with the aims of building communism."[82] Any "exercise of . . . rights and freedoms" in Communist systems " is inseparable from performance of . . . duties and obligations."[83] Citizens must work within the system as it exists or in effect find themselves outside the pale of society.[84]

The 1977 Soviet Constitution clearly states in Article 6 that the interests, aims, goals, obligations, and duties are defined by the "leading and guiding force of Soviet society and the nucleus of its political system . . . the Communist Party of the Soviet Union." All ruling Communist parties either explicitly or implicitly follow a similar pattern.

Table 9.1 provides basic information on the 17 ruling Communist parties (15 if one counts Afghanistan and Kampuchea as states in pre-Communist developmental stages.) It is interesting to note that so far no Communist party has ever lost power once it has gained it, and, if in power, has never allowed an opposition to exist for long. Nonruling Communist parties have taken part in coalition governments where they were a minority party, but none has ever acted as a liberal–democratic party and left power once it was gained—and power has never been gained by the ballot.

Internal attempts at removing a Communist party in power have so far been unsuccessful. Such removals were attempted by domestic opposition: in East Germany in June 1953, but this was quickly put down by the Soviet Army; in Hungary where a revolt was crushed by Soviet military forces in 1956; and in Czechoslovakia where an attempt at creating "socialism with a human face" (January–August 1968) was eliminated by a lightning Warsaw Pact invasion led by the USSR on the night of August 20/21, 1968. The invasion of Czechoslovakia was followed by a reestablishment of Soviet Communist orthodoxy.[85]

Poles have been very active in attempting to get rid of the Soviet-imposed Communist regime. In 1956, 1968, 1970, 1976, and 1980 to 81, various workers and intellectual groups have tried to either remove or limit Communist party control. In each case some manuever of the Polish United Workers' Party has brought it back to full power. The last instance was the declaration of martial law on December 17, 1981, by the party's First

Table 9.1 Ruling Communist Parties: Mid-1984

Country	Official party name/ Founding date	Population (estimated)	Claimed or estimated no. of CP members/ approximate percentage of population	Date of seizure of power	Method of seizure of power	Existence and names of "allied" parties	Orientation
THE AMERICAS							
1. Republic of Cuba	Communist party of Cuba/1965	9,852,000	434,143/4%	1959	Civil war	None	Pro-Moscow
ASIA							
2. Democratic Republic of Afghanistan	People's Democratic party of Afghanistan/ 1965[a]	14,448,000	120,000 claim (10–20,000 probable)/6%	April 1978	Coup Soviet military support from December 1979	None	Pro-Moscow
3. People's Republic of China	Chinese Communist party/1921	1,034,907,000	40,000,000/4% claim	1949	Civil war	None	Independent
4. People's Republic of Kampuchea	Kampuchea People's Revolutionary party/ 1951 (also Khmer Communist party/ 1960 in armed opposition)[a]	6,118,000	700 estimate		Vietnamese invasion	None	Pro-Moscow
5. Democratic People's Republic of Korea (North Korea)	Korean Workers' party/1949	19,630,000	3,000,000/17% claim	1945	Soviet army	Korean Social Democratic party and 1 other	Neutral, Beijing and Moscow influence
6. Laos	Lao People's Revolutionary party/1955	3,732,000	35,000/0.9% estimate	1979	Civil war	None	Pro-Moscow
7. Mongolia	Mongolian People's Revolutionary party/ 1921	1,860,000	76,240/4% claim	1920–1921	Soviet invasion	None	Pro-Moscow
8. Socialist Republic of Vietnam	Vietnamese Communist party/1930	59,030,000	1,730,214/3% claim	1953/1975	Civil war	None	Pro-Moscow
EAST EUROPE							
9. People's Socialist Republic of Albania	Albanian party of Labor/1941	2,906,000	122,000/4% claim	1944/5	Civil war	None	Independent

282

	Party/year founded	Population	Membership/% claim	Year to power	Method	Satellite parties	Orientation
10. People's Republic of Bulgaria	Bulgarian Communist party/1903	8,969,000	825,876/9% claim	1944	Soviet invasion	Bulgarian Agrarian National Union	Pro-Moscow
11. Czechoslovakia (Czecho-Slovak Socialist Republic)	Communist party of Czechoslovakia/1921	15,420,000	1,623,000/10% claim	1948	Coup	Slovak Freedom party, Slovak Rebirth party, People's party, Socialist party	Pro-Moscow
12. Germany Democratic Republic (East Germany)	Socialist Unity party of Germany/1918	16,717,000	2,202,277/13% claim	1949	Loss of WWII, Soviet occupation zone	Liberal Democratic party of Germany, National Democratic party of Germany, Christian Democratic Union, Democratic Farmers party of Germany	Pro-Moscow
13. Hungarian People's Republic	Hungarian Socialist Workers' party/1918	10,681,000	852,000/7% claim	1945	Loss of WWII, Soviet occupation	None	Pro-Moscow
14. Polish People's Republic	Polish United Workers' party/1918	36,887,000	2,186,349/6% claim	1944	Soviet occupation	Peasant party, Democratic party	Pro-Moscow
15. Socialist Republic of Romania	Communist party of Romania/1921	22,683,000	3,400,000/14% claim	1944	Soviet occupation	None	Moscow influence
16. Socialist Federative Republic of Yugoslavia	League of Yugoslav Communists/1920	22,997,000	2,500,000/9% claim	1944	Civil war	None	Independent
SOVIET UNION							
17. Union of the Soviet Socialistic Republics	Communist party of the Soviet Union/1898	274,860,000	18,500,000/6% claim	1917	Coup	None	—

[a] The Soviet Union refers to these two parties as "vanguard parties"; that is, something less than full ruling Communist parties.

Source: Richard F. Staar, ed., *1985 Yearbook on International Communist Affairs* (Stanford, CA: Hoover Institution Press, 1985); and Richard F. Staar, *Communist Regimes in Eastern Europe*—several editions (Stanford, CA: Hoover Institution Press); copyright by the Board of Trustees of the Leland Stanford Junior University.

Fidel Castro, First Secretary of the Cuban Communist Party.

Secretary, Prime Minister. and General of the Army, Wojciech Jaruzelski. A
modified form of martial law continues today.

Because officially there is only one ruling party in each Communist
Party state, only an examination of Communist parties in general and that of
a given state in particular would allow a political scientist to reach a basic
understanding of that Communist state (or Second World politics in the
broad scope).

THE THIRD WORLD

Except in countries such as Saudi Arabia and United Arab Emirates where
royal families do not permit the formation of political parties, and in some
military regimes where political parties are banned, parties are important
components of the political systems in the Third World. As the social setting
and political environment of the Third World are substantially different from
those of the First and Second Worlds, the nature of Third World parties is
unique. Parties in the First World developed through decades of evolution in
a social setting of rapid industrialization and a political environment of
representative democracy and expanding suffrage. Parties in the Second
World began as ideological and revolutionary forces that mobilized the
masses in order to topple the existing regimes; they then began the task of
establishing and maintaining totalitarian governments. Parties in most Third
World countries, on the other hand, developed as a response to a combination of factors that included colonial rule or foreign influence, ethnic and

tribal diversity, slow economic progress, a concern for social justice and modernization, and the need to mobilize the masses.

Emergence of Political Parties

Africa and Asia. The most important stimulus for the emergence of political parties in Africa and Asia was the colonial experience. Many parties in these two continents developed as nationalist movements whose primary objective was to end the colonial rule by mobilizing the masses against it. These parties attempted to inculcate a national identity among the masses. The development of a national identity contributed to the end of foreign rule. The initial reaction of the colonial powers to the nationalist movements was to oppose them, often with force. The colonial powers, especially the British, also tried to weaken these movements by introducing limited self-government. The plan was to placate the members of a colony's elite, who provided the leadership for the nationalist movement, by giving them some political power. With the introduction of self-government, however limited, the nationalist movement parties learned the art of bargaining and in some cases electioneering (when elections were permitted). Sometimes new parties arose to claim a share of the available political positions. In most cases, however, the introduction of self-government divided a country's elite into the supporters and opponents of the colony's changed political structure. Invariably the limited self-government was opposed by a growing number of the elites and the masses and even though the colonial government, again typically the British, increased the degree of self-government for the colony's indigenous population, opposition to the colonial rule continued unabated. As the costs of retaining a colony far exceded its benefits and it became clear to the colonial power, sometimes after protracted armed struggle (as in Algeria and Indonesia), that the colonial rule must end, political parties were again needed. The terms of transfer of power to a colony's people and had to be negotiated between the colonial power's representatives and some individuals who would be considered representatives of the colony's people. The latter were generally the leaders of the nationalist movement party. Thus, colonial rule was not only responsible for the emergence of nationalist movement parties, it also contributed to the strengthening of these parties through the introduction of self-government and the eventual transfer of power.

Some scholars contend that organizations that developed into nationalist movement parties in Africa and Asia were not formed with the object of ending colonial rule. According to these scholars, the leaders of such organizations were middle-class men or the members of the national elites whose primary purpose was to win privileges for their class.[86] When the

Indian National Congress was formed in 1885, for example, its leaders sought "responsive cooperation" with the British colonial government.[87] It took three to four decades before the Indian National Congress developed into a nationalist movement party and waged a struggle for the end to the British rule in India. In several other African and Asian countries, nationalist movement parties began as organizations primarily intended to gain concessions for the elites from the colonial powers and only later did they become nationalistic in their outlook.

The nationalist movement parties not only sought an end to the colonial rule, they also functioned as agents of social change in the colonies. An Indian scholar writes ". . . historically the Congress (the Indian Nationalist movement party) had developed as a movement of protest, not only against the colonial regime but also against some of the most stubborn features of traditional society: social regeneration was as much at the heart of its program as was national independence."[88] Most nationalist movement parties in Africa and Asia were concerned about social reform in their countries. Of course, it is debatable to what extent this concern was translated into the reform programs that were implemented.

Political scientists generally agree that political parties emerge as a response to major crises in a society. LaPalombara and Weiner consider three types of crises in this context—the crisis of legitimacy, the crisis of integration, and the crisis of participation.[89] The nationalist movement parties in Africa and Asia were clearly responding to the crisis of legitimacy. The national elites of the colonies began to question the legitimacy of foreign rule. It was felt that the colonial regime did not meet the demands of the major groups in the society and that in its place a regime controlled by the national elites and acceptable to the different groups was needed. Because geographical areas of a colony were poorly connected by transportation and communication, and were even more separated by tribes, castes, or other similar groups, integration of a colony was necessary. In order to challenge and defeat the colonial power, the support or at least acquiescence of the masses was essential. Thus, the crises of integration and participation were also present in the colonies and the nationalist movement parties entered the political arena of the colonies in order to respond to these crises. The crises of legitimacy, integration, and participation are far from resolved in the former colonies of Africa and Asia. As a consequence, the regrouping of old parties and the formation of new parties often take place in the African and Asian countries that permit party competition.

The nationalist movement parties in the colonies had attempted to unify the different segments of populations under their umbrellas. Considering the diversity of populations in the African and Asian countries, this was an extremely difficult task. When only one major nationalist movement party existed in a colony, factions emerged within this party. The Congress party of India, considered the classical example of a nationalist movement party, has always been faction-ridden. Besides, although the Congress party represented a large number of diverse groups from the time of its inception, it was challenged by rival parties during the period of colonial rule. The most prominent of these parties was the Muslim League established in 1906, which claimed to represent the Muslims, the largest religious minority in India. The membership of this party in the early twentieth century was "middle class and concerned primarily with jobs, better educational opportunities, and higher social and economic status."[90] The Muslim League refused to accept the nationalist claims of the Congress party and later demanded a separate nation for the Muslims—a demand finally met in 1947 by the partition of India into two nations, India and Pakistan. (Over 95% of Pakistan's population is Moslem.) In some other former colonies, notably Indonesia, Nigeria, and Zaire, nationalist parties supported by a large number of diverse groups never emerged. The parties claiming to be nationalist in these countries were in fact parochial and represented only some tribes or other groups.

Many of the factions formed separate parties after independence from colonial rule was achieved. With increased opportunities for political power, this development was not unexpected. The diversity of the African and Asian countries also worked as a stimulus for the formation of new parties in the postindependence era. Many of these parties were in reality interest groups. The poor economic conditions of the new countries and the concern for the redistribution of wealth encouraged the formation of leftist parties. However, in a majority of the African and Asian countries party activity was short-lived. Many of the newly emerged competitive political systems were soon replaced by military regimes with no parties, or one official party, or by one-party regimes. In some cases the single-party regimes were modeled after the Soviet system, as for example Angola and Mozambique, both former colonies of Portugal. In 1977 the liberation movement parties of these two countries—Popular Movement for the Liberation of Angola (MPLA) and Front for the Liberation fo Mozambique (FRELIMO)—declared themselves "vanguard parties of the proletariat." The label "vanguard parties" signaled a refusal to share power with any other group—a process in progress in these countries for some time.[91] In 1984, following the same path, the political leaders of Ethiopia and Zimbabwe declared Marxism–Leninism to be the basis of their ruling parties.

Modernization has also served as an impetus for the emergence of political parties in the Third World as well as in the First and the Second Worlds. Crises alone are not adequate for the formation of political parties. Transportation and communication are also essential. Highways and rail-

Robert Mugabe, leader of Zimbabwe.

roads are important links between regions; increased literacy and newspapers, radio, and television help a party spread its message throughout a country. If modernization is too rapid and the demands generated by it are not met by the political system, instability and even chaos can occur. In some cases reform parties emerge whose goal is to establish order by appealing to the nationalist sentiments of the populace.[92] Some prominent examples of such parties in the Third World are the Destourian Socialist party of Tunisia, the Institutional Revolutionary party of Mexico, and the Democratic Action party of Venezuela.

Latin America. The Latin American countries achieved independence from the colonial rule of Spain and Portugal in early nineteenth century. However, political parties did not emerge in Latin America as a result of the colonial experience. Nor did the parties develop in this region as a response to representative democracy or an extension of the franchise. In some Latin American countries parties did emerge in the nineteenth century and used political labels such as "conservatives," "liberals," "federalists," "unitarians," and in Brazil "monarchists" and "republicans."[93] These parties seldom won much support from the masses, even in the more advanced Argentina and Chile. Nineteenth-century immigrants from Europe in Latin America brought with them radical ideas of socialism and Communism, which gave rise to the socialist and Communist parties in this region. Soviet influence in Latin America, especially the Caribbean and Central America,

Voting secrecy is part of Costa Rica's democratic election process.

came much later. Indigenous radical parties have been also quite prominent in Latin America. These parties were often formed with a view to ending military rule and instituting radical economic and social reforms. The American Popular Revolutionary Alliance (APRA), formed in Peru in 1924, is one of the best known of such parties. Several reform parties in other Latin American countries were patterned after APRA. In some Latin American countries, especially Chile and Venezuela, Christian Democratic parties have emerged with "inspiration mainly from the Vatican's social encyclicals."[94] Finally, under some military leaders such as Peron of Argentina and Vargas of Brazil, political parties have been established that combine "a blend of traditional *caudillismo* [military dictatorship] and a professed concern for social justice."[95]

There are very few stable democracies in Latin America or for that matter, in other parts of the Third World. Scholars on Latin American politics consider only Costa Rica and Venezuela in this category. Regular elections in which parties compete for political power are not common in the Third World. In Africa and Asia, the experiment with democracy and competitive elections after independence failed in many countries. In Latin America, also, democracy is not widely accepted. Parties in Latin American countries are often dominated by authoritarian leaders and seldom are supported by the masses. A scholar of Latin American politics comments, "Personalism, particularism, disinterest in grass roots organization, lack of a mass popular base, and the transient nature of both parties and their membership are typical of Latin American organizations."[96] This statement is applicable to several parties in African and Asian countries also.

Types of Party Systems

A two-party competitive system in which two major parties alternate in control of government is virtually nonexistent in the Third World.[97] Some Third World countries have multiparty systems. Examples of such countries include Costa Rica, Nigeria (during democratic rule), and Venezuela. In some states in India several parties compete for the control of government. During periods of democratic rule, Argentina, Brazil, and Chile have also enjoyed multiparty systems. In Thailand many parties exist, but since the establishment of a constitutional monarchy in 1932, this country has experienced several military coups resulting in the curtailment of party competition. Malaysia is among a minority of Third World countries where several parties exist and competitive elections are held. However, a coalition of certain parties, the National Front Coalition, is virtually assured of control of government after every election, making Malaysia a single-dominant-party rather than a multiparty system. In most other Third World countries where party activity is permitted, a single-party system is the norm. There are three major single-party systems in the Third World: *single-dominant party*, *single-mass party*, and *single-control party*.

Single-Dominant-Party System. Some Third World countries allow party competition and several parties exist in these countries. However, one party is nearly always assured of winning the elections and controlling the government. Such a party dominates the political system. The most prominent example of a single-dominant party is the Institutional Revolutionary party (PRI) of Mexico. The PRI has won every major election in Mexico since its formation in 1929 and has uninterruptedly controlled the presidency and the Congress. Although a number of opposition parties and groups exist in Mexico and are able to win a few seats in the Congress and the state legislatures, PRI's dominance is apparent throughout the Mexican political system. A study of Mexican politics mentions two fundamental advantages enjoyed by the PRI over its opposition: (1) ". . . the public treasury is drawn upon to finance the perpetuation of the PRI, including electoral campaigns, its image building rituals, and its repression of rival groups . . . ; and (2) . . . the PRI controls the political registry and can make the rules for establishing one's political *bona fides* as easy or as difficult as seems convenient."[98]

India presents another example of a single-dominant-party system. From 1947, the year of its independence from Britain, until 1967 when the fourth general elections were held in India, the Congress party controlled the national government as well as governments in most of the states. The decline of the Congress dominance in the states began in 1967. At the national level, however, the Congress party has continued to control the government except for the period of 1977 to 1980 when a coalition of opposition parties gained power.[99] Some other Third World examples of a single-dominant-party system are the Nationalist party (the *Kuomintang*) in Taiwan, People's Action party in Singapore, and the Botswana Democratic party in Botswana.

Single-Mass-Party System. In a single-mass-party system only one party is permitted by law. Such a party claims to represent all the different groups of the society whether they are tribal, religious, linguistic, or economic. Partly because of the difference in ideology and partly because of the lack of resources and experience, the single-mass parties are not as all-embracing in their activities as the totalitarian parties of the Second World. Some single-mass parties, for example, the Revolutionary party of Tanzania and the Destourian Socialist party of Tunisia, do have elaborate organizational structures throughout the country reaching down to the villages. The rationale generally given for the single-mass-party system is that it is essential for political stability, nation-building, and economic development.[100] As social and religious diversity in the new countries of the Third World is considerable and the people lack a feeling of belonging together in a nation, it is said that permitting more than one party would be detrimental to political stability and nation building. It is also argued that national unity ensured by a single-mass party is conducive to the much-needed economic development.

A more convincing explanation for the existence of the single-mass-party system (and other forms of single-party systems) is that Third World countries lack the political tradition of opposition parties that come to power by election. These countries also lack the tradition of resolving conflicts and making policy through the expression of different viewpoints by parties. In considering the erosion of democracy in the new states, Rupert Emerson provides another explanation for the single-mass-party system. According to Emerson, in Asian and the African societies "the native inclination is generally toward extensive and unhurried deliberation aimed at an ultimate consensus," and ". . . the voice of the elders, the wise, and the specially qualified" is entitled to "extra or even decisive weight."[101] Such traditions are obviously in conflict with the Western concepts of party system and majority rule.

Single-mass-party regimes have been established by different processes. In several African countries such regimes were established by the "total electoral success of a leading party, by the merger of parties, and by coercion—by the banning or repression of opposition parties."[102] The single-mass-party-regimes formed by coercion did not last long and virtually all of them were replaced by military governments.[103] In some countries where the single-party system has survived, competitive (one-party) elections have emerged. Tanzania, Zambia, and Malawi, all three former British colonies, hold one-party competitive elections. Such elections are of three types: (1) a competitive primary election exists within the party; (2) more than one candidate of the official party runs in the election, and (3) competition within the party is permitted both in the primary and the election.[104] In most other single-mass-party regimes, however, such competition is not tolerated. In the one-party regimes of some former French colonies in Africa—Ivory Coast, Senegal, and Guinea, for example—the elections are "plebiscites quite strictly speaking."[105] In these countries elections are little more than endorsements of the party-sponsored candidates and the party policy.

Single-Control-Party System. As a general rule, the single-mass parties grew out of the nationalist movement parties. The single-control parties, on the other hand , have been created by authoritarian, generally military, rulers with the specific purpose of controlling the populace. A single-mass party attempts to represent virtually everyone in the society and at least in some cases permits electoral competition. A single-control party is far less representative and does not tolerate any intraparty competition. It mobilizes the masses in support of the government policy and attempts to keep a lid on their political awareness. A single-mass party also mobilizes masses in support of the government policy, but it is much less dictatorial than the control party.

Egypt, Ethiopia, and Zaire are among Third World countries with single-control parties. In Egypt, Gamal Abdel Nasser, who remained the undisputed military leader of his country from 1954 until his death in 1970, established the Liberation Rally soon after coming to power mainly as a means of controlling the country. In 1959 the Liberation Rally was replaced by the National Union, which in turn was superseded by the Arab Socialist Union in 1962. The Arab Socialist Union was more representative of different groups and urban areas than the earlier two parties; like its predecessors, however, it too was a single-control party. For a short period in the late 1970s under Anwar Sadat's leadership (Sadat succeeded Nasser as Egypt's president), Egypt experimented with a multiparty system, but soon abandoned it. Sadat replaced the Egyptian Arab Socialist party, as the Arab Socialist Union had come to be called, with the National Democratic party. The National Democratic party is as much a control party as any of its predecessors. This party captures most of the seats in the national legislature and permits some "positive" opposition candidates to win the rest.[106] The regimes in Ethiopia and Zaire are even more authoritarian than in Egypt. The Ethiopian single-control party, the Workers' party, was formed by the military leader Colonel Mengistu in 1984 and the Zaire single-control party, the Popular Revolutionary Movement (MPR), was established by President Mobutu when he came to power in 1965.

Functions of Political Parties

In a few Third World countries that permit party competition and that have developed some tradition for it, the parties aggregate the demands of the major interest groups. Even in these countries—examples include India, Sri Lanka, Malaysia, Venezuela—interest aggregation is done much less effectively than in the Western nations, because interest groups in the Third World are not well organized. In a single-dominant-party system the interest groups become part of the dominant party. In Mexico the PRI has coopted the major interest groups. The internal structure of the PRI has "separate sectors for labor, agrarian, and middle class interests."[107] The smaller parties in the single-dominant-party regimes are often indistinguishable from interest groups. Even in countries of the Third World with multiparty systems, several parties are essentially interest groups. One scholar comments, "in Latin America sometimes it is difficult to locate the boundary between interest associations and political parties."[108] This comment is equally true of Africa and Asia.

Unlike in the First World, the political mobilization function of the parties in the Third World is not to motivate people to participate in democratic politics. Instead, in most cases the Third World parties urge the masses to support the governments and their policies. This includes the task of informing people, however imperfectly, about the government policies. Often the major functions of the political parties in the Third World are to unify the diverse segments of the population, and (as discussed earlier) in some cases to control them. Because in several countries the parties are indistinguishable from the governments, some of their functions also overlap with government functions.

The function of facilitating opposition is obviously performed by the relatively few multiparty systems in the Third World; however, even the single-party systems perform this role to some extent. In the single-party systems, factions generally arise, some of which work as an opposition to the dominant factions. Of course, the degree of freedom permitted to these factions varies in different countries. A few single-mass-party countries have institutionalized factions by permitting electoral competition.

Parties in some Third World countries provide certain services for the people. For example, the local party organization may help people find jobs.

This is particularly true of single-mass parties that have organizations down to the village level. Most parties in the Third World, however, are not well organized and lack a well-developed structure. Their efforts to link the masses to governments are hindered by the lack of effective organization. It is the totalitarian parties that are able to link the masses to the governments with their all-pervasive organizations.

NOTES

1. Michael Curtis, *Comparative Government and Politics: An Introductory Essay in Political Science*, 2d ed. (New York: Harper & Row, 1978), p. 151.
2. Peter H. Merkl, *Modern Comparative Politics* (Hinsdale, Ill.: Dryden Press, 1977), p. 109.
3. Karl W. Deutsch, *Politics and Government: How People Decide Their Fate*, 3d ed. (Boston: Houghton Mifflin, 1980). pp. 494–495.
4. For a discussion of the 1980 election see Ellis Sandes and Cecil V. Crabb, Jr., eds., *A Tide of Discontent: The 1980 Elections and Their Meaning* (Washington, D.C.: Congressional Quarterly Press. 1981).
5. Deutsch, p. 60.
6. Joseph LaPalombara, *Politics Within Nations* (Englewood Cliffs, N.J.: Prentice Hall, 1974), p. 507.
7. Roy C. Macridis, ed., *Political Parties: Contemporary Trends and Ideas* (New York: Harper & Row, 1967), pp. 9–23.
8. Ibid., p. 14.
9. Ibid., p. 11.
10. Ibid., p. 12.
11. Ibid., pp. 12–13.
12. For a discussion of this theme in the United States and Great Britain see William J. Crotty and Gary C. Jacobson, *American Parties in Decline* (Boston: Little, Brown, 1980); and Samuel H. Beer, *Britain Against Itself: The Political Contradictions of Collectivism* (New York: Norton, 1982).
13. For a discussion of these functions see LaPalombara, pp. 543–553; and Merkl, pp. 98–106.
14. For a discussion of the opposition function, see LaPalombara, p. 553.
15. Kay Lawson, *The Comparative Study of Political Parties* (New York: St. Martin's Press, 1976), p. 167.
16. Ibid., pp. 166–167.
17. Deutsch, p. 61.
18. Deutsch, p. 59.
19. Curtis, p. 175.
20. For a discussion of coalition governments in the states of the West see Eric C. Browne and John Dreijmanis, eds., *Government Coalitions in Western Democracies* (New York: Longman, 1982).
21. For a discussion of this point see LaPalombara, pp. 510–515.
22. For a discussion of this theme see Joseph LaPalombara and Myron Weiner,

eds., *Political Parties and Political Development* (Princeton, N.J.: Princeton University Press, 1966).

23. Leon Epstein, "Political Parties in Western Democratic Systems" in Macridis, p. 135.

24. Everett Carll Ladd, Jr., *American Political Parties: Social Change and Political Response* (New York: Norton, 1970), pp. 1–11.

25. This concept is employed by Karl Deutsch, p. 61.

26. Judson L. James, *American Political Parties: Potential and Performance* (New York: Pegasus, 1969), pp. 16–20.

27. This limited view of popular sovereignty is part of the revisionist theory of democracy known as democratic elitism. For a comparison of this and the traditional theory of democracy see Henry S. Kariel, ed., *Frontiers of Democratic Theory* (New York: Random House, 1970).

28. Robert A. Dahl, ed., *Political Oppositions in Western Democracies* (New Haven, Conn.: Yale University Press, 1968), pp. xiii–xxi.

29. Ibid., p. xiii.

30. For a general discussion of the Fascist attack on European political institutions see Juan J. Linz and Alfred Stepan, eds., *The Breakdown of Democratic Regimes: Europe* (Baltimore: Johns Hopkins University Press, 1978).

31. Mark N. Hagopian, *Regimes, Movements, and Ideologies*, 2d ed. (New York: Longman, 1978), p. 135.

32. F. L. Carsten, *The Rise of Fascism* (Berkeley: University of California Press, 1971), p. 154.

33. Carl Friedrich and Zbigniew K. Brzezinski, *Totalitarian Dictatorship and Autocracy* (New York: Praeger, 1966), p. 45.

34. Deutsch, p. 60.

35. Lawson, pp. 151–153.

36. Deutsch, p. 60.

37. Ibid.

38. Kishimoto Koichi, *Politics in Modern Japan: Development and Organization* (Tokyo: Japan Echo, 1982), pp. 87–101.

39. Lawson, p. 168.

40. Cited in LaPalombara, pp. 512–513. See also Lawson, pp. 167—168.

41. Lawrence C. Mayer and john H. Burnett, *Politics in Industrial Societies: A Comparative Perspective* (New York: Wiley, 1977), pp. 253–255.

42. Ibid., p. 253.

43. Epstein, p. 132.

44. Ibid. (British parties are used as an example of European parties.)

45. Mayer and Burnett, p. 293.

46. Deutsch, p. 63.

47. Ibid., p. 62.

48. Epstein, p. 135.

49. Deutsch, p. 62.

50. Mayer and Burnett, p. 294.

51. Ibid.

52. Gordon Smith, *Politics in Western Europe* (New York: Holmes and Meier, 1973), p. 50.
53. Mayer and Burnett, p. 301.
54. Smith, p. 81.
55. Ibid.
56. Mayer and Burnett, p. 300.
57. Epstein, pp. 136–137.
58. Ibid., p. 132.
59. Ibid., p. 131.
60. For a brief discussion of the evaluation of the SPD in the German Federal Republic see David B. Conradt, *The German Polity*, 2d ed. (New York: Longman, 1982), pp. 86–93.
61. Everett Carll Ladd, Jr., *Where Have All the Voters Gone? The Fracturing of America's Political Parties* (New York: Norton, 1978), p. xvi.
62. For a discussion of this trend see Beer, pp. 149—194.
63. Utopia is the name given to the society described in Thomas Moore's famous work *Utopia* published in 1516. In it he described a more or less ideal agricultural society with communal living but without money and war. See Lee C. McDonald, *Western Political Theory: From Its Origins to the Present* (New York: Harcourt Brace, 1968), pp. 223–226.
64. Emile B. Ader, *Communism: Classic and Contemporary* (Woodbury, N.Y.: Barron's Educational Series, 1970), pp. 33–35.
65. J. L. Talmon, *The Origins of Totalitarian Democracy* (New York: Praeger, 1960), pp. 1–2.
66. Ibid., p. 2.
67. Karl Marx and Friedrich Engels, "Manifesto of the Communist Party" in Robert C. Tucker, ed., *The Marx-Engels Reader*, 2d edition (New York: Norton, 1978), pp. 483–484.
68. Irving M. Zeitlin, *Marxism: A Re-Examination* (New York: Van nostrand, 1967), p. 78.
69. Henry B. Mayo, *Introduction to Marxist Theory* (New York: Oxford University Press, 1960), pp. 142–143.
70. Ibid., pp. 152–153.
71. Zeitlin, pp. 152–155.
72. Georg von Rauch, *A History of Soviet Russia*, 6th ed. (New York: Praeger, 1972), p. 9.
73. Eduard Bernstein, *Evolutionary Socialism* (New York: Schocken Books, 1961).
74. Lenin, "What Is to Be Done," in Tucker, pp. 12–114.
75. See Tucker's quote of G. Plekhanov in his "Introduction," p. xlii.
76. Mayo, p. 141.
77. Lenin, "Imperialism: The Highest Stage of Capitalism," in Tucker, pp. 204–274.
78. Though seldom officially acknowledged today, the role of Stalin was decisive. In the USSR he is considered a second-level figure; in the West he is simply condemned as an unprincipled murderer during the purges of 1934 to 1939 and

1946 to 1953, the war, and the collectivization period. The only recent work that accepts Stalin as a serious revolutionary leader and writer is Bruce Franklin, ed., *The Essential Stalin* (New York: Doubleday, 1972), p. 511. The role and relationship of Lenin, Stalin, and Trotsky (Lev Davidovich Bronstein, 1879–1940) is examined in Bertram Wolf, *Three Who Made Revolution*, 2 vols. (New York: Time Inc., 1964).

79. Jerry Hough and Merle Fainsod, "Leading Party Organs," in *How the Soviet Union is Governed* (Cambridge, Mass.: Harvard University Press, 1979), chap. 12.

80. Harold Berman and John Quigley, trans. and eds., "Communist Party Rules— Intra-Party Democracy," *Basic Laws on the Structure of the Soviet State* (Cambridge, Mass.: Harvard University Press, 1969), pp. 66–68.

81. *Constitution (Fundamental Law) of the Union of Soviet Socialist Republics*, any edition of 1977 Constitution, Article 50.

82. Ibid., Article 51.

83. Ibid., Article 59.

84. Ibid., Article 60–63.

85. Journalist M., *A Year is Eight Months: Czechoslovakia 1968* (Garden City, N.Y.: Doubleday, 1971), p. 204.

86. For such a view on African political parties see Donald Rothchild and Robert L. Curry, Jr., *Scarcity, Choice, and Public Policy in Middle Africa* (Berkeley: University of California Press, 1978), p. 59.

87. Rajni Kothari, *Politics in India* (Boston: Little, Brown, 1970), p. 48.

88. Ibid., p. 153.

89. LaPalombara and Weiner, pp. 3–42.

90. Robert L. Hardgrave, Jr., *India: Government and Politics in a Developing Nation*, 3d. ed. (New York: Harcourt Brace Jovanovich, 1980), p. 30.

91. This development in Angola and Mozambique was similar to the process of the gaining of power by the Communist parties in Eastern Europe in the late 1940s and in Cuba in 1960 to 1961. See Michael Radu, "Ideology, Parties, and Foreign Policy in Sub-Saharan Africa," *Orbis* (Winter 1982): 981.

92. On the influence of modernization on the emergence of political parties see LaPalombara and Weiner, pp. 3–42; and Gary Bertsch, Robert Clark, and David Wood, *Comparing Political Systems: Power and Policy in Three Worlds*, 2d ed. (New York: Wiley, 1982), p. 433.

93. Paul H. Lewis, *The Governments of Argentina, Brazil, and Mexico* (New York: Crowell, 1975), p. 110.

94. Ibid., p. 112.

95. Ibid.

96. See Mary Jeanne Reid Martz, "Studying Latin American Political Parties: Dimensions Past and Present," *Journal of Latin American Studies* 12 (May 1980): 147.

97. One scholar of Latin American politics considers Colombia, Uruguay, and Honduras two-party competitve systems; however, another scholar disputes him. Ibid., p. 153.

98. Kenneth F. Johnson, *Mexican Democracy: A Critical View*, 2d ed. (New York: Praeger, 1978), p. 140.

99. The Congress party split into two parties in 1969; the dominant faction remained under the leadership of Indira Gandhi with the designation Congress Party-I (I stands for Indira).

100. See Benjamin Neuberger, "Has the Single Party State Failed in Africa?" *African Studies Review* 17 (April 1974): 173–178.

101. Rupert Emerson, *From Empire to Nation: The Rise to Self-Assertion of Asian and African Peoples* (Cambridge, Mass.: Harvard University Press, 1967), p. 284.

102. Ruth Berins Collier, "Parties, Coups, and Authoritarian Rule: Patterns of Political Change in Tropical Africa," *Comparative Political Studies* 11 (April 1978): 70.

103. Ibid., p. 73.

104. Ibid., p. 76.

105. Ibid., p. 75.

106. See David E. Long and Bernard Reich, eds., *The Governments and Politics of the Middle East and North Africa* (Boulder, Colo.: Westview Press, 1980), p. 329.

107. Gabriel A. Almond and G. Bingham Powell, Jr., *Comparative Politics: System, Process, and Policy*, 2d ed. (Boston: Little, Brown, 1978), p. 221.

108. Martz, p. 148.

10

Politics and Economics in Three Worlds

All states have a system for the distribution of life chances. This system is called the political economy. The political economy consists of five social facts that determine the limits of economic opportunities available to the citizens of a state. The social facts are (1) the domestic political culture, (2) the domestic economic infrastructure, (3) domestic social and political institutions, (4) international economic opportunities and constraints, and (5) the domestic and foreign policies of a state. In today's political world, two basic types of political economic systems are prevalent: (1) those that rely primarily on the market for distribution of economic values, and (2) those that rely primarily on government authority for distribution.

Despite postindustrial affluence in the West, in the 1970s the Western states experienced a deterioration of life chances, brought about by sociopolitical, infrastructural, and economic crises. In the United States and the northern states of Europe a "conservative impulse" developed. Voters responded to the crises by electing conservative and centrist candidates committed to policies designed to increase domestic productivity. France, Italy, Spain, Portugal, and Greece, however, have elected socialists pledged to the politics of equality. In terms of government policy, the politics of productivity and the politics of equality represent competing approaches for dealing with the economic recession. Neither prescription has been entirely successful, and government elites have often been forced to incorporate elements of both approaches in their policies.

POLITICAL ECONOMIC SYSTEMS

Modern political systems actually consist of a number of different systems that are related to one another. In Chapter 3 political culture and political ideology were discussed as we explored the belief systems of states. In Chapters 6 and 7 we considered how government structures (executive bureaucracies, legislatures, and courts) interact with one another to form government systems. Chapters 8 and 9 discussed interest group systems and political party systems. As we have seen, these systems are interrelated. For example, the political attitudes of the belief system influence the behavior of persons within the government system, and government policies help to determine the number and nature of interest groups. Modern states also have a system for the distribution of what may be termed "life chances." This system is called the *political economy*. Life chances include wealth; employment opportunity; occupational status; education; job training; welfare benefits; safe working conditions; national health insurance; consumer goods; the right to change jobs; the right to participate in decisions in the work place; and a healthy environment with minimum air pollution, water pollution, and hazardous waste materials (see Figure 10.1). In short, the political economy allocates the economic benefits that provide an individual with security, independence, luxury, and a high quality of life. Because of the importance of these values in the lives of most people, it can be argued that the political economy is the most important system in modern politics. As the term indicates, the political economic system involves political institutions as well as social and economic institutions. Before we examine political economic systems in the three political worlds, the concept of a political economy must be understood.

POLITICAL ECONOMY MODELS

American social scientists traditionally considered decisions about wealth, employment, occupational status, and consumer goods to be the subject matter of the field of economics. The acquisition of these values was thought to occur through the interaction of private individuals in the marketplace. This conception of economics is known as the model of economic individualism. According to this concept, individuals freely exchange money, labor, and consumer goods in the marketplace where economic success or failure is determined by such factors as the law of supply and demand. Government was thought to be only marginally involved in the exchange process. The establishment of Communist political systems in the Second World caused a reconsideration of the model of economic individualism. Though it was acknowledged that in Communist political systems such as the Soviet Union important economic decisions were made by government, the model of economic individualism was still thought to apply to the West and most of the world. A study of economics written in the 1960s summarized the two types of economies in the following way:

Economic opportunities	Protections against the hazards of life and entitlements	Safe environment and maintenance of the quality of life
Employment	Unemployment insurance	Clean air
Education	Workers compensation	Clean water
Job training	Old-age pensions	Protection from hazardous wastes
Consumer goods	National health services	
Stable currency	Aid to dependent children	Protection from noise pollution and overcrowding
Freedom from employment discrimination	Vocational retraining and resettlement	Safe food and drugs
Worker participation in decision making (industrial democracy)	Housing subsidies General welfare	Freedom from crime and violence Privacy
Safe working conditions	Child subsidies	Full participation in political life
Right to unionize	Leisure and recreation opportunities	Opportunities for cultural and religious expression
Right to change jobs		
Wealth	Protection from arbitrary dismissal and unfair labor practices	Opportunities for personal expression

Figure 10.1. Life chances.

Under economic individualism, productive enterprises are privately owned and managed. Under economic collectivism, ownership and management are in the hands of government. But this is not the most significant difference between the two. The difference is to be found, rather, in the contrasting methods employed in the two economies to determine the allocation of resources. Under individualism allocation is determined by the process of buying and selling in free markets. Under collectivism, it is determined by the process of politics. The difference in methods leads to a difference in results.[1]

According to this viewpoint, the "process of politics" determines economic outcomes only in socialist political systems where there is public (government) ownership of at least some of the means of production, or in Communist political systems in which there is public ownership of all forms of wealth (both producers' and consumers' goods).[2] Students of modern comparative politics accept that the "process of politics" influences the allocation of values in all political systems, but they believe that a new model, that of the political economy, more accurately describes the social reality in modern political systems than does the model of economic individualism. As Charles Lindblom has noted, the principal activities of government are heavily economic: taxation, national defense, education, energy conservation, transportation and communication, social security, stabilization, and the promotion of growth.[3] The study of politics cannot be isolated from economic questions because even in political systems in which production, wealth, and consumer goods are in private hands, political values, laws regarding economic bargaining, and government decisions profoundly affect economic outcomes.

Today, such diverse government actions as funding technology research, granting draft deferments to students training for particular careers, and establishing environmental protection standards may have a profound economic effect. In addition, in all political systems, political values and attitudes influence the behavior of economic actors in a variety of ways. For example, attitudes toward group violence may influence the nature of strikes, and attitudes toward political demands may determine whether unions seek the creation of a national health program to protect workers against the medical hazards of life. The model of the political economy takes into account the influence of political values, political institutions, and political decisions on economic outcomes. Its central focus is on the effects of political power and authority on the allocation of economic values in society. John Gurley summarized the differences between political economics and conventional economics:

> Political economics, as distinguished from . . . conventional economics, studies economic problems by systematically taking into account in a historical context, the pervasiveness of ruler-subject relations in society. "The realm of the political," as political scientist Robert Tucker has written, "is the realm of power and authority relations among people. . . ."
>
> I will add that it is these pervasive relations of domination and servitude, these relations of power and authority that lead to conflict, disharmony, and disruptive change. A political economist sees the power structures and puts them at the forefront of his analysis; a conventional economist—who sees society as

free, self-interested economic men interacting as equals in the marketplace—
does not.[4]

We believe that the use of the model of the political economy is one of the
best ways of comparing and contrasting the life chances available to citizens
in each of the three worlds. The political economy approach is also useful in
demonstrating how political decisions often involve difficult choices or
"trade-offs" between such goals as greater social equality or increased
system productivity.

Social Facts

The political economy model recognizes five factors that determine the life
chances available to any particular group in a political system.[5] Collectively
these factors constitute the *social facts* that establish the limits of economic
opportunities available to the citizens of the state. The social facts include
one international factor and four domestic factors. They are (1) international
economic opportunities and constraints, (2) domestic political culture, (3)
domestic economic infrastructure, (4) domestic social and political institutions, and (5) domestic and foreign policies of the state (see Figure 10.2).
International economic opportunities and constraints include the geographic
location of the political system, its place in the international economy (the
products and natural resources it has to sell to other states), membership in
regional economic organizations, and overseas territories and resources
controlled by the political system. The *political culture* is sometimes termed
the *substructure* of the state because its underlying values and beliefs
influence the operation of all social and political organizations.[6] Of special
importance are attitudes about equality, individualism, collectivism, the role
of government, and work and productivity. The domestic economic *infrastructure* consists of the physical foundations of the economy, including the
transportation system, the communications system, and the level of technology available to industry and business. The relevant domestic institutions
are of two types: *social institutions* and *political institutions*. Social institutions are divisions in the population with economic significance (e.g., social
classes and groups within the work force). Political institutions include
government structures, political parties, and interest groups. Political institutions develop the official foreign and domestic policies. Government
policies, both foreign and domestic, are strategies for dealing with the social
facts that confront the political system. In this sense no real difference exists
between foreign and domestic policies because foreign policies are decisions
directed toward international social facts,[7] and domestic policies are strategies and decisions directed toward internal social facts. The objective of

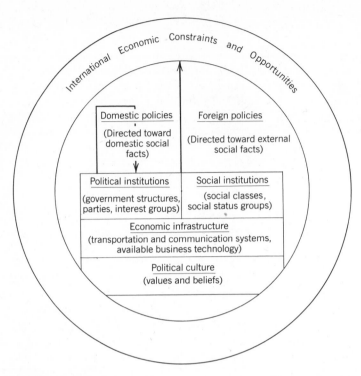

Figure 10.2. Social facts, determinants of life chances. (Adapted with permission from Robert A. Isaak, *European Politics*, 1980, p. 10.)

government institutions is to obtain the maximum amount of scarce values from the international environment and then to allocate them within the domestic population.

Collectively the social facts constitute an inescapable environment for all political action. For the individual, social facts determine the limits of economic opportunity and also provide a frame of reference by which one assigns meaning to political life. Individuals' perceptions of whether existing social conditions are likely to bring them the values they desire from life (wealth, status, a job, and so on) are major determinants of political behavior. Persons and groups who believe that existing social conditions will provide them with substantial life chances and political values usually hold political beliefs and engage in political actions designed to maintain existing political and social institutions. Those dissatisfied with existing social facts usually hold contrary ideas and undertake different actions designed to transform existing institutions. Political ideologies and political strategies are also directly related to social facts. A political ideology is a system of beliefs that provides the basis of political action to promote the interests of a certain group.[8] It is also a statement about existing social facts, specifically, whether or not the existing conditions are morally acceptable and just. Marxist–Leninist thought is an example of such an ideology. As a statement about social facts, it condemned social conditions in Europe in the late nineteenth and early twentieth centuries. As a guide to political action, it advocated revolution by the proletariat (the industrial working class) and the destruction of capitalist social and political institutions. Historically, modern political ideologies have advocated three political strategies: (1) to preserve existing institutions, (2) to reform or transform existing institutions (with the implications of only moderate change), and (3) to destroy existing institutions and replace them with new ones.[9] Political power is also related to social facts. Groups possessing political power can have more of their needs satisfied under existing social conditions than can other groups.[10] Powerful states are countries capable of acquiring more scarce resources from the international environment than other states. Powerful states and groups are likely to adopt ideologies and pursue strategies designed to preserve existing social and political institutions, while groups and states perceiving themselves to be disadvantaged by existing social facts are likely to seek the transformation or destruction of these organizations.

Market versus Government Authority

In the three political worlds, two basic types of political economic systems are prevalent: first, those that rely primarily on the market and exchange for the distribution of economic values, and second, those that rely primarily on government authority for the distribution.[11] Although some political theorists have argued for the creation of systems based entirely on the market mechanism or on a command economy controlled by political authorities,[12] real political systems are a mixture of the two alternatives. For example, the political systems of Western Europe are primarily market-oriented private enterprise systems,[13] but in several states certain sectors of the economy (transportation, steel production, mining, and utilities) are state-owned. Similarly, in the Soviet Union where the economy is under the direction of Communist party authorities, some weak market forms are present in the agricultural sector. (Between one-fifth and one-third of the gross value of agricultural output in the Soviet Union comes from private plots.)[14] In terms of their reliance on one of the two alternatives, contemporary political systems should be seen as occupying points along a continuum, ranging from those systems most reliant on the market mechanism to those most reliant on government authority. The development of either of the two alternative political economic systems is the result of the dominant social facts in the political system. The market-oriented systems of the Western world are the product of the political values of liberalism—primarily individualism and materialism (see Chapter 4)—and the influence of democratic political institutions (see Chapter 6). The relative affluence of the West is the result of a favorable position in international economic life, well-developed economic infrastructures, and the success of past government policy decisions. The authority or government-oriented systems of the Second World are the product of Marxist–Leninist and Communist political values (see Chapter 4) and totalitarian government and party structures (see Chapter 6). The mixed record of economic achievements and frustrations in the Second World is also the result of international opportunities and constraints, the state of the infrastructure, and the wisdom of past policy decisions. Authority systems dominate in the Third World, but because some Third World states have adopted Western values and institutional forms, market-oriented systems also exist (e.g., in India, Nigeria, the Ivory Coast, and Brazil).[15] Many Third World states are confronted with a disadvantageous position in the international economy, and the term "less-developed country" (LDC) has been applied to denote the lower productivity of their economic systems and nascent infrastructures.

The following discussion compares the political economies of the three worlds. Our focus will be on the distribution of life chances in each of the three worlds and on the social facts that determine those chances. As noted earlier, government policies are strategies for dealing with existing social facts. As students of political science, our focus will be on political decisions that affect economic outcomes and on the extent to which market mechanisms or government commands determine the distribution of values. Our task is to develop an appreciation of the differences between the welfare state politics of the West, the centralized bureaucratic state in the Communist World, and the politics of underdevelopment in the Third World. Of course, differences exist in the distribution of life chances within each of the three political worlds as well as among them. For example, more life chances are available in Third World states possessing important natural resources (e.g., oil) than in those without them. It is necessary to keep in mind (1) international opportunities and constraints, (2) domestic social facts, (3) the relative strength of markets and government authority, and (4) public policies affecting life chances.

POLITICAL PROCESS AND ECONOMIC OUTCOMES: THE WEST

Changing Social Facts and Declining Life Chances

Life chances in the Western states are shaped by two seemingly contradictory forces, societal affluence and deteriorating social facts. Compared with

President Ronald Reagan of the United States of America and
Chancellor Helmut Kohl of the Federal Republic of Germany.

the political systems of the Second and Third Worlds, the states of the West
have retained their position as affluent societies. This fact is supported by
such indices of economic and social progress as GNP, per capita product,
literacy, and life expectancy (see Table 2.4). Although individual Western
states differ in their economic potential, by world standards they all possess
well-developed infrastructures, established education systems, and businesses and industries employing sophisticated technology. The most affluent
states of the West have attained postindustrial development, a condition not
yet achieved in the other worlds (see Chapter 3). The economies of the
postindustrial states are considered especially strong because they contain
well-developed agricultural, industrial, and service sectors. Among the
contemporary states of the world, the United States is the only country that
can claim the status of a superpower in both economic and military affairs,
whereas Japan and the German Federal Republic have come to symbolize
economic innovation and productivity.

Despite their affluence, however, since the 1970s the states of the West
have been beset by economic problems: increased unemployment, inflation,
decreasing productivity, and balance of payments deficits. These problems
are the result of changing social facts, especially lower rates of domestic

productivity and changes in the international environment. The most important changes have occurred in the international system. The West is
confronted with decreasing international opportunities and increasing international constraints; these have resulted from complex changes affecting the
economic relationship of the Western states with the Third World, the
Communist World, and with one another. Changes in the infrastructure and
in the ability of businesses and industries to compete have also affected life
chances in some states. For example, in Great Britain aging industries and
obsolete business practices contribute to a decline in productivity. Although
Western states are primarily market-oriented systems, their economic
problems have sometimes been aggravated by flawed government policies at
various administrative levels.

The cumulative effect of the changes in social facts has been a decline
in life chances for many groups in the West. This fact has become painfully
clear to industrial workers confronted with unemployment, college graduates forced to accept underemployment, and elderly pensioners threatened
with a loss of security by inflation. The decline in life chances has been a
great psychological shock to many in the West who expected economic
growth to continue. By the late 1970s, anxiety produced by double-digit
unemployment and/or double-digit inflation produced a demand for government solutions to the West's economic problems. These demands placed a
great burden on both Western political structures and Western policy
makers who attempted a wide variety of policy solutions. The political
responses in the Western states took two distinct forms. In the United
States, Canada, Japan, and the states of northern Europe the "politics of
productivity" prevails.[16] Conservative and centrist political actors have
been elected who attempt to deal with the economic difficulties through
policies to increase productivity. President Ronald Reagan and British Prime
Minister Margaret Thatcher are typical proponents of this approach. Both
have favored tax cuts and government austerity to stimulate savings and
business investments to increase productivity. In the Mediterranean states,
the "politics of equality" prevails. Socialist political candidates have been
elected who seek to deal with current economic difficulties through policies
to achieve a more equitable distribution of society's present resources.
French President Francois Mitterand and Italian Prime Minister Bettino
Craxi, both socialists, are typical of the political leaders of southern Europe.
Both campaigned on platforms to increase welfare benefits and subsidies to
the disadvantaged and on the pledge to protect the jobs of workers. The
different responses to declining life chances are the result of domestic social
factors, especially the political culture and the nature of domestic political
groups. In the next section we first examine the changes in the international
system and then consider the cultural and institutional factors that determine

the political response of individual states. Finally, we consider the two public policy approaches that have emerged in the West.

INTERNATIONAL OPPORTUNITIES AND CONSTRAINTS

Since the 1970s the world has experienced a shift in the balance of economic power, which has presented the states of the West with decreased economic opportunities and increased constraints. The most dramatic illustration of this development occurred between 1973 and 1975 when the Organization of Petroleum Exporting Countries (OPEC), an international cartel with 13 member states, raised the price of oil by more than 400%. This action had an immediate adverse effect on the economies of the Western states which are, as a whole, heavily dependent on foreign oil. Higher oil prices contributed to increased unemployment, inflation, growing balance of payments deficits, and decreasing productivity as financial resources were diverted from investment and business expansion to pay for oil. More than any other single development, higher energy costs helped to create an awareness of two new realities of international economic relations: (1) the period of unchallenged Western dominance in international economics was ended, and (2) the Western economies were vulnerable to actions undertaken by states in other parts of the world. As important as the OPEC price increases proved to be, they represented only the "tip of the iceberg" of international economic change. By the 1970s, three factors combined to end Western economic hegemony: (1) the international monetary system established by the United States and Great Britain at the end of World War II weakened; (2) Third World states, previously colonies and suppliers of cheap natural resources, sought higher prices for their products and a more equitable distribution of the world's wealth; and (3) international competition and lower productivity caused business failures and increased unemployment in the less-competitive sectors of the economy in many Western states. Each of the three factors deserves individual attention.

Weakening International Monetary System

At the end of World War II, the Western states established a liberal international economic order that maximized opportunities for unrestricted trade among private groups in different countries. A *liberal international order* represents the application of capitalist, free market principles to the international system. Proponents of a liberal order are opposed to most forms of economic nationalism in which governments develop policies restricting free trade in order to give special preference to their nationals. Common forms of economic nationalism include tariffs, quotas, exchange controls, export controls, embargoes, and preferential trading systems. Beginning in 1944, at the urging of the United States and Great Britain, a series of international conferences were held to gain agreement on a liberal international order. During these meetings the Western states advocated freer trade (as opposed to restricted trade), low and nondiscriminatory tariffs, and currencies freely convertible in the exchange market.[17] The liberal international monetary system that developed from these meetings is often referred to as the Bretton Woods system because the first of the conferences, attended by 44 nations, was held at Bretton Woods, New Hampshire, in July 1944. By 1947, three institutions had been created as the core of the new system: the International Bank for Reconstruction and Development (IBRD), the International Monetary Fund (IMF), and the General Agreement on Tariffs and Trade (GATT). The IMF helped to establish stable currency values to facilitate exchange. In 1947 it set up a system based on the U.S. dollar, backed by gold. The price of gold was set at $35 an ounce, and all other currencies were to be measured according to the dollar or an ounce of gold.[18] By 1980, 132 nations had joined the IMF, and additional programs had been created to promote international liquidity. The IBRD, also known as the World Bank, was developed to provide loans to rebuild the infrastructures of nations devastated in World War II. The rebuilding of roads, bridges, and communications systems was considered the first step for the return to normal participation in international economic life. By 1982, 141 members participated in World Bank deliberations. Finally, GATT has served as a forum for agreements between states to reduce tariffs and other barriers. The GATT encourages countries to grant "most favored nation status," maximum benefits and immunities granted to any trading partner, to all states. By the mid-1970s GATT had 83 full members and 23 associate members.

Collectively the IMF, IBRD, GATT, and subsequent agreements created what may be called an *international regime*, a network of rules and institutions that influence world economic behavior.[19] The Bretton Woods system provided an international environment conducive to the expansion of the economies of the Western states because it gave them an opportunity to utilize their economic advantages as the most developed states—advantages ranging from the most competitive and modern industries to the largest merchant marines. It also promoted a psychological attitude of confidence and optimism among economic circles in the West.

Since the mid-1970s, the continuance of the Bretton Woods system has been in doubt. Several factors contributed to its decline. In 1972, the Nixon administration announced that the United States was departing from the gold standard and that the U.S. dollar would no longer be converted into gold on demand. The United States was forced to take this step because government

Prime Minister Yasuhiro Nakasone of Japan.

expenditures for the war in Vietnam and declining productivity contributed to a huge balance of payments deficit, which, in turn, produced increased claims against a dwindling gold supply. The U.S. action did not produce a breakdown of the Bretton Woods system, but it did contribute to its weakening. After 1972, fixed (and thereby stable) exchange rates were replaced by floating rates, and the price of gold rose dramatically.[20] Despite subsequent agreements by IMF members to deal with these changes, confidence is waning in some currencies and in the general future of the international monetary system. More important than the convertibility problem, however, was the fact that for the first time since 1947, the United States withdrew its support from an institution of the liberal international economic order. Many students of international economics argue that a liberal international system can only be maintained if the dominant country in the world economy is sufficiently confident in its financial superiority to place the preservation of the system ahead of short-term, national economic considerations.[21] The chronic productivity and balance of payments problems experienced by the United States since the end of 1960s have raised doubts about both the will and the ability of the United States to support the system.

One more development has threatened to undermine the liberal international system—the movement toward protectionism. Faced with declining productivity, the states of Western Europe and the United States have begun to adopt protective trade restrictions against Japan and one another. The debate on the wisdom of this policy is presently one of the most controversial political issues in the West. Regardless of the way this issue is ultimately resolved, the threat of protectionism has contributed to the growing mood of economic pessimism and insecurity in the West.

Challenge from the Third World

The increase in the price of oil initiated by OPEC in 1973 dramatized another challenge to Western economic affluence, namely, the efforts by Third World states to obtain more resources from the industrialized world. Third World efforts to achieve a redistribution of resources have included two particularly important developments. First, in 1964 a number of Third World states demanded the creation of the *New International Economic Order* (NIEO) to replace the liberal international order created under the Bretton Woods system. By 1980, more than 120 LDCs supported the concept of the NIEO in deliberations in the United Nations (see Chapter 12). These states share the belief that the present economic order places them at a permanent economic disadvantage, and they demand new international rules and programs to bring about a more equitable distribution of the world's wealth. The NIEO poses a long-term threat to many of the international conditions upon which Western economic affluence is based. The NIEO proposals include demands for redistributive taxes on rich countries, the right to form cartels like OPEC, the right to renegotiate debts owed to the rich nations, "most favored nation status" for LDCs, guaranteed prices for natural resources and other commodities, and the transfer of technology from the developed countries to the Third World.[22] As many sources have pointed out, the LDCs supporting the NIEO presently lack the economic and political power to implement a new international order, but the individual demands contained within the NIEO will remain points of confrontation between the West and the Third World. Gains made by LDCs will reduce the comparative economic advantage of the Western states and cause economic dislocations.

The quest by Third World states for increased resources from the West produced a second initiative, the formation of cartels. Unlike the NIEO debate, the formation of cartels had an important and immediate economic impact on the states of the West. The oil price increases initiated by OPEC were a chief factor in the economic recession that began in the West in 1973. In addition, the oil embargo imposed by a second cartel, the Organization of Arab Petroleum Exporting Countries (OAPEC), demonstrated the extent of dependence of the states of Western Europe on natural resources from the Third World. Third World states also favor the creation of similar organizations (with concomitant agreements on prices and levels of production) for natural gas, coffee, sugar, copper, wheat, tea, cotton, rubber, tin, beef, and olive oil. Although these cartels have been generally unsuccessful, they constitute both an economic and a political challenge to the West. As organizations controlled by governments and devoted to economic nationalism, they represent a challenge to the liberal international order favored in the West. They also clearly demonstrate that the age of cheap natural resources and cheap commodities is ended. From the perspective of the West, the increased costs of primary goods is one of the most important, adverse developments at the international level. It has increased the cost of industrial production, caused balance of payments problems (as developed countries have had to spend more for natural resources), and contributed to a mood of insecurity and uncertainty among Western economic and political elites.

Competition and Protectionism

In addition to the changes in the Bretton Woods system and the challenge from the Third World, many Western countries also face increased economic competition from other states in the West. This competition has been especially intense in the steel, electronics, and automative industries. During the peak years of Western prosperity in the 1960s, the steel and automotive industries were among the most profitable sectors of the economy in the older industrial states such as Great Britain and the United States. Since the mid-1970s, however, these industries have lost much of their international and domestic business to companies in Japan and, to a lesser extent, West Germany. The result has been lost profits, business failures, increased unemployment, and balance of payments deficits. For example, in the 1960s the U.S. automobile industry controlled almost 70% of the world market but today it controls less than 30%. French exports to Japan in 1982 amounted to only 37% of imports from Japan.[23] These developments reflect the fact that unequal competitive conditions prevail in the states of the West, which have caused a shift in the balance of world trade away from the United States and Western Europe toward Japan. The uneven competitiveness has resulted in threats of protectionism, economic nationalism, and economic retaliation from the United States and the EEC (see Chapter 5). Although since 1981 some progress has been made in negotiating voluntary limitations on Japanese imports, the problems of uneven competitiveness and policies of protectionism have contributed to a decline in the volume of trade between Western countries. Trade with other industrial states is of vital interest to all of the states of the West, but for most Western states this

Canadian Prime Minister Brian Mulroney.

aspect of the international environment is less favorable at present than it has been at any time since the 1950s.

DOMESTIC ECONOMIC ENVIRONMENT

Factors related to the domestic economic environment, including the state of the infrastructure, the nature of markets, and the use of technology, are still generally favorable in the West. They provide the states of Western Europe and North America with economic advantages not available to the rest of the world. However, before beginning a discussion of these factors, it must be pointed out that not all states, regions, and businesses enjoy the same competitive advantages. In recent years it has become clear that traditional sectors of the economy in the older industrial states (e.g., Great Britain) cannot compete with newer firms in Japan and West Germany. It is also clear that the benefits of technology and economic modernization have not been received equally in the states and regions of Europe. In many areas the failure to apply new technology and to achieve equal competitive conditions has resulted in economic dislocations and human suffering.

Infrastructure

By world standards, the states of the West have well-developed and sophisticated infrastructures. The importance of economic infrastructures to

Western prosperity was recognized by the United States after World War II when the United States announced that it would assist in the rebuilding of roads, bridges, and transportation and communications systems in war-torn Europe. Through the European Recovery Program (ERP) or Marshall Plan, the United States dispensed over $12 billion in loans and grants-in-aid to 16 European nations between 1948 and 1952. The U.S. aid was conditional on the requirement that European reconstruction be undertaken on a regional rather than a national basis. In June 1948, the Organization of European Economic Cooperation (OEEC) was created to allocate U.S. aid and to assess the regional needs of Europe. Priority was given to the rebuilding of the European infrastructure in a manner that would produce increased economic activity between the various states. After the creation of the EEC in 1958, emphasis was again given to the development of the European infrastructure. For the first 25 years after World War II the task of rebuilding the infrastructure created a need for labor and products which worked to stimulate the European economy. In the contemporary period the hub of Western Europe, roughly encompassing the territory bounded by Birmingham (Great Britain), Dortmund (Federal Republic of Germany) and Paris, is the most-developed area.[24] Three EEC programs, the Coal and Steel Fund, the European Social Fund, and the European Investment Bank, supply funds for the construction of transport facilities and water and electricity supplies in economically depressed areas.[25] Despite these programs, however, serious deficiencies in infrastructure remain in some areas of Western Europe, for example the Mezzogiorno (southern Italy), Brittany, mid-Wales, the Borinage region of Belgium, and southwest France.[26] Generally, however, infrastructure factors in both Europe and North America are favorable.

European Common Market

A discussion of the economic environment of Western Europe would be incomplete without reference to the meaning and importance of the EEC (see Chapter 5). In developing the EEC, the states of Western Europe created one of the largest and most affluent economic units in the world. The EEC currently encompasses Germany, France, Italy, Belgium, the Netherlands, Luxembourg, Great Britain, Ireland, Denmark, and Greece. (Spain and Portugal have been accepted as members although the process of adding them to the EEC will take several years.) In 1980 the states of the EEC collectively exceeded the United States in area, population, density of population, employment in agriculture and industry, GNP, imports, exports, steel production, and merchant marine tonnage.[27] (The EEC trailed the United States in per capita income and private consumption, however.)[28]

The advantages to business of a large market are obvious: production of items on a large scale leads to lower costs per item, large-scale producers have easier access to sources of capital, and wider competition stimulates technical improvements.[29] The formation of the EEC permitted the states of Western Europe to offer businesses the competitive advantages available in the United States, which has a population of over 230 million and an infrastructure that has escaped the ravages of war.

Technology and Business

Business structures in the West have certain common characteristics that influence the nature of economic life. First, businesses in the West lead the world in the application of new technology to the problems of industry and business. Since the onset of the industrial revolution, the application of scientific research to economic problems has been the most important factor in increasing productivity and achieving economic affluence. In the present era of economic slowdown and intensified competition, high-technology firms and their employees have generally fared better than traditional low-technology sectors of the economy which have suffered high rates of business failure and unemployment. Selling sophisticated technology to states in the Second and Third Worlds offers Western businesses the promise of new markets and high profits, but political factors often complicate such sales. The United States and the states of Western Europe are presently divided over the issue of the sale of technology to the Soviet Union. Since 1980 the U.S. government has placed an embargo on the sale of certain types of technology to the USSR, citing the fear that the possession of such technology might adversely affect the strategic balance of power between the East and West. The states of the EEC have imposed no such restrictions and remain the center of East–West trade.[30]

In addition to the technological factor, a trend exists in the West toward large-scale industrial and business enterprises. In the postwar era the "trend to bigness" was first apparent in the United States, but it is now discernible throughout the Western world. The concentration of business assets can be explained by the fact that modern technology makes large-scale production possible, and the large-scale production (known to economists as economies of scale) means lower costs per unit.[31] In an age of declining productivity many Western states have adopted promotional policies toward large-scale businesses ranging from tolerance of mergers to government subsidies and grants. Of course, the concentration of business is not equally advanced in all of the states of the West. One type of large-scale business, the multi-national corporation (MNC), has special political significance. The MNCs are firms that conduct business such as manufacturing, assembly, sale, export and import of products, in more than one country. Since the 1960s both the number of MNCs and the number of foreign subsidiaries have increased. Of the world's largest 500 corporations, over 300 are U.S., but Japanese and European multinationals are among the largest and most aggressive in their business practices.[32] The MNCs have become subjects of controversy in the industrialized world. They are criticized for exporting jobs, investing money overseas, and making it impossible for products produced in the home country at higher costs to be exported.[33] The conflict surrounding MNCs illustrates the problem confronting Western societies in this period of rapid technological change; profits for one sector of the economy often result in losses in other sectors.

The Substructure: Political Economic Values

Conditions in the international system and in the domestic economic environment are always subject to interpretation by human beings. From a political economy perspective, international and domestic social facts are not objective or neutral; they are subjective because they are viewed from the perspective of a particular set of economic and political values. Before such groups as political parties and interest groups take policy positions and before governments develop public policies, political actors must decide on the meaning and significance of events and conditions. They must also decide what political responses are normatively (morally) appropriate given the prevailing values in the society.

In the states of the West, political and economic leaders share certain values, and it is this fact that gives the West a political economic outlook distinct from that of the Second or Third World. Western values prescribe a *mixed system* for allocating life chances, combining competition in the marketplace with government authority.[34] The states of the West have been called "market-oriented systems" because many important economic decisions are made through a system of competition based on private property, free enterprise, and occupational choice.[35] The market system is one in which "economic activities are left to men and women freely responding to the opportunities and discouragements of the marketplace, not to established routines of tradition or to the dictates of the governments command."[36] The marketplace combines the various factors of production including labor, capital, ideas, and land to establish the general nature of economic life. Labor negotiates with management for the highest possible wages, businesses seek the highest profits when offering their goods to consumers, and consumers seek high-quality items at the lowest prices. In addition, the market mechanism works to establish priorities about what should be produced in society as consumers and businesses decide which products to buy and sell. Although Western theorists concede that the market system is not perfect and that modifications are frequently necessary, they believe that a system based on incentive and choice is the best method of organizing people for economic activity.

Since the 1870s, however, Western political values have also embraced the belief that, as markets are imperfect mechanisms, the intervention of government authority is essential for economic prosperity. Western values stipulate that decisions about who should hold positions of government authority and to what extent the government should intervene in the economy must be made through a process of political competition open to all groups. In the states of the West, citizens are provided with formidable political rights that enable them to participate in the political conflict process, including freedom of expression, the right to join associations, the right to vote, access to alternative sources of information, and eligibility for public office.[37] The rules for political competition stipulate free and fair elections as the way of selecting those who will be given the authority to make and implement political decisions.[38] Western political–economic values also prescribe a process of interaction for reaching political decisions. In this discussion we are most interested in political decisions about the economy, for instance, the extent to which government should attempt to regulate economic activity, redistribute wealth, or undertake economic planning. This process involves negotiation, bargaining, and conflict among all interested groups. It has been described as the political equivalent of the marketplace. Several analysts have noted that collectively the rights and procedures established by Western values constitute the core of the democratic political process, and that political democracy has been unable to exist except where coupled with a market-oriented system.[39] Democratic political procedures and the market system exist side-by-side in the West because both emerged from the same liberal political tradition. (see Chapter 4).

How Much Government Intervention?

Although it is now accepted in the West that government has a role to play in the economy, there is no consensus on how much the government should intervene. Since the 1920s the theories of the English economist John Maynard Keynes (1883–1946) have gained acceptance, including his central assumption that there is no self-correcting element in the marketplace to keep the capitalist system going.[40] All states of the West now accept the Keynesian theory that government fiscal policies (spending policies) and monetary policies (money supply and interest rate policies) must be adjusted to prevent cyclical downturns in the economy. In addition, the theory of the welfare state assumes a permanent need for government programs and subsidies to aid the disadvantaged members of society. Much of Western domestic politics is devoted to what one political analyst has called the "benefits scramble," the competition between interest groups for government grants and subsidies.[41] However, the size of the programs varies considerably from state to state, and the question of the proper scope of government activity is the source of perpetual political conflict. Social democrats in Western Europe have been the most consistent advocates of government intervention, including public (government) ownership of some sectors of the economy. Social democrats believe that there are major shortcomings or "incompetences" in the market system that can only be redressed through intervention by government authority.[42] The political economic program of the social democrats centers on four points:[43]

1. Markets often fail to produce sufficient aggregate demand (total demand for products) to achieve full employment. Government purchases, tax policies, or government ownership of some businesses are necessary to create sufficient demand.

2. The market system inevitably creates an extreme inequality in the distribution of property and income. This inequality threatens to deprive low-income groups of a decent standard of living. Government programs, including direct government subsidies financed by progressive taxation, must redistribute resources to improve the life chances of low-income groups.

3. Market systems overproduce private goods sold for profit and underproduce public goods such as transportation facilities, schools, parks, and pollution control systems. Government has the responsibility of providing society with such public goods.

4. Decisions made by strategically important private industries (banks, natural resource industries, utilities, and broadcasting companies) have a great impact on the entire population. Consequently, ownership of these industries should be transferred to public ownership.

Social democratic values have had the most influence on public policy in states where socialist political parties have the greatest support. In the period of economic uncertainty since 1973, socialist governments or prime ministers have been elected in France, Italy, Spain, Portugal, and Greece.

The most consistent opponents of government intervention in the economy have been groups representing the business community. This opposition has been based both on the normative belief that the market system is superior to government authority as a mechanism for allocating values and on the pragmatic desire to avoid higher taxes and increased government business regulation. Groups opposing government intervention

Table 10.1 Growth Rates of Selected Western States in Real Gross National Product,[a] 1976–1985 (Percentage)

Country or country group	1976–1980	1979–1983	1981	1982	1983[b]	1984[c]	1985[c]
All developed market economies	3.5	1.6	1.6	−0.2	2.1	3.8	3.1
Major industrial countries	3.7	1.7	1.7	−0.3	2.4	4.1	3.2
Canada	3.1	1.2	3.4	−4.4	3.0	4.0	3.5
France	3.3	1.3	0.3	1.8	0.2	0.5	1.5
Germany, Federal Republic of	3.5	1.1	−0.3	−1.1	1.4	3.0	3.0
Italy	3.8	1.4	0.1	−0.3	−1.2	2.0	2.5
Japan	5.1	4.1	4.0	3.3	3.2	4.5	4.0
United Kingdom	1.6	0.4	−2.0	1.5	2.7	3.0	2.5
United States	3.7	1.3	2.6	−1.9	3.3	5.5	3.5

Source: United Nations, *World Economic Survey, 1984: Current Trends and Policies in the World Economy* (New York, 1984), p. 75. Cited with permission.
[a] Constant 1980 prices and dollar exchange rates. For France, Italy, the United Kingdom, and all of the "Other industrial countries," the measure used is gross domestic product.
[b] Preliminary estimates.
[c] Secretariat forecasts.

have been strongest in the United States and Canada,[44] but in the period since 1973 centrist governments seeking lower taxes, less government spending, and less government regulation also have been elected in the states of northern Europe.

State of the Economy in the West

Before discussing the response of political institutions, it is necessary to summarize the economic problems experienced in the West in the 1970s and 1980s. Between 1945 and the late 1960s, the states of the West experienced a period of steady economic growth. This growth was the result of three factors: (1) the demand created by the need to achieve postwar reconstruction, (2) the shift of the labor force from agriculture (a low-productivity sector) to industry (a high-productivity sector), and (3) the development through scientific research of new technology to achieve higher productivity.[45] In the late 1960s, however, productivity rates began to slow in the United States, the economic leader of the Western World. (Productivity is the amount of goods produced per person in the society.) By the mid-1970s a similar trend developed in the states of Western Europe. Table 10.1 compares the annual rates of growth in GNP in the major states of the West. Although many theories have been offered to explain the decline in productivity, changes in the three factors that had spurred economic growth in the years immediately after 1945 had a major effect. By the end of the 1960s the task of rebuilding the infrastructure of Europe was finished, the shift from

Table 10.2 Changes in Consumer Prices in Selected Western States (Change from Preceding Year)

Country	Average 1967–76	1979	1980	1981	1982	1983	1984[a]
Canada	6.0	9.2	10.2	12.5	10.8	5.9	4.3
United States	5.8	11.3	13.5	10.3	6.2	3.2	4.3
Japan	8.9	3.6	8.0	4.9	2.6	1.8	2.6
France	7.3	10.6	13.3	13.3	12.0	9.5	7.3
Federal Republic of Germany	4.3	4.1	5.5	5.9	5.3	3.0	2.4
Italy	8.5	14.8	21.2	17.8	16.5	14.7	9.4
United Kingdom	10.0	13.5	17.9	11.9	8.6	4.7	4.6

Source: Organization for Economic Cooperation and Development (OECD).
[a] Forecasts.

agriculture to industry was also largely completed, and the application of new scientific achievements to industry became more difficult.[46]

In response to the decline in productivity, many Western businesses sought higher prices for their goods in order to achieve the higher profits, which are necessary to invest in new, more-efficient capital equipment.[47] This development resulted in a wage–price spiral, as workers sought increased wages to protect their purchasing power. Both higher prices and higher wages contributed to increased rates of inflation. Table 10.2 compares the rates of inflation in the major states of the West. By the mid-1970s, Western governments responded to the higher rates of inflation with anti-inflationary economic policies (tight money, reduced government spending, and so on) which increased unemployment.[48] Table 10.3 compares the rates of unemployment in the major states of the West. As the tables indicate, unemployment and inflation have not had an equal impact in every state. The term "stagflation" is sometimes applied to the present economic crisis to show that the Western states are confronted simultaneously with severe problems of inflation and unemployment. The fact is, however, that in some states unemployment is clearly the more serious problem, whereas

Table 10.3 Unemployment Rates in Selected Western States[a]

Country	1973	1979	1980	1981	1982	1983	1984
United States	4.8	5.8	7.0	7.5	9.5	9.6	7.5
Japan	1.3	2.1	2.0	2.2	2.4	2.6	2.7
Germany	0.8	3.2	3.0	4.4	6.1	8.2	8.2
France	2.6	5.9	6.3	7.3	8.0	8.2	9.2
United Kingdom	3.3	5.6	6.9	10.6	12.8	11.5	11.7
Italy	6.2	7.5	7.4	8.3	8.9	9.7	10.0
Canada	5.5	7.4	7.5	7.5	10.9	11.9	11.5

Source: Organization For Economic Cooperation and Development (OECD).
[a] Standardized rates—percentage of total, civilian labor force.

Table 10.4 Balance of Trade in Selected Western States (in National Currencies)

Country	1977	1979	1980	1981	1982	1983	1984[a]
United States (in billions of U.S. dollars)	−31.1	−27.6	−25.5	−28.1	−36.4	−62.0	−99.7
Japan (in billions of U.S. dollars)	17.3	1.8	2.1	20.0	18.1	31.6	37.3
Germany (in millions of deutschmarks)	46.0	32.0	18.9	40.0	64.3	56.3	58.5
France (in billions of francs)	−16.2	−13.5	−56.6	−54.0	−105.4	−58.1	−24.0
United kingdom (in billions of pounds sterling)	−2.3	−3.4	1.2	3.0	2.1	−1.0	−2.5
Italy (in trillions of lire)	−0.1	−0.8	−14.0	−12.0	−10.7	−4.7	−4.2
Canada (in billions of Canadian dollars)	3.0	4.4	8.8	7.4	18.3	16.9	15.0

Source: Organization For Economic Cooperation and Development (OECD).
[a] Estimates.

in others inflation far exceeds the rate of unemployment. The term stagflation does seem applicable in the cases of Great Britain, Italy, and France, which have experienced high rates of both unemployment and inflation.[49]

Two additional elements contribute to the economic turmoil in the West. First, the oil price increases announced by OPEC in 1973 and 1979 had a very detrimental effect on the Western economies. The 1973 increase, raising the price of oil by over 400%, necessitated sharply higher prices for industrial goods. These higher prices fueled inflation and contributed to a general economic slowdown in which there were fewer buyers for expensive goods. In 1975 and 1980 the states of the West underwent major recessions with significantly higher unemployment rates. (Recessions are periods in which a nation's productive forces are not fully utilized.) The oil price increases also contributed to growing balance of trade deficits as Western currencies were transferred to other parts of the world to pay for oil. Table 10.4 compares the balance of trade in the major Western states. Second, since the mid-1970s a trend toward protectionism has developed which threatens to disrupt trade between the industrial states. Facing the dual threats of inflation and unemployment, domestic political groups such as unions and businesses sought quotas and other protectionist measures to ensure jobs and markets. The trend began first in Western Europe, but by 1980 came to include the United States.[50] Protectionism threatens to disrupt the free trade patterns established under the Bretton Woods system. After 1980 it was possible to identify two major economic problems in the West: the need to increase productivity and the need to protect groups in the general population against unemployment and the loss of life chances.

POLITICAL INSTITUTIONS AND PUBLIC POLICY RESPONSE

Since the early 1970s, economic issues have dominated the domestic political scene in the West. As the general population has become increasingly aware of the threat of reduced life chances, political institutions both inside and outside government have been forced to respond. Unions, farmers' organizations, and business groups are intensifying the struggle for a piece of the shrinking national economic pie. Unions seek to protect the jobs of their members, farmers and other groups work for the continuation of government subsidies, and businesses try to protect declining profits from the dual threats of inflation and higher taxes. Strikes and public demonstrations have become commonplace in all of the states of the West. Violent strikes and protests have occurred in France and Italy, which have a strong tradition of collective political action.

The economic crisis has also been the focal point of intense political party rivalry. The initial reaction of political parties was to "nationalize" the economic problems of the 1970s. The general economic slowdown was blamed on individual governments or on specific policies. Opposition political parties effectively capitalized on the general atmosphere of insecurity. The past decade has not been an easy time for incumbent candidates and governing political parties. In the United States, Great Britain, West Germany, Sweden, Belgium, the Netherlands, Luxembourg, Denmark, and Norway, centrist candidates have replaced liberal reformers and social democrats. In France, Italy, Greece, Portugal, and Spain, socialists have replaced center-right and conservative parties which had monopolized political power for the entire postwar period. The only clear trend in the West has been dissatisfaction with the current state of the political economy, rejection of incumbent politicians, and the search for new ways of maintaining Western affluence.

In several cases, recent electoral outcomes represent major departures from past political patterns. In Great Britain's 1983 election, more than 70% of the electorate voted to the political right of the once powerful Labour party whose programs had shaped the British welfare state. The defeat represented rejection of the policies of the left wing of the Labour party, including the extension of public ownership and greater control of the national economy.[51] Dissatisfaction with the government's handling of the economy was also the major factor in the defeat of the Social Democratic party in West Germany. In the 1982 elections the Christian Democratic coalition headed by Chancellor Helmut Kohl ended 13 years of rule by Social Democratic-led governments. Public opinion polls demonstrated clearly that concern for high unemployment, budget deficits, and the general end of the "economic miracle" in Germany were the most important factors in the election. The move to the center-right was also a major political trend in Scandinavia. The election of 1982 produced the first Conservative prime minister in Denmark in 81 years, and in Sweden the defeat of the government of Social Democratic Prime Minister Olaf Palme by a center-right coalition in 1976 ended a period of socialist rule dating from the 1930s. Interestingly, dissatisfaction with the economic performance of the Conservative party subsequently led to the return of Palme as prime minister in 1982. Again, the incumbents were apparently blamed by the electorate for the poor perform-ance of the economy.

The election of socialists in France, Italy, Greece, and Spain repre-sented equally dramatic political reversals. In France the election of Francois Mitterand as president in 1981 and the subsequent victory of his Socialist party in the legislative elections were without precedent in the 23-year history of the Fifth Republic (established in 1958). Mitterand won election by directly attacking the economic policies of the center-right which, he argued, had failed to protect middle-class and working-class Frenchmen from *déclassement* (downward mobility).[52] The extent of the discontent in France was demonstrated by the fact that the Socialist party received 271 seats, an absolute majority, in the 491-seat National Assembly. In addition, Mitterand's Communist coalition partners won 44 seats (in 1984 the Communists left the government to express their dissatisfaction with Mitterand's economic policies). In Italy, the Socialist party did not win an electoral victory, but the so-called secular parties, the Socialists, Demo-cratic Socialists, Republicans, and Liberals, captured 26.4% of the vote in the election of June 1981. (This was the third highest vote total.) As a result of parliamentary maneuvering and his party's strong showing in the elec-tions, Socialist party Secretary Bettino Craxi became the Italian prime minister in 1982. The parliamentary elections of 1981 and 1982 also resulted in the victory of moderate socialists in Spain and Greece. The victory of Andreas Papandreou's Panhellenic Socialist Movement (PASOK) in Octo-ber 1981 marked the election of the first democratic socialist government in Greek history, and in Spain the Socialist party (PSOE) received the most votes in the 1982 election. Why have the socialists been successful in the Mediterranean states? Gianfranco Pasquino of the University of Bologna suggests an explanation consistent with the trend of voting against incumbents.[53] He argues that the Socialist parties in southern Europe are new. The Socialist party of Mitterand dates to 1969, the Panhellenic Socialist

Movement of Papandreou to 1974, and the current Socialist party in Spain to 1976–77.[54] As new parties, these socialist parties are not identified by the general electorate with the economic policies that have failed to overcome unemployment, inflation, and other economic ills. Voting for socialist parties in southern Europe means voting against the economic dislocations of the past two decades.

Government and Public Policy Response

The most visible political reaction to the current economic crisis has been the public policy response of the Western governments. The economic problems of the past decade have placed a great burden on government institutions as the general population demands policy solutions to a wide range of economic problems, including unemployment, inflation, a low rate of economic growth, budget deficits, and an unfavorable balance of trade. With the notable exceptions of Margaret Thatcher and Ronald Reagan, incumbents in most Western governments have been unable to produce policy solutions satisfactory to the general electorate. This fact is no surprise to anyone familiar with the contemporary political economy of the West. Today's economic problems are extremely complex, and there is substantial disagreement among economists and other experts on how to proceed. Whether the present economic problems are the result of a cyclical downturn in the economy, the failure of businesses to employ creative and productive methods, or a long-term shift in the balance of world economic power, they have proven resistant in the short run to the policy solutions of any single government. It must be remembered that the Western economic systems are mixed systems combining the market mechanism with government authority. In many cases economic decisions made by larger private institutions (e.g., major corporations and national unions) have an important and immediate effect on the economic condition of consumers, employees, and businesses. These decisions, of course, are made independent of government authority. Despite the very real limitations on government authority, it is accepted in contemporary Western political culture that government has the responsibility for overall economic management. In every industrial democracy, government is the single largest purchaser of goods and services, the single largest distributor of income, and the single largest borrower of money.[55] As such, governments are expected to use their taxation and spending powers, as well as the ability of central banks to control the supply of money, to promote economic well-being. In the industrial states of the West economic well-being is defined as full employment, stable prices, and steady levels of economic growth.[56]

There have been two general approaches in the industrial democracies for coping with the current economic problems—one places primary emphasis on increasing productivity, the other places primary emphasis on promoting equality of opportunity. Earlier in this chapter we referred to these policy patterns as the *politics of productivity and equality* rather than as *policies* of productivity and equality. The term *politics* is preferable because in no state has there been a consistent and systematic policy response. In both the northern industrial states where governments have been elected on platforms of increasing productivity and southern Europe where socialists have pledged to increase societal equality, political commitments have been as much rhetorical as real. The concepts of productivity and equality have been useful in mobilizing electoral support because they identify the groups in society whose interest a political party seeks to promote. Once in power, however, political leaders have often been forced by economic and political necessities to modify major policy commitments.

The Politics of Productivity

Between 1976 and 1983, centrist political elites pledged to increasing productivity won elections in the United States, Great Britain, West Germany, Canada, the Netherlands, Belgium, Denmark, Norway, and Sweden.* Although proposing different methods, the new centrist governments identified inflation, excessive government spending, and declining rates of productivity as the major economic ills. As remedies, the centrists proposed in various combinations reduced government expenditures, balanced national budgets, tax cuts, "tight money" (restricting the money supply), and in some cases public subsidies to businesses and industries.[57] In theory, lower taxes provide incentives for entrepreneurs who may keep more of what they earn, balanced national budgets restore faith in the government's ability to manage the economy and permit lower taxes, and tight money counters inflationary trends and intensifies competition in a sluggish business environment. By placing primary emphasis on controlling inflation, centrist governments have been forced to accept higher rates of unemployment. In general, centrist policies have been disadvantageous to groups dependent on government entitlements and subsidies, young persons not yet established, and groups vulnerable to unemployment (such as unskilled laborers, workers in low-technology industries, and government employees in poorly funded units). Centrist policies are especially beneficial to high-income groups, professionals, investors, business owners, and

---

*After losing power in 1976, the Social Democratic coalition returned to power in Sweden in 1982.

farmers. The dominance of the politics of productivity is the result of several factors. In the United States and Canada it reflects the relative weakness of labor unions in the political process; in Great Britain it resulted from a public perception that labor unions have had too much influence and have harmed the economy by excessive strikes. In West Germany the victory of the centrist Christian Socialist coalition was a reaction to the end of the period of rapid growth known as the "Economic Miracle" and the resulting loss of markets and jobs.

Despite the commitment to the politics of productivity, consistent policies have not been developed. The centrists have been confronted by economic complexity and the need to do what is politically acceptable in the context of the modern welfare state. Conditions such as money supply and rate of inflation have not been readily susceptible to government manipulation. In addition, beneficiary groups have continued to demand public subsidies and have made the political costs of abandoning government programs high. The United States and Great Britain illustrate the inconsistencies in the politics of productivity. In Great Britain the Conservative party of Margaret Thatcher was elected in 1979 on a platform that included monetarist and supply-side economic principles. Central to Thatcher's plan for improving the economy was the "sacred triad of monetarism," tight money control, lower taxes, and expenditure cuts.[58] After five years in office, the Thatcher government was unable to realize any of these three conditions. The money supply had been increasing at about double the government's target range, many middle-income taxpayers were paying a higher proportion of their income in taxes than before the Conservatives took power, and government expenditures as a proportion of national output had actually increased from 41 to 44.5%.[59] Similarly, in the United States Ronald Reagan campaigned for the presidency in 1980 on a pledge to reduce government expenditures, cut taxes, and balance the budget. By the end of his first term, a balanced budget seemed a more distant goal than before his election, and cuts in government programs in the human services areas were exceeded by new increases in defense spending. In 1984, the Reagan administration was forced to consider a tax increase in order to deal with soaring budget deficits.

The Politics of Equality

In France, Italy, Spain, Portugal, and Greece the politics of equality prevails.[60] In these states the dominant political concern of the general population has been to avoid downward mobility and the loss of life chances. Trade union members, low-income groups, students, and voters dissatisfied with political economic outcomes under previous center-right governments have combined to elect socialist parties. Socialists have pledged to continue to increase government programs to the less advantaged and to protect jobs even if this requires the government ownership of faltering industries. In France and Italy the Socialist and Communist parties have traditionally enjoyed strong electoral support. In Spain, Portugal, and Greece the victory of the socialists was a reaction against political control by conservative, antidemocratic groups in the periods between 1945 and the mid-1970s. An element of protest and reaction was also present in the victories in France and Italy. In Italy the strong showing of Bettino Craxi and the Italian Socialist party was a reaction against the indecisive economic policies of the center-right Christian Democrats who had governed Italy since 1947.[61] In France Socialist party leader Francois Mitterand campaigned on the theme that the center-right coalition (which had governed since the creation of the Fifth Republic in 1958) had subsidized the development of private industry at the cost of failing to protect the life chances of the majority of the population. Mitterand further attacked the concentration of wealth and power in specific private sectors of the economy which, he argued, exercised too much control over the economic well-being of the general population. As a remedy the Socialists promised nationalization of certain industries.

Like their counterparts in the states of northern Europe, the socialists have been unable to develop public policies consistent with the politics of equality.[62] The new socialist-led governments have been forced to direct their attention to the high rates of inflation and large budget deficits they inherited. For example, in 1983 the Spanish government of Prime Minister Filipe González and the Portuguese government of Prime Minister Mario Soares faced inflation rates of 15% and 25%, respectively.[63] Both governments announced austerity programs that included reduced government spending and the reduction of state-owned industries. The Greek socialist government of Papandreou, also facing a high inflation rate (20%) and huge deficits in foreign trade, took similar austerity measures. The government of Craxi in Italy faced the largest budget deficit in Western Europe, in 1983 equal to 22% of the economy's yearly total output.[64] Faced with this deficit, Craxi was unable to expand government programs. Instead, he spoke of the need to finally come to grips with Italy's long-term economic problems. The actions of the French government of Mitterand best illustrate the relationship between socialist ideals and economic realities. After the Socialist party's victory in 1981, the Mitterand government nationalized 5 leading multinational corporations (aeronautics, electronics, chemical, communications, and armaments firms), 36 private banks, and all private insurance companies.[65] Although the nationalizations fulfilled campaign pledges made during the 1981 election, they were undertaken more to provide jobs for the party's new technocratic, middle-class supporters than to conform to

French President Francois Mitterrand.

socialist ideals. Within 18 months of assuming office, huge trade deficits and several other problems forced the Mitterand government to institute traditional austerity measures, including higher taxes, reduced government spending, and wage–price freezes.[66] In addition, like their center-right predecessors, the socialists used government institutions and public subsidies to promote private industry.

The performances of the governments of the industrial democracies, north and south, indicate the difficulty of dealing with modern economic problems according to traditional theories and models. Western governments have been forced to deal with the present crisis through the imposition of pragmatic and short-term strategies—a process some might call "muddling through." Government policies are nonetheless important. The states of the West are both partners and competitors in the present recession. They are partners in the effort to maintain Western control over the international economic system, but they are in competition for the declining volume of world business in this period of recession. Public policies are political decisions specifying steps that must be taken to prepare the state to be more competitive and to increase the collective political–economic strength of the West. As such, public policies have a great effect on the life ,chances available to the citizens of the state both at present and in the future. At present, neither the states embracing the politics of productivity nor the states dominated by the politics of equality can claim to have identified the policies necessary to overcome the major economic problems confronting the West.

NOTES

1. Clair Wilcos, Willis D. Weatherford, Jr., Holland Hunter, and Morton S. Baratz, *Economies of the World Today: Their Organization, Development, and Perform-ance,* 2d ed. (New York: Harcourt Brace & World, 1966), pp. 6–7.
2. Ibid.
3. Charles E. Lindblom, *Politics and Markets: The World's Political-Economic Systems* (New York: Basic Books, 1977), p. 8.
4. Cited in Dwayne Ward, *Toward a Critical Political Economics: A Critique of Liberal and Radical Economic Thought* (Santa Monica, Calif.: Goodyear, 1977), p. 12.
5. The terms and the general model of social facts and life chances are taken from Robert A. Isaak, *European Politics: Political Economy and Policy Making in Western Democracies* (New York: St. Martin's Press, 1980), pp. 1–26. Concepts are also taken from Michael H. Best and William E. Connolly, *The Politicized Economy,* (Lexington, Mass.: Heath, 1976).
6. Isaak, p. 2.
7. Ibid., pp. 21, 22.
8. Ibid., p. 7.
9. Ibid., p. 6.
10. Ibid., p. 11.
11. For a discussion of these systems see Lindblom, pp. 17–52. Lindblom also recognizes a third type of political economic system, which he calls the persuasion and preceptoral system. See Lindblom, pp. 52–64.
12. See William N. Loucks and William G. Whitney, *Comparative Economic Systems,* 9th ed. (New York: Harper & Row, 1973), pp. 19–32 and pp. 163–185.
13. Ibid., p. 107.
14. Ibid., p. 283.
15. For a discussion of African capitalist states see Crawford Young, *Ideology and Development in Africa* (New Haven, Conn.: Yale University Press, 1982).
16. See Isaak.
17. Gottfried Haberler, "The Liberal International Economic Order in Historical Perspective," in Ryan C. Amacher, Gottfried Haberler, and Thomas D. Willet, eds., *Challenges to a Liberal International Economic Order* (Washington, D.C.: American Enterprise Institute for Public Policy Research, 1979), p. 43.
18. James Lee Ray, *Global Politics,* 2d ed. (Boston: Houghton Mifflin, 1983), p. 242.
19. Robert O. Keohane and Joseph S. Nye, *Power and Interdependence: World Politics in Transition* (Boston: Little, Brown, 1977), p. 19.
20. Ray, p. 249.
21. See Hollis Chenery, "Commentary," in Amacher *et al.*, p. 76; also see Ray, pp. 251–253.
22. See Ervin Laszlo, Robert Baker, Jr., Elliot Eisenber, and Venkata Raman, *The*

Objectives of the New International Economic Order (Elmsford, N.Y.: Pergamon Press, 1978).

23. *Ramses: Annual Report by the French Institute for International Relations, The State of the World Economy* (Cambridge, Mass.: Ballinger, 1982), p. 82.
24. Anne Daltrop, *Political Realities: Politics and the European Community* (Hong Kong: Wilture Enterprises, 1982), p. 96.
25. Ibid.
26. Ibid.
27. Roy C. Macridis, ed. *Modern Political Systems: Europe,* 5th ed. (Englewood Cliffs, N.J.: Prentice-Hall, 1983), 273.
28. Ibid.
29. Daltrop, p. 7.
30. *Ramses: The State of the World Economy,* p. 106.
31. Robert Heilbroner and Lester Thurow, *Economics Explained* (Englewood Cliffs, N.J.: Prentice-Hall, 1982), p. 53.
32. Ibid., p. 221.
33. Ray, pp. 347–350.
34. For the most current discussion of this point see Lindblom, pp. 107–119.
35. Ibid., pp. 162, 164.
36. Heilbroner and Thurow, p. 6.
37. See Lindblom, p. 133.
38. Ibid.
39. See ibid., pp. 116 and 133.
40. Heilbroner and Thurow, p. 31.
41. Samuel H. Beer, *Britain Against Itself: The Political Contradictions of Collectivism* (New York: Norton, 1982), pp. 23–47.
42. Lindblom, p. 64.
43. Each of these points is taken from Loucks and Whitney, pp. 168–170.
44. See Charles Andrain, *Politics and Economic Policy in Western Democracies* (North Scituate, Mass.: Duxbury Press, 1980), pp. 10–29, 213.
45. Alexandre Faire, "Ten Years of Crisis for the Advanced Capitalist Economies," in *World View 1983: What the Press and Television Have Not Told You About the Years's Mega-Issues* under the general direction of Francois Geze, Yves Lacoste, and Alfredo Valladao (New York: Pantheon Books, 1982), pp. 39–41.
46. Edward Jay Epstein and Jeffrey Steingarten, "Europe: End of a Miracle," in Christian Soe, ed., *Comparative Politics 83/84* (Guilford, Conn.: Dushkin, 1983), pp. 110–113.
47. Faire, p. 41.
48. Ibid.
49. David Wood, *Power and Policy in Western European Democracies,* 2d. ed. (New York: Wiley, 1982), pp. 40–41.
50. Faire, p. 42.
51. Philip Norton, *The British Polity* (New York: Longman, 1984), pp. 139–142.
52. Isaak, p. 77.
53. *Time,* November 8, 1982, p. 41.

54. Ibid.

55. Arnold J. Heidenheimer, Hugh Heclo, and Carolyn Teich Adams, *Comparative Public Policy: The Politics of Social Choice in Europe and America,* 2d ed. (New York: St. Martin's Press, 1983), p. 127.

56. Ibid., p. 104.

57. For a discussion of these proposals see Paul Lewis, "Europeans Debate Ways to Spur Their Lagging Economic Upturn," in Soe, pp. 114–117.

58. Stuart Butler, "Why Thatcheromics Isn't Working," in Soe, p. 113.

59. Ibid., pp. 113–114.

60. See "Sunbelt Socialism," in Soe, pp. 68–69.

61. See Isaak's discussion of the political economy of Italy, pp. 126–150.

62. Lewis, pp. 69–71.

63. Ibid., pp. 69–70.

64. Ibid., p. 70.

65. John Ardagh, *France in the 1980's: The Definitive Book* (New York: Penguin Books, 1982), p. 117.

66. Heidenheimer et al., p. 135.

CHAPTER 11

Political Process and Economic Outcomes: The Second World

The Second World is guided by the philosophy and principles of Karl Marx, Friedrich Engels, and Vladimir Lenin, as interpreted by the ruling Communist party of a given country. These principles lead Communists to believe that their system is superior to any other and that other systems must eventually give way to the Communist version and disappear. Theoretical principles clash with reality, however, as the First World remains economically strong in the contemporary period.

Second World states have adopted a "command" economic system. The theoretical and practical aspects of this system are in conflict. A command economy provides social benefits, but it also has many problems. As is the case in several states in the First and the Third Worlds, a second (underground) economy exists in the Communist states.

The Communist party has policy-making and supervisory roles in the Communist economic system. Members in the higher echelons are given special privileges. Although the Communist system does not make available the same amount of values as does the First World, it generally is more successful than many Third World economic systems in satisfying the needs of the general population.

In the nineteenth century Kark Marx's principal effort and life's work were directed at understanding the mainsprings of modern society—the underpinnings or foundations on which social structure was built. He spent considerable time arguing against the so-called classical political economists, Adam Smith and especially David Ricardo. Marx developed a theory that "confronts [classical and] neoclassical theory with a radically different perspective and a contrasting analytical structure."[1] Marx apparently thought his achievement was within the realm of social science, that is, "a piece of scientific analysis which, therefore, is capable of refinement and susceptible to error."[2]

In practice, in the twentieth century, however, his work is used mainly as the basis for a Leninist approach to political economy. This is not to say that purely Marxist (non-Communist) academic political economists do not exist, for they do,[3] but in the 17 ruling Communist party states political economy is said to be based on Leninist principles. Strictly speaking, this does not appear to be the case because, as previously mentioned, much of what is done in the Communist world is really "Stalinesque." Joseph Stalin as a person was discredited (despite recent attempts to rehabilitate his image) because of "distortions during the cult of the individual" period, that is, slave labor camps and secret police terror. Herbert Block, in an appendix to Edward Luttwak's recent book *The Grand Strategy of the Soviet Union,* wrote that "Lenin's economic ideas were harebrained, and he had to retreat from their topsy-turvy implementation" and finally "Stalin's command economy" was instituted which is more or less a *"sui generis* war economy."[4] This Stalinistic approach dogmatizes Marx into something akin to a natural or exact science. Today in the Communist world the official political economy is viewed as "the science of the laws governing the production and exchange of the material means of subsistence in human society at the various stages of its development. It studies the social structure of production."[5] Modern Communism assumes "that human society, like nature, develops according to the definite laws. These are objective laws which means that they do not depend on the will and the consciousness of people."[6]

Communist theoreticians view the present world as the ground for a gigantic struggle between the forces of dying capitalism (essentially the Western World's system of political economy) and those of advancing socialism (the Communist party-ruled states). Capitalism is in its final stage of "imperialism," a stage beyond which there is no other; it is decaying and in general crisis. Imperialism may be a worldwide system but "socialism's development into a world system has convincingly proved capitalism's inevitable doom."[7]

Let us look at what is said to be wrong with capitalism and why Leninist (Stalinist) political economy claims to be superior before we examine the actual practice of this political economic system in regard to international opportunities and constraints, the domestic economic environment, political economic values, and public policy outcomes.

Capitalism (according to *Webster's New Collegiate Dictionary*) is an economic system characterized by private or corporate ownership of capital goods, by investments that are determined by private decision rather than by state control, and by prices, production, and the distribution of goods that are determined mainly by competition in a free market.

Capitalism and ownership of capital (possession of money and/or goods designated for production of more money or goods, rather than for immediate consumption) are condemned by Leninist political economists. The principal reason for this is found in the notion of "private." By their own definition Communists say private ownership is a kind of stealing of value from the workers, and despite capitalism's ability to industrialize society and to produce enormous amounts of goods, this "stealing" creates an undesirable economic situation for the masses. Capitalism generates "its own contradictions . . . unemployment, inflation, rampant crime and violence, urban decay, the breakdown of authority patterns, as well as . . . many other ills."[8] Private control of the economy is an evil that must be eradicated.

The socialist system is offered as a remedy. Socialism is theoretically claimed to be a system of drawing people together for the common good; that is, there is no conflict between private ownership and the working masses, but rather a common activity of all people to develop the political, economic and social system. The Communist party directs the efforts of everyone, first by setting economic policy and then by using the state mechanism to achieve the specified goals. The state-planning apparatus sets up 20-year prospective plans, 5-year near-future plans and a 1-year plan for the specific year at hand. The planned and proportionally developed economic system theoretically obviates conflicts and satisfies the individual's needs. No longer do private individuals exploit others; all supposedly work for the common good.[9]

Despite these theoretical notions Marxist–Leninists recognize that they must live for a long time in a world in which an economic system exists opposed to their own. Until their superior system triumphs, they understand that they are in an interdependent system with the other two worlds and that fluctuations in other worlds effect their own economics.

INTERNATIONAL OPPORTUNITIES AND CONSTRAINTS

The clash between theoretical constructs and reality is most clearly seen in the international arena. The Communist party-ruled states recognize *de facto* that the Western World is not going to suddenly disappear and that a militarily assisted "push" to end the Western system is not in the cards. Barring a nuclear war between the two camps, Communists see competition as occurring on the social, political, and economic planes. They, however, emphasize the economy as the "main arena."

The superiority of the *command economy* and central control by a Communist party will be demonstrated in international economic competition. The proper organization of Communist domestic production will yield results in the international sphere because the rapid development of socialism will attract Third World countries and Communism will gain new adherents.[10]

Initially, though, the international economy was of little interest to any of the newly communized states. During the struggle to gain and maintain power all other concerns took a backseat. In the Soviet Union the first economic period was called "Workers Control," a time in which workers were encouraged to seize control of the factories and economic system. This was a short-lived period lasting only from November 27, 1917, to July 1, 1918. At this time the new Soviet Russian government and the Bolshevik party were looked upon by the West as German tools because Lenin received German assistance in returning to Russia in April 1917, and negotiated a peace treaty with the Central Powers. The Western Allies clamped a blockade on Russia and subsequently began a military intervention. Accordingly, there was no international dimension to the new economy; in fact, "Industrial production was grinding to a complete halt, the workers in many cases evicting their managers as well as proprietors and workers' committees trying to run factories, usually with disastrous results."[11]

The growing domestic anarchy, domestic resistance to Bolshevik control, and foreign intervention caused Lenin to jettison Marx's idea of a workers' democracy within eight months and to institute a period called "War Communism." Beginning on July 1, 1918, strikes and other disturbances in vital production were seen as counterrevolutionary. During summer of 1918 "all large-scale plants were seized . . . and from then on the nationalization of industry gradually spread downward to even small machine shops."[12] Nevertheless, state control initially proved a failure because, among other things, there was a civil war going on. By 1920, industrial production was 13.2% of the 1913 level. In the agricultural sector, also, there was failure. In 1916 there were 90 million hectares of land in production with a harvest of 74 million tons of grain; by 1921 there were only 60 million hectares under cultivation and in 1919 the estimated production of grain was 30 million tons. Additionally, there was a drought in 1920 and a famine in 1921.[13] Industrial and agricultural production in Russia was in need of a dramatic change.

In order to revive the economy and to break out of isolation, Lenin, at the Tenth Congress of the Communist party, in March 1921, decreed the New Economic Policy (NEP), which allowed for private control of small-scale

Magnitogorsk metallurgical complex in the Ural Mountains of the Soviet Union.

industry and agriculture. Large-scale industry, the "commanding heights," remained in government hands.

The NEP period (March 1921–December 1927) coincided with Lenin's physical decline and death and the rise to power of Josif Stalin. During this period the Soviet Union's domestic economy recovered and the USSR reached out economically and politically to the rest of the world. The country was in desperate need of peace and quiet to heal the deep wounds of war. Further, "normal and extensive commercial intercourse with foreign countries was required to bring in badly needed capital and foreign specialists" and foreign technology.[14] Commercial and political treaties were negotiated with foreign countries, some foreign commercial concessions were granted within the USSR, and foreigners were hired to work in Soviet industry. During this period of the struggle with those who opposed him, Stalin came up with the slogan "Socialism in One Country" and a program for bootstrap (self-help) industrialization.

The impact of Stalin's industrial and economic program began to be felt in 1928 and continued up to his death in 1953. This program is the basis for all Communist regimes. (Its structure will be discussed in the next section.) This policy initially pursued *autarky*, "a policy of establishing a self-sufficient and independent national economy," free of foreign influence. The

Soviet Union, the only Communist State before 1945,* looked inward to forced draft industrialization with 100% state control and an absolute minimum of outside influence (except for the import of technology, stripped of any ideological baggage). Since 1945 all the newly communized states went through a longer or shorter period of turning inward. The Soviet Union, and to some extent China, were the only states that actually had some capacity to carry out an autarkic policy because the amounts and types of raw materials available made it possible to attempt autarky. The first impetus to end autarky came after World War II with the establishment of the "Socialist camp" under the Soviet aegis. In April 1949, in response to U.S. activity in Western Europe (the Marshall Plan), the Soviet Union called a meeting of its satellites to found the Council for Mutual Economic Assistance (CMEA). The founding countries were the USSR, Bulgaria, Czechoslovakia, Hungary, Poland, and Romania. A second meeting was held in August 1949, when Albania joined (Albania has not, in fact, participated in CMEA since 1961). The third meeting took place in 1950, when the German Democratic Republic joined. Richard F. Staar points out in his *Communist Regimes in Eastern Europe* that actually the Soviet Union did not really give up its economic policy until after Stalin's death because CMEA did not really begin to function until March 1954.[15] CMEA has since been expanded by the inclusion of Mongolia (1962), Cuba (1972), and Vietnam (1979) as full members. Yugoslavia entered limited participation in 1965, and observer status has been granted to the Communist party states of North Korea and Laos (1979) and to Afghanistan (1980). The Communist-leaning states of Angola, Ethiopia, South Yemen (1979), and Mozambique (1980) have also been admitted to observer status. Additionally, the non-Communist countries of Finland (1973), Mexico (1975), and Iraq (1976) have signed agreements with CMEA.[16] One might also say that Kampuchea, by virtue of its occupation by Vietnam, is a member by proxy. China, however, has never taken part in CMEA and has been isolated from the rest of the Communist World since the early 1960s.

The CMEA is a very ambitious project, as can be seen from Figure 11.1 indicating its organization. The CMEA is intended to be the Soviet bloc's answer to the EEC and the growing integration and free trade in the Western World. It fails in this endeavor for two reasons. First, the Soviet Union is the

*One Communist author says, however, that "This statement is formally not accurate since in 1921, under the influence of the October Revolution, a people's-democratic revolution was won in Mongolia. However, to the beginning of the 1940s, a revolutionary antifeudal process was going on removing remnants of the feudal order and of backward civilization." Adam Koseski, *Rozwiete Spoleczenstwo Socjalistyczne* (Warsaw: Wydawnictwo Ministerstwa Obrony Narodowej, 1975), p. 5.

predominant economic force in the Soviet bloc (not to mention political and military force) and much trade is done on a bilateral basis within the bloc bypassing the CMEA mechanism. Second, CMEA does not form a common market in actual practice because there is no tariff barrier surrounding the CMEA states and internal barriers remain; thus, it is not a single market. Though trade is encouraged within the bloc, many high-technology items and some "know-how" information are available only from the West. Moreover, there has been resistance by some CMEA countries to supranational planning. There has been a tendency for the Soviet Union to "divide" the labor, for example, assigning agricultural production to Bulgaria and Romania and aircraft production to itself. As Table 11.1 indicates, trade among major CMEA members in 1979 was not insignificant. The figures available, however, do not tell us what portion of trade was done through CMEA and what portion was determined by bilateral trade agreements, which the various Soviet bloc countries often prefer to sign among themselves in order to better plan production. In sum, the large CMEA bureaucratic apparatus has not yet fulfilled its promise.[17]

Besides the perceived need to consolidate the Soviet bloc through the Council of Mutual Economic Assistance there were several other reasons for the Communist states to seek trade with the rest of the world. First, Nikita Khrushchev's rise to power in the USSR (1953–1955) and the failures of the Great Leap Forward (1958–1959) and the Great Proletarian Cultural Revolution (1966–1969) in China caused both Communist powers to recognize the vital economic need to deal with the West in order to acquire the latest technology (equipment and know-how). Despite what Leninist and Maoist dogma would have the population believe, there had been no special flowering of scientific achievement in Communist lands, and the West, despite its "oppressive" capitalist atmosphere, was leaving the rest of the world far behind in technology. Second, there are two related political reasons for the change in policy. The Soviet Union and its satellites see the possibility of outflanking Western "encirclement" by reaching out to the recently decolonized Third World. Furthermore, the Soviet Union and China have been in conflict since the early 1960s (the so-called Sino-Soviet dispute) and rivalry between the Second World giants affects relations with the First and Third Worlds. (These themes will be discussed in Chapter 14.)

The international opportunities the various Communist states see in trade with the First and Third Worlds (that is, the acquisition of scarce scientific data and machinery, the purchase of useful raw materials, and political influence) are limited by some real constraints. Many of these constraints are caused by self-imposed limitations. In as simple an area as tourism, the Second World has much to offer: the architecture of medieval Cracow, the wonders of the Kremlin of Moscow, the Chinese antiquities.

Structure of the Council for Mutual Economic Assistance

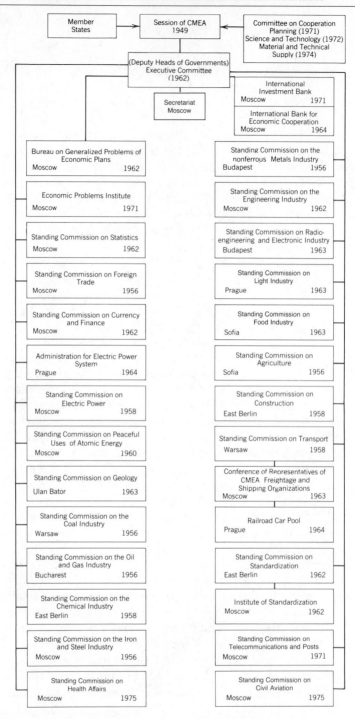

Figure 11.1. CMEA structure as of 1981 with founding date and headquarters location of each unit.

Sources: A Survey of 20 years of the Council for Mutual Economic Assistance (Moscow: CMEA Secretariat, 1969), p. 24. Richard F. Staar *Communist Regimes in Eastern Europe*, 4th ed. (Stanford, CA: Hoover Institution Press, 1982), p. 310; copyright 1982 by the Board of Trustees of the Leland Stanford Junior University.

Table 11.1   1979 Trade in Millions of U.S. Dollars for Selected CMEA Countries

Country	CMEA area dollar amount	(%)[a]	Rest of world dollar amount	(%)	Total trade dollar amount
Bulgaria	13,082	(75)	4,472	(25)	17,554
Czechoslovakia	18,395	(65)	9,866	(35)	28,261
German Democratic Republic[b]	12,070	(33)	24,380	(67)	36,450
Hungary	14,381	(62)	8,655	(38)	23,036
Poland	19,539	(55)	15,385	(45)	34,924
Romania[b]	3,270	(15)	17,379	(85)	20,649
USSR	55,131	(45)	67,743	(55)	122,874
Total	135,868	(48)	147,880	(52)	283,748

Source: Richard F. Staar, *Communist Regimes in Eastern Europe*, 4th ed. (Stanford, CA.: Hoover Institution Press, 1982), p. 313; copyright 1982 by the Board of Trustees of Leland Stanford Junior University.
[a] Percentages rounded off.
[b] Trade with USSR only.

However, in order to encourage tourists to bring their money, the Second World would have to ease or eliminate visa impediments, the sometimes onerous border formalities, and the restrictions on freedom of travel. Sufficient tourist facilities of a high-enough quality would have to be constructed. However, with the exception of Yugoslavia and to some extent Bulgaria, the Communist party states refuse to reduce political control both of their own and foreign citizens. Foreigners go to the Second World out of curiosity but hardly ever for relaxation.

Tied in with tourism but extending well beyond is monetary policy. As part of general Communist policy, free markets are condemned. Thus, even the value of one country's currency in relation to other currencies within the Second World is stated by government fiat. In order to prevent, as much as possible, development of a free market, import and export of currency are forbidden (with the partial exception of Yugoslavia and Hungary). On the paper money itself can be found the statement that the currency is valid for internal transactions only. One might suppose that the official rate of exchange not only between Communist states but also with currencies of the rest of the world would have some relation to reality. This, however, is not the case. Officially, one German Democratic Republic (East) mark is equal to one Federal Republic of Germany (West) mark, but actually the GDR mark can purchase only about one-quarter of the value in East Germany as one mark can in West Germany. The rate of the Soviet ruble to the U.S. dollar is nearly confiscatory: $1.35 (U.S.) purchases one ruble, which in turn can buy about 30¢ of value in the Soviet market. Once there were five official rates, for various types of transactions, of the Polish zloty to the U.S. dollar, with the tourist "premium" rate the second worst. Also impeding tourist, business, and scientific travel is the obligatory minimum daily exchange. Depending on the type of visa or status one has, one must exchange a certain amount of hard currency (that is, so-called freely convertible money, money of the countries of the Western World, which has no restrictions on its ability to be exchanged for any other country's money) for the local currency without the right of reconversion. In order for a citizen of a Communist state to travel to any other state—Communist or not—state bank permission is required for conversion of local currency to other currencies, and even then the permission may be for a very limited amount and at an unfavorable rate or with a hefty surcharge. Certain domestic and Communist products and nearly all Western products cannot be bought with local currency. There are special trading corporations and shops where foreigners in general, foreign relatives of local citizens, and, in some cases, local citizens themselves may purchase these desirable goods with hard currency if they possess it. These special hard currency arrangements and the nonconvertibility of local currency create a thriving black (illegal) market in Communist states, which is repressed with greater (Soviet Union, Romania), or lesser (Poland, GDR) severity.

The monetary situation forces the Communist states to trade with the First and Third Worlds in hard currency, using marks, U.S. dollars, Swiss francs, and so on. Among the members of CMEA, a fictional currency is used, the convertible ruble—strictly an accounting term.

Second World trade with the First World is limited to the amount of hard currency the Communist states can acquire by sale of raw materials and some finished products to the First World. Soviet sales of natural gas to Western Europe and China's anticipated sales of petroleum are part of this type of trade. Also, the Soviet Union has sold some of its gold reserves directly in the Swiss gold exchange to finance purchases.

Trade with the Third World is impeded because Third World countries wish to acquire hard currency too. They prefer to sell to the First World, if possible. Communist states, however, often offer barter arrangements to Third World states and frequently accept goods that could not be sold in Western markets. Despite these advantages, Third World states cannot obtain the advanced technology they desire from the Second World, so they look to the First World for the most modern items. In the area of arms purchases, however, Third World countries frequently buy or receive Soviet weapons as these weapons are relatively cheap and less sophisticated than the Western variety and thus are, to some extent, more suited to Third World conditions.

Some mention should be made of military limitations on First and Second World trade. As has been mentioned several times, the technological backwardness of Second World states poses a major problem. This back-wardness extends to weapons and weapons systems. In order to overcome Western superiority, all Communist states have exerted efforts to obtain know-how and hardware to bring their armed forces up to date. A major claim of the Soviet Union to superpower status is its military might. Clearly it is not in the interest of the West to sell outright advanced equipment, military hardware, atomic materials or information to the USSR or other Communist states—China is the only major exception. But what about dual-use materials? An imported jet engine may be installed in a passenger plane or in a fighter plane. An advanced computer can calculate equations for subatomic particles or atomic weapons. To prevent West–East strategic technology transfers, the Western World has established a Coordinating Committee (COCOM) to prevent militarily relevant technology from reach-ing Communist hands. The COCOM operates with a low budget and without much enforcement power, however. The Communist states have been able to circumvent much dual-use technology restrictions by purchases from COCOM states that do not agree with the Coordinating Committee about a specific piece of dual-use technology, from non-COCOM states, through third parties, or outright theft.[18]

A final major constraint on Communist World international trade with First and Third World countries is that it is unpredictable. It is possible to trade among Communist states based on bilateral or multilateral trade agreements because in each case the regime maintains a foreign trade monopoly. Trade monopoly is one of the hallmarks of a Communist political economy. The monopoly is exercised through government enterprises; it is illegal for private individuals to enter into foreign trade even if some internal private trade might be allowed in a specific country.

Intra-Second World trade can be integrated into the state plans for economic development. However, trade with First and most Third World countries is done not with monopolistic state enterprises but with the hundreds of thousands of large and small private enterprises. This trade is subject to all the vagaries of the free market, including boom and bust times, inflation, and currency exchange fluctuations. Despite great efforts to insulate their economies, the Communists find that their ability to sell goods, to barter goods, and to purchase in the world market is greatly affected by the economic health of the First World. The economic situation of the First

World has had very strong effect on the rest of the world. The cliche is that when the First World sneezes, the Second World catches a cold, and the Third World gets pneumonia. When the United States and its allies wish to show dissatisfaction with the internal and external policies of a Communist state, they can exert quite considerable pressure on the given state by economic means. In the case of the USSR,

> [T]he United States announced sanctions against the Soviet Union in the wake of its invasion of Afghanistan. In 1981, following the imposition of martial law in Poland, President Reagan announced suspension of Aeroflot service, the closing of the Soviet purchasing commission, postponement of negotiations on a new long-term grains agreement, suspension of negotiations on a maritime agreement and a new regime of port access. . . . He also expanded controls on exports to the Soviet Union of oil and gas equipment and technology and then suspended action on all license applications to sell either high-technology oil and gas equipment or technology to the U.S.S.R. . . . the President later decided to expand to subsidiaries and licensees abroad our sanctions on the export of oil and gas equipment and technology.[19]

Many of these sanctions were later lifted. In the case of Poland, when fishing rights, airline landing rights, freezing of credits, and other controls were imposed, the Polish regime itself claimed an exaggerated $10 billion loss. These restrictions were imposed because of the regime's declaration of martial law in December 1981, and the subsequent repression of the Solidarity labor union.[20]

Before looking at the domestic economies of Communist states some mention should be made concerning the ambivalent nature of their response to the Bretton Woods agreements of 1944 and United Nations activities in the international economy.

The Bretton Woods Conference, as has been mentioned, was held in July 1944 to bring some order to the international economy and to end the "beggar your neighbor" policies of the major economic powers. Out of this conference came the IMF, which was formed in 1945 and began functioning in 1947, and the IBRD (World Bank), established in December 1945. The headquarters of these two United Nations agencies are near each other in Washington, D.C., and their boards of directors are virtually identical. Though these institutions are open to all nations, most Communist countries do not belong and, as a group, are the largest bloc outside them.[21] The Communist states, especially the USSR, see the IMF and the World Bank as tools of the United States to support its economic dominance in the world; the location of their headquarters in Washington, D.C., certainly makes them suspect.

Table 11.2 Communist States' Participation in Western Economic Organizations

State	World bank	IMF	GATT
Afghanistan[a]	*	*	—
Albania	—	—	—
Bulgaria	—	—	—
China[b]	*	*	—
Cuba	—	—	*
Czechoslovakia	—	—	*
German Democratic Republic	—	—	—
Hungary	—	*	*
Kampuchea[a]	*	*	—
Korea (North)	—	—	—
Laos[a]	*	*	—
Mongolia	—	—	—
Poland	—	—	*
Romania	*	*	*
USSR	—	—	—
Vietnam[c]	*	*	—
Yugoslavia	*	*	*

Source: Henry W. Degenhardt, ed., *Treaties and Alliances of the World*, 3rd ed. (Detroit: Gale Research Co., 1981), pp. 50–54.
[a] Joined by predecessor of current Communist regime.
[b] Membership acquired by replacing Taiwan.
[c] Membership acquired by taking over the Republic of Vietnam.
* Indicates membership.
— Indicates nonmembership.

The GATT established under United Nations' auspices in 1947 and located in Geneva, Switzerland, is also suspect in that its role is to assist in reducing worldwide trade barriers. This assistance is seen as mainly supporting the Western countries and discriminating against the Communist states. Table 11.2 indicates the current status of each Communist state in regard to GATT, World Bank, and IMF.

DOMESTIC ECONOMIC ENVIRONMENT

Soviet economists are not loath to articulate some very bold statements:

> The World socialist economic system gains a victory over capitalism owing to its historical superiority.[22]

> Capitalism increasingly proves itself to be a society without a future. Theory

and practice of the world development visually confirm that the future belongs to Communism.[23]

What makes Communist economists so certain that their methods are correct? Basically, it comes from the belief that only Communist states are able to rationally organize an economic system, and economics is the decisive area for determining social and political structure. Although Communist states call themselves "Communist," they only claim that they are in the "socialist" phase of development. Full-scale Communism lies in the future.

The political economy of the type of socialism espoused by the 17 ruling Communist party states features socialist property, planned economic development, increased size and efficiency of production, technological progress, distribution of income to laborers according to their work, and contributions to social consumption funds.

Establishing socialist property is the first step to developing a socialist economy. As soon as a Communist party seizes power it moves to gain control of the means of production. This includes the *nationalization* (seizure by the state in the name of the people) of factories, power houses, mines, raw materials, natural resources, and the railroad system. Then, the means of transportation (buses, trams, airplanes), the economic control mechanisms (banks, insurance companies, clearing houses), and the utilities (gas, water, electricity, telephone) are put under state control. The purely Marxist idea of workers' control—as opposed to control by a state mechanism on behalf of the workers—has been little used with the exception of Yugoslavia's workers' self-management in factories. It is claimed that it no longer becomes possible for exploitation to take place in a system where the economic mechanism is controlled by the state, the state being the political expression of the workers. Thus, everyone is a co-owner of the productive system. Additionally, there exists cooperative property. This is property controlled by some of the people, for instance collective farms or collective fishing activities. Some Communist states (Poland, East Germany, China, Hungary) also allow some private property which is used by individuals to make an income (taxi cabs, small farms, small shops, small restaurants, and minor consumer manufacturing), but this is never allowed to threaten state control in any sector.

The state owns the economic system, which is to say, Communist party ownership prevails. The system is thus placed in a "command" structure. Charles Lindblom identifies a *command system* as an authoritarian one in which "the intellectual leaders [have produced] a comprehensive theory of social change that serves to guide the society."[24] Society is characterized by a "great concentration of political authority in the hands of one man or a

Vegetable growers harvest tomatoes and cucumbers in a greenhouse of the Sijiqing People's Commune near Beijing, China.

ruling committee . . . authority is less constrained by rules . . . less contrained by constitutionalism.'' Lindblom notes that ''leadership is committed to collective goals . . . rather than personal liberty . . . [and] government is near all-encompassing. . . . Government owns most productive assets . . . and government immediately and directly organizes the economy.'' Moreover, government ''reaches as well into the control of religion, all education, family, labor unions, all organizations, and details of personal behavior usually outside the scope of government.''[25] Government uses a ''full range of methods of control, including terror and indoctrination to the saturation point. It seeks to control the mind as far as possible by controlling all forms of communication.''[26]

  In order to accomplish these goals, the state mechanism becomes a huge bureaucracy that gathers information (state statistical bureau), formulates plans (state planning commission), and issues orders through the bureaucratic apparatus setting the production level for all types of goods to be produced. The Communist party sets the policy and oversees the state apparatus in its functioning.

Josif Stalin was the first to use these techniques on a broad scale. In 1928 he brought the Soviet Union out of the NEP period by means of massive centralization and bureaucratization of the Soviet economic system. This entailed not only a "militarization" of the economy (a "command" structure not unlike an army was established with the party's General Secretary in charge, and the Politburo, Central Committee, and Council of Ministers in the chain of command), but also a collectivization of agriculture (elimination of private farms). Included was a thorough cleansing ("purge") of social life so that only committed Communists and neutralized people remained. Stalin instituted the five-year system whereby giant steps in economic growth were planned and ordered. Those unable (and possibly unwilling) to fulfill the five-year plan were regarded as enemies of the people and were treated accordingly. Forced industrialization was the order of the day.

All ruling Communist party states use the Stalin-type Soviet system today. Planning is a central theme with 20-year or 10-year prospective plans, long-range plans on a 3 to 7 year basis, and the yearly plan on the immediate basis. Planners attempt to carefully calculate development and to fit the pieces together as a jigsaw puzzle. But, as Stanislaw Wellisz points out:

> Since the system of planning is rigid, the entire economy requires frequent overhauls. A weakness is tolerated as long as possible in order to avoid rearrangement of all the pieces. Finally, when the situation becomes unbearable, radical steps are taken to remedy it. Thus the economy proceeds by starts and jolts, with successive drives or campaigns to eliminate this or that mistake. At one time it may be excessive employment, at another it may be poor quality of product or lack of technical progress.[27]

It is presumed by Communist thinkers that the workers, freed of perceived exploitation in the capitalist system, would work together more harmoniously and efficiently, and because work was no longer oppressive, the productive capacities of collective labor would prove themselves. Technical progress also would be more rapid under socialism because of better working conditions and increased interest of the workers in their work. That this has not happened is well known in both East and West.

At various times ruling Communist parties have attempted to introduce "Communist" wage relations; that is, equal pay for everyone. In each case these attempts foundered. The general rule today is that workers are paid according to the value produced. There is a wage differential. The principle of equality, however, is partially maintained by diverting part of the general wage fund into the so-called social consumption funds used to provide benefits for all such as health care, education, libraries, children's camps, pensions, and so on.

To sum up, a Communist-type economic system

1. Is state owned.
2. Is highly centralized.
3. Is a command system.
4. Is state planned.
5. Receives policy direction from the Communist party.
6. Is supervised by the Communist party.
7. Maintains a foreign trade monopoly.
8. Pays workers according to value produced.
9. Diverts resources into social consumption funds.
10. Provides social benefits.
11. Maintains a large government bureaucratic apparatus, a massive defense establishment, and an enormous social control/security apparatus.

It should be added that the Soviet Union has the capacity to be nearly self-sufficient considering its manpower, natural resources, and technical capacity, if it could organize its system efficiently. The Soviet bloc countries are bound to the USSR by unbreakable economic and military ties and can be considered in this sense as part of the Soviet Union.[28] Communist China too has sufficient natural resources, but its population burden and technological backwardness, despite its growth in military technology (especially tactical and strategic atomic weapons systems), prevent it from becoming more self sufficient at this time.[29]

THE SUBSTRUCTURE: POLITICAL ECONOMIC VALUES

The official political, social, and economic values and features of a socialist Communist party-ruled state are fairly straightforward. Robert Wesson, in his *Communism and Communist Systems,* lists 23 characteristics, which include collectivism; the Communist party's right and duty to rule; and a centrally directed Stalinist economy with state control of raw materials, production, and distribution.[30]

However, there is a second level of political economic values, the unofficial ones. This is the so-called second economy. Insofar as second economy activities are system-supportive or neutral they are tolerated; activities in this gray area that are considered dysfunctional are repressed.

Tolerated activities are small-scale private transactions in selling of meat and vegetables bypassing official channels; repair of automobiles and other mechanized equipment in private garage–basement workshops; private painters, plumbers, and carpenters doing apartment repairs; and the like. These activities are system-supportive because they ease the daily life of citizens. Once, however, these activities begin to grow or to draw the attention of state supervisors, they are put to an end. Unfortunately, because of a general lack of building materials, spare parts, and consumer goods, second economy activities frequently involve diversion of state property to private use. Sometimes diversion of state materials and private use thereof for profit become quite substantial. In the USSR it is commonly believed that malfeasance in the neighborhood of 1 million rubles is equivalent to a death sentence upon conviction (most capital crimes are economic in the USSR).

In the area of the tolerated second economy are two activities known by the Russian words *blat* and *tolkach*. *Blat* is "the real lubricant of the ponderous economic machine."[31] It is a system of favor for favor: "you scratch my back, I'll scratch yours." It consists of reciprocal assistance in obtaining the required materials, permissions, and papers to carry out the economic plan. A *tolkach* is a person who acts as an expediter or pusher for an enterprise, one who extralegally moves raw materials and products through the system. Extra-legal exchange of raw materials and spare parts may be the only way for an enterprise to complete a project. These informal aspects of the economic system are not repressed "as long as [managers] are successful in fulfilling their plans."[32]

POLITICAL INSTITUTIONS AND PUBLIC POLICY RESPONSE

As mentioned in the beginning of Chapter 10, the political economy is the method of allocating economic benefits throughout the system. It determines the quality of life of different groups within the system.

Officially, the policy of Second World states is that of equality. They do note that in the "socialist" stage of development a differential in life rewards still exists. Only in full-scale Communism will true equality be possible. At this present stage, then, inequality exists and is officially recognized. The reasons for inequality can be found in differing levels of social awareness in the population and in the not-yet-fully-developed productive forces. As production is not yet sufficient to fulfill social needs, some way (whether formal or informal) is needed to distribute the social product.

The formal or official system is found in the distribution and consumption scheme established by the state (retail outlets and the transport system needed to supply these outlets), the pricing mechanism of the government, and the allocation of resources to social consumption funds. Communism's claims to the allegiance of people is based on its alleged fairness and justice in distributing goods and services. The Russian Revolution occurred, in part, because of special treatment received by the nobility, land and factory owners, and public officials in the Tsarist regime; the Chinese Revolution because of oppressions by landowners; the Vietnamese Revolution because of unfairness of "colonial oppressors" and their "puppets." Certainly, Communist systems *do* provide a more equitable and generous distribution of values than did their predecessor regimes in countries (Russia, China, Cuba, Yugoslavia, Albania, Mongolia, Vietnam) where the revolution was indigenous and directed against domestic enemies. It is a matter of opinion, though, in countries where Communism was imposed by outside force, whether the populations are necessarily better off than under previous regimes. In their constitutions, the citizens of Communist party states are guaranteed a number of social and economic rights such as the right to work (guaranteed employment), right to rest and leisure, health protection, old-age and disability pensions, housing, education, and cultural benefits.[33]

The full-employment economy is a great claim of Communism (though China and Yugoslavia admit problems in this area); indeed everyone receives some kind of work. Provisions are made for resorts and travel and vacation time for workers. Health protection is available without direct payment for the majority of the population. Old-age and disability pensions are available, though never enough to cover all the needs of the aged and disabled, a problem also common to First World countries. Housing continues to be a problem in all Communist states and assignment to living "space" (not necessarily a self-contained apartment) may take 10 to 15 years from date of application, although some sort of space is available for everyone. Education is generally through the tenth-grade level, but higher education in not easily accessible and places are not always fairly distributed. Party members' children usually are given the first choice. Culture is heavily subsidized by the state; theater, music, dance, and other arts are considered valuable as long as what is produced "supports Communism."

The problem, however, lies in the amount and quality of social-economic benefits that are available. All of these values are in short supply and the best-quality benefits are especially sought after. It is not necessarily a question of money; for example, access to a high-quality Black Sea resort in the USSR cannot be gained by cash. Rather one needs "permission" from some authority to be admitted. In order to obtain adequate housing in a reasonable time, one needs some method of cutting in front of the line of waiting people. Who gets what? Who has access to the values first?

The important members of the various Communist parties clearly have first access to values. This is justified because inequality still exists in the

People wait in two lines for their ration outside a meat shop in Warsaw, Poland.

socialist stage, and because the Communist party is the leading and guiding force of society, so it only makes sense to allow top Communists to have first access to housing, health care, schooling, and so on. This is not to say that all Communists have special access; only top controlling personnel of the party can claim these privileges. The party retains for itself the right of *nomenklatura,* a Russian term meaning that certain designated positions throughout the economic, social, military, and political structure can only be filled by people cleared by the Communist party leadership. In the USSR, for example, some of the power of *nomenklatura* resides in the Communist party of the Soviet Union's central Secretariat's Department of Party and Organizational Work: "appointments within the apparatus itself . . . must be cleared in advance by this department," and "the Department processes appointments in the [Communist Youth League] and in the Trade Unions."[34] Other central party departments control appointments in other areas.

This *nomenklatura* system is one of the mechanisms of retaining party control in all Communist states. It sets up, perhaps unintentionally, a system of trading favors among party members ("If you get me that desirable position I will reward you with first access to the values I control"). Others with privileged access to values are people whose main work lies outside the party apparatus itself but who are party members. These include career military officers, members of the security apparatus, managers and planners of the economic system, and government officials.

The only people who have privileged access without being at least peripherally attached to the party are highly qualified scientists—who are encouraged to produce by material benefits—and cultural figures (ballet dancers, singers, film stars, artists, athletes, and even Russian chess players or Chinese ping-pong players) who bring international renown to their state and the Communist system.

Thus, the scramble for values, referred to as the "rat race" in the West, occurs in Communist systems with greater intensity because the pool of values is smaller, although the situation certainly is not as critical as in the Third World, where simple physical survival may be at stake.

NOTES

1. M. C. Howard and J. E. King, *The Political Economy of Marx* (Thetford, England: Longman, 1975), p. vii.
2. Ibid.
3. See, for example, Irving M. Zeitlin, *Capitalism and Imperialism: An Introduction to Neo-Marxian Concepts* (Chicago: Markham, 1972).
4. Edward N. Luttwak, *The Grand Strategy of the Soviet Union* (New York: St. Martin's Press, 1983), pp. 119–120.
5. L. Leontyev, *A Short Course of Political Economy* (Moscow: Progress Publishers, 1968), p. 7.
6. Ibid., p. 9.
7. Ibid., p. 186.
8. John G. Gurley, *Challengers to Capitalism: Marx, Lenin, Stalin, and Mao*, 2d ed., (New York: Norton, 1975), p. 3.
9. See G. A. Deborin *et al.*, *Socialism's Historic Mission and the World Today* (Moscow: Progress Publishers, 1978).
10. John M. Carfora and Joseph A. Parker, "The Soviet Model of Democracy and Development: Paradigm for Progress or Persecution?" paper delivered at the sixth annual Third World Studies Conference, October 1983, University of Nebraska, Omaha.
11. Adam B. Ulam, *A History of Soviet Russia* (New York: Praeger, 1976), pp. 17–18.
12. George Vernadsky, *A History of Russia* (New York: New Home Library, 1944), p. 285.
13. Ibid., p. 292.
14. Adam B. Ulam, *Expansion and Coexistence: The History of Soviet Foreign Policy, 1917–1967* (New York: Praeger, 1968), p. 133.
15. Richard F. Staar, *The Communist Regimes in Eastern Europe*, 4th ed. (Stanford, Calif.: Hoover Institution Press, 1982), p. 300.
16. Ibid., p. 301.
17. Ibid., pp. 320–322.
18. Richard N. Perle, "The Strategic Implications of West-East Technology Transfer," *Adelphi Papers* part II, no. 190 (Summer 1984): 20–27.

19. W. Allen Wallis, "Review of East-West Economic Relations," *Current Policy* [U.S. Department of State], no. 567 (March 29, 1984): 2.
20. Ibid.
21. "International Monetary Fund," *Deadline Data on World Affairs,* December, 1983, pp. 1–5.
22. A. M. Rumyantsev *et al., Political Economy* (Moscow: Progress Publishers, 1983), p. 666.
23. Ibid., p. 668.
24. Charles E. Lindblom, *Politics and Markets: The World's Political-Economic Systems* (New York: Basic Books, 1977), p. 249.
25. Ibid., pp. 238–239.
26. Ibid., p. 239.
27. Stanislaw Wellisz, *The Economies of the Soviet Bloc: A Study of Decision Making and Resource Allocation* (New York: McGraw Hill, 1964), p. 233.
28. See I. P. Gerasimov *et al., Natural Resources of the Soviet Union* (San Francisco: Freeman, 1971).
29. See Jonathan D. Pollack, "China's Role in Pacific Basin Security," *Survival* (July/August 1984): 164–173.
30. Robert G. Wesson, *Communism and Communist Systems* (Englewood Cliffs, N.J.: Prentice-Hall, 1978), pp. 217–218.
31. Kenneth R. Whiting, *The Soviet Union Today: A Concise Handbook* (New York: Praeger, 1966), p. 205.
32. Ibid.
33. See the *1977 Soviet Constitution,* any edition, Articles 40–46.
34. Darrell P. Hammer, *U.S.S.R.: The Politics of Oligarchy* (Hinsdale, Ill.: Dryden Press, 1974), p. 199.

CHAPTER 12

Political Process and Economic Outcomes: The Third World

The availability of life chances in the Third World is far more limited than in the First World and in some cases in the Second World. The primary concern of the Third World countries is to increase economic opportunities. In general, the quality of life receives less attention in the Third World than in the other two worlds.

The economies of the Third World countries are often dependent on those of the First World countries, especially in the areas of trade, investment, and technology. Third World countries demand a restructuring of the international economic system to reduce such dependence and to improve their economies.

Third World countries' share of production of goods and services of the entire world is quite low. The domestic economic environment in most Third World countries has been an impediment to increased production. Some Third World countries do possess important natural resources; however, they are dependent on Western technology for extraction or utilization of these resources. Substantial scientific and technological progress has occurred in only a few Third World countries. Infrastructures are also poorly developed in most Third World countries.

Social and religious divisions in the Third World are more pronounced than in the other two worlds. Many Third World countries have authoritarian governments. Economic development in several Third World countries has been sought by combining private and public enterprise. Religion, especially the resurgence of Islam, and the values of elites and masses add further dimensions to the politics and economics of the countries in the Third World.

Policy outcomes in the Third World indicate a persistent inequality in the areas of wealth, housing, and education. Only a few Third World countries have made significant economic gains. Most are struggling to provide the basic necessities of life for the masses.

The availability of life chances in the less-developed economic systems of the Third World is far more limited than in the developed economic systems of the First World and in some cases of the Second World. Because the allocation of life chances is influenced by the political process, inequities exist throughout the world, but they are more severe in the Third World. The extremes of opulence and abject poverty of most Third World countries are virtually nonexistent in the Second and Third Worlds. Of course, in some oil-rich countries of the Middle East, economic opportunities have expanded for the masses and the lot of even the very poor has improved to some extent. The elites in these countries have brought more opportunities to the masses without any adverse effect on their own wealth and status. In a few Third World countries, notably South Korea, Singapore, and Taiwan, which have experienced significant industrial growth, the number of people enjoying economic opportunities has risen substantially. In some other countries, such as Argentina, Brazil, India, Malaysia, Pakistan, and Venezuela, which have experienced somewhat less rapid growth, the number of people enjoying such opportunities has also increased. In most other Third World countries, a limited number of elites continue to enjoy life chances, while the masses lead lives of deprivation.

Third World countries are much more concerned with the availability of basic economic opportunities than with more sophisticated quality of life issues, such as environmental protection, privacy, and increased chances for personal expression (see Chapter 10). The availability of these values is determined by external as well as internal factors (discussed as social facts in Chapter 10). Several problems that beset the Third World countries affect life chances. Population in the Third World, particularly in Africa and Latin America, is increasing at a much faster rate than in the First or Second World. Population increase, combined with slow economic growth in most of these countries, adversely affects the availability of life chances. Very few countries in the world have homogeneous populations, but the heterogeneity of the populations in many Third World countries is more pronounced than in the First or Second World. The internal divisions in the former are along several dimensions such as race, religion, region, language, tribe, and caste. In several cases these differences have led to the outbreak of violence, including civil war. Such outbursts have a further negative impact on the economic opportunities available to the people of a country. Another serious problem related to life chances faced by the Third World countries is the fatalistic attitude of the masses and the acceptance of life as it is. The values of personal achievement and optimism are uncommon among the masses of Third World countries, with the result that the desire to increase life chances lacks any intensity.

Ethiopian victims of starvation.

INTERNATIONAL OPPORTUNITIES AND CONSTRAINTS

As indicated, a few Third World countries have made substantial gains in their living standards by industrialization or oil revenues, yet a vast majority find the related goals of economic development and increase in life chances for the masses rather elusive. In Table 12.1 the growth of gross domestic product (GDP) in the less-developed countries, 1960 to 1990 is shown.[1] The growth of GDP in the African countries is the lowest and is projected to be between 2 and 3%. Although growth rates of 4 and 5% or higher have occurred in some parts of the Third World, population increase has substantially reduced any real gains in living standards. Besides, the base for computing the growth rates of GDP is rather low in the Third World, so even an apparently high growth rate does not amount to a great deal.

The economies of the Third World countries are inextricably linked to those of the First World countries. Any fluctuations in the economies of the latter affect the economies of the former. According to a recent World Bank report, "developing countries are directly affected by fluctuations in the industrial world. Overall their growth rates have been higher, but even those that have grown fastest have not been able to avoid the cyclical influence of industrial countries (of the West)."[2] Figure 12.1 indicates the linkage of GDP growth rates of the Third World countries to those of the First World.

It is often argued that the linkage of the economies of the Third World

Table 12.1   Growth of GDP in Developing Countries (Average Annual Percentage Change)

Country group	1960–70	1970–80	Gross Domestic Product 1980–90 High	Low
All developing countries	5.9	5.1	5.7	4.5
Oil importers[a]	5.7	5.1	5.4	4.1
Low-income[b]	4.2	3.0	4.1	3.0
Sub-Saharan Africa	4.0	2.4	3.0	1.9
Asia	4.3	3.2	4.4	3.2
Middle-income[c]	6.2	5.6	5.6	4.3
East Asia and Pacific	7.9	8.2	8.1	6.4
Latin America and Caribbean	5.3	6.0	5.6	4.6
Africa	4.1	4.9	4.1	3.2
Sub-Saharan Africa	4.1	3.5	3.1	2.8
Oil exporters[d]	6.5	5.2	6.5	5.4

Source: World Bank, *World Development Report 1982* (New York: Oxford University Press, 1982).
[a] All the developing countries not classified as oil exporters are included in this category.
[b] 1980 GNP per person of $410 or less.
[c] 1980 GNP per person above $410.
[d] Algeria, Angola, Bahrain, Brunei, Congo, Ecuador, Egypt, Gabon, Indonesia, Iran, Iraq, Malaysia, Mexico, Nigeria, Oman, Peru, Syria, Trinidad and Tobago, Tunisia, and Venezuela. The World Bank considers Kuwait, Libya, Qatar, Saudi Arabia, and the United Arab Emirates "high-income oil exporters" (1980 GNP per capita in this group ranges between $8640 [Libya] and $26,850 [United Arab Emirates]) and does not include them in the list of developing countries.

countries to those of the First World countries is in fact dependence of the former on the latter. Dependence (or *dependencia*) theory was very popular in the 1970s and is still accepted by some scholars. It is said that the African and Asian countries continue to depend on their former colonial masters for trade and aid, and that the Latin American countries have a similar relationship with the United States. It is also asserted that the Third World countries still supply raw materials to the First World countries and buy finished products from them. Furthermore, it is on the developed countries of the West and the international organizations such as the World Bank controlled by them that the Third World countries must depend for investment capital. An equally serious form of dependence is technological. Indeed, Third World countries depend on the First World for most of the research in technical areas. Even the research for high-yield strains of wheat

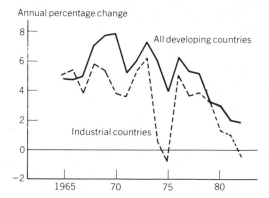

Figure 12.1. Gross domestic product growth rates, 1965–1982. (World Bank, *World Development Report 1983* [New York: Oxford University Press, 1983]).

and rice, which led to the so-called Green Revolution (dramatic increase in food production) in several Third World countries, was conducted in the First World. Lack of resources is an obvious impediment to technological research in the Third World. In many cases research done in the affluent West is of little use to the poor countries of the Third World. As Hans Singer and Jared Ansari write:

> The problems of the poor countries, however, are not the same [as those of the richer countries]; for instance, they need research to design simple products, to develop production for smaller markets, to improve the quality of and to develop new uses for tropical products, and above all to develop production processes which utilize their abundant labor. Instead, [in richer countries] emphasis is placed on sophisticated weaponry, space research, atomic research, sophisticated products, production for large high-income markets, and specifically a constant search for processes which save labor by substituting capital or high-order skills.[3]

It is also true that the Third World countries continue to depend on the First and Second Worlds for investment capital. Loans are taken from governments (governments also provide grants) and international agencies, and from private sources (in the First World). The increase in private lending ''rose at an average rate of 22 percent a year in 1970–80 and provided about half of total medium- and long-term capital flows [to the less-developed countries] during the period.''[4] Aid from oil-rich countries of the Middle East is another source of investment capital. As a result of borrowing from various sources, the debts of the Third World countries have been mounting and the dependence of the Third World countries in this area is not only on the First World and private banks, but also on the Second World, especially

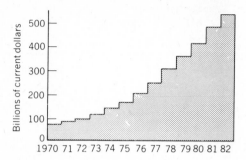

Figure 12.2. Debt (total medium- and long-term, disbursed and outstanding) of all developing countries, 1970–1982. (World Bank, *World Development Report 1983* [New York: Oxford University Press, 1983]).

the Soviet Union, and on some Middle Eastern countries. Figure 12.2 indicates the continuously increasing debts of all developing countries in the period 1970 to 1982. In Table 12.2 foreign debts of five Latin American countries are given to show how rapidly these debts are increasing, at least in some cases. The creditors, especially in the First World, have had no choice but to reschedule loan payments. (Defaulting countries cannot be repossessed!) Even some bankers are now advocating rescheduling of loan payments for the Third World countries.[5]

For a majority of Third World countries trade dependence on the West continues in the form of exports of raw materials and imports of manufactured goods. The exports of many Third World countries usually consist of one primary commodity. Some examples of such countries and their one-commodity exports are: Burundi and Colombia (coffee), Ghana (cocoa), Mauritius (sugar), and Zambia (copper).[6] On the other hand, Third World countries have become important exporters of manufactured goods and fuel (e.g., the oil-rich countries). Overall, the proportion of agricultural commodities in the exports of the Third World countries has declined substantially. This led the World Bank to remark that "developing countries can no longer be caricatured as exporters of primary products and importers of manufactures."[7] The largest exporters of manufactured goods in the Third World are Brazil, South Korea, Singapore, and Taiwan. Others, such as Argentina, Hong Kong (still a British colony), India, and Malaysia, also have a significant share of the manufactured goods exported. These countries export manufactured goods to the developed as well as to the less-developed countries. As one study notes, "the South has its North."[8] (The terms "North" and "South" are often used to denote developed countries and less-developed countries, respectively.) In Table 12.3 the value of manufactured exports from some developing countries to the LDCs in 1973, 1978, 1979, and 1980 are given. All these exporters are from Asia or Latin

Table 12.2 Total Foreign Debts of Selected Latin American Countries (in Billions of U.S. Dollars)

Country	1977	1983[a]
Argentina	11.9	38.5
Brazil	42.5	94.4
Chile	8.2	19.1
Mexico	40.8	90.6
Venezuela	9.1	31.5

Sources: World Bank, *World Tables* (Baltimore: Johns Hopkins University Press, 1980); and *Time*, September 19, 1983, p. 69 (the source of *Time* estimates was Morgan Guaranty Trust).
[a] The figures for 1983 are estimates at year end.

America, not from Africa or the Middle East. Although the Middle East has its share of oil exports, Africa's trade volume is very low. "Africa's trade amounts to a mere three percent of the South's industrial trade."[9] The poor growth rate of the GDP in the African countries is reflected in their share of the trade of the Third World. Moreover, there are some significant differences between the manufactured exports from the Third World to other Third World countries and the exports of the Third World to the developed countries. Equipment, chemicals, and steel products are major components of the former, whereas clothes and other consumer goods are predominant in the latter.[10]

On the whole, the economic progress and the availability of life chances in the Third World lag far behind the developed countries, especially the

Table 12.3 Manufactured Exports from Some Developing Countries to Other Less-Developed Countries (in Billions of U.S. Dollars)

Country	1973	1978	1979	1980
Korea	0.33	2.80	3.56	4.86
Taiwan	0.72	2.17	3.50	4.70
Singapore	0.73	2.33	3.39	4.52
Brazil	0.43	1.85	2.71	3.92
Hong Kong	0.55	1.45	1.79	2.46
India	0.41	1.23	1.50	1.70
Argentina	0.42	0.89	1.25	1.32
Mexico	0.21	0.53	0.75	1.20
Malaysia	0.15	0.47	0.69	—
Pakistan	0.25	0.31	0.35	0.47
Thailand	0.12	0.29	0.45	—
Colombia	0.11	0.32	0.33	—

Source: Ramses: Annual Report of the French Institute for International Relations, The State of the World Economy (Cambridge, Mass.: Ballinger 1982). Reprinted with permission.

West. The Third World countries' desire for economic development and increased life chances, combined with frustrations in achieving them, have contributed to the demands for a new international economic order (NIEO). The demands for NIEO were first voiced at the United Nations Conference on Trade and Development held in Geneva, Switzerland, in 1964. It was at that conference that the Third World states formed the Group of 77, still known as such in spite of increase in its membership to well over 100 countries. The Group of 77 has been exerting pressure on the First World to restructure the world's economic order. In order to establish NIEO, the Third World countries demand a redistribution of the world's wealth by means of foreign aid and trade concessions (such as higher prices for their commodity exports and lower tariffs on their manufactured goods exports) from the affluent, especially Western, countries. Demands are also made for an augmented role in the decision-making processes of the international lending agencies such as the World Bank and the International Monetary Fund and for a greater control over the subsidiaries of the multinational corporations operating in the Third World.

DOMESTIC ECONOMIC ENVIRONMENT

Internal social facts (discussed in Chapter 10) are the domestic determinants of a country's political economy and life chances. A country's resources, technology, infrastructure, social and political institutions, and political culture are the major determinants in this respect. Technology can be considered a resource as well as a part of the infrastructure.

Natural Resources

The countries of the Third World produce a relatively small proportion of the world's goods and services for meeting the needs of their citizens. One expert estimates that "the LDCs [less-developed countries] with over 70 percent of the world's population, produce about 20 percent of the world's goods and services."[11] Domestic determinants as well as external factors, as discussed earlier, are responsible for such low productivity. A country's resources are the lifeline of such determinants, both external and internal.

Several Third World countries possess important natural resources. Indonesia and Malaysia are the primary sources of world's natural rubber; Brazil and Gabon produce a major proportion of the world's manganese; and Bolivia, Malaysia, and Thailand possess large supplies of tin. It is the Third World countries that have the lion's share of the world's oil. The Middle East alone possesses well over half of the world's known oil reserves.[12] The major producers of oil in the Middle East are Algeria, Iran, Iraq, Kuwait,

Press conference before the opening of OPEC meeting in Helsinki, Finland during July, 1983.

Libya, Qatar, Saudi Arabia, and United Arab Emirates. All of these countries are members of OPEC. The non–Middle Eastern members of OPEC are Gabon and Nigeria in Africa, Indonesia in Asia, and Ecuador and Venezuela in Latin America. Although not an OPEC member, Mexico has one of the largest proven oil reserves and is among the major suppliers of oil to the world. Argentina, Brunei, Egypt, India, Malaysia, Oman, and Trinidad are also significant producers of oil.[13]

Third World countries are major producers of natural gas and uranium, a valuable resource for nuclear energy. Africa and the Middle East have 30% of the world's potential gas reserves.[14] Algeria, Iran, Nigeria, Qatar, and Saudi Arabia are among the top 12 countries in world's proven gas reserves.[15] Mexico and Venezuela are also in this group of 12 countries. Among the major natural gas producers in the Third World are Argentina, Indonesia, Iraq, Kuwait, Libya, and United Arab Emirates. Africa and Latin America have some of the richest sources of the world's uranium. Argentina, Brazil, Gabon, Namibia, Niger, and Zaire are among the largest producers of uranium in the world.[16]

Coal is the only major energy source that the Third World countries lack. Coal reserves are mostly located in the northern hemisphere in the First and the Second Worlds. Although dozens of countries all over the world produce some amounts of coal, ten countries possess over 90% of world coal reserves.[17] Of these ten countries only one—India—is in the Third World; the other nine are in the First and Second Worlds. Some Third World countries have harnessed hydropower for energy. Most other forms of energy (such as solar or geothermal) which require sophisticated technology are largely confined to the First and Second Worlds.

Technology

Only a few Third World countries, notably Argentina, Brazil, India, South Korea and Taiwan, have made substantial progress in science and technology. The fields of science and technology continue to be dominated by North America, Europe, and the Soviet Union. As Figure 12.3 reveals, Asia is the only region in the Third World with a significant proportion of the world's scientists and engineers and of the world's research and development expenditure. In general, Africa presents a bleak picture in science research and technology, although, the scientific resources of Egypt, Kenya, Libya, Nigeria, and Zambia are substantially greater than those of others in Africa.[18] There are also sizable variations in the amounts of research and development expenditures in the African countries. One scholar questions the accuracy of the UNESCO expenditure figures for Africa on the ground that "only a few countries, Nigeria, Kenya, and Senegal, for example, identify [research and development] expenditure as a separate item in their budgets."[19] According to this scholar, "many countries include expenditures for research and development within broad sectoral categories— agriculture, health, transportation—and the actual expenditures may be in reality higher than indicated."[20] The UNESCO expenditure figures may not be entirely accurate, but the backwardness of Africa in science and technology is a generally accepted fact. Some studies, for example, have pointed out that in the Third World the published contributions of the African scientists lag far behind those of their peers in Asia, the Middle East, and Latin America.[21] Notwithstanding impressive strides by some of the Third World countries, the First and the Second World countries are far ahead in science and technology. The result is that the former often find themselves dependent on the latter.

An important question facing the Third World countries is the choice of appropriate technology suitable to the environment of abundant labor and inadequate capital. The obvious temptation is to adopt technologies that use small amounts of capital and large amounts of labor. Labor-intensive technologies are quite popular in the Third World. After studying the textile and pulp and paper industries in four countries—Colombia, Brazil, Indonesia, and the Philippines—Michael Amsalem concludes that "the potential

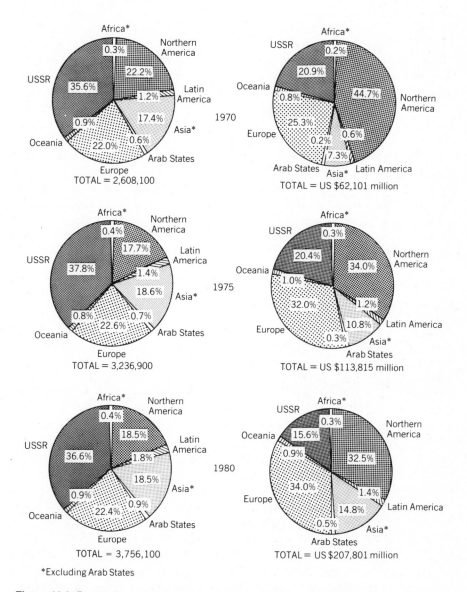

Africa*
Northern America
USSR
Latin America
Oceania
Asia*
Europe
Arab States
1970
TOTAL = 2,608,100
TOTAL = US $62,101 million

1975
TOTAL = 3,236,900
TOTAL = US $113,815 million

1980
TOTAL = 3,756,100
TOTAL = US $207,801 million

*Excluding Arab States

Figure 12.3. Research and development scientists and engineers and expenditures. (*UNESCO Statistical Yearbook 1983* [Paris: UNESCO, 1983]).

rewards from choosing adapted technologies are important: a potential for more rapid economic development and for increased employment and a heightened ability to compete in world markets."[22] Any technology adapted to the environment of a Third World country would have to emphasize employment as well as productivity.

Whatever adapted technologies the Third World countries use, projections of their economic development are not optimistic. Not only would they continue to depend on the First and Second Worlds for technology, they would also need help in meeting the most basic life need—feeding themselves. Food deficits in some of the major countries in the Third World are expected to increase substantially.[23] A majority of the Third World countries will continue to experience food deficits. According to one authoritative study, "the total deficit of staple food crops in the non-Communist LDCs in 1990 will be about 120 to 140 million tons. This deficit would be made up of 40 percent in Asia, 25 percent in North Africa and the Middle East, over 20 percent in Sub-Saharan Africa, and over 10 percent in Latin America."[24] These deficits will have to be met by imports and food aid from the First World countries. That would drain the foreign reserves of the Third World countries and continue their dependence on the First World.

Capital Resources

Along with natural resources (or raw materials) and technology, capital is needed for economic development. Third World countries' major sources of capital are savings, export earnings, remittances of citizens who work abroad, foreign aid, commercial debts, and private investment. Except in sub-Sahara African countries, savings in the Third World are over 20% of the countries' GDP and are not expected to decrease during the next decade.[25] The export earnings of several Third World countries are substantial and have increased significantly during the last decade. However, these earnings are not adequate for the rising oil prices and the import of capital goods and food from the First World. The workers' remittances, especially from those working in the Persian Gulf countries, have increased severalfold for some countries. For example, in Benin, Bangladesh, Egypt, India, Mali, Morocco, Pakistan, Sudan, Tunisia, Turkey, and Upper Volta, workers' remittances constitute well over 10% of the value of their exports.[26] The sources of foreign aid for development are the Western nations and Japan, OPEC, and the Communist countries, particularly the Soviet Union. The first group of countries provides the bulk of aid to the Third World; countries in OPEC contribute about 25% of such aid and the Communist countries give approximately 6%.[27] Despite misgivings about aid, it appears that the Western countries will continue to advance aid to the Third World countries at somewhat higher levels.[28] The prospects of commercial loans and private investment are less encouraging because of the growing debts and the political instability of the Third World countries.

Infrastructure

Less developed infrastructures are also responsible for the inadequate availability of life chances in the Third World. Not only are the means of transportation and communication underdeveloped in the Third World countries, the facilities for processing and marketing of products are poor too. In this area, black Africa presents the bleakest picture in the Third World. The African countries are basically agricultural, but they have done little to develop the infrastructure to promote agriculture. Some African countries have embarked on impressive projects to increase productivity in agriculture; however, the infrastructural foundation to support these projects is missing. Appeasement of urban elites, on whose support a majority of the African governments depend, is a primary concern of African governments. The result is that the creation of jobs for the elites in the public sector is given a higher priority than the establishment of a sound infrastructure for agriculture.[29]

The countries in Asia, the Middle East, and Latin America have made greater efforts to develop their infrastructures. Oil-rich countries, especially in the Persian Gulf region, have allocated some of their oil revenues to the development of transportation and communication systems. Some, notably Saudi Arabia, are also increasing their technical personnel by opening engineering colleges. The new industrializing countries of Asia and Latin America—Argentina, Brazil, India, South Korea, Singapore, and Taiwan—have made ingenious attempts to improve their infrastructures. In addition to investment in the means of transportation and communication, these countries have spent money on research and on developing new methods of processing and marketing of goods. For example, the Green Revolution in the state of Punjab, India, which doubled wheat production in this state in less than ten years (the Green Revolution in Punjab began in the mid-1960s), was made possible by the government's emphasis on infrastructure, particularly roads, irrigation, rural electrification, marketing, and research.[30] India also achieved somewhat of a revolution in milk production and distribution in the 1970s through the establishment of dairy cooperatives.[31] These cooperatives are owned by the private milk producers, mostly small farmers, and "form an integrated system for marketing and processing."[32] Another such success story is that of Brazilian soybeans. "Before 1960 production was insignificant, but by the end of 1970s soybeans surpassed coffee as the principal Brazilian crop in value, covered 17 percent of the cropped area, and constituted 14 percent of world soybean output."[33] The World Bank considers research "a critical factor" in the dramatic increase in Brazil's soybean production.[34]

INSTITUTIONS AND POLITICAL ECONOMIC VALUES

As pointed out earlier in this chapter, social and religious divisions are more pronounced in Third World countries. These divisions contribute to the instability of political institutions and threaten the availability of life chances. In many cases the different religious and social groups function as interest groups. However, most such interest groups are poorly organized and do not have a significant impact on public policy. As a large number of Third World countries have authoritarian governments, interest groups are not expected to exert much influence on them. Even in the democratic countries of the Third World the influence of such groups on the public policy is not substantial.

In Chapter 7 a variety of government structures in the Third World were considered. These government structures and political institutions in the Third World, the ideologies of the elites, and the values of the masses are among important determinants of life chances. Although authoritarian government structures are predominant in the Third World, a study on Latin America claims that "the wave of authoritarianism has spent its force and is receding."[35] David Becker, the author of this study, states:

> In Colombia, Costa Rica, Mexico, and Venezuela, capitalist democracy has functioned continously for ten or more years. In Argentina, Brazil, the Dominican Republic, Panama, and Peru, processes of transition from authoritarianism to capitalist democracy are underway or have recently been completed. In Chile and Uruguay [Uruguay became democratic in late 1984], military authoritarianism persists but is under increasing challenge from a wide spectrum of forces, including many members of the bourgeoisie and middle class. In El Salvador [El Salvador held elections in 1984 for the presidency], Guatemala, Haiti, and Paraguay, capitalist authoritarianism of the traditional, antidevelopmental oligarchic type remains. In Cuba and Nicaragua, nationalist-popular rebellions have led to the implantation of authoritarian socialism (not yet consolidated in the latter). And in Bolivia, Ecuador, and Honduras, fragile and unstable capitalist democracies rest uneasily on largely backward socio-economic underpinnings.[36]

The predominant economic system adopted by the Latin American countries has been private enterprise. Becker points out that "Latin American capitalism has not previously been hospitable to democracy."[37] A recent form of authoritarianism that emerged in Latin America has been called "bureaucratic authoritarianism" by Guillermo O'Donnell.[38] O'Donnell considered Argentina and Brazil the "modal type" of bureaucratic authoritarianism.[39] In bureaucratic authoritarian government the military rules with the help of civilian technocrats. These governments achieve modernization, but pay little attention to equality or political participation by the masses.

In several Latin American countries, authoritarian rule has been challenged and is being replaced by government by election; in Africa the trend appears to be quite the opposite. Nigeria, the most populous and one of the richest West African countries, resumed a military government in early 1984 after a four-year experiment with democracy. Ghana, another important country in West Africa, followed a similar course. In several African countries, democracy has become almost an endangered species.[40] Rule by the military or by one party is the predominant form of government in Africa.

An important factor in the political economy of a country is the ideology that its elite groups espouse and the impact of such ideology on public policy. In a study of African countries, Crawford Young has shed some light on this question.[41] Based primarily on "the ideological self-ascription of a regime's leadership," Young classifies African governments in three groups:

> The first set of regimes is distinguished by an official, explicit declaration for Marxism–Leninism as state ideology. The second group consists of states that espouse a socialist orientation but that either do not stress or expressly reject Marxism. The third cluster consists of regimes that pursue a market-economy, or capitalist policy though they generally deny any ideological attachment at all; "pragmatism," it is said, is their only creed.[42]

He considers the third group as the most numerous, consisting of about one-half of the total number of African countries and views the Ivory Coast, Kenya, and Nigeria as exemplary states in this group. Angola, Benin, Congo, Ethiopia, Madagascar, Mozambique, São Tomé and Príncipe, and Somalia are placed in the category of the Afro-Marxist countries and Algeria, Egypt, Ghana, Guinea, Mali, and Tanzania are classified as the populist socialist countries.[43] Regarding the impact of ideology on public policy, when a commonly used measure, real per capita GNP growth, is considered, the performance of the African capitalist group is the best, followed by the populist socialist group, and then the Afro-Marxist group.[44]

Some countries in Asia, the Middle East, and Latin America can also be considered populist socialist or capitalist states. Burma, Iraq, Peru (1968–1975), Sri Lanka (until late 1970s), and Yemen can be placed in the former category and Brazil, South Korea, Malaysia, Mexico, and Taiwan, in

Itaipu, the world's largest dam, on the Parana River between Brazil and Paraguay.

the latter.[45] The economic performance in the capitalist states has been better than in the populist socialist states.

By classifying countries as Marxist–Leninist (Afro-Marxist), populist socialist, and capitalist, it is not suggested that any of these countries has a command or a market economy in the strict sense. As explained in Chapter 10, most economic systems are combinations of these two economies, with leanings toward one or the other. Examples from two countries—Brazil and India—illustrate the combination of market and command economies. Although Brazil is considered a capitalist state, the success of some of its projects is built on mixed state–private enterprise. An annual report of the World Bank states: "Brazil's manufactured exports grew at 19.5 percent a year between 1965 and 1981. . . . The example of aircraft exports is typical. . . . The drive for export market began in 1969 with the formation of Embraer, a mixed State-private enterprise."[46] India, on the other hand, has a socialist-oriented economy, but it is the combination of public and private enterprise that is responsible for its Green Revolution. The example of Indian seed industry is pertinent here. According to the World Bank, "since its infancy two decades ago, the (seed) industry has grown enormously. It now comprises one national corporation, a dozen stateowned seed corporations, and some 300 private companies."[47]

Third World countries have sought economic development not only by a combination of public and private enterprise, but also by major institutional changes, particularly in the civil service. With new and diverse economic enterprises in which the government is an active participant by virtue of ownership or regulation, it becomes essential to train civil servants suitable for these enterprises. Countries such as Brazil and India have developed ambitious plans for training civil servants for economic development programs. The impetus for civil service reform in the Third World has come from two other, not entirely unrelated, sources—the end of colonial rule and military coups. The end of colonial rule necessitated the training of indigenous civil servants. "Africanization of civil service" has worked as a political slogan for winning the support of the urban elites for governments in African countries; it has also been necessary in order to replace foreign civil servants of the former colonial power. Military leaders in the Third World seek an efficient civil service in order to solidify their power. Countries as diverse as Chile, Ghana, Indonesia, Mali, and the Philippines have attempted major civil service reforms under military governments.[48] As in the cases of Argentina, Brazil, and South Korea, authoritarian bureaucratic regimes achieved modernization with the help of technocrats.

A recent development—the resurgence of Islam—has added another dimension to the politics and economics of the Moslem countries in the Middle East and South Asia. The resurgence of Islam, spearheaded by fervent religious leaders, seeks a radical change in the values of the people as well as in the institutions of a country. Although the economic systems of the Islamic countries continue to combine market and command economies, forces of religion are demanding a substantial, in some cases a virtually complete, restructuring of the society. Religion in these countries has become a combined social, political, and economic force. Both Western materialism and Marxism are rejected by the radical adherents of Islam.[49] Such a religious fervor has occurred not only in the well-known case of Iran, but also in Algeria, Iraq, Pakistan, Saudi Arabia, and several other Moslem countries in the Middle East.

Besides religion, certain other factors shape the ideologies of the governments and the values of people in Third World countries. Some of these factors were considered in Chapter 4. Earlier in this chapter it was mentioned that the masses in the Third World countries have a fatalistic attitude toward life, which hinders their achievement of life chances. The elites of the Third World countries, on the other hand, are achievement-oriented and the governments of these countries pay far greater attention to the elites than to the masses. One study points out that the African governments' concern for the urban elites determines their policies on agriculture. According to this study:

> Agriculture tends to be neglected by African governments whose political survival depends, after all, on the urban elites: official prices for agricultural products are set very low for the sake of the urban consumer, but this heavily penalizes the rural producer.[50]

It is not suggested here that the masses are completely ignored in the Third World countries, because their support, or at least their acquiescence, is essential to the survival of any government in these countries. There is no doubt, however, that the concerns of the elites are given a much higher priority than those of the masses.

POLICY OUTCOMES

A government's policy affecting life chances is determined by the three groups of factors considered earlier: opportunities and constraints in the international system; resources, technology, and infrastructure; and institutions and values. It influences the four basic values pursued by most people in every country—wealth, housing, education, and health. The availability and distribution of these values are, to a considerable extent, the policy outcomes of a government.

In the First World, GNP per capita of over $10,000 (U.S. dollars) is common. In the Third World, several countries still have GNP per capita of less than $500 (U.S. dollars). In the World Bank report of 1983, almost one-third of the Third World countries are listed with GNP per capita of less than $410 (U.S. dollars).[51] Except for a few oil-rich exporters in the Middle East, the rest of the Third World countries are considered to have middle-income economies; a middle-income economy is defined as a 1981 GNP per person of $410 or more.[52] In the 1983 report, 16 Third World countries are grouped as having upper-middle incomes with a GNP per capita from $1700 to $5600. However, when income distribution is considered, in most of these upper-middle-income countries the highest 10% of the households have a substantial share of the total income, in some cases as high as 50.6% (Brazil) and 44.2% (Panama). A similar pattern is discernible in Third World countries with lower incomes. The income distribution in the Third World countries is in sharp contrast with the income distribution in the First and Second Worlds. Although comparable data for the Second World countries are not available, we can assume a far more equitable income distribution in the Second World than in the Third World. In the capitalist countries of the First World where economic inequality is inherent in the economic system, income concentration in the hands of the top few is less than in the Third World.[53]

Similar inequities exist in Third World housing, education, and health care. There is a high positive correlation between income and these three categories. In comparison to the First and Second Worlds, the Third World is far behind in income, housing, education, and health care. As the data in Table 12.4 reveal, an adult literary rate of 50% or lower, life expectancy of less than 50, and infant mortality of 100 or higher are still common in the

Table 12.4   Adult Literacy Rate, Life Expectancy at Birth, and Infant Mortality in Selected Third World Countries

Country	Adult literacy rate[a]	Life expectancy	Infant mortality[b]
Afghanistan	20	37	205
Argentina	93	71	44
Bangladesh	26	48	135
Brazil	76	64	75
Egypt	44	57	75
Guinea	20	43	163
Haiti	23	54	112
India	36	52	121
Korea, South	93	66	33
Liberia	25	54	152
Mali	10	45	152
Mexico	83	66	54
Niger	10	45	143
Pakistan	24	50	123
Senegal	10	44	145
Singapore	83	72	12
Sudan	32	47	122
Tanzania	79	52	101
Trinidad and Tobago	95	72	31
Upper Volta (Burkina)	5	44	208

Source: World Bank, *World Development Report 1983* (New York: Oxford University Press, 1983).

[a] Percentage of persons, age 15 and over, who are literate.

[b] The number of infants who die before reaching age one, per 1000 live births in a year.

Third World, especially in Africa. Similar data for housing are not available; the situation, however, is not any better in the Third World in this category.

Some experts believe that extreme inequality in income (and other areas) is unavoidable in the early stages of development in any country. Charles Frank, Jr., and Richard Webb postulate that "a developing economy will first experience a worsening and then an improvement in the distribution of income."[54] It is argued that it is a "natural effect" of the development process and that the government policies reinforce it.[55] It is true that the government policies in the Third World countries aimed at economic development benefit the affluent segments of the urban areas more than the rest of the population. Programs in housing, education, and health care are generally initiated in the urban areas and are more accessible to those with money. An interesting aspect of this argument is that programs for population control increase income inequalities in a less-developed country.[56] The affluent and educated strata of a society are more receptive to the population control programs with the result that they further increase their per capita income in comparison to the poor, who are less receptive to population control.

If the foregoing hypothesis is valid, income inequalities in the Third World countries should begin to decrease, as programs in housing, education, health care, and population control gradually reach the poor segments of the countries. So far, however, there is little evidence of narrowing of the gap between the rich and the poor in the Third World.

The elites in most of the Third World countries are making concerted efforts to continue their privileged position in the society. The "political economic machinery" of the state is used by the elites for this purpose.[57] The consequence is that instead of narrowing, the chasm between the rich and the poor in the Third World countries may actually widen.

NOTES

1. The better-known measure, the gross national product (GNP), includes the total value of goods and services produced in a country over a certain period of time. When income from investments abroad and remittances of workers employed abroad are excluded from GNP, the measure is called gross domestic product (GDP). "Less-developed countries," "developing countries," and "underdeveloped countries" are used interchangeably.
2. World Bank, *World Development Report 1983* (New York: Oxford University Press, 1983), p. 2.
3. Hans W. Singer and Jared A. Ansari, *Rich and Poor Countries* (Baltimore: Johns Hopkins, University Press, 1977), p. 50.
4. *World Development Report 1983*, p. 16.
5. See Walter Wriston, "LDCs Just Need a Little Help from Their Friends," *Wall Street Journal*, March 13, 1984, p. 30.
6. *World Development Report 1983*, p. 10.
7. Ibid.
8. *Ramses: Annual Report of the French Institute for International Relations, The State of the World Economy* (Cambridge, Mass.: Ballinger, 1982), p. 98.
9. Ibid.
10. See Ibid., p. 99.
11. William W. Murdoch, *The Poverty of Nations* (Baltimore: Johns Hopkins University Press, 1980), p. 275.
12. See International Energy Agency, *World Energy Outlook* (Paris: Organization for Economic Cooperation and Development, 1982), p. 203.
13. Ibid., p. 247.
14. Ibid., p. 363.
15. Ibid.
16. Ibid., p. 340.

17. Ibid., p. 286.
18. See Atul Wad, "Science, Technology and Industrialization in Africa," *Third World Quarterly* 6 (April 1984): 333.
19. Ibid., p. 332.
20. Ibid.
21. See some of the statistics cited in Wad, esp. p. 336.
22. Michael A. Amsalem, *Technology Choice in Developing Countries* (Cambridge, Mass.: MIT Press, 1983), p. 153.
23. See Murdoch, p. 111.
24. Ibid., p. 110.
25. See *World Development Report 1983,* pp. 37–38.
26. See World Bank, *World Development Report 1982* (New York: Oxford University Press, 1982), p. 13.
27. See *World Development Report 1983,* p. 18.
28. See *World Development Report 1982,* p. 36.
29. See *Ramses: The State of the World Economy,* pp. 266–267.
30. See *World Development Report 1982,* p. 70.
31. Ibid., p. 83.
32. Ibid.
33. Ibid., p. 50.
34. Ibid.
35. David G. Becker, "Development, Democracy and Dependency in Latin America: A Post-Imperialist View," *Third World Quarterly* 6 (April 1984): 418.
36. Ibid., p. 419.
37. Ibid., p. 413.
38. See Guillermo A. O'Donnell, *Modernization and Bureaucratic Authoritarianism: Studies in South American Politics* (Berkeley: University of California, 1973 and 1979).
39. Ibid., p. 110. Note that according to David Becker, Argentina and Brazil were in "the processes of transition from authoritarianism to capitalist democracy." At the time of this writing (in mid-1985) both Argentina and Brazil were democratic.
40. See Peter Blackburn, "Recent Coups Make W. Africa Democracies Endangered Species," *Christian Science Monitor,* April 9, 1984, p. 9. An important gain for democracy in northern Africa occurred in 1984 in Egypt, which held elections for its parliament.
41. Crawford Young, *Ideology and Development in Africa* (New Haven, Conn.: Yale University Press, 1982).
42. Ibid., p. 12.
43. Ibid., p. 325.
44. Ibid.
45. Ibid.
46. *World Development Report 1982,* p. 29.
47. Ibid., p. 76.
48. See *World Development Report 1983,* p. 118.
49. See *Ramses: The State of the World Economy,* p. 236.

50. Ibid., p. 267.

51. *World Development Report 1983,* pp. 148–149.

52. Ibid., p. ix.

53. See ibid., pp. 200–201.

54. Charles R. Frank, Jr., and Richard C. Webb, eds., *Income Distribution and Growth in the Less-Developed Countries* (Washington, D.C.: Brookings Institution, 1977), pp. 10, 45–77.

55. Ibid.

56. Ibid., p. 11.

57. For an argument along these lines see Hugh M. Arnold, "Africa and the New International Economic Order," *Third World Quarterly* 2 (April 1980): 297. The phrase "political economic machinery" is taken from this article.

CHAPTER 13

Women in Politics in Three Worlds

In virtually every country that holds elections, women and men have an equal right to vote. Sexual equality in voting is largely a twentieth-century development. In most countries, whether or not they hold elections, political power is controlled by men. Very few women have held the top positions such as prime minister or president. In most First World countries no more than 5% of the members in the national legislatures are women. Women's proportion in elective state and local positions is higher, generally in the 10 to 15% range.

In the Second World, in theory women are equal to men in politics. More than Marx and Engels, Lenin was concerned with the rights of women. Communist party state constitutions grant equality to women with men in all walks of life. In reality, however, Second World women's political power in the higher echelons is severely limited.

With very few exceptions, Third World women's role in politics is chiefly limited to positions at the lower levels. Women who do hold important positions at the national levels in the Third World countries are mostly from upper classes; their positions reflect the power of their class rather than gender.

A number of explanations have been advanced for the limited power and relatively lower political activity of women. Of these explanations, socialization patterns and the related tradition of patriarchy are most convincing. Religion also plays a significant role. In the Third World, colonial experience is another influencing factor.

In the First World, and to a lesser extent in the Third World, we expect an increase in the political activity and power of women. We are less optimistic about women's increased political activity in the Second World.

In a study on the political role of women in France, the German Federal Republic, Norway, and Yugoslavia, the noted French political scientist Maurice Duverger wrote over three decades ago:

Vice-presidential candidate Geraldine Ferraro during 1984 campaign.

> So far as elections are concerned, the proportion of women taking part in political life [in voting] is large, and does not differ materially from that of men, as regards their number or composition. . . . So far as government, in the broad sense of the term, is concerned, the position is quite different. Here the political role of women is extremely small and grows still smaller as we approach the "center" of political leadership.[1]

Notwithstanding some progress in a majority of the countries of the world in the entrance of women into government positions, even at higher levels, political power is still predominantly controlled by men in most countries. On the eve of the nomination of Geraldine Ferraro as vice-presidential candidate by the U.S. Democratic party—a historic event indeed—a rhetorical question posed by *Time* was: "Why do more than 50 percent of Americans still hold less than 5 percent of the elected political positions?"[2] Equally important is the fact that a relatively small proportion of these 5% of the elected positions is near the "center" of politics.

WOMEN'S LIMITED POLITICAL POWER

In virtually every country that holds elections, women and men have an equal right to vote. Sexual equality in voting is mostly a twentieth-century development, and in many cases such equality was not realized until after the Second World War. New Zealand (1893), Australia (1902), Finland (1906), and Norway (1913) were the first to grant the right to vote to women. In the United States, the ratification of the Nineteenth Amendment to the Constitution in 1920 brought suffrage to women. Britain granted the franchise in 1918 to women in three categories—married women, female householders, and women university graduates at least 30 years of age. It took Britain another decade to recognize equality of all women and men in voting. Two prominent First World countries—France and Japan—extended the right to vote to women only after the Second World War. In the Second World, Communism brought voting and other political rights to women. In the Soviet Union women gained the right to vote in 1917, and in China in 1949. In the former African and Asian colonies of the Third World, women as well as men were able to vote after the end of colonialism. (In some colonies, especially those controlled by Britain, limited voting rights to men as well as to women were given before independence was granted.) A majority of the Latin American countries granted the right to vote to women after the Second World War; Paraguay was the last to do so in 1961 and Ecuador was the first in 1929.[3]

Attainment of the right to vote does not necessarily mean that this right is exercised. In the first decades after women obtained suffrage, their turnout rate was lower than men's. In 1920, the first year American women had the opportunity to exercise their hard-won franchise, only about 30% did so.[4] As the voting habit became part of female political culture, gender differences in turnout rates declined substantially. According to survey data gathered by the University of Michigan, female turnout increased to 56% by the 1948 presidential elections.[5] The Second World War brought a large number of U.S. women into the work force and made them more aware of their political rights. However, in 1948, 69% of men—13% more than the women—voted in the presidential election. By 1968 that difference had shrunk to only three percentage points. Women are now exercising their franchise in as great or perhaps greater numbers than men in the United States. Gender does not seem to be a major determinant of voting any longer.

In other countries of the First World, a similar reduction in the difference between percentages of male and female voting has taken place. In Europe and Japan voter turnout is substantially higher than in the United States, but gender seems to make little difference in the turnout rates.[6] In the Second World, governments strive for a voter turnout close to 100%. In theory at least, men and women are equally active in voting in these countries. In most of the Third World countries that permit voting, female voter turnout is substantially lower than male voter turnout. Female voter turnout in some of these countries is as low as 10 or 20%.[7]

The right to vote has brought only limited political power to women. All over the world women have gained far more power at the lower levels than at the higher levels. Female power gains thus resemble the structure of a pyramid. In the United States women have achieved near parity with men in the number of delegates at the presidential nominating conventions of both major parties.[8] However, this is the only major political area at the "top" where sexual equality has been attained. So far as appointive or elective government positions are concerned, women at the top form a very small group in proportion to men. Only one woman has been appointed to the Supreme Court and only eight women have been members of the Cabinet. Women holding executive ranks in the federal government are less than 10%.[9] Jeannette Rankin of Montana was the first woman elected to the House of Representatives in 1917 (women could run for office even though they could not vote.) Yet it was three decades before the number of congresswomen reached 10 and another three decades before it exceeded 20 in a house of 435 members. In the U.S. Senate no more than two women have ever served at the same time. At state and local levels women have made far more gains than at the national level. "The proportion of women in state legislatures tripled between 1971 and 1983, and the number of cities (of populations over 30,000) with female mayors went from seven to 76."[10] However, women legislators in the states are still not much over 10% of the total number of legislators[11] and the same is true of the female mayors in comparison with the total number of mayors.[12]

With the exception of Scandinavian countries, the proportion of women in national and local offices in the First World is similar to that of the United States. In Canada, Japan, and most West European countries no more than 5% of the members in the national legislatures are women. (Austria, West Germany, and the Netherlands have a somewhat higher proportion of women legislators.) The proportion of women holding office at state and local levels is higher, generally between 10 and 15%. In Scandinavian countries 10 to 20% of national legislators are women; the percentage of female office holders at the local level is higher. One study notes that "with a combined population of less than 20 million, the three Scandinavian monarchies have more women serving in their legislatures than have been elected to the Congress of the United States since 1917, when Jeannette Rankin broke the sex barrier on Capitol Hill."[13]

In the Second World countries the proportion of women serving in the government positions at the national and local levels is much higher than in the First World. However, in the top party positions where real power rests, women are as uncommon as in the upper rungs of the First World political hierarchy. As one scholar remarks about the Soviet Union, "it is clear that within the party itself there is considerable hesitation in promoting women to positions of real authority."[14] A similar situation prevails in other Second World countries. In the Third World the proportion of female legislators in national assemblies is similar to that in the First World (except Scandinavian countries).[15] Third World women in local elective positions also do as well as women in similar positions in the First World (except in Scandinavian countries).[16]

EXPLANATIONS FOR LIMITED POWER

Several explanations have been offered for the limited power and generally limited political activity of women. Of these explanations, we find socialization patterns and the related tradition of patriarchy most convincing. In most societies, preadult males and females learn through socialization in the family and other institutions of the society that a woman's place is at home as a wife and a mother and not in politics or business. Women are portrayed as unsuitable for the aggressive and demanding roles expected of political elites. Political activity is considered a male preoccupation. In a study of political participation (activities such as discussing politics with others, attending a political meeting or rally, working for a political party or candidate, and voting in national elections), M. Kent Jennings discovered that socialization generated a male participation bias in most of the eight Western countries (Austria, Finland, Germany, Great Britain, Italy, the Netherlands, Switzerland, and the United States) that he considered.[17] Finding "strong residues of differential socialization in several of these Western democracies," he poses a question, "what might we expect to find in other countries?"[18] His answer is that "political participation as a male gender role is virtually an inevitable lesson of political socialization in nations where socially, religiously, and often legally women are invested with less worth, as being less fit, able, or destined for fully active political lives."[19] Socialization patterns reinforcing less political activity by women than by men are stronger in most Third World countries than in the First World countries. Evidence indicates that in the Second World countries such socialization patterns also are well entrenched.[20]

Societal values and attitudes establish socialization patterns. The tradition of patriarchy developed from these values, attitudes, and socialization patterns. Lynn Iglitzin writes that "the crux of patriarchal thinking is a belief in male superiority and female inferiority."[21] According to her, four sources have legitimized this assumption through the ages.

First, the justification for patriarchal rule is biological in that it emphasizes the greater physical strength of the male animal. Second, patriarchy has been legitimized on cultural and anthropological grounds: primitive societies, in the process of evolving toward civilization, moved away from matriarchy and toward patriarchy, and anthropological evidence shows the universality of the patriarchal family. Third, Western and non-Western religious authority is cited as incontrovertible proof of the rightness and the inevitability of male rule. Fourth, changes in the mode of production and distribution, particularly the shift from communal to private property, are used to explain patriarchal developments.[22]

There is no doubt that patriarchal thinking prevails in most countries of the world in varying degrees. Of the four sources, religion has played the most prominent role in legitimizing patriarchal thinking. Major religions of the world have assigned a secondary, if not subordinate, status to females in relation to males.

Other explanations for the limited power and generally restrained political activity of women concern their situation and roles within the family, societal institutions, and political climate of a country.[23] Almost universally a woman is still considered primarily a homemaker, a wife, and a mother. When a married woman works, she usually carries a greater burden of the household responsibilities than the husband. These two jobs, one to earn a living and the other to manage the household, leave little time for political activity. When a married working woman participates actively in politics, it may require the ability to manage three jobs.[24] Societal institutions in areas such as education and occupation deny equality of opportunity to women. Although literacy rates for men and women in the First and Second Worlds are practically the same, women generally are less educated than men. In the Third World educational inequality is even more glaring, as substantially larger numbers of men are literate than women. Certain occupations are male-dominated and others are female-dominated. It is from the male-dominated occupations such as law, business, and banking that political elites are recruited. It is uncommon, if not rare, that a nurse or a secretary runs for or holds a political office. (In most countries of the world nursing and secretarial jobs are predominantly held by women.) The political climate of a country also determines the political role of women to some extent. When laws are passed providing equality to women with men in different walks of life, and more important, when attitudes start changing to accept such equality, political activity of women increases.

WOMEN AND MODERNIZATION

It is argued by some that as a society modernizes, in other words, as it advances in technology and the economy becomes complex and society moves away from tradition, it approaches equality between men and women. John Stuart Mill, the celebrated nineteenth-century English philosopher and political economist, perceived a trend toward equality of the sexes with the progress of civilization. Contemporary writings on modernization have also assumed such a trend. However, for the past several years this assumption has been debated, especially with regard to the impact of modernization on the equality of the sexes in the Third World. An extreme view is that often with modernization the status of women declines.[25] A balanced and convincing viewpoint is that as a society modernizes and becomes complex, the status of women declines, but with greater advancements and complexity, women again gain in their position relative to men.[26] There is thus "a curvilinear relationship between societal complexity and sex equality."[27]

Economic advancement and technology play a major role in the curvilinear relationship between modernization and sexual equality. When women and men participated almost equally in the economic enterprise of hunting and gathering in a primitive society, they were probably nearly equal in status. With the introduction of agriculture, when men did more of the actual farming than women, women's position declined. When industrialization brought greater opportunities for education and employment for both sexes, women's status began improving. There is no doubt that men have benefited far more in education and jobs from industrial progress than have women. There is, however, considerable truth in the view that in industrial societies the degree of sexual equality is greater than in the agrarian societies. We do not believe that sexual equality has increased with modernization in every country. Several other factors, notably societal norms and societal structures, also determine the role of men and women in a society. Furthermore, colonialism had an adverse impact on the status of women in the Third World, providing another intervening factor in the relationship between modernization and sexual equality. (The impact of colonialism on the status of women in the Third World is considered later in this chapter.)

CHANGING ROLES OF WOMEN

There is no doubt that perceptions of women's roles in society are undergoing a change in a majority of the countries of the world. Indeed there is increased awareness that women should make greater contributions in government as well as other areas. According to available evidence, the attitudes of men as well as of women with regard to women's role in politics are changing. Equally or perhaps even more important is that at least in some First World countries, the proportion of women in occupations such as law and business is increasing. It is these occupations that are the recruiting grounds for political elites in the West. In the Second and the Third World similar occupational changes are less visible. However, the designation of

1975 as International Women's Year (IWY) by the United Nations and the IWY Conference held in Mexico City, in 1975, indicated a greater role for women in politics and other areas.

THE FIRST WORLD

In 1848, the year of the publication of the *Communist Manifesto* and the revolutionary "Springtime of Nations" in Europe, a document was issued in a small town in New York State. The Seneca Falls Declaration of Principles called for the opening of both education and the professions to women. It stated that women should have property rights and the right to vote; it further called for the ending of a double standard in morality.[28]

This call for a change in status for women was one of the bases for organized efforts to advance the cause of women. Before this time most women in what was to become the modern Western world found themselves caught in the web of custom, tradition, religion, and the theory of male dominance. To be sure, there had been powerful individual women in Western society before (Elizabeth I of England or Maria Theresa, Empress of Austria and "King" of Hungary, are two examples). It is also true that women had occasionally functioned as specific pressure groups. During the struggle between king and Parliament in Great Britain in the 1640s, a group of women petitioned the House of Commons, "based upon their equality with men before Christ," demanding, among other things, peace and the preservation of the reformed Protestant religion.[29] Early in the French revolutionary period Parisian women were particularly noted for activism and radicalism.[30] However, it was not until the nineteenth century that a sustained effort for women's emancipation found support. The women's movement developed as barriers fell before advancing secularism and scientific thought. Theological arguments for women's inequality with men have increasingly lost their force as new interpretations of religious sources have developed. The notion of God as "male" has come to be questioned as has the necessity for a male-only clergy. Some religious groups now ordain females in the roles of ministers and teachers.

Scientifically, the notion of the "weakness" of the female has been discredited. Though males may be stronger in gross musculature, they are, in fact, weaker in many other aspects and they die sooner. This decline of scientific and religious support for female subservience and the rise of women's activism on their own behalf have forced some major changes in the political, legal, economic, and social situation of women in the First World. These changes, however, have met with considerable resistance and have not yet produced complete equality, as has already been mentioned.

Limited Political Power

In all First World countries today women are afforded the right to vote and hold office, but the percentage actually holding office remains small. Despite the fact that women are more than 50% of the population, the Margaret Thatchers of the Western world are few and far between. The First World has the most advanced economic system, the highest output of consumer goods and labor-saving devices, universally available education and, generally, a lack of legal impediments to action. Yet, women cannot be said to be playing the political role their proportion of the population would entitle them to. Why?

Many commentators explain the lack of political power as having its source in the First World's political economy. Modern Western societies are dominated by large-scale wealth and corporations. Historically, few women had access to the tools to gain wealth, so while great fortunes were amassed in the nineteenth and twentieth centuries, women had to stand on the sidelines. In the United States, for example, men "earn, own and control most of the wealth in . . . [the] country."[31]

> Fifty-eight percent of stock shares are owned by institutions whose boards of trustees and brokers are almost exclusively male. Individually, women own approximately 18 percent of privately held stock shares; men approximately 24 percent. In terms of privately held real estate holdings, only 39 percent belong to women, despite the fact of female longevity. Approximately 60 percent of persons with financial assets over $60,000 are male.

> These statistics are quite liberal estimates of wealth of women, because it is common for men to place holdings in the names of their wives, daughters, or mothers for tax purposes.[32]

Further, relations between the corporate elite are developed through an interlocking network of nonformal contacts. "Men-only" private clubs abound, civic and business organizations (e.g., Rotary International) do not admit women, sports facilities catering to the managerial set rarely have women members. Without access to these so-called old-boy (note the masculine noun) networks many a business deal would never be made.

The legal profession, though accepting women in the lower rungs, is ruled by males and only a rare female becomes a partner in prosperous law firms. Only recently in the United States did a court decision affirm that refusal based on gender alone to offer a partnership to a female was a case of illegal discrimination.

In the area of labor unions too the pattern is for women rarely, if ever, to make it to the top. Not until 1980 did the first women serve on the

Women form a large proportion of students in higher education in the First World.

Executive Board of the AFL-CIO, despite the fact that women hold 22% of union membership.[33]

Most executives are trained in the colleges and universities. Here too, the number of women in controlling bodies, boards of trustees, or administration, is low. Women find themselves relegated to social service functions, such as assisting international students or providing hospitality for visitors.

Women have attempted to assert themselves in higher education, especially in the United States, Canada, and Scandinavia. The introduction of women's studies as a separate program has met with mixed success. Resistance by the standard university departments and traditional-minded faculty creates real obstacles to development of such programs.[34] Another approach being used to draw attention to the role of women is to introduce materials dealing with women in heretofore male-oriented courses.[35] The success of such approaches in enlightening and raising the consciousness of the college and university population will only be seen after some time.

Mass media in the Western world are also dominated by men. Executives controlling radio, television, and print media are nearly always male. Emphasis on male sports and other male activities reduces coverage of women's activities to social events and homemaking programs. Although more and more women are appearing in significant roles on television, some countries, notably Japan, use women simply as background props to male commentators.

In the First World women have little power in control of property, in the corporation, in the legal profession, in education, and in the media. This lack of power is also reflected in party politics and government. In the bureaucracy of governments of First World it is not easy to find women above the levels of typing pools and middle management. Although little formal sex discrimination occurs in selection of higher-level managers and supergrade administrators, only a small number of women reach these levels.

Up to now, because of all the factors mentioned here, women do not have leadership positions in political parties in the First World. The president of Iceland and the prime minister of Great Britain are exceptions rather than the rule. In sum we can agree with Laurel Richardson: "Because women are not influential members of the corporate elite or any of its subsidiaries and partners—government, mass media, universities, and foundations—they have no direct access to power."[36] Is the situation all that bleak or can women look forward to greater access to power? Two ongoing processes—modernization and the changing role of women—allow us to give an affirmative answer to the latter part of the question.

Modernization and Changing Roles

Nearly everyone admits that women are essential to the modern industrialized state. With the rapidly increasing competition between the countries of the First World for technological advancement and markets, can any country afford to have half its population fulfilling the classical roles of "Kinder, Küche, Kirche" (children, kitchen, and church)? Should a top-flight mathematician be sent to teach kindergarten, should a computer expert be married off because of parental wishes? It makes no economic sense to do so. The force of the wave of modernization propels able women forward. Even the most retrograde of First World countries in the area of sex equality, Japan, finds its most-qualified women being hired by foreign firms operating in Tokyo.[37] Can Japan afford to let this occur on a regular basis?

Advancement for women in the economy, politics, education and other spheres of life in the First World has been slow. There have been years of struggle to gain the vote, then a lull in the women's movement. World War II brought a surge of women into formerly masculine roles to support the war effort. In the immediate postwar period women were expected to return to the home.

Changes in the economy, however, have brought women back into the job market. The "two-working-parents" family is now the rule rather than the exception in most First World states. This situation strengthens the desire for power among women, a desire to have some control over their lives rather than being an object of male decision makers.[38] This desire can be seen in demands for equal pay for equal work, for opening of employment opportunities heretofore reserved for males, and for access to advancement in the power structure. As more women begin to work in the legal structure, there has been a noticeable increase in litigation to advance these demands.

As women become more active in the marketplace, they begin to realize the necessity of political activity in order to gain desired values. Some women have been appointed to positions as cabinet members in First World countries. Political candidates now are careful to nur ture an image of being pro-women no matter what their personal views. The simple fact is a politician must take into account the existence of female voters and must accommodate them in order to attract them to his or her political party.[39]

Sweden and Japan—Two Extremes

The Scandinavian countries (Sweden in particular) have made great efforts to raise the level of women in their societies. Beyond formal, legal equality in Swedish legislation, the Swedish state is attempting to move women toward financial, social, and familial equality. In the area of education both males and females are afforded access to the full range of liberal arts and vocational training. Financial aid for education is gender-free and based on need alone. In the family, spouses are considered to have separate finances—incomes, assets, and debts; children are the equal responsibility of both parents. The Swedish state provides allowances for children, kindergartens and nurseries, and special assistance to mothers before, during, and after childbirth. A complete system of social insurance covers both males and females in regard to health, disability, and pensions. In the marketplace women have equal rights as entrepeneurs, workers, and managers. In the political sphere women are as active as men in exercising their franchise though they do not yet make up 50% of the national legislature. Leaders of the five largest political parties in Sweden have publically pledged themselves to further participation of women in the political and economic process.[40]

Japan, on the other hand, has pursued a less activist role in regard to women. Until 1945 women were expected to be obedient not only to their parents, especially their fathers, but also to their husbands, or even to their eldest sons, if they were widows. Despite the inclusion of women in the war efforts of 1933 to 1945, no formal amelioration of the woman's burden occurred.

A radical change began for Japanese women with the occupation of the country by American forces in 1945. General Douglas MacArthur, in one of his first acts as military governor, brought about the enfranchisement of women. He did this by "encouraging" the Japanese government itself to create a legal base for women in politics. Women first voted in Japan on April 10, 1946, and the Shōwa Constitution of November 3, 1946, confirmed this right.[41]

It has proven insufficient, as in other countries, to have simply the right to vote. The weight of centuries of patriarchy still oppresses Japanese women. Socialization processes continue to encourage traditional values and roles. Education, however, is open and used equally by both sexes. The tendency, however, is for a family to favor the male child over the female in making educational choices. Japanese women themselves also have been slow to change. It was as late as 1979 before a majority of women believed that it was acceptable for the woman to work outside the home and that women with the desire and ability should be allowed to enter areas of work hitherto reserved for men.[42]

Economically, women have made slow progress; 48% of Japanese women now constitute one-third of the labor force but, as in the United States, their salary level is 60% of that of men. Major Japanese businesses believe, as did North American companies 20 years ago, that hiring women, who are expected to leave for homemaking as soon as possible, is economically unwise, so they do not bother to recruit women above a menial level.[43] It is not unknown for Japanese firms to ease out women in their late twenties because they do not wish to promote them.

Politically, women are quite active in voting; in fact in 1980 a greater percentage of eligible women voted than men (75.4–73.7%), but this has not resulted in appreciable gains in women's representation.[44] Women occupy 26 out of 761 seats in Japan's Diet and there have only been two women cabinet ministers; there are no powerful Japanese female politicians today.[45]

Is the situation of a Japanese woman hopeless vis-à-vis her Swedish counterpart? Perhaps not. Robert Christopher, writing in his book *The Japanese Mind* is of the opinion that change will come very incrementally in Japan. Factors favoring sexual equality are the "shortage of new entrants into the labor force brought about by Japan's low birthrate" and the consensus which is gradually building in Japan, favoring modernization in equality of the sexes. In regard to the latter, Christopher indicates that Japan has been particularly amenable to advanced ideas in technology and industry and "all in all . . . a shrewd businessman in Japan these days would make a special point of recruiting female university and college graduates . . . they constitute an unexploited pool of talent."[46] As some Japanese have commented about themselves, "the Japanese are economic animals"; it may be the reality of economic profit that will accelerate the advance of women in Japan.

A final word about women in politics: in the First World it is possible to organize freely to advance one's causes. To petition for the redress of grievances is recognized as a political right. It is in this right that women find hope. Unlike in the Second World, women in the First World are not required to be system-supportive if they wish to make an organized effort for change. They need not fear political instability or government coercion which frequently is exerted in the Third World. Thus, the political role of women in the First World can be seen to be expanding. To paraphrase and adapt Evelyne Sullerot's conclusion in her book *Women, Society and Change*, we may say that women are essential to the solution of all modern political, economic, and social problems. The most powerful male leaders in the First World cannot implement policies without the positive contribution and assent of women.[47]

THE SECOND WORLD

Profound changes have taken place in the last 30 years in the GDR [German Democratic Republic], and many have fundamentally affected women's lives. . . . Women during the Fascist period were seen as little more than breeders of children. . . . Today, in the 30-and-under group, equal numbers of men and women receive university diplomas and skilled worker's certificates. There are guaranteed jobs for everyone, equal pay for equal work, abortion on demand, state-supported kindergartens for children between 3 and 6 . . . paid pregnancy leaves . . . special provisions for the further education of working women, full pay to take courses on job time, and special tutors for women.[48]

The quote is from a study by Joan Ecklein, a U.S. sociologist who, after examining East Germany, concluded that the GDR was as close to Marx's paradigm (model) for a proletarian state as any of the present Communist states. She noted that in the 35 years of its existence there had been a real change in East Germany for women.

The writers in the socialist–communist countries state quite explicitly in their literature that "Socialism has radically changed the status of women in society. It has ensured their equality in all spheres of political and social activity."[49] After all, if one wishes to revolutionize society, to mobilize the population to radical change, it would be foolhardy to ignore half of the population that in the past had suffered oppression based on sex.

Theoretical Bases for Women's Liberation

Alfred G. Meyer, writing about Marxism and the women's movement, mentions the personally ambivalent attitudes of Marx and Engels in regard to women. Karl Marx, in his private life, was quite conventional for the nineteenth century. He treated his wife and daughters in a patriarchal manner. He once indicated that a manly virtue was strength and a feminine one weakness. Friedrich Engels, on the other hand, was more apt to treat women as equals, although he appeared to surround himself with "serving women."[50] Both men were products of the Victorian age. Apparently, neither Marx nor Engels developed a full critique of *sexism* (the philosophy of male dominance); rather, along with racism, they considered the problem as part of the greater one of oppression in capitalist society.

Despite personal foibles and an incomplete approach, Marx and Engels did have a view concerning equality of the sexes. First, they agreed with the early nineteenth-century French socialist Charles Fournier who stated that "the change in a historical era can always be determined by the progress of women towards freedom . . . the degree of emancipation of women is the natural measure of general emancipation."[51] Second, they felt that the male–female relationship in bourgeois society was one of exploitation. "The bourgeosie . . . has reduced the family relation to a mere money relationship."[52] Workers for industry are recruited from the ranks of men, women, and children, and "all are instruments of labor, more or less expensive to use, according to their age and sex."[53] The solution to exploitation can only be found in the working class, the proletariat, for it "alone is a really revolutionary class."[54] This class, upon coming to power, will destroy the bourgeois family in which the wife is merely an instrument for producing children. It will eliminate prostitution caused by economic injustice, and it will emancipate everyone. "In the place of old bourgeois society . . . we shall have an association, in which the free development of each is the condition for free development of all."[55]

Beyond this general view of women's emancipation as part and parcel of the general emancipation of humanity by revolution, one work, by Engels, deals explicitly, though incompletely, with the sexual equality question. This work, *The Origin of the Family, Private Property and the State* (first edition, 1884) is frequently referred to by feminist thinkers around the world. In this book Engels developed a full-scale explanation of the wellspring of a society based on private property. In that discussion he included the role of women.

Engels' argument, based in large part on the work of American anthropologist Lewis Morgan, may be summarized in the following way. In the earliest stage of human history, the primitive communal prehistoric stage, women were on the highest level and society was defined as matriarchal, without a nuclear (pairing) family. This earliest stage of human development is a supposition. The change from a matriarchal to a patriarchal family occurred in the transition from primitive communal society to the slave state. This change can be inferred from remnants found in ancient writings and among primitive tribes. "We know nothing as to how and when this revolution was effected among the civilized peoples. It falls entirely within prehistoric times."[56] The change was part of the origins of the state, private property, and the exploitation of the many by the few. Engels, and all Marxist–Leninists since, consider that

> the overthrow of mother right [was] the World historic defeat of the female sex. The man seized the reins in the house also, the woman was degraded, enthralled, the slave of the man's lust, a mere instrument for breeding children.[57]

The subjugation of women continued through the slave, feudal, and capitalist epochs of history. The monogamous family allows a man to procure and own cheaply a servant, a cook, and a wife for his children. Monogamy, however, applies to the wife alone—the male is free to have extramarital affairs. The situation of the woman as a kind of property in capitalist society will be ended by the revolution. Private property, not biology, is the cause of oppression of women. Property relations will disappear from marriage and marriage will be based on love; a woman will not have to get married for reasons other than love.[58]

Engels, concentrating on history, did not concern himself with the political importance of women or their political development. Lenin, however, had a more active approach. Writing as early as 1900 in his first major work, Lenin noted that women were entering industrial production and payment to them was at a very low level based on the owners' rationale that they were merely making a supplementary income for their family. He particularly criticized rural home piecework exploitation.[59] Lenin was consistent in supporting the rights of all the oppressed, among whom he included women. The various programs of the Communist party reflected this support, as do Communist party state constitutions today. Lenin recognized that it is not possible to involve the masses in politics without the involvement of women as well. The double oppression of women—both as household drudges and as legal unequals of men—would be ended by Soviet power. Lenin fully realized that he needed support from all sources if his group wished to gain power.

The Revolution and Women

Communist revolutionaries sought to mobilize all discontented groups in their efforts to overthrow existing regimes. Appeals to wage workers, farmers, colonial peoples, oppressed races, and women were common. In the struggles for power that took place in Russia, Yugoslavia, Albania, China, Cuba, and Vietnam, women did not, however, play a decisive role; rather they were supportive of male activities. No major revolutionary leader was female. In the rest of the Communist states, where the revolution was imposed by outside force—Poland, GDR, Czechoslovakia, Hungary, Romania, Bulgaria, Mongolia, North Korea, Laos, Cambodia, and Afghanistan—the role of women was nearly nonexistent.

However, to consolidate and maintain power, all Communist states have made great efforts on behalf of women. Clauses were inserted in constitutions guaranteeing women equal rights with men not only politically but also socially and economically. Additionally, mothers receive assistance granted by constitutional articles. The family laws of the Communist states allow divorce, abortion on demand, equal property rights with men, the right to alimony, and overall equal treatment with males. In return for these benefits, women are expected to support the existing regime. Generally speaking, the Communist policies toward women during the revolutionary and consolidation of power periods affirm that (1) class struggle is more important than specific female struggle, (2) women must join the general proletarian revolutionary movement, and (3) women do have particular problems that can be addressed within the general socialist movement but which must never be separated from it.[60]

The role of women in present-day Communist party states is limited. Politically, women have equal rights with men to vote and hold public office. However, as has been noted previously, it is not in the formal political structure of Communist party states that power lies. Women may be seen in window-dressing positions, such as chairpersons of legislative assemblies or as members of delegations going abroad, but these are essentially powerless posts. Power lies within the party and no woman has yet reached a power position on her own in the party structure.[61] Women are afforded equal rights in society and notable women are found in the arts, education, and medicine, but not in controlling positions. In the economic sphere, women have equal rights in obtaining training, jobs, and advancement. Equal numbers of men and women enter the professions, but men are the only ones to advance to top positions.

The political role specifically allocated to women in a ruling Communist party state is that of regime support within directed special interest groups. Examples of these groups include the Soviet women's organization (which publishes the widely distributed monthly, *Soviet Women*, in several languages), the Czechoslovak Women's Union, the Women's Federation of China, and the Soviet-sponsored Women's International Democratic Federation based in Czechoslovakia.

Let us look at the role of women in the USSR and China in light of the foregoing statements. One of the Soviet Union's major claims concerns the emancipation of women in that country. Women are more than half of the workers and students in the USSR. They hold 73% of educational positions, 84% of public health positions and 71% of positions in culture and entertainment. Nearly 85% of working-age women work in the USSR. Equal pay for equal work, special pay for maternity leave, earlier pensions for women, and day-care centers and nurseries for working mothers are available. Women

A surveyor in the USSR; many women are found in the middle levels of the professional work force of the Soviet Union.

also work in a variety of positions that were once dominated by men, such as construction and mining.[62]

In political activities, however, women are not as well positioned. "There were over 81 million women at least 25 years of age in the Soviet Union in early 1976 compared with under 63 million men [but] only 3,800,000 . . . were Communists compared with 11,800,000 men," and among women over 30, in that year only 4.5% belonged to the party (20% of the men were party members).[63] Presently there are only 7 women in the 300 plus-member Central Committee of the Communist party of the Soviet Union and none at all as heads of divisions of the central party Secretariat or in the Politburo. In the government, a few women are prominent in the Supreme Soviet (the legislature), but there are no women among 115 members of the Council of Ministers. Further, in the scientific community there are only 3 women among the 260-member Soviet Academy of Sciences.[64]

China's vast population, the prolonged turbulence of the revolution, and sparse data prevent us from seeing the political situation of Chinese women clearly. Women started from a very low level with nearly universal illiteracy and a long-entrenched, traditional place in society. Also, as in the Soviet

Union, women's problems were not seen as different from male problems. "We must remember that the liberation movement of women cannot be separated from the liberation of the proletariat. It is a component part of the proletarian revolution."[65]

During the years of Mao Zedong's power, there were attempts to mobilize the whole of China in the periods of the Great Leap Forward and the Great Proletarian Cultural Revolution. This included bringing women into the industrial work force during the former and into political activity during the latter. In both periods, however, the national legislature was in decline and during the Cultural Revolution the party was eclipsed by the People's Liberation Army, which began administering much of the country.

The Chinese Women's Federation recently noted that women are not fully represented in the policy-making process or in decision-making bodies. "The present situation of our women [in political positions] resembles the shape of a pagoda. The higher the level the fewer the women."[66] It is reported, though, that a fairly large percentage of women (21.1% in 1978) take part in (are elected to) the National People's Congress, the formal legislature of the country. This, however, is not a decisive forum, for the Chinese Communist party takes that role.

Second World women, as a group, have relatively little effect on the party and state apparatus because they generally do not have important positions in the power structure. Yet women have been substantially affected by party policy. The extent of this influence depends on the social and political level of women when a given country comes under Communist party control. The Communists attacked the old social order and attempted to mobilize large groups of people in their struggle. Women, of course, stood out as a force to be drawn into the party. In China, for example, though there already were laws on the books about free choice in marriage and elimination of concubinage, the Communists reissued and enforced these laws and abolished parentally arranged marriages. Further, they made it illegal for females to marry under age 18 or males under 25. The Communists also gave women social, economic, and political equality, and the right to divorce. The revolutionary reforms shook Chinese society, as did similar reforms earlier in the USSR. Attacks on family traditions tended to attract youth to party values.[67]

Industrialization makes it necessary to bring more people into the labor force. One way is to bring women out of the home. To accomplish this, some governments provide certain social services (such as day care). If the government is pursuing pronatalist (propopulation expansion) policies (e.g, in the USSR or GDR), incentives must be provided to encourage women to both work and bear children.

Prospects for Change

The political role of women in Communist party states is not substantial. One cannot predict much change in this area in the near future. The lower level of consumer goods and labor-saving devices in the Second World requires working women to spend an inordinate amount of time on shopping, cooking, childrearing, and housekeeping. It is also universally noted that despite "liberation" of women in Second World states, the males have not taken up the slack at home. Patriarchal attitudes among both males and females permeate the entire Communist society. Despite appeals and exhortations, even the leadership, with few exceptions, does not take women seriously in politics or economics. Women are not advanced to decision-making positions. Present analysis does not indicate any immediate change in this situation, especially as women's support groups and the feminist movement are not allowed to exist outside the formal structure of Communist party-directed, system-supportive interest groups.

THE THIRD WORLD

Compared with the First and Second Worlds, women in the Third World lag far behind men in education and employment, two of the major determinants of one's role in politics. Illiteracy rates of over 50% are common in the Third World. In Africa, Asia, and the Middle East, illiteracy rates are substantially higher (in many cases over 20%) among women than among men; in Latin America illiteracy rates are relatively low and the difference between male and female illiteracy is usually less than 10% (see Table 13.1). The proportion of women completing high school or college is substantially lower in the Third World than in the First or the Second World. Even in those Third World countries where men and women are in nearly equal proportions in higher education, a pattern with regard to the choice of subjects of study emerges, indicating greater involvement of men in politics. In her study of political participation of women in Latin America, JoAnn Aviel observes that "even in those countries where the percentage of women and men attending university is almost equal, women are not to be found in equal numbers in the most politicized faculties—those of law and social sciences."[68]

Women in the Third World constitute a much smaller proportion of the total work force than is the case in the First and Second Worlds. Whereas women constitute almost one-half of the work force in the Second World and well over one-third of women in the First World are employed, in most Third World countries less than one-third of women are in the labor force. The lowest percentages of women in the work force are in Latin America and the Middle East. In Latin America, "only 13 percent of all women are active in

Table 13.1   Percentage of Illiteracy by Sex in Selected Third World Countries

Country	Female illiteracy	Male illiteracy
Afghanistan	94	67
Argentina	8	7
Bangladesh	87	62
Brazil	26	22
Egypt	71	43
Ghana	82	47
Haiti	83	74
India	81	52
Iran	76	52
Korea, South	19	6
Kuwait	52	32
Liberia	88	70
Mali	94	87
Niger	94	86
Nigeria	77	54
Pakistan	90	70
Singapore	26	8
Tanzania	30	22
Trinidad and Tobago	10	5
Upper Volta	96	85
Venezuela	27	20

Source: UNESCO Statistical Yearbook 1983 (Paris: UNESCO, 1983).

the labor force."[69] The proportion of working women in the Moslem countries of the Middle East is even smaller.[70] Working women in the Third World are largely in low-paying occupations. A striking example is in Latin America where "two of every five employed women are domestic servants.[71]

It is true that the Third World women are not far behind the First World women in their representation in national and local assemblies. More so than in the First World, women in positions of power in the Third World are from upper classes and have been appointed or elected to these positions because of their class rather than gender. On the whole, women in the Third World are less aware of the political processes in their countries and participate less in these processes than do women in the First and Second Worlds. In a study based on interviews with women in six Third World countries—Egypt, Kenya, Mexico, Sri Lanka, Sudan, and Tunisia—Perdita Huston notes that the rural women "had little knowledge of the world beyond their village."[72] (Third World countries are predominantly rural.) Even in urban areas, a very small proportion of women—those from the upper classes—are aware of the world beyond their immediate surroundings and participate in politics. There is no doubt that lack of education and meager income are among the major reasons for the low political participation by a majority of the Third World women.

Tradition and Religion

Societal norms, based on tradition and religion and reinforced by socialization patterns, determine to a considerable extent the role of women in politics in the Third World. Tradition all over the world stipulates that a woman's primary place in society is at home in the roles of wife and mother. Although this traditional attitude has been changing for some time, Third World countries, especially in Latin America and in the Moslem Middle East, have been slow to change. Small proportions of women in the work force in Latin America and the Moslem countries of the Middle East indicate the pace of this change. Traditional attitudes that isolate women in the home environment and deny them education and employment also deprive them of political participation. The Latin American tradition of *machismo–marianismo* reflects the implications of such attitudes. Mary Elmendorf comments that "the *machismo–marianismo* syndrome makes female subordination a sign of male virility. . . ."[73] Interpreting the same syndrome somewhat differently, Roderic Camp writes:

> Many Latin American and Mexican women are content with a traditional role within the home, not because of the negative male psychological restraints exemplified in the well-known *machismo* cult in Mexico and Latin America but because of a positive cultural exaltation known as *marianismo*, which has connotations similar to the traditional stereotype of southern, white females in the United States.[74]

As stated earlier, major religions assign a secondary, if not subordinate, role to women. In several Third World countries, especially in the Middle East where Islam is the predominant religion, societal norms governing the status of a woman in the family and in society are shaped by religion. The Moslem countries of the Middle East, with the exception of Tunisia and Turkey, follow Islamic law, rather than a secular code. Islamic law prescribes a status for women so inferior to men and relegates them to roles so confining that any economic or political activity for women becomes extremely difficult.[75] Several Moslem countries (Egypt, Iraq, Morocco, Syria, Tunisia, and Turkey) have instituted reforms, particularly in the areas of marriage and divorce, to reduce inequality of women. (Iran, under the Shah, had introduced similar reforms; however, those reforms were overturned by the Ayatollah Khomeini in 1979.) In spite of these reforms, Islamic

Women shop in Kuwait.

law, as practiced by the Moslem countries, still treats women as inferior to men.

The Islamic code of behavior, reinforced by the tradition of *purdah* (seclusion of women) prohibits social contact between men and women. Women are, therefore, excluded from most occupations. Although women from middle and upper classes have acquired education and entered professions in Moslem countries, a vast majority of the Moslem women are denied the opportunity to receive education or to work. Women are not even hired as domestic servants, as the work would bring women into contact with men.

Except in Turkey where the right to vote was granted to all women and men under the dictatorial rule of Mustafa Kemal (1924–1938), enfranchisement of women in Moslem countries is a relatively recent development. In the Moslem Middle Eastern countries that permit elections, women have enjoyed the right to vote and to run for political office for over two decades. In practice, however, these rights, especially the right to run for or hold political office, are mostly for women of upper economic strata. Beginning in 1979, when the Shah of Iran was ousted by a religion-inspired revolution, the political and economic gains made by women in the Moslem world have declined or even reversed because of the resurgence of Islam in several Moslem countries.

In other parts of the Third World, especially in Latin America and South Asia, religion plays a major role in determining the extent of women's political activity. Only in black African countries has religion been less prominent in this respect, perhaps because organized religions (i.e., Christianity and Islam) were introduced later in these countries than in other parts of the Third World. Tribal and in general societal traditions have been more important than religion in determining the political role of women in Africa.

It is difficult to prove that women in traditional African societies were equal to men in the political arena before European colonial rule began, yet there is no doubt that women in these societies did indeed enjoy a considerable degree of freedom and in many cases wielded political power.[76] Women have always been an important segment of Africa's economy and at present constitute over one-fourth of the labor force. In some African countries, especially West Africa, women traditionally had an active role in trade. Colonial rule and modernization adversely affected the economic and political roles African women had gained through tradition. The impact of colonial rule and modernization on women's political participation in Africa and other parts of the Third World is considered in the next section.

Impact of Colonial Rule and Modernization

In acquiring colonies in what is now called the Third World, European powers were primarily motivated by economic, political, and military objectives. They wanted to exploit the colonies for economic benefits and considered them as means of extending their political and military power. However, colonial rule also brought some modernization to the Third World. To administer the colonies, new political institutions were introduced, and for carrying on trade, highways and railroads were built. Schools were needed to educate small numbers of indigenous populations in European languages and other subjects so that the colonial powers could continue ruling with the help of the educated elites in civil service and other jobs. In some cases egalitarian and humane concepts of Western civilization helped women. For example, in India the cruel practice of *suttee,* in which a Hindu widow was required to burn alive on the funeral pyre of her husband's body, was abolished by the British. In a study of African women, Judith Van Allen observes:

Missionaries and colonial governments appear to have mitigated some of the harsher treatment of women in some places, by suppressing the slave trade, by reducing husbands' power of life and death over their wives, and by rescuing women who were left in the bush to die for having given birth to twins.[77]

Van Allen also points out that peace brought about by colonial rulers by the reduction of tribal warfare in Africa, the construction of new roads, and European imports "sometimes gave women greater mobility and increased their trading profits,"[78] though as she states, "too much is often made of this."[79]

The benefits of colonial rule for women in the Third World are outweighed by its baneful effects. Although patriarchal attitudes have existed in most countries of the world for centuries, colonial rule reinforced these attitudes in the Third World. According to Lynn Iglitzin and Ruth Ross, "the roots of women's gradual loss of power, in places such as Ghana, other parts of Africa, and South America, is found in the new patriarchal values imposed by Western colonialism."[80] Colonial administrators had little regard for the status of women in the territories that they controlled and, as Marjorie Mbilinyi states, they "sought spokesmen or headmen."[81] Education was provided primarily for males. Whatever schooling existed for females, its objective was not to train them for employment. The colonial education for females was intended to prepare them for roles at home, not for the outside world. That bias still exists to some extent in the Third World countries. In some areas where women had traditionally enjoyed relatively high status in their relations with men, patriarchal values imported from the West disrupted such tradition. A striking example in this respect occurs in Ghana, where women had considerable economic power in the traditional society and were held in high esteem. Colonial rule substantially reduced the status of women in that society. In present-day Ghana the government claims that there is no discrimination against women on the basis of sex. In practice, however, women's role in the economic and political life of the country is much reduced compared with their role in the precolonial, traditional society. Barbara Callaway comments that "the obstacles to women's full participation would appear . . . to be the result of practices which rest on cultural and institutionalized attitudes introduced into Ghana by male colonial agents, traders, and missionaries."[82]

In several colonies, women as individuals or groups joined men in the nationalist struggle for independence. The independence movements were dominated by men and the number of women prominent in these movements was relatively small. Furthermore, these women were generally from the upper classes. Nevertheless, their role in independence movements helped the cause of women in politics in the sense that after independence was achieved women could not be ignored altogether. In some cases women did achieve significant gains as a result of their participation in the independence movement. One such example is Guinea in West Africa, where "women's activism resulted in their obtaining positions in the National Assembly and in the party after independence."[83]

Leaders of the Third World countries were committed to continue modernization at an accelerated pace after independence was achieved. Modernization to these leaders has meant technological advancement as well as decrease in societal and sexual inequality. Virtually every Third World country has experienced at least some technological progress, yet neither societal inequality, based on economic or some tradition-related factors, nor sexual inequality has lessened appreciably. In fact, evidence indicates that technological progress, along with the reinforcement of patriarchal attitudes brought about by Western influence, has adversely affected the position of women in relation to men. India illustrates this trend very clearly. India has industrialized at a faster pace than most other Third World countries and, despite widespread poverty, it is considered a relatively advanced country technologically. However, men have gained far more from this advancement than have women. What is worse, in some areas men have gained at the cost of women. India had a woman prime minister—Indira Gandhi—for several years and the proportion of women in the Indian Parliament has consistently been higher than in far more developed countries such as Canada, Britain, and the United States. Indian women are also quite visible in some of the elite professions, notably medicine and civil service. Yet, Indian women's overall position has steadily declined with modernization. The proportion of Indian women in the work force has declined substantially with industrial progress. Such decline has been greater in the nonagricultural sector than in the agricultural sector.[84] In other areas, notably health and life expectancy, modernization has brought much greater gains to men than to women. Even more striking and disturbing is the fact that the proportion of female population in India has almost continuously declined since the beginning of this century.[85] Infant mortality, though reduced with progress, is substantially higher for females than for males in India. Preference for sons and neglect of female children are largely responsible for uneven gains of men and women in health and life expectancy.

Industrialization requires new skills and specializations. In the early stages of industrialization these skills and specializations, combined with new machines, create fewer jobs than are lost in traditional sectors of the economy. As industrialization advances and the economy expands, employment increases. India and most other Third World countries are still in the early stages of industrialization. Unemployment and underemployment are high in these countries because of the insufficient expansion of their

Indira Gandhi, the late prime minister of India, with the Indian masses.

economies by industrialization. The unemployment situation in the Third
World is aggravated by a high population growth rate. Because patriarchal
values predominate in the Third World, men have received preference over
women for education and skills needed for the scarce jobs. Consequently,
women's proportion in the labor force has declined in India and several other
Third World countries. Furthermore, many more women than men have
been left in lower-paying occupations that require fewer skills. Women in the
Moslem world are an exception to this general development. Because of
religious norms, women did not constitute a significant proportion of the
labor force in the traditional Moslem economies. With modernization their
proportion in the work force has increased, but as noted earlier, in most
Moslem countries this proportion is still very small.

Prospects for Change

Economic activity is a chief determinant of political participation. Women
are more active economically and politically in traditional societies than in

societies in early stages of modernization. At later stages of modernization, women are again likely to become active economic and political members of the society. It is evident that some postindustrial societies of the West, notably the United States, will experience a much-increased role of women in economics and politics in the near future. If the experience of the First World countries is any indication, women in the Third World countries may have a long way to go.

The class structure in the Third World is more rigid than in the First and Second Worlds. Most members of political elites in the Third World come from upper classes; this is even more true for women than for men. Rigid class structure, combined with patriarchal attitudes, is a major detriment to an active role for Third World women in politics. Another great obstacle to the political activity of women in the Third World is the military rule in so many of the countries. Military forces all over the world are predominantly male. In countries that recruit women into the armed forces, women seldom occupy positions in the upper echelons. It is not surprising, therefore, that military regimes do not place women in leadership positions. Of course, a change from military to civilian rule does not necessarily mean a greater role for women in politics.

Despite the odds against an active role for women in politics in the Third World, we believe that women in several of these countries will make significant progress in this area in the near future. Women and men are increasingly aware in the Third World that women have been denied equality for too long. Women's organizations exist in many Third World countries to advance women's causes. Anticipated First World women's gains will certainly encourage sexual equality in politics in at least some Third World countries.

NOTES

1. Maurice Duerger, *The Political Role of Women* (Paris: UNESCO, 1955), pp. 122–123.
2. *Time*, July 23, 1984, p. 37.
3. See JoAnn Fagot Aviel, "Political Participation of Women in Latin America," *Western Political Quarterly* 34 (March 1981): 158.
4. Stuart A. Rice, *Quantitative Methods in Politics* (New York: Knopf, 1929), pp. 246–247.
5. Survey statistics of the University of Michigan used in this paragraph are taken from Marjorie Lansing, "The American Woman: Voter and Activist," in Jane S. Jaquette, ed., *Women in Politics* (New York: Wiley, 1974), pp. 5–24.
6. See Ruth Ross, "Tradition and Role of Women in Great Britain," in Lynn B.

Iglitzin and Ruth Ross, eds., *Women in the World: A Comparative Study* (Santa Barbara, Calif.: ABC-Clio, 1976), p. 170.

7. See Janet Zollinger Giele, "Introduction: Comparative Prospectives on Women," in Janet Zollinger Giele and Audrey Chapman Smock, eds., *Women: Role and Status in Eight Countries* (New York: Wiley, 1977), p. 16, for female voter turnout statistics in Bangladesh and Egypt.

8. According to a survey conducted by *USA Today*, August 20, 1984, p. 5A, women constituted 47% and 53% of the delegates at the 1984 Republican and Democratic presidential nominating conventions, respectively.

9. See Laurel Walum Richardson, *The Dynamics of Sex and Gender,* 2d ed. (Boston: Houghton Mifflin, 1981), pp. 243–245; and Sarah Slavin Schramm, "Women and Representation: Self-Government and Role Change," *Western Political Quarterly* 34 (March 1981): 55.

10. *Time,* July 23, 1984, p. 34.

11. Schramm, p. 52

12. Marnie S. Shaul, "The Status of Women in Local Governments: An International Assessment," *Public Administration Review* 42 (November/December 1982): 494.

13. Ingunn Norderrah Means, "Scandinavian Women," in Iglitzin and Ross, p. 381.

14. Gail W. Lapidus, "Changing Women's Roles in the USSR," in Iglitzin and Ross, p. 314.

15. See Giele, p. 18.

16. See Shaul, pp. 494–495.

17. M. Kent Jennings, "Gender Roles and Inequalities in Political Participation: Results from an Eight-Nation Study," *Western Political Quarterly* 36 (September 1983): 364–385.

18. Ibid., p. 383.

19. Ibid.

20. See ibid.

21. Lynn B. Iglitzin, "The Patriarchal Heritage," in Iglitzin and Ross, p. 8.

22. Ibid., pp. 8–9.

23. See Jennings, pp. 264–265; Shaul, pp. 495–497.

24. See Shaul, p. 497.

25. Sue Ellen M. Charlton, *Women in Third World Development* (Boulder, Colo.: Westview Press, 1984), p. 34.

26. See Giele, pp. 9–15.

27. Ibid., p. 9.

28. Lois W. Banner, *Women in Modern America: A Brief History* (New York: Harcourt Brace Jovanovich, 1974), p. 41.

29. Harriet B. Applewhite, "Women and Political Power," paper delivered to the National Council of Women of the United States, October 26, 1978, New York, N.Y., p. 4.

30. For more on this interesting period see Darline G. Levy, Harriet B. Applewhite, Mary D. Johnson, *Women in Revolutionary Paris: 1789–1795* (Urbana: Univer-

sity of Illinois Press, 1979); and Harriet B. Applewhite and Darline Gay Levy, "Responses to the Political Activism of Women of the People in Revolutionary Paris, 1789–1793," in Barbara J. Harris and JoAnn K. McNamara, eds., *Women and the Structure of Society* (Durham, N.C.: Duke University Press, 1984).

31. Shirley Bernard, "Women's Economic Status: Some Cliches and Some Facts," in Jo Freeman, ed., *Women: A Feminist Perspective* (Palo Alto, Calif.: Mayfield, 1975), quoted in Richardson, p. 236.

32. Richardson, p. 236.

33. Ibid., p. 238.

34. See Walter Goodman, "Women's Studies: The Debate Continues," *New York Times Magazine,* April 22, 1984, pp. 39ff.

35. See "Feminism in the Academy," *Academe: Bulletin of the American Association of University Professors* 69, no. 5 (September/October 1983): pp. 11–37.

36. Richardson, p. 246.

37. Louis A. Wright, Neil Gross, Yurinori Ishikawa, "Japan: Goodbye Kimono, Opportunities in Foreign Firms," *Time,* December 12, 1983, p. 46.

38. See Juanita M. Kreps, *Women and the American Economy* (Englewood Cliffs, N.J.: Prentice-Hall, 1976).

39. See Jane Perlez, "Women, Power and Politics," *New York Times Magazine,* June 24, 1984, pp. 27ff.

40. See Edmund Dahlstrom, *The Changing Roles of Men and Women* [in Sweden] (Boston: Beacon Press, 1971).

41. Dorothy Robins-Mowry, *The Hidden Sun: Women in Modern Japan* (Boulder, Colo.: Westview Press, 1983), pp. 85–86.

42. Robert C. Christopher, *The Japanese Mind: The Goliath Explained* (New York: Simon & Schuster, 1983), p. 115.

43. *Time,* "Japan," p. 46; and Christopher, p. 104.

44. Robins-Mowry, p. 319.

45. Christopher, p. 104.

46. Ibid., 117.

47. Evelyne Sullerot, *Women, Society and Change* (New York: McGraw-Hill, 1971), p. 248.

48. Joan Ecklein, "Women in the German Democratic Republic: Impact of Culture and Social Policy," in Janet Zollinger Giele, ed., *Women in the Middle Years: Current Knowledge and Directions for Research and Policy* (New York: Wiley, 1982).

49. Y. Z. Danilova, *et al., Soviet Women: Some Aspects of the Status of Women in the U.S.S.R.* (Moscow: Progress Publishers, 1975), bookjacket introduction.

50. Alfred G. Meyer, "Marxism and the Women's Movement," in Dorothy Atkinson, *et al., Women in Russia* (Stanford, Calif.: Stanford University Press, 1977), pp. 101–102.

51. Ibid., p. 86.

52. "The Communist Manifesto," in David McLellan, ed., *Karl Marx: Selected Writings* (Oxford: Oxford University Press, 1977), p. 244.

53. Ibid., 227.

54. Ibid., 229.

55. Ibid., 238.

56. Friedrich Engels, "The Origins of the Family, Private Property and the State," in *Karl Marx and Frederick Engels: Selected Works* (New York: International Publishers, 1968), p. 495.

57. Ibid., p. 496.

58. Ibid., p. 517.

59. V. I. Lenin, *The Emancipation of Women* [a selection of writings] (New York: International Publishers, 1978), pp. 13–14.

60. A. Richard Stites, "Women and the Russian Intelligentsia," in Atkinson, p. 61.

61. The notable exceptions of Elona Ceausescu in Romania and Jiang Qing in China are really the result of their marriages to politically powerful men—Nicolae Ceausescu, president of Romania and chief of its Communist party and Mao Zedong, chairman of the Communist party of China.

62. Vadim Medish, *The Soviet Union,* 2d ed. (Englewood Cliffs, N.J.: Prentice-Hall, 1984), pp. 279–280.

63. Jerry Hough and Merle Fainsod, *How the Soviet Union Is Governed* (Cambridge, Mass.: Harvard University Press, 1979), p. 343.

64. Medish, pp. 279–280.

65. Wang Zi quoted in Elisabeth Croll, *Feminism and Socialism in China* (New York: Schocken Books, 1980), p. 317.

66. Elisabeth Croll, *Chinese Women since Mao* (Armonk, N.Y.: M. E. Sharpe, 1983), p. 118.

67. Lucian W. Pye, *China: An Introduction,* 3d ed. (Boston: Little, Brown, 1984), p. 278.

68. Aviel, p. 157.

69. Ibid., p. 158.

70. Ibid.

71. Ibid.

72. Perdita Huston, *Third World Women Speak Out* (New York: Praeger, 1979), p. 102.

73. Mary Elmendorf, "Mexico: The Many Worlds of Women," in Giele and Smock, p. 164.

74. Roderic A. Camp, "Women and Political Leadership in Mexico: A Comparative Study of Female and Male Political Elites," *Journal of Politics* 41 (May 1979): 421.

75. See Nadia H. Youssef, "Women in the Moslem World," in Iglitzin and Ross, pp. 203–215.

76. See Judith Van Allen, "Memsahile, Militante, Femme Libre: Political and Apolitical Styles of Modern African Women," in Jaquette, pp. 304–305.

77. Judith Van Allen, "African Women, 'Modernization,' and National Liberation," in Iglitzin and Ross, p. 33.

78. Ibid.

79. Ibid.

80. Iglitzin and Ross, p. 186.

81. Quoted in Van Allen, "Memsahile, Militante, Femme Libre: Political and Apolitical Styles of Modern African Women," p. 306.
82. Barbara J. Callaway, "Women in Ghana," in Iglitzin and Ross, p. 199.
83. Shaul, p. 494.
84. See Charlton, p. 220.
85. Ibid., pp. 34–35.

14

International Relations
of Three Worlds

Interactions between states, along with the interactions of groups and private individuals across state boundaries, are called international relations. States are the primary actors in international relations; groups and private individuals are secondary actors. States pursue two broad categories of goals in their relations with one another: (1) political–strategic and (2) economic. The interactions of states in order to achieve these goals are of two types—cooperation and conflict. In interacting with other states, every state must function within certain external and internal constraints.

The states of the First World have played a dominant role in the international relations of the twentieth century. According to some analysts, the power of the West has declined since the 1960s; however, the West remains a predominant force in international relations. Since World War II, Soviet–U.S. rivalry, often referred to as the Cold War, has overshadowed all other international problems. In the Third World, Western policy makers have encountered failure in pursuit of their goals on several occasions.

Theoretical goals of the Second World are derived principally from the writings of Marx, Engels, and Lenin. In practice, Second World states often pursue their historical national interests in international relations. The most powerful of the Second World states, the Soviet Union, has developed a military might on par with that of the United States, in order to pursue its interests.

Most of the Third World states claim to pursue the policy of nonalignment, though in reality only half are truly nonaligned. Third World states demand a restructuring of the world economic order to improve their economies. The resources of the Third World states are limited. In the interactions of states, there are far more conflicts in the Third World than in the other two worlds.

Throughout this book we have presented an analysis of the different aspects of politics and considered the relationship between politics and economics. We have been concerned with the working of the political and economic forces within the boundaries of individual states. The states do not function in isolation from one another; every state, whether in the First, Second, or Third World, interacts with several other states. The interactions among states take place within each world as well as across the three worlds. Such interactions, along with the interactions of groups and private individuals across state boundaries, are called international relations.

ACTORS IN INTERNATIONAL RELATIONS

States are the primary actors in international relations; groups and private individuals are secondary actors. We are concerned far more with the states here, although some groups and even some private individuals play significant roles in international relations. Of particular importance are the groups called intergovernmental or international organizations. The United Nations, European Community, Organization of Petroleum Exporting Countries, North Atlantic Treaty Organization, and the Warsaw Treaty Organization are some prominent examples of intergovernmental organizations. Intergovernmental organizations have states as their members and function in accordance with their constitutions or charters. Decision-making institutions of these organizations are established as stipulated in their constitutions. Of all the intergovernmental organizations, the institutions of the European Community are most developed. European Community institutions are modeled after a state's governmental institutions, namely, the legislature, executive, judiciary, and the civil service. Decisions made by the intergovernmental organizations have an international impact. An obvious example is the oil price per barrel fixed by OPEC. Decisions of other intergovernmental organizations also have wide-ranging impact, though the general public is less aware of them than of the decisions by the oil cartel.

A large number of organizations have individuals or nongovernment groups as their members, yet they have an international character because of the nature of their activities. Such organizations are called nongovernmental instead of intergovernmental.[1] Nongovernmental organizations include multinational corporations. Individuals and institutions hold stocks in MNCs and although such a corporation has its headquarters in one state, it functions through its subsidiaries in more than one state. Other examples of nongovernmental organizations are global associations of professionals such as political scientists, economists, or physicists. These organizations facilitate the exchange of ideas of their members from different states.

With some notable exceptions such as the release of a U.S. naval officer

The United Nations headquarters in New York City.

from captivity in Syria and freedom for some Americans jailed in Cuba, both accomplished in 1984 as a result of Democratic presidential candidate Reverend Jesse Jackson's efforts, the role of the private individual in international relations is not decisive. Individuals' roles in international relations are mostly limited to travel, attendance at foreign universities, and exchanges of a private nature. These interactions are not as significant as the roles of intergovernmental or nongovernmental organizations in international relations.

GOALS AND RESOURCES

In their relations with one another, the states of the three worlds pursue certain goals that can be divided into two broad categories: (1) political–strategic and (2) economic. Self-preservation, security, maintaining or increasing one's power, and peace are major political–strategic goals; economic development is the chief economic goal. States strive not only to defend their borders, but also to preserve their economic and political systems and their cultures. Security and self-preservation have the same meaning for most states in the Third World; for the former colonies in Africa and Asia security has the added significance of preserving newly won independence. To the smaller states in the First and the Second Worlds, the two goals are indistinguishable. However, the major powers of the First and Second Worlds perceive security as different from self-preservation. To the United States and the Soviet Union, security means maintaining and possibly increasing their power in the world vis-à-vis each other. Thus, invasion of a smaller state is a step toward security, as is the deployment of missiles on the territories of allies.

Maintaining or increasing power, whether it is perceived as indistinguishable from security or as a distinct goal by itself, is important for virtually every state in the world and has been so throughout most of history.[2] Smaller states seek power to secure themselves against interference in their internal affairs by unfriendly neighbors or major powers. Power is also pursued by smaller states to carry out aggressive designs on neighboring states. Major powers are less concerned about interference in their internal affairs; their object in seeking power is to maintain a position of parity with their rivals and, if possible, to achieve a position of dominance in the world. It is often said that the United States and the Soviet Union want to expand their ideologies of democracy and Communism into other states. They are, however, more concerned about extending their power rather than their ideologies into other states.

Peace is often mentioned as a goal pursued by states in international relations. Although practically every state professes the goal of peace, few states have qualms about ignoring this goal if war serves the goals of self-preservation, security, and power. We do not intend to minimize the importance of peace in the world, especially because we live under the shadow of a nuclear holocaust, however small this possibility may be. States possessing nuclear weapons consider them as an effective deterrent against a nuclear war; they argue that the possibility of nuclear retaliation would prevent an enemy state from initiating a nuclear attack. A similar deterrent is not available against the use of conventional weapons, which are still used in wars fought around the world.

Economic development is sought by rich and poor states alike. Success in realizing this goal often determines the political future of those in power. It is no coincidence that many Third World states with low eonomic development have experienced rather frequent government changes by military coups. The economic record of the political leaders in the Third World as well as in the First and Second Worlds is a major factor in the retention or loss of their power. In pursuing economic development states cooperate as well as conflict with one another. Thus, trade, aid, and investments abroad result from agreement and cooperation among states. The same factors can also lead to conflicts.

Goals can only be achieved with resources. States differ in the amount and extent of resources that they possess. An overall measure of a state's economic resources is its GNP—the total market value of goods and services produced in a state over a certain period of time. The growth rate of a state's GNP indicates to what an extent these resources are increasing or decreasing. The annual per capita GNP and its annual growth rate are often used to compare the economic resources of different states. By computing the value of goods and services produced in a state in a year, GNP per capita measures more resources of a state than does any other index. The value of agricultural as well as industrial products, coal, natural gas, oil, electricity, steel, thousands of consumer goods, and even weapons—conventional as well as nuclear—is included in the GNP per capita. The GNP indirectly measures a state's level of technology and the productivity level of its workers, because they are crucial to the production of goods and services. The average annual growth rate of a state's GNP per capita, if computed for several years, indicates the resiliency of its economy.

In Table 14.1, GNP per capita and its average annual growth rate for selected states are given. About 30% of Third World states have GNP per capita below 500 U.S. dollars, and a majority's GNP per capita is well below $1000. In most cases the average growth rate of GNP per capita in the Third World is under 3% and in some cases it is even negative. China's GNP per capita is in unison with that of the Third World rather than the Second World. The GNP per capita of Second World states such as Hungary and Romania is closer to that of the upper-income states in the Third World. The GNP per capita of the Soviet Union is toward the highest end of the Third World and the lowest end of the First World. As expected, the highest per capita GNP and the highest average growth rates are in the First World and in some of the oil-exporting states.

A state's population, geographic location, and military capabilities are also important resources. In several Third World states with high population growth rates and low economic growth rates, population has become more of a burden than a resource. Nevertheless, it is the people who develop and utilize the nonhuman natural resources and technology, so population must be considered as a resource in every state. A strategic geographic location can be used by a state as an important resource. On the other hand, if a state is land-locked and has no direct access to sea, geography limits its resources. The military capabilities of a state depend not only on weapons and technology, but also on the armed forces—their number as well as their training and morale.

The resources of a state include its alliances (and the help it can expect from allies in achieving certain goals) and additional territory it may occupy in case of victory in a war. Skills of diplomats, intelligence officers' expertise

Table 14.1   GNP Per Capita and Its Average Annual Growth Rate for Selected Countries

	GNP per capita U.S. dollars, 1981	Average annual growth rate, 1960–81
United Kingdom	9,110	2.1
Japan	10,080	6.3
France	12,190	3.8
United States	12,820	2.3
Federal Republic of Germany	13,450	3.2
China	300	5.0
Hungary	2,100	5.0
Romania	2,540	8.2
USSR	4,766	[a]
Chad	110	−2.2
India	260	1.4
Ghana	400	−1.1
Indonesia	530	4.1
Egypt	650	3.5
El Salvador	650	1.5
Nigeria	870	3.5
Republic of Korea	1,700	6.9
Brazil	2,220	5.1
Mexico	2,250	3.8
Venezuela	4,220	2.4
Saudi Arabia	12,600	7.8
United Arab Emirates	24,660	Not available

Source: The World Bank, *World Development Report, 1983* (New York: Oxford University Press, 1983). GNP per capita for the USSR is computed from estimates for 1980 in *Hammond Almanac, 1983*.
[a] *World Development Report, 1983* does not list the average annual growth rate for the USSR. According to another source this growth rate varied between 2.7 and 5.2% in the period 1960 to 1980. See U.S. Congress Joint Economic Committee, *Soviet Economy in the 1980's: Problems and Prospects*, Part 1 (Washington, D.C.: Government Printing Office, 1983), p. 154.

in gathering information, quality of leadership, and people's morale are also important resources, albeit intangible, used by states for achieving goals in international relations.

No state can utilize all of its resources in the pursuit of its goals in international relations. Constraints on the use of resources in pursuit of goals in international relations arise not only from the need for allocation of resources at home, but also from the political orientations of the elites and the masses in a society (and from the anticipated reactions of a state's allies in the world). The constraints caused by the political orientations of the masses in the West may also be a significant factor in the utilization of resources abroad, but that is not the case in the Second and Third Worlds.

Control over resources is the power of a state in international relations. As certain constraints limit the use of resources for realizing goals in international relations, only a portion of the total power at the disposal of a state can be exerted at any given time. A state as powerful as the United States had to withdraw from Southeast Asia partly because it felt constrained not to utilize all of its resources for achieving its goals in that region.

INTERACTIONS AMONG STATES

States achieve their goals in international relations by interacting with one another. Interactions among states can be divided into two broad categories—cooperation and competition.[3] Although cultural exchanges between states indicate cooperation with little competition and war between two adversaries reflects competition (or rather hostility with no cooperation), most interactions among states combine both cooperation and competition. Even relations between states which on the surface appear to be based primarily on cooperation contain elements of competition. The United States imports a large number of automobiles annually from Japan. This trade relation is largely based on cooperation and mutual benefit. Japan gains by selling its surplus automobiles to the United States, and the latter benefits by increased competition in the automobile industry at home and consequently higher-quality automobiles for the U.S. consumers. However, this relationship also has elements of competition. Japan may like to export more cars than it does to the United States. The United States is not willing to accept an unrestricted increase in imported Japanese cars because it would affect adversely the domestic automobile industry—a consequence that the powerful lobbies of U.S. car manufacturers and auto workers would not tolerate.

Relations between the United States and the Soviet Union are often competitive and sometimes openly hostile. Both superpowers seek to maintain and possibly increase their power in the world. Both also fear each other and engage in a seemingly endless arms race. These two powers, however, do cooperate at times. Cooperation is apparent in trade relations and scientific, educational, and cultural exchanges, and even in the area of the arms race. For years negotiations have been ongoing (with occasional interruptions) between the United States and the Soviet Union for agreement on weapons reduction. Considering the importance of an arms control agreement to world peace and the effort and time expended by negotiators of the two superpowers on this issue, the agreements so far on arms control are not impressive.[4] There is, however, no doubt that although the primary aspect of this interaction is competitive, cooperation on arms control will also continue between the two superpowers.

Elements of cooperation and competition can be discerned in the relations of other states also. The relations of states in the First World are mainly cooperative, though competition is often present and in some cases becomes significant. In the relations of the Soviet Union with its East European allies, cooperation is even more noticeable than in the First World, although even in these relations competition is far from absent. The relations of the Soviet Union and China are predominantly competitive, but these two powers also cooperate. In the relations of the states in the Third World the element of competition is greater than that of cooperation. Cooperation among the Third World states should not be underrated, however, because in bilateral relations in many cases and in some of the intergovernmental organizations, especially the United Nations, they cooperate more than they compete. In the relations of states across the three worlds, cooperation as well as competition exists.

The major instruments of cooperative and competitive interactions used by states in pursuit of their goals are diplomatic, economic, psychological, and military. Exchange of diplomats is a practice that states have undertaken for centuries. The role of a state's embassy as its representative in other states has declined in modern times, as it is now possible for a government to convey instant messages directly to another government by telephone, cable, or radio. Political leaders or diplomats specially appointed for the task of negotiating with a foreign government can reach any part of the world by jet in a few hours. Of course, embassies still play a significant, though markedly reduced role as instruments of interactions between states. They regularly send reports to home governments regarding their relations with the host governments and conditions in the host states. Moreover, the consulates, which have a status similar to the embassies, protect the citizens of their states abroad. Consulate offices in major cities are also responsible for trade and travel and immigration of foreigners to their (consulates') home states.

Trade, aid, monetary policy, and investments abroad are economic instruments of interaction among states. Virtually every state has trade relations with other states. Third World states expect trade concessions from affluent states, especially of the First World; in fact they demand a redistribution of the world's wealth through their campaign for the establishment of NIEO (see Chapter 10). Trade and aid are also used as punitive measures in the form of boycotts (refusal to buy), embargoes (refusal to sell), and aid reductions or stoppages.

Governments control the supply of money in their states, and in some cases abroad, through their monetary policies. As only the states of the First

World control the internationally exchangeable hard currencies, their monetary policies have an impact in the Western states and in the states of the Second and Third Worlds. The monetary policy of the United States is the most influential in the world. Investments abroad are also largely in the hands of the Western states. It is mistakenly believed by some that the bulk of Western investments is in the Third World. The fact is that corporations based in Western states have substantially larger investments in the First World than in the Third World for the obvious reason of higher profits in conditions of political and economic stability. In the Third World states, foreign corporations fear nationalization of their subsidiaries.

The major psychological instrument of interaction among states is propaganda. (Of course, in negotiations between governments and even in statements of the leaders of the states, elements of psychology are present.) Large amounts of money are spent by the United States and the Soviet Union to convince the world of their righteousness and to instigate rebellion among the people of certain states against their governments. China uses propaganda for similar purposes, though not to the extent that the two superpowers do. Other states, including those in the Third World, also resort to propaganda against their adversaries. The major vehicles of propaganda are radio, film, television, books, magazines, and newspapers.

Cooperation through military interaction is apparent in military alliances such as NATO and WTO, in the placement of troops and missiles on the territories of allies, and in some special arrangements or treaties stipulating joint military maneuvers or consultation among allies during crises. The arms race, armed conflicts, wars, and the chances for a nuclear war represent the competitive, darker side of this interaction.

CONSTRAINTS ON FOREIGN POLICY

A state's interactions with other states in pursuit of its goals in international relations constitute its *foreign policy*. In formulating and conducting its foreign policy, every state must function within certain external and internal constraints.[5] External restraints are determined by the power distribution among states and by the nature of a state's relations with other states. When the United States, for example, makes and implements policy on Lebanon, it is constrained by the amount of power that it can use in this case as well as by its relations with Lebanon, Israel, other states in the Middle East, and, of course, the Soviet Union.

Every state formulates goals and makes decisions in foreign policy in order to protect and promote its *national interest*, defined here as the well-being of a state's population, especially of the dominant groups. Such goals and decisions are influenced by the history and traditions of a state and by its ideology (prevailing belief system such as democracy or Communism). The demands of a society, the nature of a state's government, the roles of the central decision makers, and the individual characteristics of the decision makers are also important internal constraints on a state's foreign policy. As explained in Chapter 8 on interest groups, in the First World demands are articulated by organized groups, in the Second World governments control most of such groups, and in the Third World there are relatively few organized groups. Second and Third World governments recognize societal demands; however, they feel less constrained by them than do the First World governments.

The nature of a state's government determines the roles of institutions and central decision makers in making and implementing foreign policy. In the United States, the president exercises vast powers in foreign policy, but cannot ignore advisors, the Congress, and the public. In the Soviet Union the General Secretary of the Communist party is the most powerful decision maker in the country. He consults with other members of the party's Politburo, but the Supreme Soviet and the public have virtually no role in foreign policy. The military in the Soviet Union is very powerful in the area of foreign policy, perhaps more so than in the United States. In the First, Second, and Third Worlds, the nature of government similarly determines the roles of the institutions and the decision makers in foreign policy.

The roles of a state's central decision makers and their individual characteristics affect their perceptions and behavior in foreign policy. The nature of government, societal expectations, and individual decision makers' perceptions and expectations of themselves determine their roles in foreign policy. The individual characteristics of a decision maker reflect his or her personality, strengths, weaknesses, and idiosyncrasies. The individual characteristics of decision makers in a state differ. When leaders from the three worlds are compared, such differences appear even more striking because of the unique socialization processes they have experienced.

THE FIRST WORLD

Western States as Actors in the International System

The states of the First World have played a dominant role in the international politics of the twentieth century. The importance of the First World becomes clear when we consider the extent to which the foreign policy actions of the Western states have determined the nature of modern international life. At the time of the outbreak of the First World War in 1914, the Western states of Europe and North America had political control of over 80% of the world's population. This control was the result of the colonization of vast areas of Africa, Asia, and the Middle East by Great Britain, France, Germany, Italy, Belgium, the Netherlands, Spain, and Portugal. The creation of colonial empires provided the West with short-term economic benefits and prestige, but in the long run colonialism left behind a bitter legacy of resentment against the West and acted as a catalyst for the states of the Third World to seek to duplicate the development of the West. Two forces, anticolonial sentiment and the desire to obtain a redistribution of the world's resources, have determined the basic relationship between the First and Third Worlds in the contemporary period. In addition to the legacy of colonialism, both World Wars were the direct result of political and military competition between the Western states. In World War I the rivalry between Germany on the one hand and Great Britain and France on the other, and to a lesser extent between Austria-Hungary and Russia, produced a conflict that was a turning point in history.[6] For the first time states waged total war in which the objective was the complete destruction of the enemy state, including the starvation and demoralization of the civilian population. The strains of war also contributed to the collapse of Tsarist Russia and the subsequent Bolshevik Revolution. The victory of the Bolsheviks was the first step in the development of a political world based on Marxist–Leninist principles. In addition, World War I began the political and economic decline of Western Europe and the rise of the United States and Japan as major powers. World War II was also a catalyst for major change. The nuclear age began in 1945 when the United States used the first atomic bomb against Japan. The war also further accelerated the political and military decline of Western Europe and temporarily produced a *bipolar* world in which the two superpowers, the United States and the Soviet Union, enjoyed hegemony in a system devoid of political and military rivals. Finally, World War II brought the borders of the Soviet Union far to the west of prewar Poland. The geopolitical gains of the Soviet Union provided the background for the intense political, diplomatic, ideological, and psychological competition with the West known as the *Cold War*.[7]

From 1945 to the late 1960s, the states of the West continued to play a dominant role in the international system. With the help of U.S. postwar economic assistance, the states of Western Europe and Japan recovered sufficiently to play a major role in international economic life. The formation of the EEC has created an economic unit equal to that of the United States (see Chapter 5). In addition, since the 1960s, Japan has emerged as one of the most productive and economically aggressive states in the world (see Chapter 10). During this period, the United States retained its position as the only state that could claim superpower status in both of the two major international issue-areas, military–strategic affairs and international economic relations.[8]

Western Goals and Resources: The Contemporary Era

Recently, political analysts have given great attention to the changes that have occurred in the international system. A constant theme is the decline of the power of the West since the late 1960s.[9] According to such arguments the Soviet Union has become a global superpower and has attained military parity with the United States. In addition, several states of the Third World have been able to defy Western military power. The West's economy has also proven vulnerable to the activities of international cartels, such as OPEC. These conditions indicate that important transformations in the international system have affected the West's position vis-a-vis both the Second and Third Worlds. The cumulative effect has been to create a diffusion or fragmentation of power in the international system.[10] From the perspective of the West three new conditions exist today: (1) power is more evenly distributed than it has been at any time since the end of World War II, (2) the absolute military superiority of the United States over the Soviet Union has ended, (3) in dealing with the Third World, the West has been forced to recognize the limits of its power in certain political and economic matters. Simply stated, since the 1960s there has been a decline in the power of the Western states relative to that of the Second and Third Worlds, and the military, if not economic, gap, between the three worlds has narrowed. This does not mean, however, that the West has lost its position of dominance in the international system. The United States remains the only state in the world with superpower status in both the military and economic issue-areas, and no major international agreement is viable without the support of the United States. Similarly, the larger states of Western Europe and Japan retain their status as middle-level powers.[11] Middle-level powers possess major influence over international economic matters. For example, the EEC and Japan continue to be among the most important economic actors. In addition, middle-level powers possess significant conventional military capabilities, and two states, France and Great Britain, possess independent nuclear strike forces. Overall, the Western states retain significant power, but that power is exercised in a world in which the Third World states are independent nations, not colonies, and the Soviet Union has used its natural and human resources to achieve military parity with the West.

Next we will examine the foreign policies of the Western states toward the Second and Third Worlds. The discussion of relations with the Second World focuses almost exclusively on the relationship between the two superpowers. One theme is apparent in the international relations of the West: in the age of the diffusion of power, the Western states are pursuing preservationist foreign policy objectives designed to protect their positions of dominance in both military–strategic and economic issue-areas. In the case of relations with the Soviet Union, the preservationist programs have included the policy of containment and the maintenance of a powerful military force to deter the Soviet Union from aggressive military action. In relations with the Third World, the Western states have sought to preserve the liberal international economic order in the face of demands by the LDCs for a new economic order.

Interaction: Relations with the Second World

Since World War II the main military–strategic issue has been the relationship between the states of the First and Second Worlds, especially the relationship between the two superpowers, the United States and the Soviet Union. After a brief relaxation of tensions in the 1970s known as *détente*, political competition and hostile rhetoric reintensified. It was clear once again that the Soviet–U.S. rivalry overshadowed all other international problems as the most serious threat to world stability and peace.[12] The Cold War refers to Soviet–U.S. competition in the period since 1945. The origins of the present rivalry date to the First World War when Lenin and his Bolshevik followers first assumed control in Russia. However, the conflict between the two powers intensified during and after World War II as the West's liberal objectives clashed with the Soviet Union's plans to control Eastern Europe and expand influence into other areas of the World.

The Western states and the Soviet Union have competed to shape the postwar world. The competition has included political maneuvering, diplomatic manipulations, psychological warfare, ideological hostility, economic warfare, a major arms race (despite some arms-control agreements), and peripheral wars.[13] As the term Cold War implies, however, the competition falls short of a direct military confrontation between the two superpowers. The initial political conflict focused on Germany and Poland, which the United States wanted open to Western influence and which the Soviet Union sought to incorporate into the Soviet bloc, its system of satellite states in Eastern Europe. Subsequently, competition for political influence extended to areas both inside and outside Europe, including Greece, Turkey, Iran, Korea, China, Jordan, Lebanon, Egypt (the Suez Canal), Laos, Cambodia, Vietnam, and Cuba. Major crises involving the use of force by one of the parties (or the potential use of force) occurred in Berlin (1948–1949, 1958–1959, 1961), Greece (1946–1948), Czechoslovakia (1948, 1968), Indochina (1947–1954), Korea (1950–1953), Suez (Egypt, 1956), Hungary (1956), Jordan and Lebanon (1958), Cuba (1962), Vietnam (1964–1975), the Dominican Republic (1965), Afghanistan (1979), and Grenada (1983).[14]

Western Perceptions of the Soviet Union. Western policy toward the Soviet Union has been the topic of continuous debate since the beginning of the

U.S. helicopter shot down during the invasion of Grenada in October, 1983.

Cold War. The debate has involved a wide range of participants including national legislators and executives, foreign service elites, political candidates, political party leaders, the news media, members of the academic community, and segments of the general public attentive to foreign policy issues. The current debate centers on three issues: (1) Soviet intentions, (2) Soviet capabilities, and (3) the possible existence of mutual shared interests with the Soviet Union.[15]

Two basic conceptions of the Soviet Union have been advanced in the West since 1945. The first, sometimes called the *essentialist school* or *essentialist mind-set*, represents the Soviet Union as a state in the service of an ideology. It places great emphasis on those ideological statements by Communist party leaders that stress continuity with the historical goal of Lenin and Marx, world revolution. As Soviet conduct develops naturally from the totalitarian, Marxist, imperialistic, and "Russian" nature of its society, there is little prospect for change in Soviet relations with the West.[16] Political conflict with the Soviet Union is inevitable, and a nuclear military confrontation is a constant possibility. Essentialists advocate maximum military preparedness and political vigilance by the states of the West. Finally, the essentialist school argues that the present Soviet military buildup exceeds legitimate defense requirements and indicates an attempt to achieve military superiority over the West. The buildup is considered to be additional proof that the Soviet Union seeks world hegemony.

A rival mind-set, sometimes called the *mechanistic approach*, represents the Soviet Union as a state pursuing the traditional goal of geopolitical expansion. Although the Soviet Union presents itself to the world as the leader of an ideological movement, it behaves in a pragmatic manner and pursues limited, low-risk strategies. Because the Soviet Union pursues traditional goals similar to those of other great powers, Soviet expansion can be minimized and controlled by the local application of political, economic, and military counterforce by the West. The *policy of containment*, which has been the most consistent Western response to the Soviet Union, is the product of the mechanistic mind-set.[17] Mechanists do not see a high probability of war between the superpowers and believe that the combination of a strong Western deterrent force and successful crisis management will be sufficient to keep the peace. The mechanists also argue that the current Soviet military buildup is a reaction to years of military inferiority to the United States, and is intended to achieve parity with the United States but not superiority. The mechanistic viewpoint has been widely accepted in the upper levels of government in the West.[18]

In the late 1960s a third approach to relations with the Soviet Union developed in the West. This school has been called the *interactionist or cybernetic mind-set*. It sees the interaction between the West and the Soviet Union as a complex relationship consisting of various perceptions, misperceptions, areas of conflict, and certain limited areas of shared interests. Rather than viewing Soviet foreign policy as the product of a permanent source (i.e., Marxist ideology), interactionists argue that Soviet behavior is at least in part reactive, that is, influenced by the West's actions toward the Soviet Union.[19] In addition, the interactionists see elements of diversity, if not pluralism, in Soviet elite politics and believe that the possibility exists for a significant evolution in the Soviet system.[20] As the name of the school implies, it places great emphasis on the relationship or interaction between the two superpowers. The decision to adopt a conciliatory or confrontational style in diplomacy today may well determine the prospects for peace or war in the future. Interactionist thinking was most influential in Western Europe during the period of détente.

The three basic approaches toward the Soviet Union can be used to explain the current foreign policy positions of the Western states. Between 1945 and the late 1960s, the mechanistic mind-set dominated in North America and Europe. Although on both sides of the Atlantic essentialists had an important impact on public opinion, the foreign policy process at the governmental level was determined by mechanists. After the mid-1960s,

European leaders increasingly came to believe that improved relations with the Soviet Union were possible. Beginning with France and the German Federal Republic, the states of Europe advocated agreements to control the growth of strategic weapons, the expansion of trade with the Soviet Union, and expanded diplomatic contacts including summit meetings. The European position was the result of both a fear of nuclear war and an acceptance of the assumptions of the interactionist school. In the 1980s, the Europeans continue to seek meaningful dialogue with the Soviet Union. In the United States, the mechanistic mind-set continued to dominate even during the era of détente. Therefore, U.S. foreign policy continues to reflect the assumptions of the mechanistic school, although many important U.S. leaders have expressed the hope for improved relations with the Soviet Union. Since the Soviet invasion of Afghanistan in 1979, there has been increased concern in the United States about Soviet intentions and capabilities. As a result of this concern, the essentialist position has gained new popularity. Both essentialist and mechanistic viewpoints are represented in the administration of President Ronald Reagan, who has personally expressed essentialist sentiments in many of his public speeches.[21]

Interaction: Relations with the Third World

The recent changes in the international system are more apparent in the Third World than in any other area. The existence of more than 100 Third World states with diverse foreign policy objectives greatly increases the complexity of world politics. It also complicates foreign policy making for individual Western actors, especially the United States, Japan, and the EEC, which are extensively involved in international economic and political affairs and maintain diplomatic relations with most Third World states. From the Western perspective the problem of dealing with the Third World is further complicated by the growing military capabilities of some of the states and the willingness of diverse groups to employ terrorism. Most problems in the Third World are no longer susceptible to simple displays of Western military force. Since the onset of the Cold War, both the United States and the Soviet Union have sought to cultivate military and political allies in the Third World through the dispensation of military and economic aid. Syria, Iran, Iraq, Egypt, and Vietnam have received sophisticated weaponry and now constitute what some sources have called "regional powers." (Regional powers are states with conventional [nonnuclear] military capabilities sufficient to inflict substantial casualties on attacking forces in their region, even the conventional forces of the superpowers.) Two regional powers, Vietnam and Iran, have demonstrated the ability to frustrate even the force of the United States. More than any other event, the American involvement in

Vietnam (1964–1975) demonstrated the limits of Western power in dealing with the Third World. The power of the West has also proven inadequate to protect Western interests for the many terrorist attacks committed since the 1960s.

Changing Factors in First World–Third World Relations. Recent foreign policy failures in the Third World have prompted a lively debate among Western analysts. Two basic explanations for the failure of Western policy have been advanced. One attributes the failure to the inability of Western states to develop clear-cut objectives in the Third World and to commit sufficient political, economic, and military resources to their pursuit. An alternative explanation sees the Western states entangled in a political environment shaped by complex factors that are increasingly unfavorable to the West. Since the 1980 U.S. election, the view has become popular in the United States that the foreign policy failures experienced in the Third World are the result of a "post-Vietnam syndrome" in America rather than of a set of factors that are largely beyond the control of the West.[22] According to the current logic, the United States' present disadvantageous position in such countries as Iran, Angola, Ethiopia, and Nicaragua is the result of the loss of U.S. military superiority to the Soviet Union, the failure to adequately aid friendly governments, and fear of another costly military intervention like that in Vietnam.[23] As a remedy the Reagan administration has increased economic and military aid to states such as El Salvador and intervened militarily in the Caribbean state of Grenada. Critics argue that although U.S. military intervention may prove decisive in a small country like Grenada, the present relationship between the West and the Third World is shaped by a set of complex factors unamenable to the unilateral initiatives of any actor.

The final resolution to the debate on the Third World is unknown, but it is clear that four major factors in the Third World have worked to frustrate Western foreign policy makers. First, there has been a proliferation of issues in First World–Third World relations.[24] These relations now involve myriad issue-areas, including economic aid, trade, arms transfers, access to natural resources, human rights, nuclear proliferation, immigration, security, terrorism, debt repayment, the status of MNCs, and the future of the international economy. Not only has the proliferation of issues complicated the task of foreign policy makers, but many Third World states have linked seemingly unrelated issues to force concessions from the Western states.[25] For example, Saudi Arabia has linked the maintenance of high levels of petroleum production, an action desired by the West, to the sale of high-performance fighter aircraft by the United States to Saudi Arabia.[26] (Interestingly, the United States has also conditioned U.S. aid on the pursuit of a rigorous human rights policy, a linkage that has caused deterioration in political relations with the governments of several Third World states, including Brazil, Chile, South Korea, and the Philippines.)

The second complicating factor is the existence of widespread political instability in the Third World. Coups, assassinations, and other forms of political violence frequently lead to the overthrow of governments, which prevents policy continuity and implementation of long-range programs. As the case of the Iranian Revolution of 1979 illustrates, decades of diplomatic effort and billions of dollars of aid can be lost if governments friendly towards the West are replaced by hostile ones.[27] In addition, governments in the Third World are frequently not in control of their territories, and nonstate actors (e.g., guerrilla groups and private armies) often have sufficient military strength to challenge the official armed forces. Lebanon stands as a case in point. In the confused political environment there, Syrians, Druse Moslems, Palestinians, Christian Falangists, groups loyal to the Ayatollah Khomeini, and troops loyal to the Lebanese government have frustrated U.S. and Israeli foreign policy objectives. The deaths of 241 U.S. marines in 1983 at the hands of an obscure terrorist group at Beirut airport brutally illustrated that such unstable areas are beyond the military and political control of the Western states.

Third, after more than a decade of minimal involvement in Third World areas, the Soviet Union has escalated its political and military involvement. The increased presence is a direct result of the growing conventional military capability of the Soviet Union. By the mid-1970s, the Soviet Union was, like the United States, a global power capable of projecting military power to most of the areas of the Third World. Since the mid-1970s, Soviet or Cuban troops have intervened in civil wars in Angola and Mozambique and on behalf of Ethiopia in its border war with Somalia. In addition, a Soviet military buildup has occurred in South Yemen (the People's Democratic Republic of Yemen), and Vietnam, a strong Soviet ally, has invaded neighboring Kampuchea. In 1979, Soviet forces directly invaded Afghanistan and established a puppet government there. From the Western perspective, the Soviet and Cuban initiatives have given new urgency to relations with the Third World. Two areas, the Caribbean and the Persian Gulf, have been singled out by Western policy makers for special attention because of their strategic importance to the West.[28]

Finally, the sharp economic differences and the ideological distance between the First and Third Worlds have retarded mutual understanding between the parties. In response to overwhelming economic problems, many Third World elites have adopted Marxist–Leninist or socialist prescriptions for development which advocate state control of the economy and economic nationalism. This condition has led to theoretical and practical political conflicts with Western governments, which embrace liberal political and economic values and favor a liberal international economic order with unrestricted trade (see Chapter 10). Western governments, especially the United States, have frequently interpreted the advocacy of socialist or anticolonial sentiments by Third World states to constitute support for the Soviet Union. In many such cases, Western states have retaliated by terminating foreign aid programs, an action that has further strained relations. Most important, as less developed systems, the Third World states demand an increased share of the world's resources to be accomplished through the development of the NIEO (see Chapters 10 and 12). Because the states of the West presently possess most of the world's wealth and control the institutions of the existing world economic system (see Chapter 10), gains by the Third World must be made at least in part at the expense of the First World states. The negotiations over a new international economic system have placed the states of the First and Third Worlds in an adversarial relationship, which is likely to continue.

The basic task confronting Western foreign policy in the Third World is that of coping with change. From the Western perspective, coping with change successfully means the achievement of four conditions in the Third World: (1) maintaining or enhancing Western political influence, (2) preserving the "open door" for Western economic penetration, (3) continued access to natural resources, and (4) limiting Soviet influence to prevent a shift in the strategic balance of power. As the previous discussion has made clear, these objectives will not be easy to realize. It must be remembered, however, that First World–Third World relations occur in an environment in which the West possesses the most military and economic power. The majority of these objectives are attainable if Western foreign policy makers demonstrate sufficient patience and skill.

THE SECOND WORLD

The Communist states appear to have the most coherent philosophical foundation for international relations of any group of states in the world. Full-scale Communism is seen as a goal toward which humanity is irresistibly driven by the forces of history. Foreign policy and international relations are defined in Communism as the program of assisting all nations along the path toward that goal. The problem, however, in trying to understand the realities of today's Second World countries lies in distinguishing between the general goal of universal Communism and the specific goals of the given countries. These countries, while proclaiming the universal goal, still pursue their historical national interests. This dichotomy is most obvious in the cases of the Soviet Union, Vietnam, China, and the People's Democratic Republic of Korea. Let us first look at the theoretical and then at the actual policies of the Communist party states.

Theoretical Goals

Neither Karl Marx nor Friedrich Engels was much concerned with the non-industrialized world of the 19th century, that is, the countries outside of Western Europe and North America, and even about the international relations of industrial states they had little to say. Their sketchy analysis of international interactions, taken from one of Engel's letters, may be summarized as follows:

1. The present goal of the industrialized capitalist states is to form a world market and to create productive forces to serve that market.[29]
2. In the future, once the industrialized capitalist states become socialistic, their enormous power will draw the "semi-civilized" non-industrial countries to socialism.[30]
3. It cannot be foreseen through what social and political phases the "semi-civilized" states will have to pass before becoming socialistic.[31]
4. These non-industrial countries cannot be coerced into socialism:

   One thing alone is certain: the victorious proletariat can force no blessing upon any foreign nation without undermining its own victory by doing so.[32]

Thus, it was not the founders of Marxism who developed a world view of socialist international relations; they apparently thought that the force of example rather than a policy of force would be sufficient. It was the successful Russian revolutionary Lenin who originated a fairly clear Marxist–Socialist policy.[33]

Five months before seizing power Lenin wrote in *Pravda* (the Communist party newspaper since 1917) that revolutionary foreign and domestic policy could not be separated. He postulated that a revolutionary Russia would reach out to "the oppressed classes of Europe . . . [and] the peoples oppressed by imperialism, primarily our neighbors in Asia" in order to "wage a revolutionary struggle against all imperialists."[34] He anticipated a "truly revolutionary alliance of the workers and peasants of the colonies and semi-colonies against the despots," and proclaimed the foreign policy of the proletariat to be an "alliance with the revolutionaries of the advanced countries and with all the oppressed nations against all and any imperialists."[35]

Lenin thus clearly differentiated a revolutionary Russia from all other world powers and appealed to the "oppressed masses" of the world. Mao Zedong also used revolutionary rhetoric to indicate China's policy; he stressed the anti-imperialist theme after the Chinese Communist party's seizure of power on the Asian mainland:

> The direction in the wind in the world has changed. In the struggle between the Socialist and capitalist camps, it is no longer the West Wind that prevailed over the East Wind, but the East Wind that prevailed over the West Wind . . . in other words . . . the forces of Socialism are overwhelmingly superior to the forces of imperialism.[36]

Leaders of all other Communist party states have expressed similar ideas about foreign policy. Let us look at the actual goals, resources, and international relations of the Second World countries.

The Soviet Union

As mentioned earlier, all Second World states stress the theme of socialism/communism versus capitalism/imperialism. They explain this conflict as inherent in the forces of history, in the laws of human social development. Nevertheless, the socialist countries do not adhere to a single foreign policy. In fact a major rivalry, that between the Soviet Union and China (the so-called Sino–Soviet split) is an important factor in world affairs.

Let us first examine the Soviet Union and its bloc before considering other socialist countries. The Soviet Union was the first Communist state established in the Second World. The Soviet Union is the most powerful socialist state because of its size, population, natural resources, industrial capacity, and military capability. The principal question about Soviet goals is, Does the Soviet Union act for Russian national goals or does it act on behalf of the goals of Marxism–Leninism?

The Soviet state is the descendant of the Russian Empire and its predecessors, Tsarist Russia and Muscovy.[37] The Bolshevik seizure of power in November 1917, at Russia's nadir, brought a vigorous new group to the helm of the Russian state, a group armed with a powerful world-encompassing philosophy and led by a political genius, Vladimir Lenin. Russia, under its new name, Soviet Russia (changed in 1923 to the Union of Soviet Socialistic Republics), recovered its power, fought a major war against Nazi Germany, emerged victorious, and became one of the two superpowers of the world.

Is the Soviet Union a state that seeks to help the oppressed of the world or a Russian Empire now clothed in Red? Zbigniew Brzezinski, former National Security Advisor to President Carter, writing in a 1984 publication of the London-based International Institute for Strategic Studies, succinctly states the case for the latter by observing that the Soviet Union today is a "Great Russian empire" and the continuation of former Imperial Russia.

According to Brzezinski, it is a state that feels territorially insecure and thus is expansive. Its power in the world is primarily one-dimensional, that is, military. It is a dangerous actor in world politics, preventing international cooperative arrangements. Further, the Soviet Union's "Great Russian" bureaucratic government, highly centralized and in fear of the other half of its population, which is not Great Russian (Great Russian is the term for the dominant ethnic group of the USSR), effectively prevents any democratization of the system. Brzezinski believes that if the West fails to offset Soviet military power, "a major disruption of the international political system could occur."[38] Many Western writers see the Soviet Union in a less harsh light, nonetheless much of what Brzezinski says appears to be true.

The Soviet Union has not only recovered all territories controlled by Imperial Russia but has added lands that were never controlled by any Russian state. The combination of Marxist–Leninist philosophy with Great Russian national goals—expansion until resistance is met—has created an immensely powerful force in the world, a force that could eventually create the long-sought-after world empire.

What resources does the Soviet Union bring to bear in world politics? In 1984 the Soviet Union had an estimated 271,800,000 population, about half of which is ethnically Great Russian. In addition, the USSR controls "a cluster of geographically contiguous states numbering approximately an additional 115 million people. In effect, about 135 million Great Russians exercise political control over a political framework that cumulatively encompasses some 385 million spread over much of the Eurasian Continent."[39] The Soviet Union has the world's largest army, air force, and largest navy, although it may fall behind the United States slightly, by some counts, in deliverable on-target nuclear weapon explosive power. In addition to its own strength, the USSR is buttressed by the Warsaw Treaty Organization (WTO). The Warsaw Pact signed in Warsaw, Poland, on May 14, 1955, established the WTO to legalize the continuation of Soviet garrisons in the East European "sovereign" states (which came under Soviet control as the result of World War II) and to add the forces of these countries to overall Soviet power.

The members of the Warsaw Pact also support the USSR politically and cannot be said to have a foreign policy of their own. The only exception is Romania, which occasionally votes against the USSR in the United Nations. Of the Second World states, Romania alone maintains diplomatic relations with Israel.

It should be noted that some military analysts question whether some East European troops would be reliable in time of war. Nevertheless, the political support given to the USSR by the Warsaw Pact in time of peace, and the military threat to NATO are most useful to the Soviet Union. In some scenarios the Warsaw Pact could be useful in wartime too.[40]

The Soviet Union can depend on several bilateral arrangements both within and outside of East Europe to further support its policies. Bulgaria, Czechoslovakia, and North Korea often export weapons to Soviet-supported foreign governments and insurgent forces. The German Democratic Republic exports both material and military advisors on behalf of Soviet objectives. The Bulgarian secret service has been accused of being involved in the attempted assassination of Pope Paul II, acting as a surrogate for the Soviet KGB (Committee on State Security).[41] Cuba has acted as the Soviet Union's cat's-paw in supplying troops to further Soviet goals in Africa.

The Soviet Union and its allies advance their cause in the First World by attempting to undermine and disrupt the Western World's political, social, and economic ties. In the Third World the Soviet bloc uses diplomatic contacts and economic and military aid in order to gain influence. The Third World is also the major area of contention between the Soviet bloc and the Western states (a third, though less important rival is the People's Republic of China; see below). That neither Soviet nor Western policy is successful here is explained by the fact that neither superpower has an agenda that matches that of most Third World states.

To sum up, the principal foreign relations actor in the Second World is the USSR. It is directly supported by Poland, GDR, Hungary, Czechoslovakia, Bulgaria, Mongolia, Afghanistan, Cuba, Vietnam, Laos, Kampuchea, Romania, and frequently North Korea. The first eight countries, Soviet allies, cannot be said to have any foreign policy other than the Soviet one. Vietnam, with its allies Kampuchea and Laos, closely adheres to Soviet policy in return for Soviet support, but at times some commentators have claimed to see some Vietnamese independent action. Romania is a bit of a maverick in the Soviet bloc, for within carefully prescribed limits it takes actions contrary to openly expressed Soviet wishes, even voting against the USSR in the United Nations. North Korea supports the USSR as it sees fit.

Soviet and Warsaw Treaty Organization objectives in the three worlds may be summarized in the following manner:

First World

1. to split the NATO alliance.
2. to decouple Japanese and U.S. security.
3. to isolate the United States from Australia and New Zealand while exacerbating U.S.–Canadian tensions.
4. prevention of the expansion of Western and especially U.S. political, military, and cultural influence.

Second World

1. prevention of Western, especially U.S., rapproachement with the People's Republic of China.
2. the return of Romania, Yugoslavia, and Albania fully to the Soviet fold.
3. isolating Communist China.
4. tying Indochina (Vietnam, Laos, Kampuchea) more closely to the USSR.
5. winning the war in Afghanistan.

Third World

1. the sharpening of Third World–First World conflicts while isolating Communist China.
2. the acquisition of raw materials and natural resources for the Soviet bloc while denying the same to China and the West.
3. support of "wars of national liberation" that are considered anti-imperialist.[42]
4. obtaining military bases for projection of Soviet power.
5. presenting the Soviet system as the only possible model on which plans for development should be based.[43]

Whether the Soviet Union will be able to sustain its "grand strategy" for an extended period of time is the real question. Whether it will be able to grind down Western resistance and in a cold war of attrition obtain its goals, remains to be seen. Optimistic observers feel a direct "hot war" between East and West is unlikely, and that in store is a long political struggle extending far into the future. Others, not so sanguine, see the possibility of a direct confrontation between the two superpowers and their allies either by design[44] or in desperation.[45]

The People's Republic of China

> For half a century, starting in 1850, Tsarist Russia forced China to conclude a series of unequal treaties, extorting many privileges and slicing off a total of 1.5 million square kilometers of China's territory.[46]

Perhaps the key to one main thrust of Communist China's foreign policy lies in the statement just quoted from a study of Chinese history. Today's China is not a world power and cannot compete with the superpowers for the simple reason that it cannot "project" its power. China has no capacity to effectively act beyond East Asia. This does not mean that China is not strong, however, for it is the strongest of the second-level powers. Even

Soviet tanks in Afghanistan.

though the 4,100,000-member People's Liberation Army is being modernized (with the phasing out of old Soviet equipment and the introduction of other imported and domestically produced weaponry), it "lacks facilities and logistic support for protracted large-scale operations of any significant distance outside of China."[47] However, the Chinese have a stockpile of several hundred nuclear weapons and a means to deliver them.[48] Except for some intercontinental ballistic missiles, China's forces are regional. China perceives no threat from Japan because that country has no offensive capacity, and Vietnam is too small to offer a serious threat. The United States and other Western powers are either too remote or too weak to threaten China with conventional weaponry.

As stated in the quote at the beginning of this section, nineteenth-century Imperial Russia was a threat to China, and in the twentieth century the Soviet Union continued this threat. All other enemies have been dislodged from their former positions in China. The roots of Chinese–Russian enmity go back to the seventeenth century when a weakened China and a strong Russia began contending for the Mongol inheritance in Siberia. By the 1860s, when China was in sharp decline, Russia added Chinese-controlled territory to lands taken in the seventeenth and eighteenth centuries, which the Chinese could not so clearly claim. Russia also forced favorable concessions in the Manchurian region. During the Russian Revolution and the interwar period China was still too weak to recover these territories. After 1949, Communist China, feeling itself just as "Communist" as the Soviet Union, started to question the continued Soviet administration of these lands and the satellite status of Mongolia, since Mongolia was long considered part of the Chinese sphere of influence. The struggle came out in the open in the early 1960s in the Sino–Soviet dispute. The Chinese accused the USSR of hegemonism. As Lucian Pye notes, national interest superceded ideological unity:

> Until Stalin's death the concept of a monolithic Communist world was accurate, but in 1969 Russian and Chinese soldiers were shooting at each other and Mao was preaching that Russian revisionism was a greater threat to China than American imperialism.[49]

The result of this conflict is the development of a Moscow–Peking–Washington triangular relationship.

Beijing looks to the United States for technological assistance, industrial "know-how," investment, and potential markets for Chinese goods. In particular China seeks advanced military equipment not only from the United States but also other Western countries. However, though both countries fear the USSR, U.S. and Chinese priorities are not the same, especially in the area of ideology. The question of sovereignty over the British crown colony of Hong Kong is settled, with Great Britain publically stating that it will end its control at the expiration of the 99-year lease in 1997. The same type of resolution is not in sight for Taiwan, however. The island's regime, the Republic of China, is supported by the United States (since 1949). This regime also claims to be "China"; moreover, it claims to be the only legitimate government for all the Chinese territory.

The United States in particular and the West in general wish "to play the China card" against the USSR, but fears prevent too close a tie with China. As both the Soviet Union and Taiwan ask, what will China do if and when it becomes an equal with the other superpowers? Taiwanese and some Western commentators also ask what would happen if a Sino–Soviet rapproachement occurred on the basis of their common ideology.[50]

China's foreign policy does not allow either of the superpowers to sleep peacefully.[51] The People's Republic first wishes to assert sovereignty over all Chinese lands, including Taiwan. Second, it wants to reestablish its historical sphere of influence in East Asia, including Korea and Southeast Asia. Third, it seeks to industrialize and modernize while retaining Chinese values. All in all,

> The Chinese are determined to recapture the sense of greatness that was theirs when they saw themselves as the Middle Kingdom, the center of the earth. The essence of the Chinese Revolution has been precisely this striving to regain national power and greatness . . . to reverse the humiliations of the last 150 years.[52]

Yugoslavia, Albania, and North Korea

Yugoslavia, since its expulsion from the Soviet bloc in 1948, has striven to maintain a nonaligned approach to foreign affairs. Depending on the period, it has leaned either toward or away from the West or the Soviet bloc. It has been able to continue this delicate balancing act for decades and has received aid from both East and West. Yugoslavia has made a permanent policy out of the late Josep Broz Tito's "nonalignment" idea,[53] and has been successful in implementing this while retaining a socialist–communist internal policy.[54]

Albania, on the other hand, has forged a policy of isolation. Claiming to be the only true Communist state in the world and the only country to have totally eliminated religion, tiny Albania (population 2,800,000 and armed forces totaling 40,400) now rejects both a Chinese and a Soviet orientation and remains sealed against the outside.[55]

North Korea represents an example of a one-goal foreign policy. Its one object is unification with South Korea, by force if necessary. The People's Democratic Republic of Korea has a defense treaty with China and owes its existence to the USSR, but is aloof from both of them. Kim Il-Sung, president of North Korea and head of its Korean Workers' (Communist) party, refers to the single most important task of his regime as forcing "U.S. imperialists out of South Korea and unifying the country."[56] The main sources of North Korean policy are its armed forces and the principle of *juche* (self-reliance), by which means North Korea maintains itself in balance between China and the USSR.[57]

Interactions and Constraints

The Second World states interact with each other and other states depending on their national or bloc interests. The Soviet bloc deals with the West both in confrontation and in cooperation in order to obtain much-needed technological information. Soviet bloc nations have negotiated cultural and scientific exchange agreements that are perceived by both sides as beneficial; the Soviet bloc gains some access to the latest technology, while the West gains access to otherwise closed societies. For example, the United States has signed 11 specialized agreements with the USSR dealing with science, environmental protection, medicine and public health, space, agriculture, oceans, transportation, atomic energy, artificial hearts, energy, housing, and other construction, besides formal exchanges of personnel.[58]

Within the Second World, the major interaction is between the Soviet bloc and China, with Yugoslavia, Albania, North Korea, and Romania taking the sidelines. In the Third World the Soviet bloc is by far the most active, with China offering a minor alternative. North Korea appears active only in supplying military training and weaponry for insurgent and terrorist groups of Latin America, Africa, and the Middle East.

The principal constraints on Yugoslavia, Albania, and North Korea are their size and capability. China, although larger and more important, is constrained by its lack of industrial development, its immense population, and its inability to project power. The main contenders for power in the arena of international relations are the United States and its allies and the USSR and its allies.

Despite internal and external constraints on their power, the Soviet Union and the United States appear to be in for a long struggle for world dominance, a struggle that could end in the victory of one or the other, a drawing together (the theory of convergence), the exhaustion of both in a hot or a cold war, or the development of a true coexistence based on a stalemate or damping down of passions.

THE THIRD WORLD

International relations of the Third World states as well as of the First and the Second World states are determined by four interrelated factors: a state's history, its share of power in the world, its level of political and economic development, and the choices made by its leaders. The colonial past of many African and Asian states influences their foreign policies. They are quick to adopt a stance of anticolonialism, which generally means a position critical of the West, especially the United States. Ironically, many of them also maintain close political and economic ties with their former colonial masters. The policies of the Latin American states reflect the influence of their history in their close relations with, and in several cases even dependence on, the United States. Close cultural ties remain with Spain and with Portugal in case of Brazil.

A state's power in international relations was defined earlier in this chapter as its control over resources. With some exceptions (e.g., oil-rich states), Third World states lack resources, especially in comparison with the developed states of the First and Second Worlds. The power exercised by most of them in international relations is, therefore, limited.

Levels of political and economic development of the states of the three worlds were considered in Chapter 3. The political and economic development of the Third World states is reflected in their search for political identity and economic progress through domestic and foreign policies. Third World states often make foreign policies aimed as much at uniting their populations as at achieving any other goal in international relations. Trade and aid are obvious examples of attempts at economic progress through foreign policy. John Spanier remarks that "the desire to modernize largely molds the LDCs' foreign policy and perceptions of the world."[59] The policy of *nonalignment* is pursued by many Third World states partly because it helps them assert their newly won independence and focuses on their political identity, and partly because it improves their prospects for foreign aid from both superpowers.

The choices made by the leaders of any state are important in domestic as well as foreign policy. The history of a state, its share of power in the world, and its level of political and economic development all influence leaders' choices as much as their personalities and their roles as determined by their countries' constitutions, people's expectations, and their own perceptions. The choices made by the leaders of a Third World state affect not only present and future policies, but sometimes political and economic viability, as many of these states are in constant turmoil.

States are the primary actors in the international relations of the Third World, even more so than is the case in the First and the Second Worlds. Although some intergovernmental and nongovernmental organizations have emerged in the Third World, they are usually less cohesive and less effective than similar organizations in the other two worlds. Consequently, such organizations of the Third World do not play as significant a role in international relations (a prominent exception is OPEC) as do the organizations of the First and Second Worlds. The role of private individuals as secondary actors in international relations is even more limited than the roles of intergovernmental and nongovernmental organizations in all three worlds.

Goals and Resources

Third World states seek goals of self-preservation and security through policies of political and economic independence and, whenever possible, through increase in military capabilities. Political independence has been pursued by many Third World states by means of nonalignment policy. Nonalignment as a Third World policy was initiated in 1955 at a conference held in Bandung, Indonesia, attended by 25 African and Asian states. Countries that had recently won freedom from colonial rule and others (such as Yugoslavia) that wanted to maintain independence from a potentially threatening superpower adopted this policy. Nonalignment became so popular in the 1950s and 1960s that it came to be known as a movement. Besides nonparticipation in an alliance with a superpower, nonalignment was interpreted as a policy that considered every issue on its merits, not on the basis of which of the superpowers supported or opposed it. It also espoused peaceful coexistence among states of different ideologies, and supported independence movements in the remaining colonies.

Judged by the number of its adherents, nonalignment has continued in popularity in the 1970s and 1980s. The number of states now claiming to be nonaligned is more than 100. However, no more than half of them can be said to be genuinely nonaligned in the sense that they avoid foreign policies that lean toward the United States or the Soviet Union. Some states in the vanguard of the contemporary nonalignment movement can be hardly considered nonaligned. Cuba, India, and Egypt are among such states. Cuba depends on the Soviet Union for its continued existence as an independent state; India signed a "treaty of peace and friendship" with the Soviet Union in 1971 and meticulously avoids any policy that might offend the latter; and Egypt, which was on the Soviet side until 1972, is currently in the U.S. camp. Most of the genuinely nonaligned states are small countries in Africa and Asia. The pro-Soviet and pro-American nonaligned states are often called radicals and conservatives, respectively.[60] Writing in the mid-1960s, J. D. B. Miller had stated that for most Third World states "nonalignment can be worn as a garland rather than a banner."[61] Even those states which now wave it as a banner rather than use it only as a symbol do so more for reasons of publicity than to indicate policy.

Of course, leaning toward the United States or the Soviet Union (or toward China) gives the Third World states hope and sometimes assurance of protection against interference in their internal affairs by an unfriendly major power or a hostile neighbor. Third World states can expect military and economic assistance from the power with which they side. It can be argued that such protection and aid help a Third World state realize the goals of self-preservation and security. Protection and aid are not given without strings; recipient states lose some of their independence in foreign as well as domestic policy.

Like states of the First and Second Worlds, Third World states attempt to improve their military capabilities for the sake of self-preservation and security. Improvements in military capabilities generally require a state to decrease expenditures in other areas. Most Third World states have scarce resources and are not in a position to spend large amounts of money on defense. The major exceptions in this case are the oil-rich states of the Third World, especially of the Middle East. With data published by the U.S. Arms Control and Disarmament Agency, Daniel Papp argues convincingly that

it is a myth . . . that Third World countries are spending ever-increasing percentages of their gross national products and governmental budgets on military expenditures . . . . both military expenditures as a percentage of gross national product and military expenditures as a percentage of central government expenditures in fact decreased during the 1970s in most areas of the Third World. The Middle East was the only significant exception.[62]

In arms imports, it is the Middle Eastern states that are the major buyers in the Third World. From 1970 to 1979 the Middle Eastern states purchased almost half of the arms imported by the Third World.[63]

It is virtually impossible for any state to be completely independent economically in the contemporary world. There is little doubt, however, that the Third World states are far less independent economically than First and Second World states. As was pointed out in Chapter 12, Third World states depend on the developed states of the First World for trade, aid, investment capital, and technology. Their economies are affected by any fluctuations in the economies of the latter. It was also noted that the debts of the Third World states have been increasing; in some cases the amounts of these debts are staggering indeed. Besides, the Third World states are dependent on the Second World and the oil-exporting countries within the Third World for aid. Third World as well as First World states are dependent on the oil-exporting countries for this energy resource.

Economic development is a crucial goal for the Third World states. A few Third World states (South Korea, Singapore, Taiwan, Argentina, Brazil, and India) have become the new industrializing countries. The economic progress of these states is noticeable and in some cases impressive. In most other states in the Third World very little economic progress has been achieved. The desire for economic development in the Third World states and the frustrations caused by the lack of achievement in this area have contributed to the demands for a new economic system, the NIEO. A redistribution of the world's wealth by means of foreign aid and trade concessions is the primary objective of these demands.

Third World states also pursue the goal of power. However, their lack of resources (oil-rich states are exceptions) and dependence on the First and Second Worlds limit their power. Like the states of the other two worlds, they profess the goal of peace as well. Most armed conflicts since World War II have, however, taken place in the Third World. Although many of these conflicts can be blamed on the former colonial powers (the artificial borders of African states, for example), some have roots unrelated to colonial rule. For example, the protracted and bloody war between Iran and Iraq which started in 1980, and the conflict between Libya and Chad have little to do with colonialism.

The resources of the Third World states to realize their goals in international relations are limited. Earlier in this chapter we pointed out how low the GNP of most Third World states is. In Chapter 12 natural and other resources of the Third World states were considered. The only Third World states that have converted their control of natural resources into power are those rich in oil. The inability of other Third World states in developing similar power is due to the present international economic order and the substitutability of some raw materials. Today's international economic order is largely controlled by the Western states. The prices of raw materials have not increased proportionally to those of the manufactured goods, which many Third World states import from the West. Steganga and Axline offer a telling example: "The jeep that Colombia could import in 1950 for 17 bales of coffee . . . cost 67 bales in 1965 and over 200 bales in 1980."[64] The substitutability of some raw materials (such as natural rubber) further undercuts the possibility of utilizing them for power in international relations.

Some Third World states have used their strategic locations to increase power by establishing close political and military relations with one or the other superpower. Some examples of such states are Angola, Egypt, Ethiopia, India, Iran (until 1979), Mozambique, Nicaragua, Pakistan, and the Philippines. Close political and military relations with a superpower are linked with close economic relations, generally in the form of economic assistance, thereby helping the Third World states in their economic development goal. It can be argued that such relations basically reflect dependence of the Third World states on the two superpowers and thus decrease the former's political (and in some cases, also economic) independence. However, the states seeking these relations often perceive them as contributing to the goals of self-preservation and security.

Population as a resource is not a major contributor to the power or other goals of the Third World states and is often a liability for them. The highest growth rates of population are in the Third World, particularly in Africa and Latin America. Economic progress and food production in most of these states have not kept up with the increase in population. Population is a major factor in keeping the growth rate of economies in the Third World states so low. Military capabilities of the Third World states, unless buttressed by close military relations with a major power or by arms purchases with oil money, are clearly limited and are not a significant resource for the realization of goals in international relations. Intangible resources, such as morale of the people, are adversely affected by the poor economies and ineffective governments of the Third World states.

Interactions among States

In an article published in 1971, Johan Galtung, a prominent European scholar, described the interactions among states as a "feudal interaction structure."[65] Galtung's ideas have some relevance to the interstate hierarchy of the 1980s. Galtung divided the world into three categories of states: core, periphery, and intermediary. Concentrating on the first two categories, he concluded that the core states dominate the periphery states and that the latter have a relationship of dependence on the former. The core states are the United States, the Soviet Union, France, West Germany, Japan, and the United Kingdom. The periphery states are most of the Third World states. States such as Canada, Nigeria, and Venezuela fall in the middle of the two categories.

Galtung described the interactions between the core and the periphery states as vertical and posited that there was a lack of interactions among the periphery states. (Vertical interactions indicate dominance of the periphery states by the core states and dependence of the former on the latter.) It is true that the Third World states depend on the core states for trade, aid, investment, technology, and military weapons, but there is no conclusive evidence to suggest that a relationship of dominance or exploitation exists between these two categories of states. It cannot be established, for example, that only the core states exercise influence over the periphery states; in fact, sometimes the reverse is also true. Research in international relations has revealed that states that receive economic and military benefits from a core state tend to support the core state on foreign policy issues. However, this relationship does not always hold and there is no cause and effect relationship between economic and military benefits and support on foreign policy. Besides, there are significant variations in this relationship. The Soviet Union is able to receive greater returns (for support of its foreign policy) than the United States for the economic and military benefits given to the Third World states. The extent of dependence of the periphery states on the core states also varies substantially. The former French colonies in West Africa and the satellites of the Soviet Union are far more dependent on their core states than are the periphery states with close relations with the United States.

Contrary to Galtung's theory, interactions among the Third World states are substantial and have increased since he wrote. This is particularly true of diplomatic interactions.[66] Exchange of visits by high-ranking officials with a view to discussing and resolving common problems is rather frequent within the Third World. Exchanges of cultural and educational nature within the Third World have increased. Another category of interactions within the Third World is economic. A number of regional organizations exist in the Third World in order to achieve the goal of economic development for its members. Most of these organizations have not been very successful in achieving their goals. (Some reasons for their lack of success were given in Chapter 5.) There is no doubt, however, that such organizations reflect growing interactions within the Third World.

Cooperation as well as conflict exists in most interactions among states. Though Third World states do cooperate among themselves and with the states of the First and Second Worlds in various ways, there are far more conflicts in the Third World than in the other two worlds. Some of the major conflicts in the Third World are in the Middle East, Southern Africa, South Asia, and Central America. We consider here conflicts in two of these areas: the Middle East and Central America. In the Middle East the establishment of Israel as an independent state in 1948 created a relationship of hostility between this new state and neighboring Arab states. Arab–Israeli conflict has led to four wars—in 1948, 1956, 1967, and 1973—and to the Israeli invasion of Lebanon in 1982. Israel wants the Arabs to accept its right to exist as an independent sovereign state in the Middle East. Besides, Israel is not willing to give up some of the Arab territories that it has occupied since the 1967 war.[67] The Arabs have not yet accepted the existence of Israel to its satisfaction. They wish to recover their territories. The Arabs also seek the settlement of the Palestinian issue. The Palestinians are Arabs who lived in Palestine before Israel was created out of this region. (Palestine was under British control as a League of Nations mandate from the end of World War I until 1948.) The Palestinians hope to establish a new state for themselves, possibly next to Israel, a demand that Israel finds unacceptable.

In Lebanon a civil war between religious factions of the Moslems and the Christians has continued since 1975. Israel, Syria, and the Palestinians have been directly involved in this civil war. The United States, France, Italy, and the United Kingdom are also directly involved, either in the multinational peacekeeping forces or by supporting one group in the civil war. At the time of this writing there appears to be no end to the conflict in Lebanon.

Central America historically has been dominated by the United States. There is evidence of Cuban and the Soviet intrusion in this area, for example, in Nicaragua. Rebel forces opposing or directly fighting the governments have become an almost inseparable ingredient of political life in this region. In Nicaragua, guerrillas opposed to the government are supported by the United States with money and weapons. In some other Central American states, for example El Salvador, guerrillas are fighting the pro-U.S. government with the help of Cuba and the Soviet Union. There appears to be no end to armed conflict in this region, either. According to some, the conflict in Central American states is internal and no outside power should intervene. However, this position is not accepted by the United States, Cuba, and the Soviet Union. Wherever internal conflict develops in the Third World states, major powers, particularly the United States and the Soviet Union, tend to intervene. Donald Puchala comments that "civil disorder in weaker states [of the Third World] invites (some will argue it necessitates) major power intervention, especially when such disorder is ideologically charged."[68]

Israeli forces in Lebanon.

Constraints on Foreign Policy

As is the case with the First and the Second World, the foreign policies of the Third World are also constrained by external and internal factors. The power distribution in the world is such that the Third World states have a disproportionately small share in it. The resources that can be utilized for wielding power are not possessed by most of these states. Even though they are not dominated by the core states in every major aspect of their foreign policies, there is no doubt that they must keep in view the policies of their economic and military benefactors in making decisions in international relations. The pursuit of national interest and foreign policy goals by the Third World states is thus influenced by the policies of the major powers.

The history of African and Asian states has brought their foreign policies closer to those of their former colonial rulers. At the same time their histories have made them support anticolonial positions. In making their foreign policies, Latin American states cannot escape the historical fact of U.S. influence (some would say dominance) over this region. Prevailing political beliefs of the elites, the nature of government, and the roles and personalities of central decision makers are also important domestic constraints on the foreign policies of the Third World states. On the other hand, demands of the masses are not a significant limit in most of these states. The authoritarian governments that rule in many Third World states do not pay much attention to popular demands. Even in states that are relatively open and permit freedom of expression, the means for the articulation and aggregation of such demands are inadequate.

NOTES

1. For an excellent discussion of intergovernmental and nongovernmental organizations see Bruce Russett and Harvey Starr, *World Politics: The Menu for Choice* (San Francisco: Freeman, 1981), pp. 51–59.
2. Some writers consider power as the central theme of international relations. The late Hans J. Morgenthau is perhaps the best known; see his *Politics among Nations: The Struggle for Power and Peace,* 5th ed. (New York: Knopf, 1978).
3. Donald James Puchala, *International Politics Today* (New York: Harper & Row, 1971), pp. 5–9.
4. For a summary of major arms control agreements, see Russett and Starr, pp. 378–379.
5. Our discussion of the external and internal constraints on a state's foreign policy is based on the following sources: James N. Rosenau, *The Scientific Study of Foreign Policy* (New York: Free Press, 1971); James N. Rosenau, "Pre-Theories and Theories of Foreign Policy," in R. Barry Farell, ed., *Approaches to Comparative and International Politics* (Evanston, Ill.: Northwestern University Press, 1966); and James A. Stegenga and W. Andrew Axline, *The Global Community,* 2d ed. (New York: Harper & Row, 1982).
6. See Jack J. Roth, ed., *World War I: A Turning Point in Modern History* (New York: Knopf, 1967); and René Albrecht-Carrié, *The Meaning of the First Cold War* (Englewood Cliffs, N.J.: Prentice-Hall, 1965).
7. See Thomas Paterson, *On Every Front: The Making of the Cold War* (New York: Norton, 1979).
8. See Kenneth A. Oye, "Domain of Choice," in Kenneth A. Oye, Donald Rothchild, and Robert J. Lieber, eds., *Eagle Entangled: U.S. Foreign Policy in a Complex World* (New York: Longman, 1979), pp. 4–11.
9. Ibid.
10. Ibid.
11. For a discussion of three middle-level powers (West Germany, France, and Great Britain) see Wolfram F. Hanrieder and Graeme P. Auton, *The Foreign Policies of West Germany, France and Britain* (Englewood Cliffs, N.J.: Prentice-Hall, 1980).
12. For a discussion of U.S.–Soviet relations since 1975 see Lawrence Caldwell and Alexander Dallin, "U.S. Policy Toward the Soviet Union: Intractable Issues," in Oye, Rothchild, and Lieber, pp. 199–228; and Alexander Dallin and Gail Lapidus, "Reagan and the Russians: United States Policy Toward the Soviet Union and Eastern Europe," in Kenneth A. Oye, Robert J. Lieber, and Donald

Rothchild, eds., *Eagle Defiant: United States Foreign Policy in the 1980's* (Boston: Little, Brown, 1983), pp. 191–237.

13. Jack C. Plano and Roy Olton, eds., *The International Relations Dictionary*, 3d ed. (Santa Barbara, Calif.: ABC-Clio, 1979), p. 165.

14. For a discussion of crisis management in the Cold War see Alexander L. George and Richard Smoke. *Deterrence in American Foreign Policy: Theory and Practice* (New York: Columbia University Press, 1974); and Alexander L. George, *Managing U.S.–Soviet Rivalry: Problems of Crisis Prevention* (Boulder, Colo.: Westview Press, 1983).

15. This discussion is borrowed from the sources listed in footnote 12.

16. Dallin and Caldwell, pp. 215–216.

17. Ibid., p. 216.

18. Ibid.

19. Ibid., p. 218.

20. Dallin and Lapidus, p. 207.

21. Ibid., p. 219.

22. Richard E. Feinberg, *The Intemperate Zone: The Third World Challenge to U.S. Foreign Policy* (New York: Norton, 1983), p. 32.

23. Ibid., pp. 32–33.

24. Oye, pp. 11–13.

25. Ibid., pp. 13–17.

26. Ibid., p. 13.

27. See Barry Rubin, *Paved With Good Intentions: The American Experience and Iran* (New York: Penguin Books, 1980).

28. For a discussion of U.S. policy toward the Caribbean and the Persian Gulf see Carl Leiden, "The United States and the Persian Gulf," pp. 54–85; and Karl M. Schmitt, "The United States and Latin America," pp. 85–113 in Robert C. Gray and Stanley J. Michalak, Jr., eds., *American Foreign Policy since Détente* (New York: Harper & Row, 1984).

29. "Engels to Kautsky," in Robert C. Tucker, ed., *The Marx-Engels Reader,* 2d ed. (New York: Norton, 1978), p. 676.

30. Ibid., p. 677.

31. Ibid.

32. Ibid.

33. At least one author would think we are misreading Marx and Engels by too lightly evaluating their ideas. See "Marx and Engels on the World State," in Elliot Goodman, *The Soviet Design for a World State* (New York: Columbia University Press, 1968), pp. 1–24.

34. Vladimir Lenin, "The Foreign Policy of the Russian Revolution," in Robert C. Tucker, ed., *The Lenin Anthology* (New York: Norton, 1975), p. 538.

35. Ibid., pp. 538–539.

36. Robert R. Schram, *The Political Thought of Mao Tse-Tung* (New York: Praeger, 1969), p. 408.

37. Any good history of Russia will offer the student a survey of Russia's develop-

ment. We recommend Jesse D. Clarkson, *A History of Russia,* 2d ed. (New York: Random House, 1969), esp. pp. 823–845.

38. Zbigniew Brzezinski, "The Soviet Union: Her Aims, Problems and Challenges to the West," *Adelphi Papers,* no. 189 (Spring 1984): p. 3.

39. Ibid.

40. See Robert W. Clawson and Lawrence S. Kaplan, *The Warsaw Pact: Political Purpose and Military Means* (Wilmington, Del.: Scholarly Resources, 1982).

41. "Bulgaria Hired Agca to Kill Pope: Report of Italian Prosecutor Says," *New York Times,* June 10, 1984, p. 1; "To Russia With Love," *Time,* February 14, 1983, p. 49; and Nathan Adams, "Drugs for Guns: The Bulgarian Connection," *Readers Digest* (February 1984): 35–46.

42. The Soviet Constitution of 1977, Article 30, specifically states that the foreign policy of the USSR includes "supporting the struggle of peoples for national liberation."

43. See John Carfora and Joseph Parker, "The Soviet Model of Democracy and Development: Paradigm for Progress or Persecution?" Paper delivered the sixth annual Third World Studies Conference, University of Nebraska, Omaha, October 1983, p. 14.

44. See Richard Pipes, "Why the Soviet Union Thinks It Could Fight and Win a Nuclear War," *Commentary* 64, no. 1 (July 1977).

45. See Edward N. Luttwak, "Soviet Grand Strategy and Its Future," in *The Grand Strategy of the Soviet Union* (New York: St. Martin's Press 1983), pp. 111–116.

46. Qi Wen, *China: A General Survey,* 2d ed. (Beijing: Foreign Languages Press, 1981), p. 32.

47. *The Military Balance: 1983–1984* (London: International Institute for Strategic Studies, 1984), p. 81.

48. Ibid., pp. 81, 83, 84.

49. Lucian W. Pye, *China: An Introduction,* 3d ed. (Boston: Little, Brown, 1984), p. 363.

50. A. G. B. Metcalf, "Red China Revisited," editorial in *Strategic Review* 12, no. 3 (Summer 1984): 7–8.

51. See Jonathan D. Pollack, "China's Role in Pacific Basin Security," *Survival* (July/August 1984): 164–173.

52. Pye, p. 370.

53. See Stanislav Stojanovic, "Tito's Concept of Foreign Policy," *Socialist Thought and Practice* 24, no. 5 (May 1984): 17–54.

54. See Mika Spiljak, "Internal and Foreign Policy of Yugoslavia," *Socialist Thought and Practice* 24, no. 5 (May 1984): 3–16.

55. See Nicholas C. Pano. *The People's Republic of Albania* (Baltimore: Johns Hopkins University Press, 1968); and *The Military Balance: 1983–1984,* p. 44.

56. Kim Il Sung, *For the Independent Peaceful Reunification of Korea,* rev. ed. (New York: Guardian Associates, 1976).

57. Jae Kyu Park and Jung Gun Kim, eds., *The Politics of North Korea* (Seoul: Institute for Far Eastern Studies, Kyungnam University, 1983), p. 183.

58. "U.S.–U.S.S.R. Exchanges," *Gist,* August 1984 (a quick reference aid issued by U.S. Department of State).
59. John Spanier, *Games Nations Play,* 5th ed. (New York: Holt, Rinehart and Winston, 1984), p. 339.
60. See Daniel S. Papp, *Contemporary International Relations* (New York: Macmillan, 1984), p. 115; and Charles W. Kegley, Jr., and Eugene R. Wittkopf, *World Politics: Trend and Transformation* (New York: St. Martin's Press, 1981), p. 99.
61. J. D. B. Miller, *The Politics of the Third World* (New York: Oxford University Press, 1967), p. 68.
62. Papp, p. 301.
63. See Stegenga and Axline, p. 83.
64. Ibid., p. 76.
65. See Johan Galtung, "A Structural Theory of Imperialism," *Journal of Peace Research,* 8 (1971): 81–117.
66. See William R. Thompson, "Center-Periphery Interaction Patterns: The Case of Arab Visits, 1946–1975." *International Organization* 35 (Spring 1981): 355–373.
67. In accordance with a peace treaty signed between Israel and Egypt in 1979, Israel withdrew from the Egyptian territory of Sinai which it had occupied since the war of 1967.
68. Puchala, p. 265.

Photo Credit List

Index